WIN YOUR UNEMPLOYMENT COMPENSATION CLAIM

Second Edition

Lawrence A. Edelstein
Attorney at Law

SPHINX® PUBLISHING
AN IMPRINT OF SOURCEBOOKS, INC.®
NAPERVILLE, ILLINOIS
www.SphinxLegal.com

Second Edition, 2002

Published by: **Sphinx® Publishing, An Imprint of Sourcebooks, Inc.®**

<u>Naperville Office</u>
P.O. Box 4410
Naperville, Illinois 60567-4410
630-961-3900
Fax: 630-961-2168
www.sourcebooks.com
www.SphinxLegal.com

This publication is designed to provide accurate and authoritative information in regard to the subject matter covered. It is sold with the understanding that the publisher is not engaged in rendering legal, accounting, or other professional service. If legal advice or other expert assistance is required, the services of a competent professional person should be sought.

From a Declaration of Principles Jointly Adopted by a Committee of the American Bar Association and a Committee of Publishers and Associations

This product is not a substitute for legal advice.

Disclaimer required by Texas statutes.

Library of Congress Cataloging-in-Publication Data
Edelstein, Lawrence A., 1970-
    Win your unemployment compensation claim / Lawrence A. Edelstein.-- 2nd ed.
        p. cm. -- (Legal survivial guides)
    Includes index.
    ISBN 1-57248-225-7 (alk. paper)
        1. Workers' compensation claims--United States. I. Title. II. Series.

HD7103.65.U6 E33 2002
368.4'1014'0973--dc21
                                                                    2002021177

Printed and bound in the United States of America.

VHG Paperback — 10 9 8 7 6 5 4 3 2 1

ACKNOWLEDGMENTS

DEEP APPRECIATION AND A SPECIAL THANKS GO OUT TO THOSE WHO AIDED IN THIS ENDEAVOR:

Michael E. Edelstein, *for first envisioning the need for a manual such as this and then helping to compile its contents.*

•

Eileen C. Edelstein *and* **Dawn Edelstein**, *for traveling in pursuit of data, via telephone, to lands as far as Alaska and Puerto Rico.*

•

Bryan Glass *for all his editing prowess.*

•

Jennifer L. Edelstein *and* **Elliott M. Edelstein**, *for all their moral support.*

•

Max T. Edelstein, **Monroe Edelstein**, *and* **Buffington Edelstein**, *for always helping in any way they could.*

CONTENTS

USING SELF-HELP LAW BOOKS

Before using a self-help law book, you should realize the advantages and disadvantages of doing your own legal work and understand the challenges and diligence that this requires.

THE GROWING TREND

Rest assured that you won't be the first or only person handling your own legal matter. For example, in some states, more than seventy-five percent of divorces and other cases have at least one party representing him or herself. Because of the high cost of legal services, this is a major trend and many courts are struggling to make it easier for people to represent themselves. However, some courts are not happy with people who do not use attorneys and refuse to help them in any way. For some, the attitude is, "Go to the law library and figure it out for yourself."

We at Sphinx write and publish self-help law books to give people an alternative to the often complicated and confusing legal books found in most law libraries. We have made the explanations of the law as simple and easy to understand as possible. Of course, unlike an attorney advising an individual client, we cannot cover every conceivable possibility.

COST/VALUE ANALYSIS

Whenever you shop for a product or service, you are faced with various levels of quality and price. In deciding what product or service to buy, you make a cost/value analysis on the basis of your willingness to pay and the quality you desire.

When buying a car, you decide whether you want transportation, comfort, status, or sex appeal. Accordingly, you decide among such choices as a Neon, a Lincoln, a Rolls Royce, or a Porsche. Before making a decision, you usually weigh the merits of each option against the cost.

When you get a headache, you can take a pain reliever (such as aspirin) or visit a medical specialist for a neurological examination. Given this choice, most people, of course, take a pain reliever, since it costs only pennies; whereas a medical examination costs hundreds of dollars and takes a lot of time. This is usually a logical choice because it is rare to need anything more than a pain reliever for a headache. But in some cases, a headache may indicate a brain tumor and failing to see a specialist right away can result in complications. Should everyone with a headache go to a specialist? Of course not, but people treating their own illnesses must realize that they are betting on the basis of their cost/value analysis of the situation. They are taking the most logical option.

The same cost/value analysis must be made when deciding to do one's own legal work. Many legal situations are very straight forward, requiring a simple form and no complicated analysis. Anyone with a little intelligence and a book of instructions can handle the matter without outside help.

But there is always the chance that complications are involved that only an attorney would notice. To simplify the law into a book like this, several legal cases often must be condensed into a single sentence or paragraph. Otherwise, the book would be several hundred pages long and too complicated for most people. However, this simplification necessarily leaves out many details and nuances that would apply to special or unusual situations. Also, there are many ways to interpret most legal questions. Your case may come before a judge who disagrees with the analysis of our authors.

Therefore, in deciding to use a self-help law book and to do your own legal work, you must realize that you are making a cost/value analysis. You have decided that the money you will save in doing it yourself outweighs the chance that your case will not turn out to your satisfaction. Most people handling their own simple legal matters never have a problem, but occasionally people find that it ended up costing them more to have an attorney straighten out the situation than it would have if they had hired an attorney in the beginning. Keep this in mind if you decide to handle your own case, and be sure to consult an attorney if you feel you might need further guidance.

LOCAL RULES   The next thing to remember is that a book that covers the law for the entire nation, or even for an entire state, cannot possibly include every procedural difference of every county court. Whenever possible, we provide the exact form needed; however, in some areas, each county, or even each judge, may require unique forms and procedures. In our *state* books, our forms usually cover the majority of counties in the state, or provide examples of the type of form that will be required. In our *national* books, our forms are sometimes even more general in nature but are designed to give a good idea of the type of form that will be needed in most locations. Nonetheless, keep in mind that your *state*, county, or judge may have a requirement, or use a form, that is not included in this book.

You should not necessarily expect to be able to get all of the information and resources you need solely from within the pages of this book. This book will serve as your guide, giving you specific information whenever possible and helping you to find out what else you will need to know. This is just like if you decided to build your own backyard deck. You might purchase a book on how to build decks. However, such a book would not include the building codes and permit requirements of every city, town, county, and township in the nation; nor would it include the lumber, nails, saws, hammers, and other materials and tools you would need to actually build the deck. You would use the book as your guide, and then do some work and research involving such matters as whether you need a permit of some kind, what type and grade of wood are available in your area, whether to use hand tools or power tools, and how to use those tools.

Before using the forms in a book like this, you should check with your court clerk to see if there are any local rules of which you should be aware, or local forms you will need to use. Often, such forms will require the same information as the forms in the book but are merely laid out differently, use slightly different language, or use different color paper so the clerks can easily find them. They will sometimes require additional information.

CHANGES IN THE LAW

Besides being subject to state and local rules and practices, the law is subject to change at any time. The courts and the legislatures of all fifty states are constantly revising the laws. It is possible that while you are reading this book, some aspect of the law is being changed or a court is interpreting a law in a different way. You should always check the most recent statutes, rules and regulations to see what, if any changes have been made.

In most cases, the change will be of minimal significance. A form will be redesigned, additional information will be required, or a waiting period will be extended. As a result, you might need to revise a form, file an extra form, or wait out a longer time period; these types of changes will not usually affect the outcome of your case. On the other hand, sometimes a major part of the law is changed, the entire law in a particular area is rewritten, or a case that was the basis of a central legal point is overruled. In such instances, your entire ability to pursue your case may be impaired.

Again, you should weigh the value of your case against the cost of an attorney and make a decision as to what you believe is in your best interest.

INTRODUCTION

How long could you sustain your current standard of living if you were fired, quit, or had your work hours or pay drastically reduced tomorrow? Perhaps you are already between jobs and learning fast. Do you deplete your lifetime or retirement savings? Do you skimp during that next holiday season? Do you fall behind on your bills and duck collection calls and threats of lawsuits?

Perhaps you would be forced to run up your credit card balances. Did you know that if you make only the minimum required payments on a credit card it may take you up to thirty-three years to pay off the debt?

Job loss can be a devastating part of life. Suddenly, often without warning, a seemingly secure lifestyle based on a regular weekly paycheck is completely thrown into disarray. Many hard-working Americans earn only enough to pay their monthly bills and have little savings from which to draw during a crisis. Taking heed of this problem, Congress enacted a statute called the Federal Unemployment Tax Act (FUTA). This statute provides each state with incentives that all but mandate establishing and administering a system to provide a safety net for workers in times such as these.

Today, each state maintains its own unemployment compensation system. Under FUTA the term *state* was broadly defined to include the District of Columbia, Puerto Rico, and the Virgin Islands. Therefore, there are unemployment compensation systems in each of these regions as well.

With a common origin, it is not surprising that the similarities among the state unemployment compensation laws far outweigh the differences. Basically, each state government requires employers to make periodic contributions to fund the system. These contributions normally are based upon the average payroll of the firm and the employment history of the firm. In the event that an employee loses his or her job "through no fault of his or her own," a periodic, usually bi-weekly, benefit check is paid to the employee to help finance living costs while he or she searches for new employment.

This book is intended for two distinct audiences. First, if you recently separated from your employment and are currently unemployed or underemployed, this is the book for you. This book will explain your rights under unemployment compensation law and provide guidance on how to maximize your chances of being awarded unemployment compensation benefits. Second, if you are still employed but fear you soon will be fired or laid-off, or feel you are being left with no alternative but to quit, again you will find this book extremely useful. It explains the law as it applies to both discharges and voluntary terminations, and details on how you can structure an argument in either of these situations to increase the likelihood of being awarded benefits.

This book has been organized to make it as user-friendly as possible. It divides the area of unemployment compensation law into ten chapters:

Chapter 1 explains the eligibility requirements for an applicant, sometimes termed a *claimant*, for unemployment benefits. There is far more to eligibility than merely being unemployed. As a matter of fact, you need not even be entirely unemployed to collect benefits in most states.

Chapter 2 explains what acts disqualify a claimant from receiving unemployment compensation benefits. A claimant can be disqualified before, during, or after the application procedure.

Chapter 3 details how to calculate the amount of benefits for which a claimant is eligible. It is possible to be officially *eligible* for unemployment compensation but to have your benefits reduced to such a low figure (or even to zero), that it is not worth your time to even apply for benefits.

Chapter 4 explains the two factors that must be considered when deciding *when* to apply for benefits. Most people do not know that there is a strategy to timing when to apply for benefits. This chapter contains some real insiders' secrets.

Chapter 5 walks you through the application procedure. It was written under the presumption that the reader knows absolutely nothing about the process, and provides details accordingly.

Chapter 6 discusses the situation where you have been fired or suspended by your employer, and explains what to say, and perhaps just as importantly, what not to say, when applying for benefits. This chapter details the arguments an attorney would develop on your behalf in such situations.

Chapter 7 discusses the situation where you have voluntarily quit your job, and explains what to say, and what not to say, when applying for benefits. This chapter details the arguments an attorney would develop on your behalf in such situations.

Chapter 8 discusses the situation where you have been laid off or had your work hours reduced, and explains what to say, and what not to say, when applying for benefits. This chapter details the arguments an attorney would develop on your behalf in such situations.

Chapter 9 discusses the appeals procedure. Appeals can be initiated by you or your employer, so you may be attending a hearing on your separation whether you want to or not. This chapter takes you into an administrative hearing and explains how to conduct yourself while there.

Chapter 10 discusses the issue of legal counsel. After reading this book you should feel significantly more comfortable with your rights under unemployment compensation law. This chapter, however, explains how to spot an unemployment compensation claim that is particularly complex and which may merit the seeking of professional help.

This book also contains a glossary and series of appendices. Appendix A includes the telephone numbers and addresses of the central unemployment compensation agency of each state. If they cannot provide you the answer you need, they can direct you to someone who can. Appendix B provides a comprehensive, state-by-state summary of relevant portions of each unemployment compensation law. Appendix C provides a series of case studies illustrating the circumstances under which claimants have been found eligible or ineligible for benefits. Appendix D provides a sampling of application, appeal, and other record-keeping forms used throughout the states.

You need to understand, however, that differences in unemployment compensation laws do exist. When reading this or any other self-help book, you should be aware of the fact that you are being presented with merely a summary of the law. You should use the information in this book to help guide you as to the important issues that exist in the law. If you find an issue that applies to your specific situation, you are encouraged to contact your state unemployment compensation agency at the telephone number or address contained in Appendix A of this book for more specific information on the topic.

ELIGIBILITY 1

When a claimant applies for unemployment compensation benefits, the state unemployment compensation office must first determine whether that person is eligible for benefits. Eligibility requirements vary from state to state. Appendix B includes a state-by-state summary of eligibility requirements. The following subsections of this chapter will explain more in depth how the most common criteria are applied.

There are generally seven hurdles that a claimant must overcome before and during the unemployment compensation benefit claims process (although the last three do not apply to all claimants):

1. A claimant must demonstrate that he or she had been employed in the past.

2. He or she must prove that such previous employment was of a substantial nature, yielding a certain minimum level of income.

3. He or she must show that at the time of filing for benefits he or she is unemployed (or has had income reduced so as to be considered underemployed), and is therefore in need of financial assistance.

4. A claimant must be able and available for work while receiving unemployment compensation benefits. In many states the claimant must make an active effort to secure employment.

5.   Those claimants who are deemed likely to have a difficult time securing employment may be required to participate in state reemployment programs.

6.   A claimant who has collected unemployment compensation benefits in the past must meet additional conditions before receiving benefits once again.

7.   A claimant who has been disqualified from receiving unemployment benefits must, in addition to meeting the other eligibility requirements, overcome another hurdle or hurdles before he or she may apply for benefits once again.

The following subsections will explain and discuss, in turn, the application of these eligibility criteria.

PREVIOUSLY EMPLOYED

The unemployment compensation system provides financial relief for those who have temporarily separated from employment. Nearly all states' unemployment compensation laws give a broad interpretation of the term *employee*. An employee typically is defined as one who performs services for an employer. This means that the vast majority of workers in the vast majority of states are classified as employees. The definitions rarely have a work hour element, and thus even part-time or casual workers are usually recognized as employees as well.

EXEMPT EMPLOYEES

The few workers who are not granted employee status typically fall in one of two categories. The first includes those who are actually employees under the broad definition, but who are specifically exempted from receiving unemployment benefits by the law itself. The second includes those who work, but who fail to satisfy the requirements of even this broad definition.

While the list of those explicitly exempted from unemployment benefits can be rather lengthy, it represents a relatively small portion of the work force. Obviously, if you are among the few and unfortunate, the rarity of this classification is of no comfort.

Simply reading the list of exemptions is unlikely to yield any clear understanding of why these particular employees were the unlucky chosen. These exemptions are usually based upon one of two factors. Some are excluded based upon the types of activities in which their employer participates. Others are excluded based upon the type or nature of work they actually perform for their employers.

The table below contains a listing of the types of employment most commonly exempted.

NOTE: *Not all of these exemptions apply in every state. Where they do apply, their application is often very limited. If you believe you are employed in one of these commonly exempted fields, you should contact your central state unemployment compensation agency for more information. (See Appendix A on "State Unemployment Compensation Agencies.")*

Adults employed by own children	Inmates in correctional facilities
Adults employed by own spouse	Insurance agents
Agricultural laborers	Medical interns
Baby-sitters	Patients employed in hospital
Commissioned employees	Real Estate broker
Corporate officers	Real Estate salespersons
Domestic workers	Sales agents of an investment company
Elected officials	Select government employees
Employees covered under other federal unemployment laws	Student nurses
Employees in certified work-training programs	Student workers employed by school they attend
Employees of foreign governments	Young children working for parent
Employees of religious organizations	Young newspaper carriers

INDEPENDENT
CONTRACTORS

The other type of worker commonly not covered under unemployment compensation law is the *independent contractor*. These workers typically are deemed self-employed because they do not have an employer and, therefore, do not satisfy even the broad definition of employee.

Seeing this loophole, many employers attempt to classify some of their actual employees as independent contractors. It is normally quite simple to determine whether your employer considers you an employee or independent contractor. If no income tax is withheld from your paycheck, your employer probably considers you to be an independent contractor.

What is more important, and what few people know, is that how your employer classifies you is nearly irrelevant under the law. This means that, even if your employer classified you as an independent contractor for the past ten years, you still may be eligible for unemployment compensation benefits if your services are terminated.

The key factor distinguishing an independent contractor from an employee is control. While both employees and independent contractors are limited, in that they have little control over the ultimate objective for which they are hired, the independent contractor has more control over the means and manner of achieving this objective. For example, an independent contractor may be hired to "build a wall," leaving it up to the independent contractor to determine how to build it; while an employee would be instructed to build the wall by first excavating the property, then pouring a foundation, and then stacking bricks in a particular pattern. However, you should know that this concept of control is incredibly vague in practice. Fortunately for some workers, this gives nearly every independent contractor a fighting chance to establish that he or she is actually an employee.

If you believe there will be a question as to whether you are an employee or an independent contractor when applying for benefits, you may be able to establish that you were actually an employee by emphasizing a number of points, to the extent they are true.

- *Discuss the regularity with which you worked.* Independent contractors are normally hired to perform a limited number of tasks, while an employee's service is typically less temporary in nature. Employees usually have a set work schedule with respect to work hours and workdays, while independent contractors usually have more flexibility.

- *Emphasize how, and how often, your work was supervised.* Note the names of those employees of the firm who watched you work, and explain how you were regularly provided with elaborate or detailed instructions on how to complete certain tasks.

- *Discuss how your job duties were necessary for the employer to complete its regular business activities, and not merely incidental to those business activities.* Explain, if it is true, how other employees did the same or similar tasks. Perhaps you could emphasize how other employees performed this task before you were employed. If you were once officially employed in this capacity by the firm, state this as well.

- *State (to the extent it is true) that you do not have any independent side business; do not work for anyone else; and do not advertise to perform the same or similar services for others.* You may be able to explain that you do not even own the necessary tools or equipment to provide such services to others, and must use your employer's equipment, tools ,and other materials in performing daily work tasks. If the employer never provided you with a written independent contracting agreement, this should be stated as well.

The more of these factors that apply to your specific case, the more successful you will be in demonstrating that you were mis-classified as an independent contractor.

UNEMPLOYED OR PARTIALLY UNEMPLOYED

Once you establish that you were employed in the past, you must then show that you are currently unemployed. The easiest case occurs if you are not currently working or earning income of any kind, from any source. As discussed previously, however, the vast majority of states often deem a claimant who only is *partially unemployed* to be eligible for benefits as well. Thus, even if a claimant is still working for his or her employer, or obtains alternate employment, he or she may still be considered as unemployed under the state unemployment law, as long as he or she experiences a recognizable decrease in weekly income.

For more information on how states define and compensate the partially unemployed, see the section in Chapter 3 on "Partial Employment." A state-by-state breakdown on how this term is defined can also be found in Appendix B.

FINANCIAL ELIGIBILITY

A claimant must also be found *financially eligible* for benefits. Whether a person is eligible or ineligible is a function of the amount of income the claimant earned during his or her *base period*. A base period is the period of time during which the state assesses how much income the claimant received in the past, in order to determine how much unemployment compensation benefits to award. Benefits usually are granted in proportion to past income. The concept of financial eligibility is really an extension of the concept of being previously employed, as discussed earlier in this chapter. After determining whether you were previously employed, it must now be determined whether you were sufficiently employed in the past to merit unemployment insurance coverage.

The concept of the base period is discussed more thoroughly in Chapter 3 in the section entitled "Determining a Base Period."

MULTIPLE
EMPLOYERS

An employee typically does not have to work for any one particular employer for any specific period of time to be ruled eligible. Financial qualification is generally determined with respect only to an employee's income history, without regard to the number of employers for which the employee worked or the length of time the employee worked for each individual employer during the base period.

CALCULATION
METHODS

In most states, when calculating whether a claimant earned a sufficient income during his or her base period to be deemed eligible for benefits, the state unemployment office considers only income earned while serving in the capacity of an employee. Income earned while working as an independent contractor or in one of the exempted positions (see page 2) will likely be ignored when performing this calculation. Thus, it is possible for a worker to have earned a significant amount of money during the base period, and yet fail to meet the state's financial eligibility requirements.

Financial eligibility requirements, relative to other eligibility requirements, differ greatly from state to state. (See "Benefit Eligibility" in Appendix B.) The simplest formulation, although not entirely common, is an absolute dollar amount requirement.

Example: The law may state that the employee must have earned "at least $1,000" during his or her entire base period. More typically, however, this dollar amount is relative to either the claimant's "weekly benefit amount," that is, the amount of unemployment compensation benefits to which he or she will be entitled, or to his or her highest base period quarter earnings. (See Chapter 3 on the "State Unemployment Compensation Benefit Calculations" and "Determining a Base Period" sections.)

The law may state that the claimant must have earned, during his or her entire base period, an amount equal to "1.5 times his or her highest base period quarter earnings," or an amount equal to "30 times his or her weekly benefit amount."

Occasionally, the financial eligibility dollar requirement is relative to some outside indicator, such as the state minimum wage or the *statewide average weekly wage*. The statewide average weekly wage is typically computed by adding all the wages earned by all employees of the particular state, dividing this by the number of employees earning such wages, and dividing this amount by fifty-two. Since this calculation is done annually, if your state uses this term you will probably have to contact your state unemployment compensation agency to get the recent calculation. (see Appendix A.)

Example: Assume for the moment that all the wages paid by all the employers to all employees in New York last year amounted to $90,500,000,000. Then assume that during this same year there were 6,300,000 workers employed in all New York. Although different states modify this formula slightly, generally the statewide average weekly wage would be calculated as: $90,500,000,000. Then that number is divided by 6,300,000 divided by 52 weeks, and thus equals approximately $276 per week.

To complicate matters, most state laws provide for other conditions of financial eligibility. It is very common for the law to mandate that the claimant must have earned income from work "during at least two quarters" of his or her base period. Legislators typically do not favor the situation where a highly paid employee only works for three months or less, then applies for benefits.

Example: The Bureau of Employment Security of Pennsylvania has determined that Meagan Methodical's base period includes the months of October, November, December, and January. During this base period, Meagan earned $3,000, with $2,500 of this income alone being paid in December. In Pennsylvania, Meagan would likely be ineligible for benefits since she has not earned, as required by Pennsylvania law, at least 20% of her base period earnings, that is at least $600, in months other than her high earnings month of December.

Still other state laws place minimum requirements on the income the claimant must receive during his or her highest-paying base period quarter. Typically this amount is provided in an absolute dollar figure, such as "$800." Legislators see this single quarter as indicative of what the claimant is trying to achieve, and award this attempt by entitling him or her to benefits if this goal is deemed satisfactory.

Conversely, some state laws place minimum requirements on the income the claimant must earn during his or her base period, but in quarters other than his or her highest-paying base period quarter. This mandate is intended to foil the claimant who strategically secures minimal employment of short duration, merely to apply for unemployment compensation benefits.

Finally, a handful of states require that the claimant must have been employed for a certain number of weeks during his or her base period. Thus, the law may say that the claimant must have been "employed for all or some part of 15 weeks" during his or her base period. This requirement is also intended to assure that the claimant is not merely playing the unemployment system like a strategic game.

If any of this subsection confuses you, do not worry. Terms such as the *weekly benefit amount* and *base period* will be thoroughly explained in Chapter 3, which discusses how to calculate unemployment compensation benefits. The financial eligibility requirements that apply in your particular state are included in Appendix B of this book. However, the vast majority of full-time workers, and a majority of the regular part-time workers, do qualify for benefits in most states despite this earnings requirement.

ABLE AND AVAILABLE FOR WORK

Generally, to be eligible for benefits, a claimant must be "able and available for work." In addition to being a requirement for initial eligibility, this is also a requirement for continuing to collect benefits. Unfortunately, few state statutes actually define what the terms *able* and *available* mean. (See "Able and Available for Work" in Appendix C, page 248.)

ABLE TO WORK It has never been the intention of state legislators to replace state and federal welfare and disability systems with an unemployment compensation system. Instead, the unemployment compensation system is meant to provide a safety net for those who are temporarily unemployed while they seek new employment. Consequently, to be eligible for benefits you must demonstrate that you are *able* to work, that is, both physically and mentally capable of working. If you are not currently able to work and are in need of financial support, you should seek aid under one of those alternative welfare or disability systems.

NOTE: *Being able to work does not necessarily mean that the person is capable of performing the same job duties as before. Similarly, and perhaps obviously, a claimant also need not be able to perform any and all job responsibilities available in the world at large to be deemed able to work.*

A claimant who is unable to perform physical labor duties due to failing health may still be able to work in a variety of other capacities. Similarly, mere age, in itself, does not disqualify a claimant from receiving benefits. Even if an employee was involuntarily retired, or forced to quit work due to real and substantial health risks associated with aging, such as failing eyesight, the employee may still be able to work as long as he or she can perform the necessary work duties demanded elsewhere in the labor market.

Similarly, disabled employees are also typically capable of performing a variety of work functions even though they may be unable to perform others. It is interesting to note, moreover, that in many states, a pregnant woman is treated in a similar manner as a temporarily disabled person for unemployment compensation purposes. Thus, unless she is bedridden, she is probably capable of working in a variety of capacities, and as such, may be eligible for unemployment compensation benefits. States differ dramatically in their treatment of pregnancy. Contact your state's unemployment compensation agency, listed in Appendix A, if you need more information on this subject.

AVAILABLE FOR WORK

You must also make yourself *available* to work. Availability for work centers on what you are *willing* to do. First of all, to be deemed available for work you must be willing to perform job duties currently in demand or those likely to be in demand in the near future. You must be reasonable in how you limit the type of employment for which you believe you are suited. This means that if you are only searching for a job in a field rendered obsolete by technological advances, you are probably not available for work.

Similarly, you must be willing to travel a reasonable distance to secure employment. A claimant who moves to a ghost town must be willing to travel a lot further, perhaps to the nearest metropolitan area, to be deemed available for work. In this respect however, the claimant need not be merely willing, but also able, to commute to work. Thus, if you do not have any regular and independent method of transportation, and you relocate to an area without sufficient public transportation, then you have probably rendered yourself unavailable for work.

While a claimant need not demonstrate a willingness to work twenty-four hours a day, he or she must be flexible and willing to work the number of hours and during the work schedules commonly demanded in his or her chosen field.

Example: A laborer in manufacturing usually must be willing to work during more than one shift if it is the norm in that particular industry. Similarly, a claimant who refuses full-time work because he or she is seeking only part-time employment likely will be deemed unavailable for work as well.

NOTE: *The many factors in determining availability do not always function independently. Thus, the claimant who seeks work in a steel mill will not necessarily be ineligible for benefits despite the fact that the last steel mill in his or her town recently closed, as long as he or she is willing to either commute or relocate to another mill in the vicinity. Conversely, the claimant who is willing to work in almost any laborer capacity may be able to place more stringent limits on his or her commuting without jeopardizing his or her availability status.*

Students. The question of the availability for work of a full-time, or even part-time, student has long plagued state legislatures. Some have concluded irrebuttably that such students are not available for work and are subsequently disqualified from receiving unemployment compensation benefits. (See the "Disqualification" section in Appendix B.)

Under the typical state law, however, the student is presumed unavailable under a *rebuttable presumption*. Thus, if the student can demonstrate that he or she worked the academic schedule around work, and not vice versa, the student probably will be eligible for benefits. Students who intend to apply for benefits are encouraged to contact their state's unemployment compensation agency for more information. (see Appendix A.)

Work-training programs. One final exception applies in the availability area. In most states, at various times, a claimant may have the opportunity to enroll in a variety of work-training programs with the approval of the state unemployment compensation office. While enrolled in such programs, claimants are typically unavailable for work in the statutory sense of the word. They usually are not willing to quit, nor required to quit, such programs before completion to accept employment. Because the state wants to encourage enrollment in these basic education and vocational classes, it does not disqualify the claimant on eligibility grounds even if the claimant temporarily takes himself or herself out of the job market during this training period.

EFFORT TO SECURE WORK

Under the unemployment compensation statutes currently in effect in the majority of states, a claimant must make an "effort to secure work" during his or her entire spell of unemployment. (See "Benefit Eligibility" in Appendix B.) Some states articulate this requirement in a slightly different manner, mandating that a claimant must "actively seek work," but in application there is little difference between these two formulations. The STATE OF FLORIDA AGENCY FOR WORKFORCE INNOVATION UNEMPLOYMENT COMPENSATION WORK SERVICES RECORD, included in Appendix D, may assist you in your efforts to maintain records on your employment search should you be required to produce this information to one or more staff members at the unemployment office.

Generally, these laws require a positive effort on behalf of the claimant to obtain work while collecting benefits. This contrasts with the "able and available" criteria which merely require the claimant to place himself or herself in a position where others can contact him or her if work becomes available.

Of the states that impose this requirement, the majority do not define the extent of the actual effort expected. Presumably, the time, effort, and methods utilized to search for employment must necessarily change with numerous factors including the type of employment being sought and the effectiveness of resources already used.

Example: A laborer may be expected to search the classified advertisements each week for suitable employment, while an unemployed executive may need to apply with one or more employment search firms. Similarly, the claimant who only has been combing the bulletin board in the state unemployment office for the past few weeks may be expected to alter his or her plan of attack if this search consistently comes up dry.

States actually have a system in place that more clearly defines what constitutes a reasonable effort to secure work. While such states are the exception and not the rule, they may require an employee, for example, to make "three contacts" during the week which are likely to further the claimant's efforts to seek employment. Other states specify that a claimant must make inquiries at local firms with a specified frequency. In those few states that do help formulate the job search, the claimants are typically provided specific instructions on these expectations after they are found otherwise eligible for benefits.

Participate in Re-employment Services

Most states have adopted reemployment service programs, with varying degrees of effectiveness. Under these programs, the state unemployment bureaucracy attempts to discern which types of claimants are likely to exhaust their unemployment benefits before securing employment. Such individuals are required to participate in certain activities intended to increase the likelihood of their finding jobs.

Claimants who are, in effect, replaced by technological advances, are common candidates for these programs. Similarly, claimants who become unemployed as a result of the relocation of certain industries to foreign nations are common candidates as well.

Under these programs state unemployment office personnel take a more active role in assisting these claimants in securing jobs. Typically the claimant is expected to participate in some form of re-training program to prepare him or her to work in another occupation.

Once again, it is important to remember that while unemployment office personnel usually try to work with the claimant in formulating the employment search, once the claimant is placed in the program he or she is required to participate. Failure to do so may render the claimant ineligible for unemployment compensation benefits.

Additional Hurdles for Subsequent Application for Benefits

In drafting state unemployment compensation statutes, legislators included provisions in their laws to protect the system from abuse. One source of foreseeable abuse arose from the potential for habitual filers. Thus, while there normally are no limits on how many times a claimant may file for unemployment compensation benefits during his or her lifetime, nearly every state places an additional hurdle or hurdles that a claimant must overcome before filing a second or subsequent application for benefits. Such claimants must still satisfy all other eligibility conditions, in addition to these requirements.

MAXIMUM BENEFITS DURING A BENEFIT YEAR

First, a claimant typically cannot file a claim for benefits during a particular *benefit year*, if he or she already has exhausted the benefits associated with the specific benefit year. A benefit year normally is comprised of a fifty-two week period, commencing on or around the day the claimant first files an initial claim for benefits. When a claimant first establishes a benefit year and is awarded benefits, the amount of benefits to which he or she is entitled is normally capped. Once the claimant receives the maximum amount of benefits associated with the original application for benefits, he or she normally will not be eligible for additional benefits until the fifty-two week benefit year has expired.

NOTE: *This limitation does not prevent the claimant from filing additional claims for benefits during a particular benefit year if the maximum has not been reached.*

A claimant may normally file for benefits an indefinite number of times during a particular benefit year if, for example, he or she is subject to numerous layoff periods. Only when the sum of the benefits he or she receives during this benefit year equals the maximum benefit amount does this restriction take effect. The maximum amount of benefits to which a claimant is entitled is discussed in more detail in Chapter 3. (See also the "Maximum Total" section in Appendix B.) By completing the **WEEKLY EARNINGS WORKSHEET**, included in Appendix D each week while collecting unemployment compensation benefits, you will be better prepared to monitor your progress to overcome this obstacle.

EARNINGS AFTER BEGINNING THE PRIOR BENEFIT YEAR

The second obstacle that a claimant must overcome concerns his or her actual earnings from employment. This limitation typically requires a claimant, who is filing for benefits after having received benefits in the past, to earn a certain level of income through employment after the beginning of the prior benefit year before he or she can establish a new benefit year. This means that in order to establish back-to-back benefit years without any time interval between such periods, the claimant must have worked during the former benefit year. (See the "Subsequent Application" section in Appendix B.)

Example: Robin Reapli, a resident of West Virginia, has just completed her benefit year which began on April 13th of last year, and ended on April 12th of this year. During her benefit year, her weekly benefit amount, as calculated by the appropriate state agency, was $500. While collecting benefits, Robin had a part-time job and earned exactly $3,000 during the entire benefit year. Robin would likely not be eligible yet to establish another benefit year, and thus she cannot continue to collect benefits. This is because she has not earned during the first benefit year, at least $4,000 which is the product of her weekly benefit amount, $500, and the state mandated times.

A handful of states express this as an absolute dollar amount of earnings necessary to requalify for benefits. This amount can range anywhere from $50 to $2,000 depending upon the particular situation. The vast majority of states, however, peg this level of income relative to the claimant's weekly benefit amount. Thus, the standard formulation states that a claimant who received unemployment benefits during a prior benefit year "must have worked and earned an amount equal to 8 times his or her weekly benefit amount" after the commencement of the prior benefit year.

This dollar amount rarely carries with it a time factor. In other words, the vast majority of states do not require the claimant to earn the specified amount during a time period of specific duration. He or she can earn the necessary income during a single week and qualify for benefits rather quickly, or the claimant can take several months to earn the funds thus delaying his or her subsequent eligibility status. Only a few states actually require the claimant to work for a period of time, perhaps a few weeks, before becoming eligible for unemployment compensation benefits once again.

There are also two variations to this requirement that are noteworthy. First, when the majority of states peg this amount relative to the claimant's weekly benefit amount, they mean his or her current weekly benefit amount. That is, the weekly benefit amount calculated for the new benefit year for which he or she is applying. A number of states, however, peg this amount in relation to the claimant's former weekly benefit amount. In other words, the amount is computed using the weekly benefit amount as calculated for the claimant's prior benefit year.

The second variation concerns what are commonly termed *lag period wages*. In a handful of states, claimants need not overcome an additional hurdle to qualify for a second benefit year. In order to protect against abuse by regular filers, however, the relevant state statute sometimes places certain restrictions on a claimant's ability to apply income he or she rightfully earned as base period earnings. Such restrictions may reduce the claimant's calculated weekly benefit amount for his or her subsequent benefit year.

Lag period wages include the income earned by a claimant after the close of the months included in his or her prior base period, and before the beginning of his or her prior benefit year. As you will soon learn, in most states, the last few months of income that a claimant earns prior to applying for benefits are normally not included in his or her base period. Thus, such income is not considered when calculating his or her weekly benefit amount. (See the section "Determining a Base Period" in Chapter 3.)

Depending upon when a claimant files for benefits, it is possible that a subsequent filer may have these lag period months included in his or her new base period. In some states, however, in order to include these earnings in his or her new base period earnings calculation, the claimant must have earned a certain amount of income between the time when the former benefit year began and when he or she files for the new benefit year. Under this variation the claimant must also earn a certain amount of income during the same time period as used in the common formulation previously described. In states that apply these lag period wage restrictions, however, the claimant risks only the benefit of using certain income earned during a particular time period for his or her weekly benefit amount calculation, not eligibility for benefits entirely as in the common formulation previously discussed.

ADDITIONAL HURDLES FOR DISQUALIFIED CLAIMANTS (PURGING DISQUALIFICATION)

A claimant who satisfies all of the eligibility requirements discussed thus far may still fail to receive unemployment compensation benefits due to one of many disqualification provisions provided for under state law. In reality, there is little difference between being *disqualified* and being deemed *ineligible* for benefits, although most state laws distinguish between these two events.

As discussed previously, a claimant who attempts to apply for unemployment compensation benefits in succeeding years must overcome an additional hurdle or hurdles before being held eligible for benefits. These hurdles were intended to protect the integrity of the system. Similarly, when a claimant leaves work under statutorily disqualifying circumstances, he or she must again overcome an additional hurdle or hurdles before being deemed eligible for benefits. In these situations, however, the hurdles are provided in the law to just make it more difficult for the disqualified person to receive benefits.

Most state laws provide for numerous factors, each of which may independently disqualify a claimant from receiving benefits. (See the section on "Disqualification" in Appendix B.) A claimant who is discharged from employment for misconduct is usually disqualified from receiving benefits. Moreover, a claimant who voluntarily terminates his or her own employment without good cause is usually disqualified as well.

A claimant who fails to accept or apply for suitable work is normally disqualified, as is a claimant who separates from work during a labor dispute. While disqualification is discussed in Chapter 2, the focus of this section is on the affect of such a disqualification upon a later attempt by a claimant to file for benefits.

Often a disqualifying separation carries with it an explicit time period of disqualification.

Example: State law may provide that one who quits work without good cause will not be eligible for benefits for "seven weeks subsequent to the disqualifying separation."

Such time periods are statutorily defined, and the claimant is powerless to alter them. A disqualified claimant will be informed on what grounds he or she was denied benefits, and how long he or she must wait before applying for benefits again (subject to any rights of appeal). A potential claimant may want to contact one of the telephone numbers or addresses contained in Appendix A to inquire further about these statutory time periods *before* separating from employment under possibly disqualifying circumstances.

In nearly every state, however, the mere passage of time will not make the disqualified person eligible for benefits. In such states, depending upon the underlying basis for the disqualification, the claimant must earn a certain amount of income through employment after the disqualifying separation before again being deemed eligible.

NOTE: *This additional requirement does not give the claimant free license to quit this subsequent employment once he or she earns the requisite income. His or her separation from subsequent employment must, in itself, not be for disqualifying reasons, or the disqualification purging process will start again.*

As with the hurdle involved with subsequent applications for benefits, the income hurdle involved with disqualifying separations is typically provided in the statute in a form that is relative to the claimant's weekly benefit amount. Thus, a claimant may, subsequent to the disqualifying act, have to earn an amount of income that ranges between one times his or her weekly benefit amount and thirty times his or her weekly benefit amount. These amounts vary greatly from state to state. (See "Purging Disqualification" in Appendix B.)

Example: Greg Gokwit has been gainfully employed virtually everyday since his high school graduation approximately fifteen years ago. About a month ago, after an argument with a co-worker, Greg decided to quit his bookkeeping position, thinking that he could probably get a similar job elsewhere. Greg was right. after only one week of unemployment, Greg secured another bookkeeping position with almost identical wages and benefits. Unfortunately, however, Greg's new employer filed for bankruptcy exactly twelve days later and was forced to lay off Greg.

Despite his recent "lay off status", Greg would still be disqualified from receiving benefits in most states. While he certainly had the right to quit his former bookkeeping position, leaving after an isolated argument with a co-worker normally is a disqualifying separation. In Greg's brief employment with his most recent employer, Greg probably did not earn enough income to purge the disqualification. If Greg typically earns $400 per week, his weekly benefit amount as calculated by the unemployment office would roughly be about $200.

If , for example, Greg lived in California, he would not be eligible for benefits until he earns, subsequent to a disqualifying separation, employment income of at least "5 x his weekly benefit amount". Thus, Greg would need to earn approximately 5 x $200 = $1,000 to purge his disqualification. In his most recent but short employment experience, he likely only earned approximately two weeks wages, about $800. Under this scenario, Greg needs to secure replacement employment and earn the balance, $200, before a subsequent separation from that newest position would render him eligible for benefits.

Even within states, however, the necessary income amounts tend to vary depending upon the type of disqualification they are intended to purge.

Example: A state may provide that a claimant who is discharged for willful misconduct is disqualified from receiving benefits until he or she earns income in the amount of "8 times his or her weekly benefit amount." The same state, however, may require a claimant who is disqualified because he or she quit work to earn an amount of at least "10 times his or her weekly benefit amount."

It is important to note that in almost half of the states this dollar amount carries with it a time factor as well. (See "Purging Disqualification" in Appendix B.) In other words, such states require the claimant to earn, through employment, the specified amount during a specified time period. Such states usually require the claimant to work between three and fifteen weeks after his or her disqualifying separation before becoming eligible for unemployment compensation benefits.

Finally, in a small minority of states, claimants who purge their original disqualification still feel the residual effects of this original disqualification. For example, in select states, even after purging a disqualification, the claimant still experiences a reduction in the benefits to which he or she would have otherwise been eligible had he or she never been disqualified. Appendix A lists contact telephone numbers and web pages for additional information.

DISQUALIFICATION ISSUES

The difference between being deemed *ineligible* to collect unemployment compensation benefits and being *disqualified* from collecting such benefits is trivial. If you are marked with either status you will not be granted unemployment compensation benefits.

However, disqualification issues tend to be contested with far more frequency than eligibility issues. The most hotly debated disqualification issues concern the circumstances of the employee's separation from work. These issues tend to be far more controversial, but far less complex, than the eligibility questions.

While employers often compile the necessary documentation, for example, to calculate financial eligibility, they rarely accept the daunting task of recalculating this amount to confirm whether the state unemployment office has properly processed the data and therefore determined financial eligibility accurately. Conversely, an employer tends to already know, or at least have its own version as to, why a particular employee separated from its employ.

Employers always think they were fair with employees and gave them every opportunity to mend their ways. Employees know they always tried their best, and can name any number of employees who perform their duties worse yet seem always to avoid employer criticism. Many separations leave both sides with ill feelings. Subsequently, these disqualification issues tend to be passionately contested.

Virtually every state law provides for at least eight sets of circumstances under which an otherwise eligible claimant will be disqualified from receiving benefits. These are discussed below:

DISQUALIFICATION
BASED ON
TERMINATION OF
EMPLOYMENT

The first three circumstances concern the reasons the claimant left work.

- The employee is discharged for committing an act of willful misconduct.

- The employee quits work without a good reason.

- The employee separates from work as a result of a labor dispute.

DISQUALIFICATION
DURING THE
APPLICATION
PROCESS

The next three circumstances include when a claimant may be rejected during the process of filing an application for benefits.

- The claimant is an illegal alien. This is a disqualifying situation in every state.

- The claimant is already receiving unemployment compensation benefits under other state or federal law.

- The claimant makes false statements to state unemployment office personnel during the application procedure or later while he or she is collecting benefits.

DISQUALIFICATION
AFTER APPROVAL

The final two circumstances render a claimant ineligible for benefits and involve his or her actions after he or she is already collecting unemployment compensation benefits.

- If after the beginning of payouts the claimant fails to apply for or accept employment which is both available and suitable, he or she will be disqualified from receiving benefits.

- Similarly, if after the beginning of payouts, the claimant makes false statements to unemployment office personnel, he or she may also be disqualified.

The following discusses the circumstances that serve to disqualify a claimant in nearly every state. To avoid duplicating materials, the making of false statements during the application process and after the application process will be treated as one topic.

DISCHARGED FOR WILLFUL MISCONDUCT

BURDEN OF
PROOF

An employee who is fired from work is not automatically disqualified from collecting unemployment compensation benefits. In fact, if an employer discharges an employee, the employer generally has the *burden of proving* that the reason for the discharge was willful misconduct on behalf of the employee. Thus, if the employer fails to provide any explanation for the discharge, the employee usually will be granted benefits. Similarly, if the employer justifies the separation by describing an act that may be willful misconduct, but the employee provides an equally convincing description of the circumstances that tends to show he or she was dismissed for reasons other than misconduct, the employee generally will be awarded benefits. In other words, the employee wins on a tie.

WILLFUL
MISCONDUCT
DEFINED

What actually constitutes willful misconduct is not an easy question. Some state statutes attempt to define the concept more definitively. For example, the law in a number of states specifically provides that an employee who is discharged for "theft," or the intentional "destruction of property connected with work," shall be disqualified from receiving benefits. Refer to the listing for your state in Appendix B to determine how your state defines this concept. (Also see the section "Willful Misconduct" in Appendix C.)

All other things being equal, it is easier for a claimant to fight a particular disqualification if the applicable law is ambiguous. For example, drinking alcoholic beverages on the job constitutes willful misconduct according to some state statutes. If your state statute does not explicitly spell this out, you will have a significantly greater chance of contesting disqualification if you were fired for imbibing at work. (See the section on "Alcohol or Drug Abuse" in Chapter 6.)

In the broadest sense, disqualifying misconduct exists where an employee intentionally disregards an employer rule, or acts in a manner contrary to that which an employer has a right to expect. A single act of major misconduct or a series of instances of less serious misconduct may both rise to the level of disqualifying misconduct. Conduct most commonly classified as willful misconduct includes: excessive absenteeism, insubordination, dishonesty, committing a criminal act, and alcohol or drug use on the job.

Appendix C more thoroughly explains the concept of disqualifying behavior and provides examples to help illustrate when an employee crosses the line. Chapter 6 discusses in more detail how to contest an accusation of disqualifying behavior.

VOLUNTARILY TERMINATED OWN EMPLOYMENT WITHOUT GOOD CAUSE

BURDEN OF
PROOF

An employee who quits work is not automatically disqualified from collecting benefits. The employee who terminates his or her own employment, however, does have the burden of proving that he or she had good cause to leave. If the employee fails to provide any explanation for his or her departure, the employee typically will be denied benefits. Similarly, if the employee justifies the separation by describing a condition of employment that may have provided him or her with good cause to leave, but the employer provides an equally convincing argument that the employee's story was false, and the employee really left the job for a less compelling reason, the employee generally will be denied benefits. In other words, the employer wins on a tie.

The distinction between the applicable burden of proof in a discharge case and the applicable burden of proof in a voluntary quit case, explains why employers often request employees who quit to provide a letter of resignation. It also explains why employers often offer employees the option of resigning, rather than being fired. Watch out for this old trick. While signing such a resignation form may be the only way of securing a much needed written letter of recommendation, be aware that it may drastically reduce your chances of receiving unemployment benefits. You may still apply, and argue that you were really fired, but it will be more difficult to prove.

What actually constitutes good cause for voluntary termination is not an easy question. Some state statutes attempt to define the concept more clearly by eliminating certain arguments. For example, the law in a handful of states specifically provides that an employee who quits employment to "marry or perform marital, parental or familial duties" shall be disqualified from receiving benefits. Refer to Appendix B to determine how your state defines good cause. (Also see the section on "Voluntarily Quit Without Good Cause" in Appendix C.)

GOOD CAUSE
FOR LEAVING

All other things being equal, it is easier for a claimant to fight a particular disqualification if the applicable law is ambiguous. For example, an employee who departs from work to care for his or her children in a state that has a statute similar to that just described will have a difficult time claiming he or she left for good cause. Conversely, if your state statute does not explicitly spell this out, you will have a significantly greater chance of contesting disqualification if you depart from work to care for your children. (See the section on "Personal Reasons" in Chapter 7.)

In the broadest sense, good cause for quitting exists where an employee essentially is left with no alternative but to leave. Before leaving, the employee generally is expected to notify his or her employer of the impending departure. Such notification provides the employer with the opportunity to make special accommodations for the employee to remain with the firm. The employee who points at his or her employer or working environment as the motivating factor for the departure generally has a greater chance of avoiding disqualification than the employee who cites other, less clearly job-related reasons for leaving.

For example, if you allege that you had to leave your job at a factory because of the excessive dust in the air, you are far more likely to receive benefits than if you claim that personal reasons compelled your departure. Justifications provided for leaving a firm that have been classified as "good cause" for quitting in the past include: material changes in the conditions of employment, transportation problems, safety or health hazards, and hostile work environments.

Appendix C more thoroughly explains the concept of good cause for voluntary quitting and provides examples to help illustrate where good cause has been found in the past. Later we will explain in more detail how to put forth a sound argument that a separation was motivated by good cause. (See the section on "Collecting benefits if you quit your job" in Chapter 7.)

SEPARATED FROM WORK AS A RESULT OF A LABOR DISPUTE

Under most situations, claimants who separate from work as a direct result of a labor dispute are disqualified from receiving benefits. This has been a hot topic in recent years among politicians on all levels. Part of the law as it stands today is due to funding issues. The legal argument is that a claimant on strike (particularly if it is in violation of a collective bargaining agreement) is voluntarily refusing to work, and thus can be dealt with under the standard voluntary quit provisions of the law. Some believe all strikers should be eligible for benefits, whereas others would limit eligibility to where a collective bargaining agreement has ended and employees have worked for a period of time without the protection of a new contract before going on strike.

Under federal law, employees have the right to unionize and participate in other concerted activities. Under certain circumstances they are even encouraged to do so. Pursuant to these laws, employees usually have the right to strike or otherwise voice their grievances against their employers. Legislators, however, have drawn a line.

In an attempt to reduce the occurrence of protracted plant shut-downs, legislators have disqualified striking workers and other employees who are unemployed due to work stoppages caused by a labor dispute. The feeling is that the cessation in production in itself will place tremendous pressure on the employer to settle the dispute. The cessation of income is intended to place similar pressure on employees to settle the dispute. Much like a parent dealing with his or her children, legislators do not care who is right; they just want the fighting to stop.

LOCKOUT
EXCEPTION

Most jurisdictions place one or more limits on labor dispute disqualification. First, many states allow the worker who is unemployed due to an employer *lockout* to collect benefits. Generally, a lockout occurs when an employer withholds work from its employees in an effort to coerce them to accept its terms to settle the dispute. For example, if an employer closes its plant down for a week in an attempt to force employees to accept a pay cut, this would be a lockout. A claimant who is unemployed under this scenario may receive benefits. See the section on "Labor Disputes (Lockouts and Violence)" in Chapter 7.

Often it is not clear whether a work stoppage resulted from a strike or a lockout. Some employers claim, for example, that they were forced to close their doors when demonstrations became violent, because they feared that employees would be hurt or machinery would be damaged. When this occurs employers claim their actions were necessarily caused by inappropriate employee behavior, and the employees cry lockout. Under these circumstances, most states attempt to assign the responsibility for the shut-down to one of the parties. If it was initiated unilaterally by the employer, the claimant has a fighting chance for benefits.

EXCEPTION FOR
CLAIMANT NOT
INVOLVED IN
STRIKE

There is another, albeit small, loophole in this area. Not every employee of a firm closed by a strike is necessarily ineligible for benefits. In many states a claimant who is unemployed during a labor dispute may receive benefits, if the claimant:

1. is not participating in, or directly interested in, the labor dispute that caused the work stoppage;

2. is not a member of the organization (i.e., the union) that is participating in, or directly interested in, the labor dispute that caused the work stoppage; and,

3. does not belong to the class of workers who are participating in or directly interested in the dispute. (Thus, if the assembly-line union goes on strike, and you work on the dock and do not belong to that union, but are unable to work due to the strike, you may be eligible for benefits.)

All three of these hurdles must be overcome to avoid disqualification. Some of these, especially the third, are subject to various interpretations. See the section on "Labor Disputes (Strikes)" in Chapter 6.

ILLEGAL ALIENS

If you are what is commonly termed an *illegal alien*, you are essentially prohibited from obtaining unemployment compensation benefits. In this respect, legislators have felt free to discriminate against such persons because, according to law, they generally are not permitted to work in the respective state anyway.

There are two classifications of workers who, by definition, are not illegal aliens:

1. **Citizens of the United States.** Every citizen of the United States, whether natural or naturalized, has the right to work in any state. If your citizenship status is questioned when you are filing for benefits, you may be required to produce one or more of a number of documents. Typically a Social Security card, United States birth or nationality certificate, current driver's license, or other state identification card with a photograph will suffice.

2. **Aliens with work permits.** If you are not a citizen of the United States you may still be eligible for benefits if you can demonstrate that you have legal authorization to work in the country. To this extent, personnel at the state unemployment office may ask you to produce a resident alien or other alien registration card (i.e., a *green card*), a certificate of naturalization, or a foreign passport endorsed by the Attorney General entitling you to work in the United States.

ALREADY RECEIVING UNEMPLOYMENT BENEFITS IN ANOTHER STATE

In nearly every state, a claimant who is currently receiving unemployment compensation benefits under another state's law, or under federal law is disqualified from additional benefit awards. Thus, a claimant cannot collect unemployment benefits from two different states during a single spell of unemployment.

A person may be disqualified in certain circumstances, even before he or she actually begins collecting unemployment benefits in another state.

Example: If you merely have applied for benefits in one state and have not received word yet on your eligibility status there, you will normally be forbidden, at least in the interim, from applying for benefits in another state.

Sometimes, this form of disqualification, however, is only temporary. If the other state finds the claimant ineligible for benefits, the disqualification in the second state will no longer apply.

Under rare conditions, a claimant who is eligible for benefits under an alternative national system of unemployment insurance may not be eligible for benefits under any of the state systems. The only set of circumstances where this really applies is where a claimant works in the railroad or maritime industries and is covered under a railroad or maritime unemployment insurance program.

FALSE REPRESENTATION IN ORDER TO RECEIVE BENEFITS

In each state, a claimant who makes a false statement to the state unemployment office personnel in order to receive benefits is disqualified from receiving such benefits. This disqualification applies both if the statement is made with the intention of rendering an otherwise ineligible claimant eligible, or rendering the eligible claimant eligible for more unemployment benefits.

Example: A claimant who is caught lying about employment search efforts, in a state that requires claimants to actively search for work, may be disqualified from receiving any benefits for the ensuing weeks.

For this disqualification to apply, the claimant generally must have intended to mislead unemployment office personnel or at least must have known that such statements would most likely mislead. However, a claimant who accidentally misinforms the unemployment office will not be disqualified merely for providing incorrect information.

In some states, even the failure to disclose *material information* is an offense that results in disqualification. In the general sense, the following may be considered material information:

- any information that can affect eligibility for benefits;

- any information that can affect the weekly benefit calculation; and,

- any information affecting eligibility or weekly calculations that the claimant has knowledge of, and knows the unemployment compensation agency does not.

Under these laws, the claimant who conceals important information from state unemployment office personnel will be denied benefits.

Example: The claimant who notices that the information in his or her file at the state unemployment office is incomplete, in that some unfavorable portion of his or her employment history does not appear, and who fails to notify office personnel of this fact, may be deemed ineligible for benefits if caught. (See the "Disqualification" section in Appendix B.)

NOTE: *State provisions punishing false statements or representations often do more than merely disqualify applicants. In most jurisdictions such lies, or even intentional non-disclosures of material information, can be prosecuted as a crime. A claimant who is convicted of one of these crimes can be fined or even imprisoned under certain conditions. Be careful with your words.*

FAILURE, WITHOUT GOOD CAUSE, TO ACCEPT OR APPLY FOR SUITABLE WORK

State unemployment compensation systems are intended to provide financial relief for the temporarily unemployed. The laws in the various states presume that a claimant will search for replacement employment while collecting benefits. The degree of effort expected and required of a claimant during this search varies greatly from state to state. Only a minority of the states actually require the claimant to "actively" search for employment. Regardless of how much effort states require claimants to exert while job hunting, all states disqualify claimants who fail to accept or apply for work that is both available and suitable. (See the "Benefit Eligibility" section in Appendix B.)

APPLYING FOR
SUITABLE WORK

While all state laws have similar provisions disqualifying claimants who fail to accept or apply for suitable work, there is great variety as to how they apply these laws. Some states require claimants to follow certain job search strategies each week.

Example: A state may require a claimant to apply for two suitable positions each week. Failure to do so would serve to disqualify the claimant. (See the section on "Suitable Work" in Appendix C.)

On the other extreme, many states only penalize claimants who fail to apply for particular positions to which the state unemployment office referred them. Ultimately, this means that the job searches of these claimants are only scrutinized where the state office provides individualized job hunting aid. If you are awarded unemployment compensation benefits, you should ask unemployment office personnel if and how the office aids in the job search process.

ACCEPTING
SUITABLE WORK

The failure to accept suitable employment has a more universal application than the failure to apply for such employment. Two parties monitor a claimant's willingness to accept employment. First, the state unemployment office expects the claimant to accept, if offered, any suitable positions for which the claimant applies. Thus, if the office requires the claimant to provide a list of the applications he or she completed in a given week, the office may follow up on this information and demand an explanation why a particular job was rejected.

Many unemployment office inquiries regarding the failure to accept employment arise from information provided by the former employer. Generally, an employer's unemployment tax rate increases when former employees collect unemployment compensation benefits. Thus, the employer has the incentive to expedite the claimant's return to work.

Employers who know the system also know how to work it. Often when an employer and employee clash, the resultant discharge is not deemed to be due to willful misconduct, and the employee is granted benefits. Employers know that, under these conditions, the last thing the employee wants and intends to do is return to the firm. The devious employer recalls the employee and notifies the state unemployment office of this action. If the employee refuses to return to the less-than-amicable environment, the employee essentially fails to accept suitable work. Thus, the employer can effectively convert a compensable separation into a noncompensable separation.

You can protect yourself from this in one of two, although perhaps not completely satisfactory, ways. First, you can accept your old job back. At least you will have a paycheck and perhaps you can seek alternate employment during off-work hours. Alternatively, you can claim that your former work environment was so hostile that it gave you good cause to quit. This is actually converting an involuntary discharge into a voluntary quit for good cause. While such devious employers may be more apt to maintain hostile work environments, unfortunately the threshold of what constitutes a sufficiently hostile environment to merit a voluntary quit is usually fairly high. (See the section on "Hostile Work Environment" in Chapter 7.)

State laws typically impose two additional limitations on a claimant's responsibility to accept and apply for work. First, a claimant may reject or fail to apply for work as long as he or she has "good cause" to do so. Unfortunately, this phrase usually is determined on a state by state and even case by case basis. Thus, in certain states, the refusal to accept a position temporarily vacated by a striking employee may be justifiable under the appropriate unemployment benefit statute. More generally, a claimant who really wants to work but is confronted with an obstacle that would cause any reasonable person to reject or fail to apply for a particular position, may have *good cause* for such action. In determining when good cause exists, the question usually revolves around the existence or absence of reasonable alternative actions. Unfortunately, the term good cause is only specifically defined on a case-by case basis such as where an illness or unique allergy, transportation problems, or obvious hostilities in the prospective work environment lead to the rejection. Appendix C contains a section on "Suitable Work," which provides specific case examples where *good cause* has been found.

Second, a claimant need only accept or apply for suitable work. Again, what is suitable work and what is not, is not very clear. The employer's trick described previously works well because former employment usually is presumed to be suitable work. Similarly, a position that provides similar working conditions, work responsibilities, and a comparable benefits package to the claimant's last job likely will be deemed suitable as well. Appendix C contains a section on "Suitable Work," which also provides specific case examples explaining when work is considered "*suitable.*"

NOTE: *Due to the ambiguity of what truly is suitable work, you must be careful. While demonstrating a willingness to consider alternative positions of various natures during a job search is normally commendable, you are cautioned to focus your job search on quality jobs, rather than on a quantity of applications. If you interview for a number of positions just to see what type of employment is out there, you may be sorry.*

If an employer offers you a position that you feel is not right for you, it may be too late. If you reject the position, the employer may notify the state unemployment office, which may conclude that you refused what it deems suitable work for you. Thus, you really should keep your job search focused on positions you truly want, or you may find out the hard way how broadly the unemployment office sometimes defines the term suitable.

AMOUNT OF BENEFITS 3

The unemployment compensation system typically provides a worker who has separated from employment between fifty and fifty-five percent of his or her former weekly wage. The actual wage-replacement percentage that will be granted, however, may vary greatly depending upon a number of factors including:

- the state in which he or she was formerly employed;

- the amount of income that he or she established in past employment; or,

- the earning patterns that he or she has established in past employment.

Although it may seem unfair, an employee who receives a substantially larger portion of income in a single calendar quarter may be eligible for higher unemployment compensation benefits than a person who has earned a relatively stable but lower income over the years.

The amount of benefits to which a claimant is entitled is normally calculated in weekly increments. Conversely, benefits are typically paid every two weeks. A claimant deemed eligible for benefits should expect to receive a check from the state every two weeks, in an amount equal to twice what the state terms his or her *weekly benefit rate* or *weekly benefit amount*.

DETERMINING A BASE PERIOD

Regardless of what method a particular state elects to use to calculate a claimant's weekly benefit amount, it first must determine his or her *base period*. A base period is the time period during which the claimant's earnings from work are assessed to determine the amount of unemployment compensation benefits he or she will receive. In nearly every state, a claimant's base period is defined as the period consisting of the "first four of his or her last five completed calendar quarters." Such quarters usually are determined relative to the date the claimant files for benefits, not relative to the date he or she separates from employment.

The states, of course, recognize four calendar quarters consisting of three months each. The first calendar quarter includes the months of January, February, and March. The second calendar quarter includes the months of April, May, and June. The third calendar quarter includes the months of July, August, and September. The fourth calendar quarter includes the months of October, November, and December.

An individual who is trying to determine which quarters are included under this base period definition must first disregard any time period that is not a complete calendar quarter. For example, if you file for benefits in the middle of December, you should not consider December or the immediately preceding November and October as part of your base period.

After ignoring this incomplete calendar quarter, you must next disregard the first immediately preceding completed calendar quarter (July, August, and September). Your base period is comprised of the four calendar quarters immediately preceding this quarter (in other words, the base period would be for the one year period ending June 30th).

The table on the next page, and the example which follows, will help explain how the vast majority of states determine which months to include in an individual's base period.

TABLE: BASE PERIOD QUARTERS

A Claimant Who Files for Benefits in...	Has a Base Period of Four Calendar Quarters, Which Ends in the Calendar Quarter That Concludes on...
January February March	September 30th
April May June	December 31st
July August September	March 31st
October November December	June 30th

Example: Jordan Jobless was laid off from her position at Aurevoir, Inc., several months ago. Jordan finally filed an unemployment compensation claim at her state unemployment compensation office on June 23, 2001. The state unemployment office will determine her base period to include the quarter containing October, November, and December of 2000, the quarter containing July, August, and September of 2000, the quarter containing April, May, and June of 2000 and the quarter containing January, February, and March of 2000.

While the vast majority of states use this method for determining a particular claimant's base period, some states (most notably California, Massachusetts, New Hampshire, New York, and Wyoming) use alternative methods. The base period in New York, for example contains the fifty-two week period concluding on the Sunday immediately preceding the claimant's application for benefits. In California, the base period contains the four quarters ending in the preceding June if the claim is filed in November, December, or January; the four quarters ending in the preceding September if the claim is filed in February, March, or April; the four quarters ending in the preceding December if the claim is filed in May, June, or July; or the four quarters ending in the preceding March if the claim is filed in August, September, or October.

Where an individual who recently separated from work earned a fairly constant weekly income, however, the choice of which calendar quarters a state chooses to include in its base period is probably immaterial. Suffice it to say that base periods typically include four quarters, and thus, one year of income. Claimants in the unconventional states listed above, who were not formerly salaried employees and who earned varying amounts from week to week, are encouraged to contact their state unemployment compensation agency at either the telephone number or address listed in Appendix A for more information concerning this topic. (See also the section on page 56 on "Estimating Calculations.")

A modified system for determining a base period may apply to claimants in the following situations:

- claimants who were disabled, ill, injured, or otherwise incapable of working during all or a portion of the base period;

- claimants who received unemployment compensation benefits in an immediately preceding benefit year; and,

- claimants who failed to meet the standard financial eligibility requirements under their state unemployment compensation law.

Individuals who find themselves in any of these situations are also encouraged to contact their state unemployment compensation agency, or discuss their particular situation with a state unemployment interviewer when applying for benefits.

STATE UNEMPLOYMENT COMPENSATION BENEFIT CALCULATIONS

Now that you have a good idea how to determine which months fall into your base period, you must understand the important part the earnings in your base period play in the calculation of your weekly benefit amount.

Different states calculate a claimant's weekly benefit amount using different computation methods. In general, however, there are four main computation methods employed by the various states:

1. the total base period earnings of the claimant;

2. the earnings received in the base period quarter in which the claimant earned his or her highest amount of income;

3. the average weekly wage of a claimant; and,

4. a statutory schedule or table is used, which bases the claimant's weekly benefit amount upon anywhere from one to several of a variety of relevant factors.

In general, most states use only one of these four computation systems, however, a few states alternate between methods, depending upon a claimant's earnings or other claimant-specific factors.

Appendix B contains a state-by-state summary of how weekly benefit amounts are calculated. This section, however, will help explain the several calculation methods more thoroughly and will provide examples to further illustrate how these systems are applied.

NOTE: *Before you frantically go scavenging through your personal records to attempt the computations, stop. It is true that in the past you have received sufficient information to make the calculations. Most of this information should be contained on your pay stubs. If by chance your personal records concerning your income are not entirely complete or up to* *date, however, do not panic. Over the years your current and previous employers have been required, under legal mandate, to maintain certain records concerning your income history. Some of these records they need only retain in their own files. Others they must periodically forward to various governmental agencies, including your central state unemployment compensation agency.*

If your records are not in the best of order, do not worry, you will not be disqualified from receiving benefits merely because you did not keep some of these important documents. This is one of the many situations where the government probably knows more about you than *you* do. (For further information see a later section in this chapter titled "Estimating Calculations.")

TOTAL BASE PERIOD EARNINGS METHOD

Several states calculate a claimant's weekly benefit amount in reference to the total amount of wages the claimant earned in his or her entire base period. The sum of these wages is then multiplied by a fixed statutory portion amount, usually written as a percentage, to arrive at the weekly benefit amount.

This computation method looks at an entire year of earnings. It presumes that periods of unusually low earnings during the base period will be cancelled out by periods of unusually high earnings, and thus result in a fair and just benefit assignment.

Example: Orville Oregon lives in a state that computes the weekly benefit amount based on the total amount of wages the claimant earns during his or her entire base period. In the four quarters of Orville's base period, he earned a total of $22,700. The fixed statutory percentage applied by this state is 1.25%. The state unemployment office will calculate Orville's weekly benefit amount as $284. ($22,700 x .0125 = $284.)

HIGHEST-PAYING BASE PERIOD QUARTER EARNINGS METHOD

The majority of states compute a claimant's weekly benefit amount with reference only to his or her highest paying base period quarter. In these states, the base period is divided into its four calendar quarters. The income earned by the claimant in each of these four quarters is compared to the income earned in each other quarter of the base period. Only the highest paying quarter is relevant in this calculation. The earnings of the remaining three are not considered. The earnings of this single quarter are then multiplied by a fixed statutory portion amount, usually written in the form of a fraction, to arrive at the claimant's weekly benefit amount.

This computation method looks at only a three-month period of earnings of a particular claimant. Thus, a claimant who had an unusually high quarter of earnings may be eligible for more benefits than a claimant who earned a stable salary, even if on average they earned the same weekly wages.

The theory behind this calculation method is that the quarter in which the claimant earned the most income is more representative of his or her income potential because it was probably the quarter in which he or she was more fully employed, both with respect to working hours and with respect to working tasks which utilized his or her particular talents and abilities. This method presumes that it is more fair to base a claimant's weekly benefit amount on this one quarter alone because the claimant should not be penalized if he or she was willing to accept employment for which he or she may have been over-qualified.

A few states apply a minor variation to this computation method. In such states the sum of wages earned in more than one quarter but less than all quarters of the base period is used in the calculation. Thus, a state may add the income a claimant earned during the two quarters in which a claimant earned his or her highest income, rather than just focusing on the single quarter in which he or she had the most earnings. This income amount would then be multiplied by a fixed statutory portion amount as with the normal computation method.

Example: Ari Zona lives in a state that computes the weekly benefit amount in reference to the claimant's highest-paying base period quarter. In the first quarter of Ari's base period he earned $2,600. In the second quarter of Ari's base period he earned $3,120. In the third quarter of his base period he was unemployed and subsequently received no income. In the fourth quarter of Ari's base period he earned a total of $1,200. The fixed statutory portion amount in this state is $1/25$. The state unemployment office will calculate Ari's weekly benefit amount as $125. ($3,120 x $1/25$ = $125.)

AVERAGE WEEKLY WAGE METHOD

A handful of states compute the weekly benefit amount with reference to the average weekly wage the claimant earned during his or her entire base period. The average weekly wage is usually derived by taking the sum of all wages the claimant received during his or her base period and dividing this amount by fifty-two (since there are fifty-two weeks during an entire base period). This average weekly wage is multiplied by a fixed statutory portion amount, usually written in the form of a percentage, to arrive at the weekly benefit amount.

Much like the total base period earnings method, this computation method also looks at an entire year of earnings. It presumes that periods of unusually low earnings during a given base period will be cancelled out by periods of unusually high earnings of the base period, and thus result in a fair and just benefit assignment.

Example: Christopher Columbus lives in a state that computes the weekly benefit amount in reference to the claimant's average weekly wage. For the first 20 weeks of his base period, Christopher received a salary of $250 per week. For the next 7 weeks, Christopher was unemployed. The next 21 weeks, Christopher secured a new job in which he earned $300 per week. During the final 4 weeks of his base period Christopher earned $500, $450, $300, and $250, respectively. The fixed statutory portion amount in this state is 50%. The state unemployment office will calculate Christopher's weekly benefit amount as $123. (Total earnings for the base period year of $8,300, divided by 52; then multiplied by .50 = $123.)

STATUTORY SCHEDULE OR TABLE METHOD

Approximately twenty percent of all states use a statutory schedule or table to compute the weekly benefit amount. Such schedules are available at local state unemployment compensation offices. The central unemployment compensation agency of each state listed in Appendix A, is also a good source to obtain a copy of one of these schedules or tables.

States using statutory schedules or tables, however, do not randomly or haphazardly assign weekly benefit amounts. The amount of benefits assigned by these tables usually depends upon one or more of the same factors that other states use to calculate benefits. Some schedules or tables base the weekly benefit amount on total base period wages. Others assign weekly benefit amounts according to the amount of income received in the base period quarter in which the claimant had his or her highest earnings. Still others base the claimant's weekly benefit amount on other factors, including the average weekly wage or the amount of income received in more than one base period quarter.

Some states use these schedules because they prefer to avoid basing benefit amounts upon a fixed statutory portion, as is typically done in other computation methods. Thus, a claimant who received a lower amount of income during his or her base period may be assigned a higher statutory portion of his or her total base period wages than the claimant who was paid very well throughout his or her entire base period. In this manner, the schedule or table method may provide additional aid to those who traditionally receive lower incomes.

States may also prefer to make a claimant's weekly benefit amounts dependent upon multiple factors rather than just one single factor. Thus, a state may assign benefits based upon both the amount of income a claimant earns in his or her highest paying base period quarter and the amount of income he or she earns throughout his or her entire base period. A claimant in such a state would have to meet one threshold test based upon his or her highest quarterly earnings, and another threshold test based upon his or her total base period earnings in order to be assigned a particular weekly benefit amount.

Example: William Penn lives in a state that computes the weekly benefit amount in reference to a statutory schedule. William earned $500 in the first quarter of his base period. He earned $3,050 in the second quarter of his base period. He earned $1,500 in the third quarter of his base period. In the fourth quarter of his base period William earned $1,750. A portion of the statutory schedule used to compute weekly benefit amounts in the state in which William lives is included below. The state assigns a weekly benefit amount according to both a claimant's *highest quarterly wage* and a claimant's *qualifying wage*.

Highest Quarterly Wage	Rate of Compensation	Qualifying Wage
2988-3012	122	4800
3013-3037	123	4840
3038-3062	124	4880
3063-3087	125	4920
3088-3112	126	4960

The state unemployment office will first look at William's highest paying base period quarter. In his second quarter, William earned $3,050. This places him on row three of the above schedule, which assigns a weekly benefit rate, termed the *rate of compensation*, of $124 to William. In order for William to be eligible for this amount, however, he must have also received at least $4,880, the *qualifying wage*, during his base period. Throughout his entire base period William earned $6,800. ($500 + $1,500 + $3,050 + $1,750 = $6,800.) This base period income is more than sufficient and so William is eligible for a weekly benefit amount of $124.

(If William would have had insufficient base period earnings to meet the *qualifying wage* threshold, for example, if he would have earned only $4,810 during his entire base period, he may have had to move to higher rows on the chart and subsequently would have been assigned a lower weekly benefit amount.)

ADJUSTMENTS TO WEEKLY BENEFIT AMOUNT

The amount of unemployment compensation benefits for which a claimant qualifies is subject to a variety of adjustments. Thus, a claimant may actually have his or her weekly benefit amount reduced under certain circumstances, or may receive other unemployment benefits in addition to the weekly benefit amount. The following sections discuss a variety of such adjustments provided under state law.

DEPENDENCY
BENEFITS

Over one-quarter of the states provide for additional benefits for claimants who have one or more *dependents*. States that provide dependency benefits tend to define the term *dependent* in a similar manner. A dependent must, by definition, be financially supported wholly or chiefly by the claimant. The term always includes dependent children of the claimant, usually includes a dependent spouse of a claimant, and sometimes includes additional dependent relatives of the claimant. (See the section on "Dependency Benefit" in Appendix B.)

Dependent children typically must be under the age of eighteen. Children over this age, however, may still qualify as dependents if they suffer from a physical or mental infirmity prohibiting them from engaging in gainful employment. Some states also deem full-time students under the age of twenty-four as dependents as well.

Finally, certain individuals may also be required to live with the claimant before a state will recognize him or her as a dependent. Some states, for example, require a spouse to live with the claimant in order to be deemed a dependent.

Typically, these dependency benefits are allotted in dollar increments. Thus, a claimant who is financially responsible for one dependent may receive between $5 and $25 of additional benefits each week in addition to his or her normal weekly benefit amount.

Normally, the amount of the dependency benefits also depends upon the number of dependents a claimant must support. Thus, a claimant who supports one dependent may receive $10 in additional benefits, while a claimant who supports two dependents may receive $20 in additional benefits. There is almost always, however, a limit to these increases. Some states, for example, will only provide dependency benefits for the first two dependents, while others will provide these additional benefits for up to five dependents.

REDUCTIONS IN BENEFITS

State laws also provide for adjustments to a claimant's weekly benefit amount in the negative direction. In other words, in circumstances where the government normally has the power to order the withholding of relevant amounts from paychecks or benefit checks before such checks are distributed. Reductions in benefits may be mandated under a variety of circumstances and vary among the states. (See the section on "Reduction in Benefits" in Appendix B.) In many states, for example, a claimant who is seeking, or already receives, disability benefits or sick leave pay will have his or her weekly benefit amount reduced accordingly. Where a claimant receives separation, dismissal, termination, or other severance pay, he or she may also find his or her benefits reduced. In some states, a claimant who receives holiday or vacation pay will have his or her weekly benefit amount reduced as well. Other common deductions are implemented where an employee is granted a back pay award or when he or she receives a bonus check from an employer.

Additional reductions commonly emerge in circumstances where governmental *garnishments* normally arise. For example, periodic benefits often are reduced by amounts necessary for an employee to fulfill child support obligations. Other situations where a claimant previously received an inappropriate amount of other assistance may also subject the claimant's benefits to deductions. Thus, if a claimant receives excess unemployment benefits or was the beneficiary of an over-issuance of food stamps in the past, he or she may experience an effective garnishment of his or her new unemployment benefits.

Still, some state statutes allow for voluntary benefit reductions. A claimant, for example, may opt for federal and/or state tax withholding where permitted. A handful of states also offer the claimant the opportunity to have health insurance premiums deducted from his or her periodic unemployment benefit checks.

While the above, non-exhaustive list of reductions may vary from state to state, there is one form of deduction that is universal. Every state reduces a claimant's weekly benefit amount where the claimant receives a governmental or other pension, or similar retirement pay. These payments usually include annuity and trust fund payouts intended for retirement purposes. Depending upon the state, the receipt of Social Security benefits may also trigger the deduction.

While most deductions discussed above are done on a dollar-for-dollar basis, the typical deduction scheme for pensions and retirement pay is more complex. Usually a reduction will only be merited if the pension or retirement plan was maintained, or contributed to, by one of the claimant's base period employers. If the pension was entirely contributed to by such employer or employers, then the entire pro-rated weekly amount of the pension typically is deducted from the weekly benefit amount. Conversely, however, if the claimant contributed to the same pension, in any amount, then typically only fifty percent of the pro-rated weekly amount of the pension is deducted from his or her weekly benefit amount.

Finally, most states do not allow any deduction where the services performed by the claimant during his or her base period did not affect the claimant's eligibility for, or increase, the amount of the pension or other retirement pay. Thus, if the claimant was already eligible for retirement benefits before his or her base period even began, and if the amounts contributed during his or her base period were so little that they did not affect his or her pension benefits, then such amounts may possibly be ignored in the unemployment compensation calculation.

PARTIAL EMPLOYMENT

In nearly every state, a claimant who is otherwise eligible for benefits may still be eligible despite the fact that he or she earns some wages through partial employment. This means that a claimant who loses his or her job and subsequently secures a part-time position may still be eligible for benefits even though he or she is working. Sometimes a claimant who loses his or her job and subsequently secures a full-time job which pays less than the prior employment may still be eligible as well.

The drafters of each state unemployment compensation law wanted to give claimants the incentive to return to work as quickly as possible, and to even accept less attractive employment or lower-paying employment where no other positions are available. While providing benefits under these circumstances is nearly universal, the manner in which a claimant's weekly benefit amount will be adjusted by virtue of such partial employment varies greatly from state to state. (See the section on "Partial Employment" in Appendix B.)

Nearly every state that provides benefits to the partially unemployed, permits a claimant to earn a certain amount of wages through partial employment and still be eligible for the full weekly benefit amount. In other words, a specified amount of the claimant's income will be ignored or disregarded. Ultimately, this means that a claimant who is collecting benefits could usually increase his or her weekly income to some extent by securing even a few hours of employment each week.

The amount of partial employment income that a state is willing to disregard is typically provided in the law in one of two forms. Some state laws specify a particular dollar amount ranging from around $5 to $100. Most state laws, however, will disregard income up to a certain proportion of the claimant's weekly benefit amount. Thus, in these states a claimant may earn anywhere from 20% to 100% of his or her weekly benefit amount, and still receive the full weekly benefit amount.

Typically, the amount of earnings that a claimant receives above the specified disregarded amount is subtracted from his or her weekly benefit amount on a dollar-for-dollar basis. In a handful of states, however, only a portion of the earned income in excess of this disregarded amount is subtracted from the claimant's weekly benefit amount. Regardless of the method used, these reductions help define and explain what each state deems as partial employment and full employment.

Obviously, beyond some point a working claimant earns too much income to be considered partially employed, and is thus rendered ineligible for benefits. Usually a claimant does not need to earn as much income per week as in his or her former employment to be deemed fully employed once again. For a claimant to be both employed and eligible for benefits, therefore, he or she must not have his or her weekly benefit amount reduced to zero through the application of the state's partial employment reduction formula.

The following two examples will help explain some of the concepts discussed above. The first will demonstrate how a typical state calculates the benefits of a claimant only partially employed. The second will illustrate how a claimant, otherwise eligible for benefits, will not receive any if he or she earns too much money in a particular week.

Example 1: Caroline South lives in a state that disregards her earnings from partial employment that do not exceed 25% of the weekly benefit amount. Income earned above this amount, however, is deducted from the weekly benefit amount on a dollar-for-dollar basis. Caroline's weekly benefit amount is $240. Caroline earned $75 this week at her part-time job. The state unemployment office will disregard the first $60 (.25 x $240) earned by Caroline. The remaining $15 ($75–$60) she earned, however, will be deducted from her weekly benefit amount. Thus, Caroline will receive a reduced weekly benefit of $225. ($240–$15 = $225.) Of course, she will still be able to keep her $75 of income, so her total income for this particular week is $300.

Example 2: Missy Ippey lives in a state that disregards the first $40 she earns from partial employment. Income earned above this amount, however, is deducted from this amount on a dollar for dollar basis. Missy's weekly benefit amount is $125. Missy earned $175 this week at her part-time job. The state unemployment office will disregard the first $40 of Missy's income. The remaining $135 ($175–$40) she earned, however, will be deducted from her weekly benefit amount. Since this deduction brings her weekly benefit amount to a negative number, Missy is not considered partially employed this week and will receive no unemployment compensation benefits.

One final warning should be made concerning income from partial employment. In determining what constitutes income from partial employment many states apply broad definitions. Thus, holiday pay, vacation pay, back wage awards, and severance pay, as well as other income sources, may sometimes be deemed income from partial employment.

In other words, sometimes legislators classify income paid from former employers as income from partial employment as well. If you are receiving income of any kind from a current or former employer, or on account of current or former employment, you should contact your state unemployment compensation agency at the telephone number or address listed in Appendix A. You may need to know whether such amounts will be deducted from your benefit paycheck. The WEEKLY EARNINGS WORKSHEET, distributed by the Florida Department of Labor and Employment Security, and included in Appendix D, may assist in your efforts to maintain earnings records for purposes of applying for partial benefits.

MINIMUM AND MAXIMUM WEEKLY BENEFIT AMOUNTS

Nearly every state places limits on both the minimum and maximum weekly benefit amounts it will pay to an unemployed or partially unemployed person. Minimum limits range from $5 to $87. Typically, if the weekly benefit amount drops below this minimum, the claimant will not be eligible for benefits. In some states, however, a claimant's weekly benefit amount is adjusted upward to reflect this minimum if the calculated weekly benefit amount falls below this amount. (See the section on "Min./Max. Weekly" in Appendix B.)

Maximum limits included in state law range from $133 to around $521. Typically, if a claimant's weekly benefit amount is calculated to be higher than this limit, his or her weekly benefit amount will be adjusted downward to the prescribed limit. In some states, the maximum does not prohibit the claimant from receiving other additional benefits such as dependency benefits. In these states, a claimant may receive the state maximum weekly benefit amount and additional benefits for one or more dependents.

One final point concerning minimum and maximum weekly benefit amounts should be addressed. Many state laws provide formulas for calculating minimum and maximum limits, rather than amounts that remain the same year after year.

Example: In many states the maximum weekly benefit amount that the state will provide to a claimant is calculated as between 50% and 70% of the statewide average weekly wage.

As discussed earlier, the statewide average weekly wage is typically calculated by adding all the wages earned by all employees covered under the state unemployment compensation system, dividing this amount by the number of workers so employed, and dividing this number by fifty-two. Thus, as the statewide average weekly wage increases, the maximum limit on the weekly benefit amount increases as well.

Some states also provide formulas to calculate the minimum weekly benefit amount limit as well. Since minimum and maximum limits are often subject to annual changes, and since such changes are calculated in different months in different states, claimants who feel their benefits may be affected by these limits are encouraged to contact their central state unemployment compensation agency, as listed in Appendix A.

MAXIMUM TOTAL UNEMPLOYMENT COMPENSATION BENEFITS

State unemployment compensation laws do not merely cap the amount of weekly benefits that a claimant may receive per week in any given benefit year. Every state also restricts the total amount of benefits that a claimant may receive throughout a given benefit year. (See the section on "Maximum Total" in Appendix B.)

While variations exist, this maximum is typically calculated using one of two methods. Most states cap benefits with reference to a claimant's weekly benefit amount. The standard limitation is somewhere between eight and thirty times a claimant's weekly benefit amount.

The second most common method of establishing a maximum benefit amount is to cap benefits at an amount somewhere between 25% and 100% of a claimant's base period earnings.

The vast majority of states actually limit the maximum total with reference to both of the methods just described. Thus, the standard statutory provision includes a limit that is pegged at "the lesser of 26 times the claimant's weekly benefit amount, and $1/3$ of his or her entire base period earnings." Once the sum of all benefits the claimant receives during a benefit year equals the lower of these two calculated amounts, he or she will no longer be eligible for benefits. (See the section on "Maximum Benefits During a Benefit Year" in Chapter 1 discussed under the subsection concerning "Additional Hurdles for Subsequent Application For Benefits.")

Under this statutory provision, two caps must be calculated and applied. First, if the claimant's weekly benefit amount has been calculated, for example, at $500 per week, the claimant can receive this full benefit amount for no more than 26 weeks during his or her benefit year. Similarly if the same claimant would be receiving $250 in benefits (half the maximum amount) because of partial employment deductions, then he or she would be eligible to receive this amount for 52 weeks (twice the amount of time). Alternatively, if the same claimant earned $15,000 during his or her entire benefit year, he or she would be eligible for no more than $5,000 of unemployment compensation benefits during his or her entire base period.

Under most state systems, the result is that claimants are typically only eligible for full benefits for a total of twenty-six weeks.

NOTE: *The ultimate amount does not necessarily dictate the number of weeks for which a claimant will be eligible for benefits. If a claimant, for example, has his or her weekly benefits reduced because of income from partial employment, or as a result of a pension or other retirement pay, he or she will typically be eligible for benefits for a greater number of weeks.*

Example: If a claimant is only receiving benefits equal to one-half of his or her weekly benefit amount due to such reductions, he or she should be able to receive benefits for twice the number of weeks before reaching the total benefit limit. Thus, once the maximum total is calculated, the claimant does not typically forfeit a portion of his or her benefits by reason of the application of one or many of the various deductions outlined previously.

A claimant should also be informed about the possibility, of receiving extended benefits. Nearly every state unemployment law covers extended benefits. If a claimant is eligible for extended benefits, he or she typically will receive the usual weekly benefit amount for up to an additional thirteen weeks. When a claimant is eligible for such benefits, the maximum total unemployment compensation benefits for which he or she is eligible is increased by an amount equal his or her normal weekly benefit amount times this thirteen week extension. In other words, the claimant may be eligible for up to 13 additional weeks of full benefits. The catch, however, is that extended benefits are really only available during times of exceptionally high unemployment. The vast majority of claimants never receive these additional benefits.

ESTIMATING CALCULATIONS

What do you do if you want to perform some of the calculations described in preceding sections but, upon reviewing your personal files, you find you have no personal files? First, you are among the vast majority of employees who really maintain little in the way of employment records. Few retain W-2 and other income tax records over the years, and fewer keep pay stubs. Second, every computation described thus far, including those relating to benefit calculations and financial eligibility, are performed by state unemployment office personnel utilizing their own records and information submitted to them by your former employers. Therefore, as long as you place full faith and trust in your former employers and the employees of the unemployment office, you need not keep any employment records at all.

Sarcasm aside, there are really three figures that are commonly required to perform unemployment compensation calculations. First, a claimant often wants to know his or her weekly benefit amount. Second, the claimant needs to have an idea how much income he or she earned during his or her base period. Third, the claimant is sometimes asked to use his or her Statewide Average Weekly Wage in calculations. The following sections will explain how to derive rough estimates of these three figures.

ESTIMATING
WEEKLY
BENEFIT
AMOUNTS

Most claimants or potential claimants are very curious as to what their weekly benefit amount should be when calculated by the state unemployment office. They may determine that their weekly benefit amount is too low to even merit applying for benefits. This is especially the case where a claimant intends to secure replacement employment in a very short time. In order to determine if a claimant is financially eligible for benefits, the claimant usually needs to know his or her weekly benefit amount as well. (See the section on "Financial Eligibility" in Chapter 1.)

The four methods of calculating a weekly benefit amount were outlined previously in this chapter. (See the previous section on "State Unemployment Compensation Benefit Calculations.") If your state uses the total base period earnings method, or the highest-paying base period quarter earnings method, you need to estimate your base period earnings to compute your weekly benefit amount if you do not have sufficient records to calculate this amount. Estimating base period earnings will be discussed in the following section.

The third system for calculating weekly benefits is the average weekly wage method. If you do not have your pay stubs to indicate how much your average weekly wage amounted to during your base period, the first thing you should do is ask yourself if your wages have really changed substantially over the past couple years. Few people experience substantial fluctuations over so short a time period. Often the best indicator of what you were earning during your base period is what you were earning when you separated from your last employer. Thus, if you have absolutely no records at all, you should start by assuming your former weekly wage equals your most recent weekly wage.

To the extent you remember changes in your pay structure, try to adjust this estimation accordingly. Did you receive any pay raises? Were you working more hours? Were you ever laid off? Did you have a weekend job as well? Try the best you can to factor these into your estimation.

The *statutory schedule* or *table method* is the fourth system utilized by states to calculate weekly benefit amounts. Again, to the extent that these tables depend upon base period earnings, see the following section. To the extent that these tables depend upon average weekly wages, see the preceding paragraphs.

If you are really in a bind, want desperately to estimate your weekly benefit amount, and either have no income records to guide you or do not understand how to perform the benefit calculation required for your state, there is a general "rule of thumb" which may be of use to you.

As discussed earlier, unemployment compensation laws are meant to provide financial relief for the temporarily unemployed. When legislators draft such legislation, however, they want to provide sufficient incentives for claimants to return to work as soon as possible. Subsequently, the wage-replacement ratio, that is, the amount of income a claimant receives while receiving unemployment benefits relative to the claimant's normal employment earnings, is rarely pegged at 100%. Most unemployment compensation laws provide employees with benefits that on the average equal about 52% of their former wages. Thus, if you must have a number now, multiply your most recent weekly wage amount by .52 and this will give you a rough estimate as to what your weekly benefit amount should equal.

ESTIMATING
BASE PERIOD
EARNINGS

Nearly every claimant needs to know his or her base period earnings to calculate a weekly benefit amount. Similarly, base period earnings are often used in the financial eligibility calculations as well. (See the section on "Financial Eligibility" in Chapter 1.) If you do not have your past pay stubs to calculate your base period earnings or just cannot figure out which months to include in your base period, there are some shortcuts you can take.

Regardless of the months a state includes in its base period, it usually defines it as one year in length. Thus, base period earnings typically include a year's worth of income.

Using the information from the prior section, it would probably not be such a bad assumption to peg your base period earnings equal to what you typically make in a year. If you understand which months are included in your base period, you should adjust this earnings assumption to the extent you received any pay raises during this time period, worked more or less hours during this period, were placed on layoff status during this period, and to the extent you held additional employment during this period.

If your state requires you to make one or more calculations using the quarter or quarters in your base period in which you earned the most income, you can be conservative by assuming you earned the same amount of income in each quarter. Multiply your total base period earnings estimate by .25 to derive a very rough estimate of your highest-paying base period quarter.

Finally, you may want to adjust this high-quarter amount, if you need it in a calculation, if your employment tends to be seasonal. If you work far more hours in the summer you may conclude that this single quarter earnings should be pegged at a substantially greater amount than your average quarterly earnings.

NOTE: *Remember that these are all just estimates for your own purposes and do not be surprised if they differ substantially from the amounts actually calculated by the state unemployment office.*

ESTIMATING THE STATEWIDE AVERAGE WEEKLY WAGE

Some states call it the *statewide average annual weekly wage*, some states may term it the *state average wage*, but either way they have the same meaning. The statewide average weekly wage is sometimes used to perform financial eligibility calculations. Sometimes this number is used to calculate dependency benefits. (See the section on "Dependency Benefit" in Appendix B.) The figure is most often used, however, to calculate state minimum or maximum weekly benefit amounts.

As discussed earlier, the statewide average weekly wage, by definition, must change each year. The easiest way of determining this amount is to contact the state unemployment compensation agency listed in Appendix A.

If you are a math whiz, there is a sneaky back door method that may help you calculate this figure. Typically, you can use the maximum weekly benefit amount provided in Appendix B and the formula provided for this amount, to work backwards and calculate the statewide average weekly wage. The following example will illustrate this method, demonstrate that this method is really complex, and that it would probably be easier to call the state unemployment office for this information.

Example: Dave D'Aljabra works in a state that required him to have earned 3.5% of the statewide average weekly wage during his base period in order to be eligible for benefits. Looking at

59

Appendix D, he knows that the maximum weekly benefit amount paid to claimants in his state is $219. He also knows by reading this appendix that the maximum weekly benefit amount is calculated as 53% of the statewide average weekly wage. Dave wants to know if he meets the financial eligibility requirement.

First, Dave needs to calculate the statewide average weekly wage ("SAWW"). He knows from appendix D that .53 x SAWW = 219. By dividing both sides of this equation by .53, he can calculate that SAWW = $413. That is, 219 divided by .53 = 413. He can then multiply this amount by .035 to determine if he satisfies the state financial eligibility requirement.

Incidentally, once you have calculated the statewide average weekly wage, you can use this figure to estimate the state average annual wage. A handful of states use this figure to determine financial eligibility. To estimate the state average annual wage you need to calculate the statewide average weekly wage, as described above, and then multiply this number by fifty-two.

When to Apply 4

When deciding the most appropriate time to file for unemployment compensation benefits, there are a number of relevant considerations. Unfortunately, sometimes these factors are in conflict with each other.

First, in the vast majority of states, benefit payments do not begin until the claimant has served what is called a *waiting week*. This means that a claimant usually will not receive benefits for the first week of total or partial unemployment subsequent to the day he or she files for benefits. Considering this factor, a claimant normally should apply for benefits as soon as possible after discovering he or she has lost a job. (See the section on "Waiting Week" in Appendix B.)

A claimant who knows the job loss is only temporary (such as a seasonal or other temporary layoff), has an even greater incentive to apply for benefits immediately. Typically a claimant is required to earn only one waiting week per benefit year. As discussed previously, a claimant's benefit year, in most states, commences on or around the date the claimant first files for benefits, and continues for one full year.

Once the claimant establishes such a week during his or her benefit year, the claimant usually will not have to serve another waiting week during this benefit year before collecting benefits. This is true even if the claimant applies for benefits numerous times during a benefit year because he or she periodically separates from, and is recalled to, employment. With each subsequent application for benefits, the claimant need not go through another waiting week. This is especially important for claimants who work for firms that regularly layoff and then rehire employees.

Another relevant consideration in determining when to apply for benefits concerns the claimant's base period earnings. As stated earlier, the base period of a recently separated employee is used to determine how much unemployment compensation benefits the claimant is entitled to receive. All other things being equal, if a claimant can show high earnings during his or her base period, he or she will be eligible to receive greater benefits than with lower earnings during the base period. Since a base period is typically determined by the date a claimant files for benefits, not the date of separation from employment, a claimant may be able to increase the weekly benefit amount by carefully choosing when to file for benefits.

For example, a claimant who has been employed relatively constantly for the past two years would be well advised to file for benefits quickly after separating from work. A three-month delay in filing could result in one quarter of no income being included in the base period. This could lower the weekly benefit amount. Conversely, if a recently separated claimant held a job for exactly one year but had been unemployed for a substantial period of time before being employed, he or she may want to delay filing for benefits until the twelve months of employment move into the base period.

Ultimately, the trick is for the claimant to move as many of the quarters he or she was actually working into the base period, and try to move quarters of unemployment out of the base period. Before attempting this strategy you may want to make sure you are well acquainted with how your specific state determines its base period. The following example will help explain this interesting loophole.

Warning: While it is true that the base period in the vast majority of states is determined relative to the date a claimant files for benefits, some states backdate the actual date a claimant files for benefits. For example, if a claimant files for benefits as late as Friday, in some states his or her filing date will be recorded as the first day of that particular week, i.e., the prior Sunday. Other states determine this "filing date" using other bizarre methods as well. Thus, claimants should be careful when strategically delaying filing not to cut it too close to the beginning of a new calendar quarter. Otherwise, the filing date may be backdated into the prior calendar quarter.

Example: Al Einstein was employed until recently in a state that includes "the first four of the last five completed calendar quarters" in a claimant's base period. In this state, there is no backdating of filing dates. Al was employed for exactly one year at his present occupation, from July 1, 2001, to June 30, 2002. For two years prior to this employment, Al had been unemployed. If Al were to file for benefits on September 15, 2002, his state unemployment office would determine his base period to include April 1, 2001, through March 31, 2002.

Since Al was unemployed between April 1, 2001, and June 30, 2001, Al's weekly benefit amount would probably not be very high. If, however, Al had the financial resources to wait until October 1, 2002, to file, his base period would include July 1, 2001, through June 30, 2002. Since Al was employed during this entire base period, his weekly benefit amount would be much higher.

FILING A CLAIM 5

You may be eligible for unemployment compensation benefits. You may even be eligible for a lot of unemployment compensation benefits. Until you file a claim for benefits, however, you will never see a penny.

States place the obligation of applying for unemployment compensation benefits upon the claimant. State agencies do not typically notify claimants when they are, or may be, eligible for benefits until after a claimant applies. Claimants are expected to know where to go, what to bring, what to do when they get there, and what happens after they leave.

WHERE TO GO

Appendix A includes a list of telephone numbers and addresses of each state's central unemployment compensation agency. These offices may be contacted to obtain local office addresses and telephone numbers. In reality, however, it is probably easier to locate the nearest unemployment compensation office by referring to your local telephone directory.

Unemployment compensation offices are typically included in the state government portion of the telephone directory. Most unemployment compensation offices are listed under the heading "Department of Labor" or "Department of Labor and Industry." The precise name given to these offices vary from state to state. Some states title them "Job Centers" or "State Employment Services," while others list local offices under more official sounding names such as "Employment Security Commission."

Typically a claimant is free to file for benefits in whichever office he or she finds most convenient. The claimant does not have to file in a location closest to his or her former employer. In fact, if the claimant moves to another state after separating from work, the claimant may even file a claim near his or her new residence.

Most states have numerous local offices. If you do not find this to be the case, or if the nearest office still seems rather far, you should contact the telephone number listed in Appendix A to inquire about a closer location. Some states establish unofficial substations where a claimant may file for unemployment compensation benefits. If these substations are still too distant from the claimant's residence, some state laws provide for the organization of provisional offices to service particular claimants.

If this is not an option in your particular state, you may want to log onto the internet and search the web page of your state's unemployment compensation agency. The web pages for each agency are included in Appendix A. There is a growing trend to allow claimants to file unemployment compensation applications on the web.

WHAT TO BRING

Usually the initial filing for unemployment compensation benefits must be in person. Telephone filing, at least initially, is either rare or nonexistent. The claimant must normally complete a few forms on his or her first visit to the state unemployment office, and doing so over the telephone would be especially tedious.

What you should bring to your first visit to the state unemployment office depends on the type of documentation you have, and the arguments you expect to make. (See Chapters 6, 7, and 8.) There are a number of documents that you should bring if you have them. The more documentation you keep concerning your employment and income history, the more you will be able to protect your interests.

In actuality, state unemployment offices expect very little with regards to records maintained by employees. Instead, the law usually mandates that employers keep records, within their own files, many of which are regularly filed with the state or federal government. To the extent that an employer errs or even loses one or more of these necessary documents, an employee may save a lot of aggravation if he or she also keeps copies of employment documents.

At a bare minimum, there are a number of documents that you really should make an effort to bring to your first visit. Certain information will be essential when you attempt to complete the required forms. While some states permit a claimant to complete these forms at home, a claimant typically has to wait in the office lobby for a period of time before his or her claim is processed and may want to take advantage of this waiting period by filling out these forms while waiting.

The following is a list of documents that a claimant should strive to bring when filing for unemployment compensation benefits:

1. *Social Security card.* This is the identification instrument of choice and many unemployment offices will not allow a claimant even to apply for benefits without one. If you cannot find your card, you should bring another document containing your Social Security number. A W-2 or other tax form usually has this information.

2. *Green cards.* If you are not a citizen of the United States, bring proof of your authorization to work in the U.S., such as your alien registration receipt card, often called a *green card*. Such documentation is especially important in states such as Texas and California where illegal immigration is very common.

3. *Layoff documents.* If you are laid off from prior employment, bring any available documentation indicating a layoff. Many employers provide employees with a layoff notice.

4. *Information about your last employer.* Such information should include the employer's name, address, telephone number, and, if available, the employer's tax identification number. You should be prepared to answer questions regarding when you first began working for this employer, and when you ceased working for this particular employer.

   You should also make an effort to bring information concerning the income you earned while in the employ of this employer. Ideally, you should not bring mere totals, but should bring a breakdown indicating exactly when such amounts were paid. Pay stubs are preferable, but tax forms such as a W-2 usually contain much of this type of information.

5. *Information detailing your past work history.* Be prepared to name all of your former employers over the course of the last two or three years. Be prepared to provide the addresses, start and ending employment dates, and employer identification numbers, if available, of such employers. At the very least, refer to your telephone directory to find the addresses of prior employers, and bring a list containing this information to the initial visit to the state unemployment office.

   Also make an effort to bring information concerning the income you earned while in the employ of these past employers. Again, you should not bring mere totals, but should bring a breakdown indicating exactly when such amounts were paid. Pay stubs are preferable, but tax forms such as a W-2 usually contain much of this type of information

6. *Union information.* If you are affiliated with any labor unions, bring the name, address, and telephone number of such organizations. This is especially important where you expect the union to aid in your job search.

7. *Benefits information.* If you currently receive pension or Social Security benefits, or expects to receive such monies within the next year, bring any documents you may have concerning such benefits.

8. *Dependent information.* If you were employed in a state that provides additional dependency benefits, bring information concerning your dependents. (See Appendix B on "Dependency Benefit.") Normally, if you are claiming one or more children as dependents, bring the Social Security numbers of your children (and your spouse's social security number, as well).

NOTE: *With the exception of the documents listed in paragraphs 1 and 2 above, you will rarely be asked to produce any other documents.*

There are essentially two main purposes for lugging all this information down to the office. First, as explained previously, much of the information contained in these documents must be included on one of the forms you will need to complete. Some of this information may also be requested by unemployment office personnel.

The second reason for bringing this information is just as important. The claimant who is armed with this information can guard against errors, either accidental or otherwise, by office personnel and former employers. While it certainly is not common practice for employers to intentionally report inaccurate income and employment data to state agencies, the motivation of tremendous tax savings through such fraudulent acts will always make this possibility a real risk.

WHAT TO DO WHEN YOU GET THERE

The layout of unemployment offices, and the manner of processing claims, varies, not just from state to state, but within states as well. This section details the inner workings of a typical state unemployment office. Generally, such offices are user-friendly. They expect, and are prepared for, a significant amount of traffic from first-time filers who are not well acquainted with the facilities.

State unemployment offices tend to be broken down into two distinct areas. The front area typically contains a lobby with a large number of chairs and a reception desk. After notifying office personnel that a claimant desires to apply for unemployment compensation benefits, the office personnel usually provide the claimant with a few forms, or direct claimants elsewhere in the lobby area where such forms are kept. Some unemployment offices assign a number to the claimant at this time for waiting purposes. Some of the busier offices actually have deli-ticket numbering systems. In some states, however, the unemployment office requires the claimant to return to the office on a later date for further processing. In such states, the claimant should bring his or her stack of documents when returning.

In many states, the claimant is expected to complete the forms while he or she is waiting for an available representative to process his or her claim. The quantity of forms, and the information requested on such forms differs from state to state. Appendix D contains a set of sample forms including the UNEMPLOYMENT INSURANCE APPLICATION, used in California, the Application For UC Benefits, used in Pennsylvania, and the APPLICATION FOR UNEMPLOYMENT BENEFITS, used in Michigan. Please note the similarities in the questions from form to form. These similarities suggest that even if a particular form has not been included in this appendix, all claimants, regardless of state residency, should be prepared to answer these questions while waiting in the lobby area.

The application forms generally request two types of information. The first type of questions are geared toward benefit eligibility issues. These questions center on information concerning the claimant's past employers. In general, claimants are advised to keep their responses short and to the point. Often these forms do not provide much room for responses anyway.

> ***Warning:*** Be sure to read the last section of this chapter and Chapters 6, 7, and 8 in this book before providing answers to questions on these issues.

The second type of questions concern employability issues. Many of these questions resemble those standard to employment applications. Questions concerning a claimant's education and experience are typical. By completing these questions the claimant is essentially registering for work as required in many states. (See the section on "Benefit Eligibility" in Appendix B.)

The standard state unemployment office has messages, brochures, and pamphlets posted haphazardly around the lobby. Some of the signs provide information on how to file for benefits. A few unemployment offices are equipped with a videotaped presentation providing instruction on, among other topics, how to apply for benefits and who is eligible for benefits. Other postings describe the resources available in the office.

Most offices are equipped with job research assistance resources. These range from sophisticated computer systems to general billboard postings on work available. Most claimants underestimate the value of the information available in these unemployment offices in their search for new employment.

Eventually, in most states, claimants are directed to the second distinct area of the unemployment office. This section normally contains several offices or cubicles where unemployment office representatives sit at desks. Formerly, each claimant would be handled individually and provided a personal orientation concerning information on filing for benefits, benefit eligibility, and calculating benefits. There is now a growing trend to provide group orientations on these matters.

After this brief orientation, the unemployment office representative normally meets one-on-one with each claimant. The representative makes certain the claimant completed the requisite forms correctly. He or she may ask several follow-up questions as well. Again, be polite and courteous, but keep your responses to these questions short and to the point.

> *Warning:* In every jurisdiction, an intentional misrepresentation of facts to obtain or increase benefits is grounds for disqualification. Such misrepresentations may even be the subject of criminal prosecution.

Purposely failing to disclose important information to personnel at the unemployment compensation office is grounds for disqualification in most states as well. (See the section on "Disqualification" in Appendix B.) Be sure to read Chapters 6, 7, and 8 before answering the representative's questions. On rare occasions, the representative will contact a claimant's former employer via telephone to ask some questions.

Often, at the completion of the discussion, the unemployment office representative will provide the claimant with a general assessment on whether he or she believes the claimant will be deemed eligible for benefits. Such assessments, however, are usually non-binding and are subject to reconsideration.

AFTER YOU LEAVE

After you leave the unemployment office, the representative normally contacts your former employer or employers. The representative normally sends one or more forms containing a series of questions to such employers concerning the income you earned and length of time you worked for the firm. Employers also provide their account of the reason for the claimant's separation. Often this account differs greatly from that provided by the claimant.

State unemployment office personnel next sort through the information provided by the claimant and the information provided by the past employer or employers. Other forms filed by former employers, mostly containing earnings information, are also considered.

Generally, within two to three weeks the unemployment office renders a decision on a number of issues. The office typically mails its decision to both the claimant and his or her former employer or employers. The decision states if the claimant is eligible for benefits, or, on what grounds, if any, the claimant has been disqualified. If the claimant is eligible for benefits, he or she is also notified at this time as to the weekly benefit amount and the maximum amount of benefits to which he or she will be entitled during the benefit year. The claimant does not necessarily receive all of this information in a single envelope. Sometimes, in fact, the claimant is informed merely whether he or she is financially eligible for benefits well before he or she is ultimately deemed eligible to receive benefits.

Once the unemployment office deems the claimant eligible for benefits, the claimant is typically charged with the responsibility of keeping in contact with the office at a specified frequency. The office normally instructs the claimant to file claims for unemployment benefits on a weekly or bi-weekly basis. Depending upon the jurisdiction, filings for continuing benefits may be done in person at the unemployment office, by mail, or even by telephone. Appendix D includes the ADDITIONAL CLAIM BY MAIL, form used in Michigan. The form contains a sampling of the questions asked of a claimant when he or she files a continuing claim for benefits.

When the claimant files for continuing benefits, normally he or she must indicate how much income, if any, was earned through partial employment for such weeks. The claimant must also certify that he or she remains eligible for benefits. (See Chapter 1.) While the speed and efficiency of processing claims varies greatly from state to state, generally the claimant will receive the first benefit check in three to four weeks, and subsequent checks on a bi-weekly basis.

In most jurisdictions the claimant must serve a waiting week before receiving benefits. (For additional information, see Chapter 4 and the section on "Waiting Week" in Appendix B.) Therefore, the claimant's first check normally includes benefits for all the weeks of unemployment the claimant has logged subsequent to filing the initial claim for benefits, excluding this one week.

MAKING YOUR CASE FOR BENEFITS

Chapters 6, 7, and 8 explain in detail how to make a compelling argument that you are entitled to unemployment compensation benefits. Your case must first be presented during your initial visit to the unemployment compensation office, when completing application forms and discussing the circumstances surrounding your separation from work with office personnel.

If you are not granted benefits after your first visit, or if you are granted benefits but your employer appeals this decision, you must make the same argument before an administrative law judge or other presiding officer at an unemployment hearing. Again, if you are unsuccessful on this level, or if your employer appeals the decision of the hearing officer, you may need to once again make your argument for eligibility. This is usually in the form of a written brief presented to a state unemployment compensation review board. Beyond this, you may have to present your argument, either in written form, oral form, or a combination of both, before a court of law.

The information provided in the following three Chapters will instruct you as to those factors which will increase your chances of being declared eligible for benefits. We will also discuss what type of information is irrelevant, and potentially damaging to your case because it tends to obscure the actual issues and confuse those who will determine your eligibility.

Before applying the following information, you should always be aware of two important points:

1. Your former employer generally has an opportunity to respond to your claims, so you should expect and prepare for inconsistencies between your version of the incidents surrounding your separation and that of your employer.

2. *Never lie to or mislead personnel of the state unemployment compensation office.* If you do, and it is discovered, you may not only have to return the unemployment compensation benefits you have received, but you also risk criminal prosecution which may result in stiff fines or even imprisonment.

In the following three chapters, the nature of a separation from employment has been divided into three categories:

1. termination or suspension (Chapter 6);

2. voluntarily quitting (Chapter 7); and,

3. layoffs and reductions in work hours (Chapter 8).

While it may be tempting to jump to the chapter and subsection that appears to cover your specific separation situation, be sure to read all of the next three chapters. Valuable information can be obtained from all of these chapters, regardless of your situation. You may find that a suggestion in the section relating to insubordination (Chapter 6) can be used in your claim based on unsafe working conditions (Chapter 7). Also, information about certain types of situations may be discussed in more than one chapter. For example, there is information about labor disputes and extended absences from work in both Chapter 6 and Chapter 7.

While no one can ever guarantee that you will be awarded benefits, you should substantially increase your chance of being awarded benefits by studying these chapters carefully. These are the arguments that an attorney attempts to develop when representing claimants.

GETTING FIRED OR SUSPENDED 6

This chapter explains in detail how to make a compelling argument that you are entitled to unemployment compensation benefits when you have been fired or suspended. Be sure to read all of Chapters 6, 7, and 8, because valuable information can be obtained from all of these chapters, regardless of the specifics of your separation from work.

YOUR GENERAL PLAN OF ATTACK

As discussed earlier, if you were fired or suspended, your employer has the burden of proving that the termination or temporary suspension was for willful misconduct in connection with your work. Thus, you will be awarded benefits unless your employer can demonstrate that you either wilfully disregarded your employer's interests, deliberately violated your employer's rules, or disregarded the standards of behavior, which your employer has a right to expect of an employee.

An employer satisfies his or her burden of proving a termination was for willful misconduct by providing the unemployment office with sufficient evidence concerning the following four elements:

1. A work rule or workplace policy existed.

2. The terminated employee knew or should have known about the rule.

3. The employee breached the rule.

4. The breach was not the result of the particular employee's mere inability to fulfill his or her work responsibilities.

If you can prove that the employer's assertion with respect to even one of these four elements is incorrect, you should be found eligible for benefits. Thus, when filing for benefits, you should launch one or more of the following five defenses:

1. Your employer never had such a policy.

2. The reason given by your employer was not why you were fired.

3. You never thought you could be fired for doing what your employer has accused you of doing.

4. You never violated the rule you are accused of violating.

5. You tried your best, but just could not do the job.

Each of these are discussed below in more detail.

"MY EMPLOYER NEVER HAD SUCH A POLICY"

Sometimes an employer will terminate an employee for violating a rule or policy that was never clearly stated in the past. Emphasizing that your employer never prepared an employee manual or distributed written detailed instructions on how to perform certain tasks is a good beginning for a defense. If your claim happens to proceed to a referee hearing, you may want to ask co-workers to attend who will vouch that they never heard of the particular policy either. (See Chapter 7.)

Sometimes you can demonstrate that your employer did not have a clear policy on the issue in question by presenting evidence that the employer enforced two or more conflicting policies, or never enforced the "formal" policy. For example, if an employer fires an employee for not washing his or her hands in direct contradiction to signs posted in the rest room, the employee may still be eligible for benefits if he or she can establish that the employer never took that rule very seriously, e.g., employees were never provided with soap or towels in the rest room.

An employee who has been terminated may want to list other times in the past that he or she violated the policy or rule without being reprimanded. If an employer knew an employee had violated a company rule many times in the past and did not discipline him or her, the representative from the state unemployment office will likely conclude that a clear policy never really existed.

Even if an employee manual was written, an employee can argue, if it is true, that he or she never received one. Perhaps an employee was only given a brief time to read the manual soon after being hired. If so, the employee can justifiably assert a lack of clear knowledge concerning many employer rules and policies.

"THAT'S NOT WHY I WAS FIRED"

As a last resort, even if the reason provided by the employer would technically constitute willful misconduct, if the employee can show that this was not the "real reason" for the suspension or firing, then the employer would then have to prove that the "real reason" constituted willful misconduct as well. For example, if an employee often disobeyed a company policy, but was not fired for disobeying this same policy until just after he had an argument outside of work with the employer's good friend, the employee may be able to show that the argument was the true reason for the dismissal.

NOTE: *Trying to shift the attention of the representative from one termination justification to another is typically more difficult than merely persuading him or her that the original reason did not constitute willful misconduct.*

"I NEVER THOUGHT I COULD BE FIRED FOR DOING THAT"

Employers are expected to make certain that employees are aware of company policies, as well as the consequences of breaching them. After all, if you were never told that you could lose your job for not abiding by a particular policy, how can the employer claim that you truly understood the intricacies of the policy? When discussing company policies with unemployment office personnel, an employee should emphasize if different supervisors enforced company rules in a different manner.

An employee who is transferred from one position to another, for example, may have less reason to know about the intricacies of company rules and policies than the employee who has held the same position under the same supervisor for a number of years. Perhaps a former supervisor was significantly more lenient than your last supervisor.

Generally, an employer is also expected to warn employees of the consequences of not following specific instructions, particularly with respect to the final incident that resulted in termination. Tell the representative from the unemployment office if you had no idea you could lose your job for violating a policy that was never really taken seriously in the past. Emphasize how other employees who violated the rule in the past were treated less harshly.

NOTE: *This duty to warn has its limits. An employer does not have to warn employees of the consequences of committing heinous acts such as stealing, lying, or fighting with fellow workers. Employees usually are expected to know that such acts will result in dismissal even if they are not specifically warned by their employer.*

"I Never Violated That Rule"

Sometimes an employer merely suspects an employee violated a company policy and terminates him or her based upon mere suspicion. If you did not breach a company rule, make your former employer try to prove his or her assertion. Vehemently deny the allegation. Feel free to display sincere emotions in front of the office representative. Most people who are wrongfully accused are angered and upset by such an assertion. Your emotional state will bolster your credibility.

"I Tried My Best, But I Just Could Not Do the Job"

Many employers believe that a fired employee can be denied benefits simply because the employee has a history of failing to follow instructions or making mistakes. In the case of being fired, the employee can usually collect benefits unless the employer proves that the final act that led to the termination constituted willful misconduct. This means that the employer must prove that your failure to do what was asked of you was deliberate or well within your control.

If you were fired for merely not being able to live up to your employer's expectations, you are probably eligible for benefits. Be sure to tell the interviewer that you tried your best and just could not do the work. If an employee, despite reasonable efforts, was unable to perform the duties an employer asks, the employee will probably be awarded benefits. Be specific in your explanation. Tell the interviewer exactly why you could not comply. (Was the job too hard for you? Did an injury prevent you from performing well this day? Were you poorly trained?)

The following categories include those reasons most often cited by an employer for dismissing a worker. Each subsection in turn explains, more specifically, how to defend against the particular accusation.

ABSENCE OR TARDINESS

Again the issue here is *willful* misconduct, not just misconduct. While an employer has a right to expect an employee to show up for work and arrive on time, reasonable explanations for failing to do so may demonstrate that even a history of absences or tardiness was not intentional or controllable. Be open with the unemployment office representative. Tell him or her the truth, that you were fired or suspended because you were absent or tardy on your last day of work. Your employer will assert this anyway.

In these circumstances, what usually is important is your *last* absence or tardy arrival. Even if you have a history of being late to work for unacceptable reasons, if your lateness on the last day was entirely out of your control, you may still be found eligible for benefits.

If an unemployment compensation interviewer asks if you have a history of absenteeism, and you do, avoid using words such as "extensive," "habitual," or even "often." These suggest that even you know that your actions may have been unreasonable. As a rule of thumb, only use adjectives to describe good things about yourself. When describing a behavior that led to your termination, be objective and report the unadorned truth. Just explain that you have been late in the past. Do not attempt to characterize your actions any further than that.

Stress to the unemployment compensation interviewer if you have had a reasonably good attendance record recently. Emphasize how you were working on the problem. You should also describe your efforts to avoid being tardy or absent. For example, did you check the bus schedule to see if you could take the bus rather than drive the morning your car broke down? Transportation problems, illness, and emergencies are generally acceptable justifications for absences or tardiness. If you provided your employer with an explanation for your failure to arrive on time, make sure you tell the unemployment compensation interviewer. Employees have been awarded benefits when frequent absenteeism was caused by an unreliable car. It was not the employee's intention not to show up, circumstances just prevented him or her from doing so.

Sometimes an interviewer will ask what actions you took to notify the employer that you were not going to work on a particular day. If your employer never specified rules on how or who to call if you were going to be late or out, make sure you tell the interviewer that no formal policy was ever conveyed to you but that you always did the best you could under the circumstances. However, if you were aware of a formal policy, but it was company practice not to enforce it consistently, tell the unemployment compensation interviewer this if you are asked about it.

By not enforcing the policy regularly, the employer may have set a precedent that invalidates the formal policy. For example, you might say "No one ever called in if they could not come to work, we were just never really expected to. I was never reprimanded for not calling when I was absent in the past."

Even if you had been reprimanded for poor attendance in the past, a discharge for a tardy arrival to work may seem a bit excessive to the interviewer. Relate if you were never warned that you actually could or would be fired for this. State, if it is true, how nobody had ever been fired for failing to arrive to work on time or to work on a particular day. Explain to the interviewer how your employer normally punishes an employee with attendance problems. Perhaps your employer suspends such employees or takes them off the schedule for a day.

Even if your employer gave you a "last chance" warning, stating that you would be fired if you were late one more time, if it was company policy not to really follow through with such threats, discuss this with the interviewer if he or she asks if you were warned. State, if it is true, how many employees were subject to one of these "last chance" warnings. Some employers abuse these warnings so that they may have the ability to discharge an employee at any time for what they claim is "willful misconduct."

FAILURE TO KEEP IN CONTACT (EXTENDED ABSENCE)

If you were absent for an extended period of time, for example, to care for a child that was injured, and then returned to work only to discover that your job was no longer yours, you may be eligible for unemployment benefits. Often, when these situations arise, an employer attempts to characterize this separation as the employee quitting, rather than a termination. This is an important distinction because if your employer is successful in establishing that you actually quit, rather than were fired, under the law the burden will shift to you to prove that you had a good reason to quit.

On the other hand, if you can convince the unemployment compensation interviewer that you were indeed fired, then the interviewer will require your employer to prove that you were fired for willful misconduct. You want the burden of proof to be placed on your employer rather than on you. As discussed earlier, if the burden is placed on your employer, and you and your employer both provide equally convincing stories concerning your separation from work, the unemployment compensation interviewer will have to award you benefits.

DESIRE TO WORK

In an extended absence situation, you should first explain to the interviewer how you returned to work and your employer refused to allow you to perform your work duties. It is often helpful to establish your desire to return to work even today if your employer would allow you.

You must next show that this desire was continuing, that is, that you always intended to return to work when your crisis ended. State that you knew the crisis was going to be of a temporary nature and that you had every intention of returning to work. Explain, of course only if it is true, how you made no attempt to secure other employment, and emphasize how your particular skills are best suited for the requirements of the job from which you were terminated. If you feel you were unsuccessful in convincing the unemployment compensation interviewer that you were indeed fired, see the section on "Extended Absence" in Chapter 7 for further instructions.

MAINTAINING
CONTACT

If the unemployment compensation interviewer or hearing officer agrees that you were involuntarily terminated, your employer can still contest your benefit application by proving that you were fired for willful misconduct. Employers typically demonstrate willful misconduct with respect to extended absences by showing that an employee did not maintain frequent contact with them, did not periodically let them know that they intended to return, or did not apprise them of the approximate day they intended to return to work. If you did periodically contact your employer, make sure you tell this to the unemployment compensation interviewer. Be as specific as possible. A telephone log or telephone bill is ideal for this purpose. Certified receipts with copies of letters written to your employer are very good proof of your assertion that you did maintain contact.

If you do not have written proof, recreate for the unemployment compensation representative a detailed history of the times you corresponded with company officials. Specificity will make you sound more credible to the representative. Give names and approximate dates of persons you contacted if possible.

FAMILY
EMERGENCIES

Often, employees on extended absences due to family emergencies may not contact their employers as often as they would have liked. If the interviewer asks questions concerning notification, first mention the few times that you did contact your employer. Explain that you contacted your employer as often as a reasonable person could during your perilous situation. Explain how your employer appeared to tacitly accept your absence and how he or she never warned of any consequences.

If you explained your emergency to your employer, tell the unemployment compensation interviewer. If a family member is undergoing surgery, for example, explain to the interviewer that you told the employer this and the employer should have known that you would be absent during the surgery and for a short period thereafter during the family member's recovery. Again, explain how your employer appeared to accept your absence and never warned you of any consequences.

If you feel emotional at the interview, do not be afraid to express this. Unemployment compensation interviewers expect these human responses and may begin to doubt your credibility when they are not displayed. A family emergency may be a time of great worry, so the expected frequency of communication is usually considerably lower. Just try to let the interviewer know that, under the circumstances, you did your best.

EMPLOYER
CONTACTING
YOU

If your employer did not attempt to contact you during the extended absence, you may have been led to believe that all was well at work. Explain to the interviewer if you assumed your employer would contact you if he or she found your absence "excessive." Discuss how, in the past, your employer would call with threats even if you were late for work. Explain if others in similar emergency situations had taken significant time off without consequences as well.

Sometimes an employer does attempt to contact the employee during an extended absence. If the employee did not get the message or messages, there may be a reason for this. Sometimes the employer leaves a message with a child or someone who is relatively irresponsible. Sometimes these same people listen to the messages left on an answering machine and do not save these messages. In either of these situations, you should communicate to the interviewer that you normally are quite responsible when it comes to returning messages. Explain any times in the past where your employer telephoned you and you returned the call promptly. Explain how you would have contacted your employer immediately if you had known that he or she was trying to telephone you.

INSUBORDINATION

If your employer claims you were fired because you were disruptive or *insubordinate* (i.e., unwilling to submit to authority), you can maximize your chances for collecting benefits by emphasizing two particular points. First, some working environments are more casual than others. Discuss with the unemployment compensation interviewer if it is common for co-workers or employees and supervisors to use bad language, call each other names, and generally behave in an unprofessional manner toward each other. You should stress that your actions were precisely what your employer should have expected, and were normally tolerated, under the circumstances.

Oddly enough, this argument is strengthened by citing past incidents where you used similar language without being reprimanded. You should also explain how others used similar language and acted in a similar manner in the past without penalty. Here, you are generally trying to prove that you had no warning that such behavior would lead to termination. Stress how surprised you were when you were terminated.

If you typically were expected to act in a more professional manner while at work, you must use a secondary, and often less successful, argument. Stress how your words or actions are acceptable under modern community standards. What constitutes "acceptable language" changes over time. Argue that your statements or actions were not vulgar, obscene, or profane.

Explain how the alleged words and phrases you used were not directed toward a particular person, but were vents of your discontent or anger about an event or situation. Describe why the particular situation aggravated you. Explain that you just responded how any reasonable person would have to the particular situation.

If you were not the instigator of the final incident that led to your termination but merely acted in response to another's unwarranted acts, you should again stress the reasonableness of your acts under the circumstances and the fact that you were provoked. Describe the incidents leading up to your outburst emphasizing how long you restrained yourself. Try pointing the finger back at your employer. Explain how he or she had no control over the workplace environment and consistently left you in a position where you had to defend yourself by reasonable means.

DISHONESTY

Allegations of dishonesty are relatively serious charges in an employer/employee relationship. In fact, because of their severity, an employer is rarely expected to give warnings before dismissing an employee for lying, misleading, the theft of objects or time (i.e., changing time cards), or other dishonest acts. An employee is expected to know that dishonesty will lead to termination and therefore deserves no notice as to this fact.

If accused of dishonesty, you really have few defensive options. First, you can explain, if it is true, how the witness to the statement or dishonest act in question must have misunderstood it entirely. This defense centers more around his or her inability to hear your statement or otherwise observe your act. Was a statement made in a loud plant or otherwise tumultuous environment? Did you have the listener's full undivided attention, or was he or she performing other duties at the time that may have distracted him or her?

Next, you can emphasize differing interpretations of your statement. Yes, the witness may have heard you properly, but perhaps he or she did not understand what you meant, or fully see what you did. The listener may not have caught your sarcastic tone, or heard the statements out of context. Perhaps you were exaggerating for effect or even joking.

Similarly, if you regularly round down when recording working hours both when arriving to and departing from work, recording your arrival time a five minutes earlier on a particular day probably should not be interpreted as an intentional dishonest act.

Perhaps the best defense in a case where dishonesty is alleged is mere error. In order for a statement to be found "dishonest" and therefore sufficient justification to fire an employee under a willful misconduct paradigm, the statement must not have been merely false, but the person who uttered the statement must have known it was false. Was your statement a lie or were you just trying to give as honest an answer as possible when you did not know all the facts?

MISTAKES   Similarly, an act that may seem dishonest on the surface may have actually been a mistake. Did you actually think it was 8:00 a.m., instead of 9:00 a.m., when you signed in? Remember, however, regardless what you have done in the past you should never lie or be misleading to an unemployment compensation interviewer or other state unemployment office personnel. You should use this defense only to the extent that you were not entirely apprised of the matters of which you spoke.

EXAGGERATIONS   The only other defense to this accusation centers around the *materiality* of the alleged dishonesty. If your employer asks you a personal question, for example, you probably have no duty to answer the question and thus if you lie rather than confront him or her on this issue, you probably have not technically committed an act of willful misconduct. Similarly, little lies or exaggerations concerning relatively unimportant issues made merely to avoid embarrassment may not be deemed sufficiently material to merit dismissal.

Example: An employee who experiences morning production problems rounds up when asked how many products he or she completed, this may under certain circumstances be tolerated by the interviewer.

If you find yourself in this situation you should explain how you were doing the best you could, how you thought you would catch up later in the day anyway, and how your employer was extremely critical of your work and would have subjected you to extreme and hurtful ridicule if you had been entirely truthful.

CRIMINAL CONDUCT

As with dishonesty, allegations of criminality are serious charges in an employer/employee relationship. Because of the severity, an employer is almost never expected to give warnings before a termination on such grounds.

> *Warning:* When defending against allegations of criminality, however, *be careful*. You may want to consult with an attorney before providing any information to an unemployment office representative or your employer. You may just provoke your employer to file charges or provide the employer or prosecuting attorney with information that can be used against you in a court of law.

Being accused of a crime you did not commit can be devastating. Many times, an act is committed by someone within an organization but there is no real proof as to whom perpetrated the act, only suspicion. This often results in the termination of the suspect, whether or not he or she is truly guilty. Luckily, as in other termination cases, an employer bears the burden of proving who committed the act, and until he or she does, a claimant normally will be eligible for benefits.

On the bright side, if you have been wrongfully accused, it is fairly common for employers who fire suspects purely on suspicion to never contest a claim for unemployment benefits. They merely want to rid the company of the suspected criminal and bring the matter to an end. They realize that they can never actually prove their allegations despite their suspicions.

If you are accused of a crime you did not commit, vehemently deny the allegation and express your abhorrence at even being accused of the crime or dishonesty. Do not be afraid to display your emotions here. If you are mad at the injustice, express your anger. Avoid, however, becoming overly sarcastic. If you are hurt, feel free to display this as well. Employers rarely become emotional, so you can pick up some credibility points here. Always be sincere, as a false performance may be interpreted as an indication of guilt.

Offer alternative theories for the crime. For example, if you were not the only person with access to a missing asset, explain this to the interviewer. Your immediate supervisor and others who perform the same work tasks as you do should be suspects as well. While it is not your responsibility to solve the crime, to the extent that you can provide other reasonable scenarios or suggest other culprits, you may provide the interviewer with sufficient doubt to rule in your favor. Did others at work recently complain about financial problems? Did others at work ever express a desire to own any property? Do not overlook the possibility that no crime was committed at all. Could your employer be mistaken even as to the commission of a crime?

If allegations of criminality go to an unemployment compensation hearing, consider cross-examining your employer. In the vast majority of crimes in the workplace, the employer rushes to judgment about who committed the crime. Ask your employer if he or she honestly considered other potential culprits. Ask your employer if he or she honestly investigated other potential culprits. Ask the employer if you had ever committed such a heinous act in the past. Then ask the employer why he or she would think you would start committing such acts now.

While cross-examining an employer, you should never attack him or her. Do not place your employer on the defensive. Calmly ask your employer if it is possible that he or she is mistaken. Even the most sadistic of employers often have a difficult time looking into the eyes of the accused. Typically the employer waivers in his or her confidence in the assertion that you committed the crime. If the interviewer senses your employer's doubts, the interviewer cannot help but harbor some doubts of his or her own.

If you have not been convicted, but have had charges filed against you, follow the above instructions but make sure you let the interviewer know that you have yet to be convicted and are looking forward to your day in court to prove your innocence. If you have not been brought up on criminal charges you may want to notify the interviewer of this and suggest that if the employer truly believed you were guilty he or she would have filed such charges.

ALCOHOL OR DRUG USE

First, it is important to distinguish between mere alcohol consumption and intoxication. While drinking or using drugs before or during work is never encouraged, as long as it is in moderation, this in itself is insufficient to constitute willful misconduct in certain states. If your employer accuses you of merely drinking alcohol, (e.g., if he or she claims your breath smelled like alcohol), you have a clear line of defense.

Of course, if you did not drink any alcohol or consume any illegal drugs on the day in question, this may be the one and only fact you need to convincingly explain to the unemployment compensation interviewer. Often cough medicines and other over-the-counter drugs have a similar odor to alcohol. Sometimes people interpret a groggy demeanor as suggesting one has consumed illegal drugs when the behavior can sometimes be explained through lack of sleep or the effect of certain types of legal over-the-counter or prescription medications.

If however, you did indeed drink alcohol either before work or during work, and your employer fires you for this reason, there are a few points you need to establish for the unemployment compensation interviewer. First, and foremost, you must explain, if it is true, how you were never explicitly notified that the mere drinking of alcohol was prohibited. Explain, how your employer never provided you with an employee manual, or even a clear oral policy on the issue. If you can, cite specific incidents where your supervisor knew you drank before or during work in the past and yet never reprimanded you.

Sometimes, by citing examples of how fellow employees drank on or before work, you can establish that supervisors must have known about this behavior and must have acquiesced to it. By describing other incidents of alcohol consumption of fellow employees, you may also establish that, even if a written or formal policy existed, the employer commonly allowed such activity. This tends to show that the company's "real" policy on the issue was far less strict than the formal policy.

After establishing that a clear policy never existed you should stress, if it is true, just how little alcohol you consumed. The primary distinction between merely consuming alcohol and being intoxicated centers around the effect that the beverage has on your behavior. Your employer has a right to expect that you will perform up to your fullest potential on any given day and that your judgment will not be impaired so as to render you a danger to yourself or your fellow employees. Subsequently, you should describe your alcohol consumption in terms of relieving thirst. If alcohol was consumed merely as a beverage during a meal, this may be important. Drinking alcohol for "relaxation" purposes is exactly what an employer fears, for a worker who is relaxed may be far more accident prone.

If you can, describe incidents on the day in question to suggest that your judgment and dexterity were not hampered. Did you drive to work that day? Did you perform your job satisfactorily for a significant amount of time before being confronted on the issue?

Example: Lori Lush woke up early Thursday morning with an incredible thirst. Finding her refrigerator barren of juice or milk, Lori guzzled down two beers with her eggs and toast before embarking to work at "Kotu Supermarket." After an hour of meat cutting, Lori's supervisor beckoned her over to discuss scheduling issues. During this discussion, her supervisor smelled alcohol on her breath and noticed other indicia of alcohol consumption in Lori's speech and other actions. When the blood alcohol test confirmed the presence of alcohol in Lori's blood stream, Kotu Supermarket promptly discharged her for alcohol consumption in violation of the employer's written policy.

Despite the clear violation of company policy, the hearing officer declared Lori eligible for benefits. The officer held that the consumption occurred prior to her work shift and not during the work day. More importantly, the officer found that Lori had competently performed her meat-cutting tasks for a complete hour on the day in question before being asked to leave by her supervisor. Lori's supervisor confirmed this by admitting that her work product did not suffer on account of the consumption. (See *Safeway Stores, Inc. v. Industrial Claim Appeals Office*, 754 P.2d 773 (Colo.App. 1988).)

UNUSUAL BEHAVIOR

If your employer terminated your employment because of alleged unusual behavior, perhaps the behavior itself can be explained. Similar explanations to those discussed previously for those who are wrongfully accused of even consuming drugs or alcohol should be considered in these situations as well. Were you groggy not from drugs or alcohol but because you were merely tired? Were you dizzy because you had the flu? Perhaps your behavior was not exactly normal because of a prescription or over-the-counter medication. You should offer any of these explanations for your apparent odd behavior, to the extent they may be true, to the unemployment compensation interviewer. State that your behavior was normal under the circumstances and make your employer prove otherwise.

SCREENING TESTS

Again, the burden of proving intoxication is on the employer. However, if you were required to undergo a drug or alcohol test at work, failed it, and were subsequently let go because you failed it, you may not have an easy time defending your benefit claim. Where an employer has a reasonable suspicion that an employee is under the influence of drug or alcohol, such drug or alcohol tests normally are legal and fairly difficult to contest. When filing for unemployment compensation benefits, however, you may have the right to require your former employer to have the test results professionally verified. If your employer fails to submit to your request for verification, notify the unemployment compensation interviewer of this fact. Suggest that maybe your employer is not as confident in the results of the test as he or she claims.

In a very narrow sense, your employer's interest in your alleged intoxicated state probably has little to do with the moral ethics of consuming the alcohol. Rather, your employer has a right to expect you to perform your duties on any given day to the best of your abilities and to do so without subjecting yourself and fellow employees to undue danger.

Alcohol when consumed in mass quantities or the consumption of illegal drugs could indeed affect your performance. Thus, if the results of a drug or alcohol test indicate you were heavily intoxicated, your best argument, though rarely successful, is that despite any verified test results, your drinking or drug consumption in no way affected your abilities on the day in question. Again, if you can, describe incidents on your final work day which suggest that your judgment and dexterity on that day were not hampered. Did you drive to work that day? Did you perform your job satisfactorily for a significant amount of time before being confronted on the issue? Do you have a particularly high tolerance to alcoholic beverages?

In any event, if you were not given a drug or alcohol test prior to dismissal, you should stress this fact to the interviewer and question why, if the employer was so certain that you were intoxicated, he or she did not conduct or request such a test. Remember, the burden is on the employer to prove you were intoxicated, not on you to demonstrate you were not. Thus, an unemployment compensation interviewer should not even ask why you did not request a test to "clear" yourself.

Explain how you would have been willing to submit to a test if the employer had requested. If pushed further by the unemployment compensation interviewer, you may want to respond with a question asking why you should have volunteered to subject yourself to a battery of tests when you knew you had been wrongfully accused. Try not to become defensive on this issue unless the interviewer really pushes you.

LABOR DISPUTES (STRIKES)

Generally, no unemployment compensation benefits are paid to strikers or those honoring a picket line of striking employees. Moreover, if you are fired for striking or honoring a picket line and are not explicitly granted the right to strike by a collective bargaining or other formal agreement, you probably will be ruled ineligible for benefits as well. See also the section in Chapter 7 on "Labor Disputes (Lockouts and

Violence)." Often both sides of a labor dispute accuse the other of closing down the plant. As discussed earlier, in most states, if you can prove that a lockout situation existed (i.e., you were willing to return to work but your employer refused to allow you to return until the dispute was settled), you may be entitled to collect benefits.

Logic dictates here. Simply explain to the unemployment compensation interviewer, to the extent that it is true, that when you showed up for work at your regularly scheduled time, the door was locked, or the guard would not let you enter. The unemployment compensation interviewer will call the employer for verification. Make sure you tell the unemployment compensation interviewer that even now you are eager to return to work but cannot because of the actions of your employer.

EXCEPTION   As discussed previously, even where a strike brings about a work stoppage, a select group of employees may still be eligible for unemployment compensation benefits. (See the section on "Separated from Work as a Result of a Labor Dispute" in Chapter 2.) To benefit from this exception, the claimant must first show that:

1. he or she is not participating in, or directly interested in, the labor dispute which caused the work stoppage;

2. he or she is not a member of the organization participating in, or directly interested in, the labor dispute that caused the work stoppage; and,

3. he or she does not belong to the class of workers who are participating in or directly interested in the dispute.

While this may be an interesting statutory loophole, it does not leave much room for clever lawyering. If you are a member of the union that is striking, you lose. If you are not a member of this union, you may have a fighting chance. First, disclose to the interviewer that you are not affiliated with the striking union. Describe the bargaining unit which the union represents and why you are not a member of it. Next, describe in detail any meetings the union organized in advance of the strike and all the activities in which the union has participated to voice its grievances.

Once you lay out all the union members have done in attempting to persuade your employer, contrast that with a narrative concerning your failure to participate or actively support these activities in any way. Explain how you or your bargaining unit planned on working through the impending strike. Remember, merely wishing your co-workers well in their endeavor to improve their working conditions does not provide you with the requisite "interest" in the labor dispute to disqualify you from benefits.

Third, describe your bargaining unit, if you are a member of one, emphasizing how your skills, work hours, wages, and other conditions of employment differ from the striking unit. Assert, to the extent it is true, how your wages and working conditions are traditionally changed independently from those of the strikers. Perhaps in the past you have found that when other employees in the firm are granted pay raises it may even have a tendency to delay future increases in your salary. Express your unrest with the work stoppage and how you desire to return to work as soon as possible.

If you were on layoff status prior to a work stoppage, in some states this fact may serve to sufficiently distance you from the strike to render you eligible for unemployment compensation benefits. You should make sure you notify the unemployment compensation interviewer of your status. If the work stoppage is caused by a strike, even if you openly support the strike, you can argue that the true reason for your separation from work had been the layoff. The unemployment compensation law was intended to provide some degree of financial security for those who are laid off. Explain how it would be unfair to allow your employer to exploit the ongoing labor dispute to re-characterize your particular separation from work.

Finally, if your employer claims you were fired because you personally participated in a strike in violation of a collective bargaining agreement, you still have one final line of defense. As explained earlier, any time an employer terminates employment, the employer has the burden of proving that the dismissal was for willful misconduct. While such a strike may indeed constitute willful misconduct, you may be able to demonstrate that your termination was not motivated by the strike itself, but by a company desire to reorganize or scale down operations.

When a firing occurs so close in time to an illegal strike, it is difficult to prove the termination was for other reasons. However, if you can provide evidence, through newspaper articles, financial reports released by your employer, or interviews provided by management of your company, that reorganization had been in the works for some time, you may be found eligible for unemployment compensation benefits. Present this information and any supporting documentation you may have to the interviewer.

If you can, for example, provide evidence that you were never replaced, or that higher ranking managers were also released around the time you were terminated, you may be able to convince the interviewer that your employer used the strike as a pretext for your termination and had intended on laying off you and perhaps your colleagues all along. Incidentally, managers who had also been dismissed may be an excellent source of information regarding former company plans. Consider requesting former managers to provide a written statement concerning these facts. If your case goes to an appeals hearing, you may want or need this person to actually attend the hearing. (See Chapter 9 on appeals.)

QUITTING YOUR JOB 7

This chapter explains in detail how to make a compelling argument that you are entitled to unemployment compensation benefits when you have voluntarily quit your job.

NOTE: *Be sure to read all of Chapters 6, 7, and 8, as valuable information can be obtained from all of these chapters on building your best argument, regardless of the specific circumstances of your separation from work.*

Many unemployed workers do not know that they still may be eligible for benefits despite the fact that they quit their job.

YOUR GENERAL PLAN OF ATTACK

One of the most misunderstood concepts regarding the unemployment compensation system concerns the collection of benefits when an employee voluntarily quits his or her job. Despite what most think, it *is* possible to be eligible for benefits even after quitting your job. There are, of course, some major differences between quitting and being fired or laid off.

When it comes to voluntarily quitting, the burden of proof rests upon the claimant to show that he or she had good cause to terminate employment. As discussed previously, this basically means that the employer and employee may provide equally convincing arguments concerning the separation. One makes it sound as though there was a good reason for the quit, the other tending to prove that the separation was not really justified, the employer will win the case and the employee will be found ineligible.

Thus, in order to be eligible for benefits after quitting, you must demonstrate that you left work "for good cause." To do this you must generally establish two points:

1. You were left with no alternative but to quit.

2. Your employer knew you were unable to continue working at the same position.

First we will discuss these two concepts in a little more detail, then we will examine some common types of situations where they apply.

"I Had No Alternative But to Quit"

To prove that quitting was justifiable, you must show that you could not continue working under the conditions as they existed just prior to quitting. Sometimes an employee is unable to continue working because the employee was subjected to an unreasonable work environment or other external stress factor that was uniquely within the control of an employer. Other times a new physical or personal limitation prompts the separation.

When discussing the specifics of what precisely provoked you to quit, you should try to emphasize the distinction between your employment situation before and after the motivating factor developed. For example, if harassment from a co-worker was the cause of your separation, do not merely explain the incidents of harassment, but also discuss how satisfied you were with your position during the period of time before the particular employee began targeting you. This focuses the interviewer's attention on the harassment as being the actual reason for your departure.

The unemployment compensation interviewer often asks about other conditions of employment which may have motivated you to leave, but which often fail to constitute "good cause" for leaving. For example, the interviewer typically attempts to discern whether you merely were uncomfortable or unhappy with your prior work situation, or whether you were truly *compelled* to leave. Make sure when discussing this, that you do not merely stress *your* particular perspective, but apply an objective *reasonable person* standard. In other words, use phrases like "no one would have endured what I did" and "any reasonable person in that situation would have had to quit." Ultimately, under the law, your subjective desire to leave is not very important. It is important that a reasonable person in your situation would have quit as well.

An employee who quits should not only emphasize how any reasonable person would have felt compelled to leave when confronted with the same conditions, but also that he or she unsuccessfully sought alternatives to quitting. Explain, if it is true, how you confronted certain persons involved, including your boss, to see if you could work things through. Systematically list all possible alternatives to quitting that you considered, and negate each one for the interviewer. Tell him or her why a transfer was out of the question. Explain why a temporary leave of absence would not have been sufficient. Show that you really thought things through, but couldn't find any alternative solution.

You should also stress how, despite your attempts, you could not control the factor that motivated your departure. Nobody really can control their health. Some automobiles have a mind of their own, and if you cannot afford a new one you may have no means of commuting to your former job in a distant city.

"MY EMPLOYER KNEW I WAS UNABLE TO CONTINUE WORKING AT THE SAME POSITION"

Ideally an employee is supposed to notify his or her employer of any grievances the employee has during the course of employment. Moreover, before departing, the employee normally has a duty to give notice as to the reason for separating and the intended date he or she will leave. This provides the employer the opportunity to make amends or to reasonably accommodate an employee's special needs if this is possible. Obviously, if an employee has spoken to supervisors prior to quitting, he or she should describe for the unemployment compensation interviewer the details of each meeting.

More difficult cases arise when an employee fails to provide his employer with notification of the intended separation. In these situations you must convince the interviewer that if you would have approached your employer, he or she would have been unmoved. You should explain to the interviewer how many times you and your fellow employees tried to express your concerns or complaints in the past, and how your employer never took any action to rectify the situation. State, if it is true, how your employer virtually ignored employee suggestions.

If you never provided direct notification of an impending departure, try emphasizing how many times you or your fellow employees informally notified your employer of your grievances through even casual complaints. Explain how your employer had been hearing such complaints for a long time and should have known that eventually one of his or her employees would leave if action was not taken.

You should also assert how your employer knew about the unsatisfactory working condition from first-hand knowledge. Did your supervisor or another manager ever break out into coughing spasms because the shop was so dusty? Did your employer ever suffer an injury due to hazardous conditions?

Finally, you may want to stress the need for urgency in your departure and your inability to provide notice either because a situation arose that demanded your immediate attention, because you were confronted with a sudden unsurmountable limitation, or because each minute you continued to perform the duties of your former employment you were subjected to great health and safety risks. In any of these situations, notifying your employer before the separation would have been to no avail because he or she could not have corrected or even offered to correct the situation in a sufficiently expeditious manner.

The rest of the chapter includes the most commonly successful *good cause* reasons for voluntarily quitting a job. Each subsection, in turn, explains how to develop and present the facts of a given justification in the light which provides the most support for your argument.

A MATERIAL CHANGE IN YOUR JOB OR YOU WERE MISLED WHEN HIRED

When you initially accept a job offer, there is a presumption that the position you have accepted is *suitable work* for someone with your particular skills and experience. If you were, however, told what your specific duties were going to be, provided a written job description, or given other promises concerning the job which proved to be false or substantially misleading once you actually started working, you may be able to demonstrate that the work was not suitable work for you.

Similarly, even if you had been employed for a particular firm for a lengthy time, and your job responsibilities have drastically changed over the years, your job may not currently be considered suitable employment for a person with your qualifications. In either case, you may be able to convince the unemployment compensation interviewer that you had good cause to quit the position.

SUBSTANTIALLY DIFFERENT WORK

Sometimes employers have difficulty finding employees to fill unpleasant positions. Subsequently they "market" a job as being substantially different or higher paying than it actually is to trap unsuspecting workers into accepting it. You should investigate such deceptive practices by questioning former co-workers as to whether they were lured into accepting a position with the firm as well.

If you feel that you have been baited into accepting a job, and consequently had to quit, you may be eligible to collect unemployment compensation benefits. You still have the burden of proving that the job was substantially different than originally described. You are also expected to first express your grievances to your employer and give your employer a chance to fulfill his or her promises to you.

When talking with the interviewer, you should start by calmly describing your qualifications, experience, and training. List jobs you have had in the past that utilized your particular skills more effectively. Also, remember to discuss any health, physical, or other limitations you may have which made it difficult to perform your new or substantially different responsibilities.

Next, explain to the representative how you discovered the job opening. Most major libraries have old newspapers in storage. You can obtain a copy of a classified ad containing the job description, if you feel it would aid your case. Using great detail, describe the duties you were actually expected to perform and how they materially differed from what was originally described to you in the ad or during the interview. If you were taken on a tour of a plant and find you were not shown the less desirable portions of the facility in which you would work, explain this to the interviewer as well.

Indicate if you had expressed your concerns about being misled or the material changes in the position from the original job description. Even if your concerns were not voiced in a formal meeting, any time that you complained in front of the employer, or a supervisor, may be sufficient notification.

NEW OR UNREASONABLE CONDITIONS

Even if you had worked for your employer for a considerable amount of time, you may still have good cause to leave if your employer materially changed your job duties or conditions of employment. Where adjustments in working conditions are found "reasonable," an employer is usually afforded broad latitude to make such changes. However, a significant pay reduction (e.g., twenty percent or more), for example, may be deemed a legally sufficient reason to quit, especially when coupled with substantially less favorable shift or hour changes.

In any case, if you claim that you quit because you were subjected to new and unreasonable conditions of employment, you must also describe the adjustments in you work situation, emphasizing the distinctions between your former and current conditions. Next, compare your situation with the conditions of others similarly employed in the same local region. Be certain to compare wages, hours, benefits, and the intangibles of the working environment, such as job security.

In the case of a significant salary reduction, you should show old pay stubs to the unemployment compensation interviewer and compare them to recent ones reflecting the salary reduction. Often, seeing the reduction in the written form has a far greater impact than mere oral assertions. You should also explain how the reduction severely affected your particular standard of living.

If your work responsibilities have changed significantly since you originally accepted your job, you may also be able to make a case that your employment was no longer suitable. You do this by making the same arguments discussed previously regarding a misleading hire. Basically, make sure you describe the work that you had originally been hired to do, and had actually done for some time. Next, describe the new duties that you were expected to perform, emphasizing the distinction between the two sets of responsibilities. Explain why the new duties are substantially less favorable than the old duties. If others were employed in the same capacity as yourself, stress, to the extent it is true, how their work responsibilities have not changed.

Try to give your job position a name. For example, the interviewer will understand what you mean if you say you work in "maintenance." Otherwise, the interviewer may misconstrue that you were a general laborer and he or she may expect you to demonstrate more flexibility.

Try to speculate about why you are now performing these new tasks. Did another employee quit and now your employer is having a difficult time replacing them? Is your employer intentionally requiring you to do demeaning tasks in an effort to force you to quit?

Make sure you relate to the interviewer each and every time you complained about these new duties. Point out, if it is not obvious, that these new duties are undesirable. If others suddenly were expected to perform these new responsibilities, tell the interviewer if they complained as well.

ODD SHIFTS OR HOURS
If you are now suddenly required to work during an odd shift or odd hours, this may or may not be sufficient cause for quitting. The key question in this respect is whether rotating shifts or sporadic hours is common to the industry. If your company is the only of its type to run a midnight shift, for example, you may be able to use this fact to prove that what your employer expects is not reasonable.

OVERTIME   Generally, an employer has the right to expect an employee to work a reasonable amount of overtime. What constitutes a reasonable amount of overtime is not clear. Factors include the number of hours, the regularity of overtime, and what overtime was discussed when you accepted the job. Thus, if a company has a particularly busy month it can expect its employees to log, perhaps, fifty to fifty-five hour work weeks for this time period. When employees are expected to log these long hours on a regular basis, however, the overtime work may be considered to be excessive.

If you are arguing that your former employer expected you to work too many hours, state how many hours you were expected to work and with what frequency you were expected to work such hours. Explain what characteristics about the job made it difficult to work so many hours. Was the job very labor intensive? Were you performing tasks which could have become very dangerous if performed when not sufficiently rested? Citing studies showing adverse health effects and increased injury rates where rotating shifts are employed, or extensive work hours are required, may bolster your argument.

Next, describe, if it is true, how the fatigue affected you. Describe your physical condition when your employer hired you and whether you voiced any limitations that such condition imposed upon your future job performance. State if your work product suffered. Relate how you complained about these excessive hours to your employer, without any indication that your work hours would return to normal anytime soon.

It may help also to explain how the excessive work negatively affected your personal life. Mention, in passing, how your children never see you anymore. As a rule of thumb, however, it is always better in a voluntary quit situation to emphasize how your employer was unreasonable more than how the change negatively affected your personal life.

TRANSPORTATION PROBLEMS

If you were unexpectedly faced with extreme difficulties in getting to work, and had consequently been forced to quit, you may be eligible to collect unemployment benefits. You must first establish to the satisfaction of the interviewer, that you relied on a particular form of transportation. Explain how long you have been working for your employer and how you had always used the same mode of transport to get to work.

Next, you must show that your normal form of transportation is no longer available. Has your car finally had it? Has the bus company cancelled your route?

Finally, explain how other transportation alternatives do not exist. Make sure you show that you really did your homework, which should include:

- finding out about bus routes and times (or other forms of public transportation) from the area where you live to your workplace;

- pricing some reliable cars, and being able to explain if you cannot afford one; or,

- finding out exactly how much it costs to take a taxi to and from work.

Tell the unemployment compensation interviewer what you have found about transportation options.

If you live a considerable distance from your place of employment, walking may not be an option, especially in the winter. Even if you had done so occasionally in the past when your car was only temporarily inoperable, employees are not usually expected to make a long trek to work everyday. Tell the interviewer if you believe you will be able to secure employment closer to your house in a relatively short time.

Sometimes, the suitability of work, including whether an employer is within a reasonable walking distance from your home, depends upon available employment alternatives. In other words, you will probably be expected to walk longer distances to your job if no other likely employers are located closer.

Before applying for benefits, make sure you notify your employer of your difficulties and request that the employer make accommodations for your transportation. In other words, ask your employer for any suggestions on how you can get to work. Be sure to inform the interviewer if your employer was unwilling to reimburse you for the additional transportation expenses.

RELOCATION

If an employer attempts to relocate you from one workplace to another, and you quit because of the move, you may be eligible for benefits. The key question again is how far you are expected to commute to work. If the commuting distance is about the same, you really have no argument based merely upon a preference to work in one place rather than another.

If, however, your employer expects you to double your commuting time, explain to the interviewer how your old car could not take this daily abuse. Stress your *inability* to make the trip rather than your mere *desire* to minimize your travel time. Employees who sincerely desire to remain with a firm but who are not able to do so, for example, due to transportation difficulties, are more likely to be awarded benefits than employees who leave merely because they feel their employer was taking advantage of them.

FINANCIAL ISSUES

Any argument concerning transportation difficulties should discuss finances. Inability to overcome difficulties may come from an actual physical inability, for example if public transportation is not available, or from financial inability. Sure, the employee owns a car, but considering the wages he or she earns, he or she may not be able to afford the additional gasoline expense. Gasoline is not the only expense associated with the commute. An employer can reimburse the employee for gasoline, but wear and tear on an automobile is not as easy to estimate.

Again, explain how, due to the transportation problem, the position is no longer suitable employment for you. Stress how a variety of other positions providing similar incomes are available in your neighborhood, and how you should be able to secure a closer job rather quickly.

Explain, to the extent it is true, how you barely have enough income to support you and your family now, and how the prospect of wearing your car out prematurely is frightening. Even if your employer reimburses you for the extra miles, and even if you routinely saved this extra money as a form of self-insurance against car troubles, how long would it take to accumulate sufficient money to actually buy another car if your current auto is no longer worth fixing? Reimbursements may be sufficient for those who need to pay for routine maintenance, but where a car is near the end of its useful life, mere reimbursements may not be sufficient.

SAFETY OR HEALTH HAZARDS

If you quit your job because of serious safety or health concerns, you may have had good cause to leave your employment. Before you may leave, however, you usually must attempt to notify your employer of your safety or health concerns. The employer typically must then be given an opportunity to either improve working conditions, quell your safety or health concerns, or transfer you to another position which does not pose the same threat to your health or safety.

When discussing your separation with the unemployment compensation interviewer, be very specific in your description of the hazards at your prior workplace. Give particular details of any incidents that resulted in injuries, and explain where injuries would have occurred had luck not been on your or your fellow employees' side.

Describe hazards. While you should emphasize your exposure to these hazards, it also helps to give examples of the dangers that your fellow employees, performing similar tasks, have confronted as well. To the extent that they are genuine concerns, include information about the following:

- leaks;

- fumes;

- airborne dust;

- spills;

- sparks;

- fires;

- general clutter;

- absence of fire extinguishers;

- toxic materials;

- exposed electrical outlets;

- gas leaks;

- lack of proper lighting;

- lack of proper safety equipment;

- lack of proper tools;

- broken equipment;

- improperly trained or supervised labor force;

- materials to that you are allergic; and,

- even your physical limitations that made it difficult for you to work in the specific environment.

When discussing your separation with the interviewer, list each time you explicitly notified your employer of your health and safety grievances. If you provided your employer with any of your grievances in writing, tell the interviewer, and provide a copy of the letter if you have one. If your claim proceeds to an administrative hearing, you may want to ask the administrative law judge or appeals office staff how you can require your employer to bring such documents to the hearing.

If you failed to explicitly notify your employer of the conditions you considered unsafe or unhealthy immediately prior to your departure, you have a far more difficult task ahead of you. Essentially, you must convince the interviewer that approaching and notifying your boss of your grievances would have been futile. If you had explicitly notified your boss or supervisors in the past regarding workplace dangers and they consistently ignored you, you may be able to argue that further notification would have been to no avail.

Emphasize how you informally notified your employer through casual complaints about safety or health conditions. Explain how grievances filed by others were systematically ignored. As a last resort, you may try to demonstrate that the entire workplace was a hazard and that it would have been impossible to list all your grievances because there were so many. Similarly, you may want to stress the existence of a few obvious and severe health and safety hazards of which your employer needed no notification.

EXTENDED ABSENCE

Although prolonged absence was discussed previously in regards to discharges and suspensions, it also appears here because a dispute often arises in this area as to whether employment separation was due to a termination by your employer or by you voluntarily quitting. (See the section on "Failure to Keep in Contact (Extended Absence)" in Chapter 6.) If, for example, an emergency arises causing you to leave work for a substantial amount of time, when you return your employer may claim you quit while you may maintain that you always intended on returning and were thus fired. This is the reason it is important to always maintain routine contact with your employer during prolonged absences due to illness, or family emergencies.

It is important to provide the unemployment compensation interviewer with a detailed history of exactly when and how frequently you maintained contact with your employer while absent. If you present enough evidence to this effect, the burden of proof will shift to the employer to show he or she fired you for willful misconduct. If you find yourself in the middle of one of these extended absence contests, you should reference the previous section on this area for more information on this topic. (See the section on "Failure to Keep in Contact (Extended Absence)" in Chapter 6.)

HEALTH PROBLEMS

If you suffer from unexpected health problems, injuries, allergies, occupational diseases or ailments (such as carpal tunnel syndrome or other repetitive stress injuries), or changes in your physical state (e.g., pregnancy) that make it impossible or inadvisable to continue performing your normal job duties, you may be eligible for unemployment benefits. Claimants with these afflictions must still prove, however, that they are able and available to accept substantial work that is perhaps less physically demanding. (See the section on "Able and Available for Work" in Chapter 1.) The key in these situations is to demonstrate that your current employment is unsuitable for a person in your physical condition.

DOCTOR'S NOTE

The best evidence of one's physical limitations is a doctor's note. Have your doctor list or describe those activities which you can, or should, no longer perform. Have him or her describe the technical cause of the injury.

NOTE: *If your claim proceeds to an unemployment hearing, you will want to be certain that the note itself is admissible evidence. You should ask the administrative law judge or appeals office personnel if you will need to have your doctor attend the hearing or if the note itself will suffice.*

If you are unable to secure a physician's note, describe in detail to the interviewer the duties you previously performed, your current physical condition, and why your current physical condition precludes you from working at your old job. Be candid about what types of activities aggravate your condition or cause you to suffer pain. Describing the origin of your physical problems, e.g., where and what you were doing when you first received the injury or became aware of the illness, lends to your credibility. If the injury was suffered some time ago, try to explain why you feel it is suddenly flaring up with more frequency or more potency. Was there one recent strain that particularly aggravated the injury?

NOTIFYING YOUR EMPLOYER

Here, it is also important to let the interviewer know that you notified your employer of the reason that you were forced to quit your job. Your employer should always have the opportunity to find more suitable work within the organization before you determine it is necessary to quit. Again, if you did not specifically notify your employer that you intended to quit, emphasize incidents where you were forced to take off work, either to rest or visit a doctor on account of your physical problems. Also, cite each time you complained, even informally, about your aches and pains in front of the employer.

The point is, you must establish that, even if you did not give your employer explicit notice, he or she had sufficient informal indications that you were having problems and should have transferred you on his or her own accord. If you can demonstrate that you did give your employer an opportunity to transfer you, you may be awarded benefits.

Example: Diane Diztrest was employed as a software technician for "Panic, Inc.," an international Web page hosting firm. After working in this position for almost two years, she began to feel very anxious, especially during her "on call" nights which, on occasion, required her to return to work as late as 2:30 A.M. Diane's job performance deteriorated as her condition worsened. In fact, her emotional problems, aggravated by the pressures of work eventually led to her hospitalization for five and one-half months. After returning to work, and despite her employer's attempt to reduce her workload, Diane again exhibited symptoms of emotional difficulties as her job performance further deteriorated. Per her physician's suggestion, Diane voluntarily terminated her employment without prior notice.

While at the unemployment compensation hearing, Panic, Inc. is likely to claim that Diane should have requested a transfer to another less stressful position before quitting. Under these circumstances, however, hearing officers often find that where an employer has actual knowledge of the employee's difficulties, such as that gained from information regarding Diane's extended leave of absence, and where a deterioration in work product and other indicia of emotional distress implicitly give notice of an employee's severe condition, the employer may be charged with the responsibility to seek alternative means of maintaining the employment relationship.

Once it was obvious that the reduced workload did not rectify the situation, the employer itself should have suggested the transfer to a new position alleviating Diane from the responsibility to seek such available alternatives. This holding is more likely in situations, such as this, where the employer would commonly have more knowledge concerning other available alternatives than the claimant. See *Central Data Center v. Commonwealth Unemployment Compensation Bd. of Review*, 458 A.2d 335 (Pa.Cmwlth 1983).).

NO ALTERNATIVE JOBS FOR TRANSFER

If you really never provided your employer any indication of your problems, you may still have a chance of securing benefits. Under these circumstances you should try to demonstrate that there were no other less demanding positions available at your former place of employment and thus your employer could not have transferred you even if he or she would have wanted. Evidence of recent layoffs or few non-labor positions may prove this well.

If your claim advances to an administrative hearing and your employer alleges that he would have transferred you elsewhere, question your employer as to the type of position in which he would have placed you. Question him as to whether such positions are currently available. Question him as to whether such a position was suitable for you. (See the section on "Suitable Work" in Appendix C.) Could you really have performed the duties of this position efficiently? Do you have an education or other skills that make the position unsuitable? Describe the benefits package of employees performing those tasks and how it compares unfavorably with what you received in your prior position.

ABLE AND AVAILABLE

Remember, in order to be eligible for benefits you must be able and available to accept other work that currently exists in the job market. You may want to list for the interviewer a number of jobs you feel you are currently able to perform. Provide a liberal list of the types of activities you can still perform. Explain again how your education or skills background make these types of employment suitable for you. Provide the interviewer with a rough idea of how much these types of employment pay.

When describing the types of employment for which you are suited, you need not provide the names of actual employers who are currently hiring for such positions. To the extent possible, however, provide a label for the type of employment you can handle. By stating, for example, that you can function as a "machinist," it will give the interviewer more confidence that such positions actually exist. A position which has a formal title must be common.

Finally, demonstrate confidence in the fact that you will be able to secure replacement employment in a relatively brief period of time. Tell the interviewer if it is true, for example, that "machinists are in demand," and that you only need a little time to interview and complete job applications.

HOSTILE WORK ENVIRONMENT

If your employer, fellow employees, or others who commonly visited or worked in or near your workplace consistently used abusive or profane language, were unnecessarily hostile, made sexual advances, or behaved in an otherwise inappropriate or unacceptable manner, you may be eligible for unemployment benefits if you were left with no alternative but to quit your employment. Arguments tending to prove that ill treatment was due to race, skin color, national origin, age, sex, disability, religious beliefs, sexual orientation, or marital status are among the most effective.

Establishing that the work environment was generally unbearable can be particularly difficult. Merely having problems with others with whom you work is usually not sufficient to demonstrate the requisite hostile work environment. Specificity is probably more important here than when other valid reasons are provided for quitting. Describe to the interviewer, in great detail, the many indecencies to which you were subjected by your employer, supervisory staff, or fellow workers. Stress the frequency of such events, especially if there has been a noticeable increase in the frequency.

POLICY AND
SUPERVISORS

Cite company policies on filing grievances and how you received no satisfaction using them. If you discussed the matter with supervisors, relate if they seemed indifferent, and especially if they became defensive during the conversation. Some supervisors attempt to blame the victim in such cases. It is not uncommon, for example, for a supervisor to suggest that the employee wear different clothing where sexual harassment is alleged. Such statements tend to show an insensitivity to such issues.

If you failed to properly go up the chain of command with your grievances as company policy required, you have a difficult task ahead of you. You must demonstrate that following proper procedures would have been futile. For example, if your company president is the culprit, you should emphasize that going to your immediate supervisor, a subordinate of the president, would have been ineffective. Similarly, you should emphasize, to the extent it is true, how the person who committed the offenses has a very close relationship with the president and is therefore likely to gain support from him or her.

If you did not explicitly notify the supervisor or your employer, you also should try to establish that he or she is likely to have heard about the situation. Explain to the interviewer how things pass through the "grapevine" at your former workplace. Discuss if your supervisor or employer has ever been in the presence of the perpetrator when he or she acted inappropriately.

If others in the firm have had similar problems with a particular individual, state this as well. If they spoke with a supervisor or to your actual employer regarding their allegations, this also could be important. If your employer either failed to react to your or your co-worker's allegations, or responses were merely patronizing or entirely ineffective, this could bolster your case as well. Any of this may have a tendency to show that your employer is not really taking the matter very seriously.

SPECIFIC EVENTS

It is also very important to recall specific events at which you very definitely voiced your displeasure with the actions to the perpetrator himself or herself. Describe his or her reaction or lack thereof. Explain why you were convinced after this confrontation that he or she had no plans to stop the inappropriate behavior. Providing the interviewer with a time line comparing when you discussed the problem with the perpetrator and when he or she committed subsequent inappropriate acts will help convince the interviewer of this fact as well.

If particular behaviors were offensive to your moral or religious beliefs, make sure you notify the interviewer. Prove to the interviewer the strengths of your religious convictions. Explain, for example, with what frequency you attend church or other religious institution. Finally, if you are angry or disgusted, do not be afraid to show this to the unemployment compensation representative. A passionate demeanor in these situations usually is associated with honesty.

LABOR DISPUTES (LOCKOUTS AND VIOLENCE)

As discussed earlier, your best defense in a labor dispute situation is typically to establish that you were the subject of a *lockout* and had attempted to return to work but were prevented from working by your employer. (See the section on "Labor Disputes (Strikes) in Chapter 6.") You may also be eligible for benefits if you fail to return to work during a labor dispute, if you can establish that your health or safety would have been jeopardized by returning.

DIRECT THREATS

To demonstrate that your health or safety was at risk, a very real and direct threat must have been present. When talking with an unemployment compensation interviewer, start by discussing if you were the direct target of any violence when attempting to return to work. Explain if you were the subject of any offensive physical touching or the use of intimidation.

Give all the details: swearing, muttering, staring, screaming, indecent gestures, etc. Describe if you were the victim of any threats, particularly of serious bodily harm, when attempting to return to work. You also must convince the interviewer that any negative experiences you have had or witnessed since the dispute began were not merely isolated incidents. The frequency of hostility directed toward you, management, or other workers is important.

If you were not personally targeted by the strikers, but others who attempted to return to work were, this may sufficiently demonstrate the unsafe conditions at the plant as well. Explain how others received threats, and list any incidents of violence. Even destruction of property may be evidence that your safety may be in jeopardy.

SECURITY PERSONNEL
Stress how law enforcement agents or security guards failed miserably at containing the dispute. Discuss any special treatment management received when entering work, which provided them with more protection than you. Did they use a special entrance? Were they permitted to enter or exit the facility at different hours than you?

ATTEMPTS TO WORK
Provide examples of your last attempt to enter the building and the results of the attempt. Even if you decided it was too dangerous while viewing the situation from across the street in your car, this is still a very relevant point. It demonstrates that you made a genuine effort to return to work.

INCREASING HOSTILITY
Describe if the feeling of hostility in the atmosphere has recently increased. Provide a time line of events to demonstrate, if it is true, that the environment is getting worse. Try to speculate, if you can, as to the cause of any escalation. If talks between the employer and workers recently broke down, for example, explain how this negatively affected the ongoing dispute the last time this occurred.

Finally, provide any indication you may have that the situation is likely to become even more hostile in the near future. Are more workers participating in the dispute? Do the participants seem more restless? Are the participants louder than previously? Do they seem more aggressive?

VOLUNTARY RETIREMENT

If you voluntarily retired from your job, you are typically ineligible to collect unemployment benefits, at least until you purge this disqualification. (See the section on "Additional Hurdles for Disqualified Claimants (Purging Disqualification) in Chapter 1.") Quitting merely because you no longer desire to work in a particular capacity typically is not for good cause. This is usually the case even if you intend to seek employment elsewhere.

There are situations, however, where retiring from employment may be compensable. If, for example you are having difficulties performing your normal work duties due to health problems related to your age, you may be eligible for benefits as discussed previously. (See the section on "Health Problems" in this chapter.) Perhaps your eyesight or strength has depreciated.

Sometimes a firm relocates an employee when he or she reaches a certain age. Employers attempt to anticipate increased health problems, or fear that older individuals cannot or should not perform the same tasks as they did when they were younger.

While the legality of such moves is questionable to say the least, the employee subject to them may have an argument for unemployment benefits. The new position, for example, may not be suitable for the employee and thus the employee may be able to argue that he or she has suffered from the unilateral imposition of a material change in his or her job. Constructing arguments for benefits where this has occurred has already been discussed. (See the previous section in this chapter on "A Material Change in Your Job or You Were Misled When Hired.")

PERSONAL REASONS

It is often quite difficult to convince an unemployment compensation interviewer that a personal justification for quitting was for good cause. In fact, some state laws automatically disqualify employees who leave work for certain, specified personal reasons. (See the section on "Disqualification" in Appendix B.) Family responsibilities are often targets of these direct prohibitions. In the vast majority of states which do not exclude specific reasons or categories of personal reasons, employees citing such reasons for quitting must generally demonstrate that they were left with no alternative.

SPOUSAL TRANSFER

In the past, a variety of personal justifications have been deemed good cause for leaving work. For example, in some states and under certain conditions, employees who quit to follow their spouse to a new geographic region have been eligible for benefits. In such situations there typically is an investigation into the underlying cause of the move. If, for example, the cause of the relocation was the transfer of the spouse who predominantly financially supported the family, the following spouse sometimes has been deemed eligible for benefits.

Similarly, benefits have been awarded where the employee had no alternative but to quit because of an inability to find a suitable babysitter for the children during specific hours. Where employees have demonstrated they can be gainfully employed elsewhere but must quit a particular job to care for a family member, they sometimes have been found eligible for benefits as well.

DOMESTIC VIOLENCE

There has also been an increasing trend to offer additional protections to victims of domestic violence. Thus, where a claimant voluntarily quits to relocate to escape from domestic abuse, many states will deem him or her eligible for benefits despite the personal aspects of the separation.

NOTE: *Remember that employability elsewhere is always important because the claimant must still establish to the interviewer's satisfaction that he or she is able and available for work.*

ABLE AND
AVAILABLE

When discussing your separation with the unemployment interviewer, be very specific in your description of your personal dilemma. It is important that you establish not only your inability to continue working under former employment conditions, but also your eagerness, ability, and availability to continue working for other employers, even at the same type of employment but during different hours or at a different location. Explain the limited nature of the restriction placed upon you by your personal situation. Perhaps you must refrain from working for only an hour or two in the morning before your children go to school.

Demonstrate your flexibility by expressing a willingness to accept other types of employment. List other types of employment which may be more able to accommodate your particular needs. Some employers have various shifts. Perhaps some work can even be done in the home. Show confidence in your ability to secure new employment in a relatively short period of time.

Explain to the interviewer how you have always prioritized work in the past. Tell him or her how long you have personally supported yourself or your children. Discuss your financial position and how you need your weekly paycheck to survive. Let him or her know, if it is true, that your unemployment compensation benefits will not even provide you with sufficient income in the interim. Assure the interviewer that you have no choice but to eagerly search for alternative employment.

DISCUSSION
WITH EMPLOYER

When claiming that your separation was prompted by a personal situation, it is particularly important that you explain to the interviewer how you gave your employer an opportunity to accommodate your personal needs. For example, if you were having difficulty finding suitable child care, did you ask your employer to change your hours so your child would be at school during your work day?

If you did not discuss your particular problem with your employer, you should try to establish that such notification would have been useless. For example, a local employer with a single factory could not possibly accommodate an assembly line worker who was compelled to move clear across the state to follow her husband. Perhaps you are only unavailable for work during a limited number of hours, but your employer only operates during those hours. Basically, you are trying to prove that your former position is no longer suitable work for you. (See the section on "Suitable Work" in Appendix C.)

ALTERNATIVES TO LEAVING

You should also demonstrate to the interviewer that you carefully considered alternatives to leaving your former employer, but found none to be appropriate. For example, explain how the distance required to commute from your new home to your old office would be impractical. Public transportation may not be available and your car may not be able to take the additional wear and tear. (See the section on "Transportation Problems" in this chapter.) Discuss how economic hardship substantially limits your alternatives. For example, explain how you could not have possibly afforded to send your children to a high-priced day care center.

Finally, emphasize how your personal problem was caused by factors outside of your, and perhaps even your spouse's, control. Tell the interviewer if your spouse's employer was closing its only local plant, forcing your spouse to move. Explain how the only baby sitter you can afford in the area suddenly became ill and could no longer watch your children during the morning.

LAYOFFS, REDUCED WORK HOURS, OR INVOLUNTARY RETIREMENT

This chapter explains in detail how to make a compelling argument that you are entitled to unemployment compensation benefits when you have been laid off or had your work hours reduced.

NOTE: *Be sure to read all of Chapters 6, 7, and 8, because valuable information on building your best argument can be obtained from all of these chapters, regardless of the circumstances of your particular separation from work.*

LAYOFFS

Layoffs may be more complex than they appear. Many workers who are still employed, but who have had their work hours or wages substantially reduced, do not know that they may be eligible for benefits. In essence, they have been the victims of a *partial layoff*.

Sometimes, an employee may be legally laid off and not even know it. In certain vocations, like teaching, an employee may be eligible for benefits before he or she is formally laid off at the beginning of the next scheduled semester or other work period (See the section on "Reasonable Assurance of Returning to Work" on page 127.). Finally, while most individuals know that a layoff is grounds for unemployment compensation awards, many claimants provide too much irrelevant information when applying for benefits, leading unemployment office personnel to improperly assess a layoff as a discharge.

YOUR GENERAL PLAN OF ATTACK

An employee who is laid off, or has had work hours or wages significantly reduced, due to a lack of work or corporate budgetary reductions, may be eligible for unemployment benefits. When employees are awarded benefits, the employer's unemployment compensation tax rate may increase, therefore, it is not uncommon for an employer to try to disguise a true layoff as a firing or as the employee having voluntarily quit. This is why it is important to take certain measures to ensure eligibility for benefits.

First, when separating from employment under these situations, always ask for a *pink slip* or other formal written documentation from your employer showing your layoff status. You should show your copy to the unemployment compensation interviewer at the time of application. If you cannot get a pink slip, ask your employer or supervisor for a letter of recommendation to be used in seeking new employment. The employer is usually happy to give one to an employee who has been laid off because it is a sign that the employee intends to seek replacement work and not just receive unemployment benefits. This letter of recommendation should be shown to the interviewer as proof that your employer was generally pleased with your performance and did not fire you. Requesting such a letter also exhibits a good faith intention to seek replacement work as soon as possible.

Describe to the interviewer the reason you were told that you were laid off. Layoffs usually come from corporate restructuring or downsizing. Where business is slow, try to speculate for the interviewer as to the cause. Has a key salesperson recently left the firm? Has a competitor recently moved into the vicinity?

Do not, however, try to speculate as to why you were among the unlucky chosen to be laid off. For example, do not complain that you believe you were laid off first because you never got along very well with your employer. The representative of the unemployment office, apprised of this information, may believe you are hiding additional information, and may probe your former employer for more details. He or she may attempt to formulate a "discharge for cause" argument on the grounds of insubordination, especially if you have had a recent and impassioned argument with your employer.

In these situations, an employer who reads the interviewer's signals that a discharge actually may have been merited, may take the bait and attempt to develop a willful misconduct argument. After all, if you collect benefits, your former employer's unemployment tax rate may be increased. Either way, such discussion may delay the processing of your claim and may even lead to disqualification.

If your employer insists you quit and were not laid off, you can still prove otherwise. Present evidence to the unemployment compensation interviewer that other employees of the organization are now fulfilling your duties and that you were never replaced. Show that a number of other employees separated from the company at the same time. Layoffs often occur in groups. If you or your fellow employees have experienced recent reductions in work hours, you should notify the interviewer of this fact as well. This demonstrates that your former employer may have had too many workers. Expressing a willingness to return to work, even at the time of application, will lend to your credibility.

WHEN YOU ARE PARTIALLY UNEMPLOYED

Many people are surprised to discover that they do not have to lose their job entirely to collect unemployment benefits. If your hours, or rate of pay, have been drastically reduced because of a lack of available work or fiscal cut backs, you may be eligible for partial benefits to supplement your reduced paycheck.

If your wages or work hours have been substantially reduced, you are essentially only partially employed. The distinction between partial employment and full employment is not universal among states. In most states, a claimant can actually earn some wages through partial employment, despite the fact that he or she is currently receiving unemployment benefits. (See the section on "Unemployed or Partially Unemployed" in Chapter 1.)

The trick to determining whether a partially employed individual is eligible for benefits is to perform the requisite benefit calculations as described in Chapter 3 of this book. First, you must calculate your weekly benefit amount. (See the section on "State Unemployment Compensation Benefit Calculations," page 49 in Chapter 3.) Then, you must apply the adjustment for partial employment mandated in your state. (See the section on "Partial Employment" in Chapter 3.) If after this adjustment, your weekly benefit amount is still a positive number, that is, greater than zero, you will likely be eligible for the partial benefits.

INVOLUNTARY RETIREMENT

Even if an employee is one hundred years old, or even if his or her former employer has an established policy of retiring employees when they reach a certain age, a person who is involuntarily retired is eligible for benefits as long as he or she is still able to perform substantial work. In cases of involuntary retirement, an employer often attempts to portray the retirement as voluntary.

When discussing an involuntary retirement with an unemployment compensation interviewer, you should first provide the interviewer with any available evidence that tends to prove that you were retired. Dispel any doubts in his or her mind that you quit or were discharged from your last job. Show the interviewer your gold watch or the plaque thanking you for your years of service. Often, companies organize retirement parties. Invitations or other notices indicating the purpose of such parties also serve as excellent evidence of retirement.

Next, make it clear that the retirement was entirely involuntary. If the mandatory retirement policy is contained in an employee handbook, show it to the interviewer. Describe the average age of employees at the firm, and, more importantly, the age of the oldest person performing the same tasks as you once did. Make a list of all those that you remember were involuntarily retired as well. Make sure you express your displeasure at being put out to pasture so early in life.

Describe all your duties under your previous employment and your willingness and eagerness to continue to perform them. Also stress your ability to perform these functions. Describe how long it took to figure out how to do these tasks. Compare your efficiency at performing these tasks when you just secured the position of employment to your efficiency when you were involuntarily retired.

If you are unable to secure employment similar to your last, it may be helpful to show your enthusiasm for working in a variety of other vocations. Be sure to provide the interviewer with a long list of the types of employment for which you are still qualified. Make sure you emphasize, however, how you would have preferred staying at your last place of employment rather than moving elsewhere, otherwise the involuntary nature of your separation may be questioned.

REASONABLE ASSURANCE OF RETURNING TO WORK

Sometimes an employee does not even know if he or she has been laid off or if his or her hours have been reduced. For example, where work is seasonal, often the employee does not know if he or she will be recalled in the following work session. Aware of this fact, many states carve out special guidelines defining when certain seasonal workers can and cannot apply for unemployment benefits.

EDUCATIONAL INSTITUTIONS

In this respect, there are some vocations that are afforded special attention in nearly every state. If you are employed as a teacher, professor, administrator, or other employee of an educational institution, you may be eligible for benefits between academic terms, during sabbatical leaves, or during a vacation or holiday recess. The same holds true for those performing services for educational service agencies in or near schools, junior colleges, and universities. Similarly, those who are paid to participate in sports or athletic events or training may be eligible for benefits during a seasonal break.

Generally, if someone employed in one of these vocations can demonstrate that he or she did not have a *reasonable assurance* of being re-employed after the interim period, he or she may be eligible for benefits. (See the section on "Reasonable Assurance of Returning to Work" in Appendix C.) In fact, the employer typically has the actual burden of proving that the employee had a reasonable assurance of returning to work.

Be careful, however, as state laws concerning the details about which particular employees are covered under this provision vary. In certain states, this special treatment is only bestowed upon *nonprofessionals* employed by educational institutions. If you believe this statutory provision may apply to your circumstances, you are encouraged to contact your state unemployment agency for more information before filing for benefits. (see Appendix A.)

STEPS TO TAKE   If you are trying to demonstrate that you did not have a reasonable assurance of returning to work, there are a number of points you should make. First, emphasize what you do not know. Typically the burden is on the employer to provide you a reasonable assurance of returning. If a particular term has ended and your employer has not mentioned the upcoming term, explain this to the interviewer. Tell him or her that you do not have a contract as of yet. Furthermore, explain how you have not received word from an administrator, a principal, or even a department chairperson, as to whether you are to return during the next semester or term.

Emphasize if you have only worked at a particular school or for a particular employer for only one or two years and have little knowledge of how decisions to hire for the following term are made. If you have worked in a variety of different capacities for this employer, for example teaching different subjects each semester, state this as well. The point you should try to make is that you held a very unstable position with your employer.

If a contrast can be made between this year and last year, make it. Did you have a contract last year? Did someone notify you by this same time last year that your services would be needed?

Sometimes events during the school year give you less confidence that you will be returning. Have changes in a particular school district made it less likely that you will be asked to come back during the following term? Sometimes when new administrators are hired they attempt to restructure a program or programs, which renders employment during these times rather uncertain. Sometimes high expectations lead administrators to hire more teachers and other employees than are actually needed. Explain to the interviewer if you felt your employer was overstaffed last year. If it seemed as if it was difficult for the administration to keep all the employees busy last term, this may suggest that layoffs are imminent.

NOTIFICATION OF RETURN

Even if you have been given oral or written notification indicating that you may be returning in the following semester, you still may be eligible for benefits. Such notification rarely provides a full commitment to re-employ your services. Point out any escape clauses in the letter. Often these letters request the particular employee to demonstrate an interest in returning, but simultaneously convey a "don't call us we'll call you" attitude. Explain to the interviewer if the letter requires you to wait for word on if and how you will be assigned a position. State how, subsequent to this letter, they have not called you, and thus your employment situation is less than settled.

CONTINGENCY VARIABLES

Next, emphasize any *contingency variables*, either explicitly or implicitly embedded in the notification. Contingency variables are those that essentially state that you will be recalled to work if, and implying only if, certain events occur. Emphasize if you have no indication as to if and when those events will occur. For example, if a letter states that you will be recalled "if student enrollment remains the same," explain how that is entirely out of your hands.

If you have any indication that enrollment may decline, moreover, state this as well. If you teach high school, decreasing class sizes at the younger levels may be a bad sign. If you teach college, are you anticipating tuition increases which may scare off students? Do the classes you teach seem to be declining in popularity? Are other colleges launching recruiting campaigns in your area?

Sometimes contingency variables are not so obvious. For example, if an employer states that it is "anticipating a need" for your services, this does not say much. Emphasize how this demonstrates absolutely no desire to commit to hiring you. Explain to the interviewer if the letter does not explain upon what these anticipations are based. Try to speculate as to what these anticipations are based upon. They may be based upon expectations about enrollment. State again if you have any indication that enrollment may be decreasing and that such decreases are likely to reduce your chances of being re-employed. They may be based upon expectations about funding.

If budgetary cuts are likely, relate this and the possible negative effect on your employment situation. They may be based upon student choice. Explain if you have any indications that fewer students will choose to take your particular class in the next term.

Finally, it may help to compare your particular situation with that of others similarly situated. Tell the interviewer if other teachers have long-term contracts. Relate if others have been assigned classes yet. The fact that your employer has made a firm commitment with others, and has to date refrained from re-employing your services, at least provides reason to be pessimistic on the issue.

APPEALS

This chapter explains how unemployment compensation determinations are appealed. While this process differs greatly from state to state, we will show how a typical state system handles an appeal. First, we will provide basic information concerning the meaning of an appeal and how to appeal a decision rendered by the unemployment office. We will then describe what transpires at an appeals hearing and what you must do when attending one.

APPEALS AND DECISIONS OF THE STATE UNEMPLOYMENT OFFICE

If you are deemed ineligible, or are otherwise disqualified from collecting unemployment benefits, you may appeal this decision. Similarly, your former employer may appeal a decision that awards you benefits. The right to appeal provides either party with the opportunity to have the original decision reversed.

APPEAL OF A
DENIAL OF
BENEFITS

If your application for benefits is denied, you will receive, usually via mail, a statement indicating this fact and explaining, at least briefly, the reason for the denial. You will normally receive instructions concerning the procedure and time limit for appealing the decision. Typically, you will have between one and four weeks to file an appeal.

Filing the appeal is usually quite simple. In some states the claimant need only indicate, on a form that is enclosed with the mailed decision notice, or available at the local unemployment office, that he or she disagrees with the decision. The EMPLOYMENT DEVELOPMENT DEPARTMENT APPEAL FORM, for California is included in Appendix D. While a bit more complicated, the minimal space allotted for each question suggests that broader explanations rather than detailed analyses are expected. To be certain, however, you should ask a representative of your local unemployment office if a brief statement is sufficient. You should also indicate that you desire an administrative hearing on the matter.

EMPLOYER
APPEAL OF A
GRANT OF
BENEFITS

If you are initially granted benefits, your former employer may file an appeal. In some states, a claimant who loses such an appeal must return any unemployment benefits paid to him or her during the appeal process. In such a state, a claimant who begins collecting benefits, and is subsequently held ineligible for benefits on appeal, must return all the benefits received.

In many states, however, if the claimant did not lie to the unemployment office in order to receive the initial eligibility determination, the claimant will not be expected to return the benefits, at least not immediately. In these situations, the claimant often will not be penalized for this overpayment until he or she applies for benefits in the future. For example, if you were overpaid for a former benefit year, and apply for and are granted benefits in a subsequent benefit year, your weekly benefits may be reduced in order to account for the overpayment in the previous year.

If either party appeals, a hearing on the relevant issues will be scheduled within a few weeks. Hearings often are conducted in special rooms located in state unemployment offices. It is not uncommon, however, for a hearing to be scheduled in an unemployment office that is in a different location from where you initially applied for benefits.

Unemployment Compensation Administrative Hearings

Appeal hearings are similar to, but less formal than, a court hearing. The hearing will be presided over by a person with a title of *administrative law judge, hearing officer, deputy, referee*, or some similar title. To simplify our discussion, we will use the term referee. The referee typically dresses in business attire, rather than in a black robe like a judge in court. Both parties usually are expected to wear clothing demonstrating some respect for the system, although casual attire is not at all uncommon.

At appeal hearings, claimants are generally free to represent themselves or have an attorney represent their interests. In some states, claimants may request a consultant or other spokesperson to speak on their behalf. Either way, you should plan to attend the hearing because a lawyer or spokesperson cannot testify during the hearing as to what you know or have witnessed. He or she can only ask the important questions of you and other witnesses. You should be aware that employers have the right to be represented by professional counsel as well.

The layout of hearing rooms vary from state to state, and even between various offices within states. A typical hearing room contains a single long table. The referee sits at one end of the table. The claimant and his or her witnesses usually sit opposite the employer and employer witnesses. Proceedings often are recorded on audio tape so they may later be transcribed into a formal transcript.

"HOUSEKEEPING" AND CATALOGING EVIDENCE

At the beginning of the hearing the referee usually conducts some quick "house-keeping" chores. He or she describes the purpose of the hearing and notes who is in the room. Next, all written evidence included in the file for the particular case, such as your written application for benefits, the employer's written response to your application, and any supporting evidence that has been offered by either side, is described and cataloged for the record. In many states, parties to the hearing have the opportunity to review the file before the commencement of the hearing. If you live in such a state, and wish to review the file, you should arrive at the hearing at least forty-five minutes before it is scheduled to begin. Of course, you should have your own copies of most, if not all, of what is in the file.

After each piece of evidence is described, the opposing party has the opportunity to object to the admission of this evidence into the record. You must pay careful attention. In most jurisdictions a party may object to the introduction of evidence on a number of grounds. Two, however, are particularly important in the unemployment compensation context.

Hearsay. First, either party can object to the admission of any and all documents containing *hearsay* information. The topic of hearsay alone is the subject of many treatises. To complicate matters, there is as much to say regarding exceptions to the hearsay rule as there is to say about the hearsay rule itself.

To try to simplify, perhaps even over-simplify the concept, hearsay generally is any statement that was made outside of the hearing that a party is attempting to admit as evidence during the hearing itself.

Example: If a manager or employee fails to attend the hearing and instead provides the employer with a written statement agreeing with the employer or even stating facts as he or she believes them to be, it would be hearsay. The statement was made, or in this case written, outside of the hearing. It would be unfair to admit this statement because if the speaker does not attend the hearing, the claimant will not have the opportunity to cross-examine the person and to probe as to whether he or she really knows what he or she is saying.

The context of the statement may also be unclear and most likely it was not made under *oath* or promise to tell the truth.

For the same reasons, a witness cannot normally testify as to the oral assertions of another. In other words, a witness cannot discuss what others have told him or her outside of the hearing.

Example: The statement, "My manager, Greg, said that you were goofing off," would probably be inadmissible as hearsay.

If you believe that a particular document or statement that has been submitted for evidence by your former employer is hearsay, you should announce: "Objection hearsay!" The administrative law judge will make a ruling on this objection. If it is deemed hearsay, the administrative law judge will say, "sustained," meaning that he or she agrees and the document will not be entered into evidence.

In rendering a decision at the end of the hearing, the administrative law judge will not consider evidence to which successful objections have been raised. It was as if the document never existed. If the administrative law judge disagrees, however, he or she will say "overruled." Thus, the document will be admitted into evidence.

Exceptions to hearsay. You should be made aware of the fact that many business documents fall into one or more of the hearsay exceptions. Do not be surprised if you are unsuccessful in keeping out, for example, annual evaluation forms.

There are so many exceptions to the hearsay rule that you should not be overly concerned when presenting your own evidence as to its admissibility. Place the burden on your employer to contest such statements or documents.

The information provided in this subsection is meant to give you a sword to use at the hearing to try to keep certain controversial evidence that your employer attempts to offer from being admitted. Your best protection against having the hearsay rule applied against you is to bring witnesses to the hearing who have first-hand knowledge regarding your separation from employment. In other words, only bring witnesses who have heard, said, seen, smelled, or felt what they intend to testify about.

Irrelevancy. The claimant also may object to the admission of certain documents into the record on the grounds of *irrelevancy*. Irrelevant evidence is evidence that is not directly related to the facts of the specific case.

Example: If an employer discharged the claimant for alleged absenteeism, the admission of time cards from one of the claimant's prior employers indicating absenteeism would not be relevant to the case at hand. The time card is clearly irrelevant because even if the claimant routinely failed to report to work during his or her former job, this in no way indicates whether or not the claimant reported to work at his or her most recent position.

If you believe that a particular document is irrelevant to the hearing, you should object to the admission of the document by announcing: "Objection, irrelevant!" Again the administrative law judge will either sustain or overrule this objection.

PRESENTING
YOUR CASE

Once the file has been reviewed and evidence has been ruled upon, each person intending to offer testimony at the hearing normally must take an oath to tell the truth. Depending upon the issues presented in the case, the administrative law judge next will ask either the claimant or the employer to tell his or her respective side of the story.

When you are called upon, you should explain why you should be eligible for benefits. (see Chapters 6, 7, and 8.) You should generally explain the circumstances surrounding your departure form your former employer. If you filed the appeal, you generally should explain why the determination by the unemployment office was incorrect.

In providing testimony you should speak slowly, clearly, and deliberately. You should avoid digressing from your main argument. It is always wise to prepare, and even rehearse, what you plan to say at the hearing.

Witnesses. After you finish testifying on your own behalf, you may call witnesses. If you know of a person who has first-hand information supporting your argument for benefits, consider calling this person as a witness. In certain situations, a witness may be compelled to attend the hearing if he or she does not agree to come voluntarily. If you have doubts that an important witness will attend the hearing voluntarily, you may want to request the aid of the referee to ensure the witness attends.

If you are not represented by counsel and you "call a witness," you will usually be expected to function as your own attorney. You will need to solicit witness testimony by asking the witness a series of questions. Initial questions should be basic, establishing, for the record, the name of the witness and why the witness was in a position to have first-hand information relevant to the proceeding. When asking questions concerning the incidents surrounding your separation from employment, ask clear and concise questions so as not to confuse your witnesses. Basically, witness testimony should provide additional support for the arguments that you made during your testimony.

Written evidence. Typically, you will have an opportunity to submit written evidence while presenting your case. When written evidence is submitted, you should have someone who is familiar with the document explain its contents. Either you or a witness may fall into this category.

Objections. During the testimony of you and your witnesses, your employer has the option of objecting to evidence submitted, be it oral or written. Such objections are normally based upon the same grounds of hearsay or irrelevancy as discussed previously.

Cross-examination. After you have made your statement, and after each of your witnesses has finished answering your questions, your employer will have an opportunity to ask questions. When answering these questions, you should never lie, but it is usually in your best interest to provide answers which are as short and to the point as possible. Never volunteer additional information beyond what was specifically asked. It is always a good idea to prepare for the hearing by trying to guess the types of questions the employer will ask, and prepare answers for these questions. The more you prepare for the hearing, the better chance you have of obtaining or retaining benefits.

In some jurisdictions, the referee will also ask questions of those who testify. In answering these questions, never lie, be very polite, and keep your answers short and to the point.

YOUR
EMPLOYER'S
PRESENTATION

As stated previously, your employer will be provided an opportunity to present his or her case, either before or after you present yours, depending on the issues involved. Employers may present their testimony, the testimony of witnesses, and written evidence. As described previously, written evidence that is either irrelevant or hearsay may be excluded if you make a proper objection. You may also object to oral testimony on these same grounds.

Oral hearsay. Oral hearsay typically is easier to spot than written hearsay. All testimony provided at the hearing must derive from first-hand knowledge. Any witness, including the employer and claimant when they provide their story, can testify as to what they specifically saw, heard, smelled, tasted, or felt. They cannot, however, testify as to what they were told by someone else. This type of testimony would be hearsay. For example, if an employer states, "my manager told me that the claimant always…," this would be hearsay. The employer can testify about what he or she personally has seen the claimant do, but not as to what others have told him or her outside of the hearing.

If you are objecting to oral testimony or written evidence, you must be quick. You should clearly, firmly, and fairly loudly (so you are sure everyone can hear), exclaim "objection." If you do not object to the statement very soon after it is offered, you may forfeit the right to have the hearsay or irrelevant information stricken from the record.

Cross-examination. After each employer witness testifies, you will have the opportunity to ask him or her questions as well. The referee may also have questions for the employer and employer's witnesses.

Response to your employer's case. If you desire to respond to testimony offered by an employer's witness, you will have the opportunity to do so after the employer brings his or her case to a close. You may also ask additional questions of your own witnesses in response to the testimony or other evidence provided by your employer.

Technically, each party has the right to respond to information presented by the other. This *rebuttal*, in theory, could continue endlessly. In reality, both sides eventually *rest* their cases because they feel comfortable with all the evidence they have presented, or because the referee informs them that they are merely repeating the same argument.

Closing statements. Normally, at the end of the hearing the referee will ask for concluding statements. Even if the referee does not ask, you should ask if you can provide a brief closing statement. In a very concise manner the closing statement should summarize your main arguments. (see Chapters 6, 7, and 8.) These statements are easiest to understand if they are presented as a list of the important issues you raised during the hearing, and a brief explanation as to why the employer's argument is incorrect.

When the referee determines that neither party has anything further to add, he or she wraps up the hearing with a concluding statement and explains to all present when they should expect to receive a decision. Depending upon the state, decisions are normally rendered within two to four weeks.

TIPS FOR
THE HEARING

As you can see, the typical unemployment compensation hearing is indeed similar to a court hearing. Try not to get intimidated by the procedures and the apparent formality of the proceeding. Remember, you are expected to know virtually nothing about the procedures of the hearing. You should not be afraid to ask questions of the referee throughout the hearing. If you do not understand what the referee is saying, ask him or her. If you are uncertain as to when you are permitted to speak, ask the referee.

Incidentally, if the referee happens to render a decision deeming you ineligible or disqualified you from receiving benefits, there is still hope. In most states there are at least two additional levels of appeal, and usually three, beyond the administrative hearing. Normally a claimant can appeal the administrative decision to a state unemployment compensation review board. If unsuccessful on that level, a claimant can appeal that decision to one or more courts of law. With each level of advancement, however, the issues tend to become more complex and subsequently the claimant may feel more comfortable with professional legal assistance.

LAWYERS AND PROFESSIONAL ASSISTANCE 10

The circumstances surrounding a separation from employment are often subject to a variety of interpretations. To present the strongest case that you should be eligible for benefits, you must present the facts in the light most favorable to your position. The importance of *truthfully* answering all questions of personnel of the unemployment compensation office, and during administrative hearings, cannot be stressed enough. As anyone knows, however, there are often many ways to make the same statement, and some, of course, will be more favorable to your interests.

This chapter will first advise on how to determine if you would benefit from professional representation. If after reading, you decide to seek professional guidance, it will next instruct on how to formulate an effective lawyer search. Finally, once you have identified two or three lawyer prospects, the chapter provides suggestions as how questioning and otherwise interacting with these attorneys can help you to make a final determination as to whom would best represent your interests.

NEEDING A LAWYER

Attorneys (and unemployment consultants in states in which they are permitted) have experience eliciting testimony and presenting evidence in the light most favorable to their clients. As discussed earlier, however, attorneys and other consultants cannot testify on behalf of a client. Thus, if your claim proceeds to an administrative hearing, you should always attend the hearing, even if you hire a lawyer.

You should not hire a lawyer because you want to avoid attending a hearing. What an attorney or consultant can do, however, is organize a set of questions to ask you, your witnesses, and even witnesses for the employer, to obtain and present testimony and evidence that aids the referee in understanding your position in the matter.

With a little knowledge, and a lot of preparation, most claimants can do a very competent job in representing themselves. Sometimes, however, even after sorting through all the information, you may feel uncertain as to whether you are prepared to defend yourself. It is difficult for a claimant who has little experience with the unemployment compensation system to know whether he or she has a particularly complicated case that may require professional help.

The following guidelines are provided to help you place your particular case into perspective. If you are still uncertain as to whether you should represent yourself or hire a lawyer, consider the following:

1. *Try to determine the number of issues likely to be contested at the hearing.* Issues can generally be spotted where an employer is expected to disagree with you on a particular point. For example, if you assert that the work environment was unsafe, you should expect your employer to retort that it is indeed safe. Many cases revolve around only one or two material issues. When there are multiple issues at play, you may want to consider seeking aid.

2. *The mere number of issues, however, may not tell the whole story.* Certain issues are more complex than others. Issues tend to be more complex when they are more legal in nature than factual. For example, if your employer claims you failed to call in when you would not be at work on a particular day, and you intend to deny this, this is more of a factual question (i.e., did you call or not?). The most an attorney really can do in this situation is to ask you to tell your side of the story. He or she can ask you questions such as when did you call, whom did you speak with, and what message you left.

Conversely, if the issue is more legal in nature, such as whether a particular personal reason constituted *good cause* to voluntarily quit a job, and your reason for leaving was not discussed anywhere in this book, there may be an issue of law, as opposed to an issue of fact in question. In this situation, there is no disagreement as to the *fact* (the reason you quit), but there is a question of whether your reason for quitting *legally* qualifies as good cause for quitting. Not even judges agree on what always constitutes good cause. When more legal, rather than factual, issues are at play, seeking the assistance of an attorney may be advisable.

3. *Consider the dollar amount of benefits at stake, and your ability to support yourself and your family without these benefits.* If you are certain you will have another job within two weeks, you may be better off representing yourself, because attorney fees may easily exceed the amount of benefits you might collect during this brief time period. However, if your employment prospects look bleak, you may want to play it safe and secure professional representation.

4. *Try to figure out who will represent your employer.* Some companies may send a manager or the president of the company. Others secure high-priced lawyers to represent them. As a rule of thumb, employers are creatures of habit. The best indicator as to whom you should expect to represent the employer's interests is past behavior. Thus, ask other employees or former employees of the firm who represented the firm at prior unemployment hearings.

Similarly, firms that retain payroll companies or other employment relations companies are also more likely to seek professional help for hearings. If you notice a corporate name on your weekly paycheck other than your employer's name, or if you notice that the company employee handbook was published by another company, this may indicate your employer's willingness to spend more money in this area. The more sophisticated the person representing the employer, the more motivation you should have to seek help.

5.   *Objectively assess your ability to speak on your own behalf.* Ask yourself if you are willing to put the time and effort into preparing the case, You should also ask yourself if you would feel comfortable speaking in front of a referee, or cross-examining your employer. If the answer to either of these questions is a resounding "no," you should consider looking elsewhere for representation.

FINDING A LAWYER

If after considering all options you determine that you would benefit from professional representation, you will have to formulate an effective lawyer search. Retaining effective and cost effective representation is often more difficult than one might think. All lawyers do not practice in all areas of law.

REFERRALS   Many seeking legal counsel overlook the most obvious source of referrals. Friends and relatives often boast that they have a great lawyer and are eager to disclose their source of legal guidance. These suggestions are not only informative with regards to professional abilities, but also with client relations issues. While you are seeking a lawyer who will aggressively defend your position, as the individual financing this engagement, you have a right to be treated with respect throughout the relationship. Some attorneys, especially *litigators*, who spend many hours at hearings or in court, find it difficult to exit attack mode. Friends and relatives are in a far greater position perhaps than any other referral source, to discuss the more personal aspects of their relationship with legal counsel.

MASS MEDIA   While searching in the mass media is often the easiest method of locating attorneys, the utility of the results of such searches may be limited. Lawyers who advertise on television often specialize in personal injury lawsuits. Advertisements in the appropriate newspaper classified sections rarely specifically identify "unemployment compensation" as a practice area. Even attorneys who advertise on public radio as labor or employment attorneys often market their services primarily for large firms perhaps representing more employers than employees in unemployment compensation cases. Thus, you may have to take a more active role in your quest for representation.

BAR ASSOCIATIONS

Local Bar Associations often are productive resources for legal referrals. Lawyers who choose or are compelled to join these associations often organize themselves in various practice areas. Membership of their labor and employment law subdivisions often are the most experienced lawyers who practice in these mentioned areas.

Telephone listings for these organizations are included in either the governmental blue pages or the business and professional organizational listings of the telephone book white pages. To locate your local bar association, you should reference both of these sections of your local telephone directory and look under the name of the county in which you reside. Thus, an appropriate listing may be found, for example, under "Allegheny County Bar Association." While you may also want to reference statewide bar associations, these organizations are rare on the city or township level unless you live near a large metropolitan area.

If contacting a local bar association, you may want to ask another question. Many counties establish lawyer referral services, which offer legal representation for those in need on a reduced fee or even free basis. Normally, a client seeking such services must demonstrate his or her need by establishing his or her current poor financial state.

Alternatively, you may research these reduced fee services by contacting your local court system. A number of contacts may be knowledgeable in this area. In the blue pages of your local telephone directory, you may want to reference your local magistrate or clerk of courts. If they can not help, they may be able to refer you elsewhere.

WEB SEARCHING

The Internet may be the most fertile source of legal referrals. The Internet typically includes web pages of local bar associations, dozens or even hundreds of local attorneys, a rather large assortment of telephone book-style directories and many local newspapers.

In essence, the Internet serves as an accumulation of the information available from most, if not all of the sources discussed thus far. However when signing on, one should remember that some attorneys have resisted the computer revolution, choosing to peddle their services through more conservative marketing media. Lest you discount the effectiveness of this sector of the attorney population, you will find that it includes many of the older more experienced attorneys. After all, what better reason to enroll in law school than to avoid all those technical math, science and computer classes.

Formulating an Internet search for legal assistance is similar to, although a bit more sophisticated, than your normal telephone book search. In the Internet search, you can combine more ideas and better target your results. Regardless which search engine you use, you should first input the two terms, divided by the conjunctive "or", "lawyer" and "attorney." While these two terms are obviously interchangeable in common usage, as you likely have experienced in the past, a search is interpreted very literally and may not otherwise yield results from the unused term.

Alternatively, in jurisdictions that permit professional consultants to compete with attorneys in the area of unemployment compensation representation, you may replace the "attorney or lawyer" terms with other more general search items. For example, you may enter "unemployment and consultant" or "unemployment and consulting." If found, these advisors may be less expensive. Unfortunately, however, you may find that these consultants usually concentrate on employer representation, preferring this possible single source of repetitive business.

Next, include a geographic limitation in your search. If you live near a large city you may include the city name in your search, such as "and Philadelphia." Otherwise, as discussed earlier, attorneys are more commonly organized into county bar membership. Thus, you may want to include the terms "and Allegheny County" to limit your search. While you may be eager to limit your search with terms such as "unemployment" in an effort to find lawyers who specialize in the particular field, unfortunately, you probably will not find this limitation very fruitful.

This area of law is not amongst the most lucrative. Thus, few attorneys allot their advertising dollars to seek clients in need of assistance in this very targeted area of law.

If you find your search is too broad without a practice area limitation, but the term "unemployment" was not helpful, you may want to limit your search with "and labor or employment." These broader concepts should yield attorneys who regularly practice in this more general area of law.

SELECTING THE BEST LAWYER FOR YOUR CASE

Developing a list of two or three attorneys who practice in a particular area of law may be simple. Concluding which of these attorneys will best represent your interests is not so easy. Through a very brief series of questions and answers you must determine experience, knowledge, competence, disposition, as well as the tangible aspects of the relationship such as fee structures.

Initially you should contact your prospects by telephone. If you are not satisfied with the progression of the conversation, it will be easier to opt for alternative representation. After a face-to-face consultation you may find it uncomfortable to seek counsel elsewhere.

YOUR
QUESTIONS

You should first inquire into whether the attorney represents employees in matters involving unemployment compensation benefits. Lawyers tend to severely limit their practice areas. This means that a self-pronounced "labor lawyer" may not handle unemployment cases or may represent only employers in these matter.

Once you determine that the particular attorney is receptive to handling cases in this area of law, you should inquire into his or her experience in the field. Try to focus their responses through a series of questions. Do not merely allow him or her to generically announce he or she is an "employment lawyer." Ask if the lawyer has experience specifically representing clients on matters involving unemployment compensation and, more specifically if he or she has experience representing employees in these matter.

Inquiry into bar affiliations may be relevant as well. As discussed previously, many local, state, and national bar associations have labor and employment law sections. While these areas are rather broad and may not guarantee experience in unemployment compensation matters, membership in these sections does suggest a propensity to practice regularly in these areas.

Moreover, sectional membership draws additional fees that finance the publication and distribution of newsletters, pamphlets, and books, to keep these attorneys abreast of new changes in the law. Thus, if your prospect is a member of the labor and employment law section of one or more bar association, he or she has at least made a minimal investment in continuing his or her education in the practice area.

FEES While experience and competency are of primary importance in your search for legal representation, affordability must be addressed at the onset as well. The fact that you are applying for unemployment compensation benefits suggests that you have lost your major income source, your employment. As addressed elsewhere in this book, both your weekly benefits, as well as your total available benefits per each unemployment compensation application, are capped. Thus, it is important that the fee for the representation does not require you to tap into your limited funds any more than necessary.

Regardless of which fee schedule you negotiate, many attorneys are willing to offer a free initial consultation. It is often to the lawyer's benefit as well as to your benefit to provide these pre-screening sessions to determine if your case has merit. Successful attorney practices thrive on referrals. If he or she accepts too many futile cases merely in an attempt to extract legal fees, this referral base may wither.

Attorney fee structures come in nearly unlimited varieties. It would be great if you could find an attorney willing to work on a *contingency* basis. Under this arrangement, the attorney only charges if you are ultimately found eligible for benefits. If your are denied eligibility, you pay nothing. Unfortunately, due to the limited caps on benefits, and often formal or informal caps on other attorney fees imposed by state law or other policies, attorneys rarely accept unemployment compensation cases on a contingency fee basis.

The most common fee structure is the hourly fee. If quoted an hourly fee, however, to make a fair and equitable comparison to your other attorney prospects you should request an estimated number of hours the attorney anticipates working on your behalf. While attorneys are typically evasive on this issue, given the number of unforeseen issues that may arise while preparing your case, you should really attempt to foster a guess from the counselor. You may in fact, want to request a fee cap per phase of the representation. In other words, ask for a flat fee to represent you through, for example, the administrative hearing, or through an appeal.

It may be in your best interest to offer the attorney even more money than he or she originally anticipated it would cost through a particular phase in order to secure a guarantee that the costs will not exceed this limit.

QUESTIONS FOR YOU

Whether at the initial consultation or after the representation has begun, the interaction between legal counsel and a client can yield valuable clues and/or warning signs concerning the continuing relationship. When discussing the details of your separation from work, you should sense that the attorney is honing in on the important issues, enunciated elsewhere in this book.

Your lawyer is not your cheerleader. While as a client you deserve to be treated with respect, you should expect him or her to ask the tough questions. He or she should politely question you and not merely accept your responses on their face. It is to your benefit for your attorney to identify the apparent holes in your proposed testimony before anyone else spots them.

Finally, as a reality and honesty check you may want to boldly ask your attorney prospects if, in their professional opinions, you need their services. As explained earlier in this chapter, you probably can competently represent yourself under certain conditions and in certain situations. You may even want to offer to pay the attorney a fee for the initial consultation, even if her or she offered a free initial discussion, as compensation for an honest answer to this query.

Ultimately, you may still veto his or her suggestion to represent yourself if you feel you would be too anxious to competently do so. The content and manner in which he or she responds to this difficult question may provide insight as to how your relationship with this attorney will develop.

GLOSSARY

A

able to work. The physical and mental capacity to accept, perform, and generally become gainfully employed.

appeal. A request by either a claimant or employer to a higher authority that a decision rendered by unemployment office staff, an administrative law judge, other hearing officer, or a courtroom judge, be reconsidered and redetermined more in his or her favor.

applicant. An individual who completes the requisite forms and otherwise seeks and requests eligibility for unemployment benefits.

available for work. The state of placing only reasonable restrictions on the terms of employment for which one is suited and willing to accept such as those relating to commuting distance, work hours, work responsibilities, and wages.

B

base period. The time frame during an applicant's past employment history during which his or her former income figures are determined for use in calculating the amount of unemployment benefits to which he or she will be eligible. In most states, this period includes the first four of the last five calendar quarters prior to application.

benefit year. The period of time, usually fifty-two weeks, commencing upon a positive determination on eligibility for unemployment compensation benefits, and during which time the maximum total benefits for which a claimant will be eligible for during his or her particular application for benefits is capped.

C

claimant. An individual who completes the required forms and seeks and requests eligibility for unemployment benefits.

covered employment. Work performed under an employer who is statutorily required to participate in the unemployment compensation system. This category includes most employers except those exempt under state law such as religious organizations or governmental employers.

D

dependency benefit. Additional unemployment compensation benefits which may be available to an unemployed or partially unemployed applicant who is responsible for the financial support of a spouse, child, or other dependent.

disqualification. A formal determination that an otherwise eligible applicant should be ineligible for unemployment benefits based upon certain acts or omissions such as willful misconduct, voluntarily quitting without good cause, the making of false statements to government officials, or the failure to accept or apply for suitable work.

E

eligibility. A formal determination of unemployment compensation factors such as prior employment, sufficient past earnings, current unemployment or partial unemployment, the current ability to perform substantial work, and the availability to perform same, that must be satisfied by an applicant seeking unemployment benefits.

evidence. Oral testimony, documentation, or information from other sources or in other forms offered to prove the assertions made by a claimant or employer to either unemployment office staff, an administrative law judge, or other hearing officer, or before a courtroom judge.

extended benefits. Additional unemployment benefits beyond the normal statutory maximum limits, which may be available to claimants periodically during times of high unemployment.

F

false representation. Incorrect statements either made with the intention of misleading or with the knowledge that such statements were likely to mislead.

Federal Unemployment Tax Act (FUTA). A national law which imposes taxes on employment income in an effort to establish a fund to temporarily support those individuals who separate from employment through no fault of their own. The edicts of this law place a series of incentives upon state legislatures, the legislative bodies of Washington D.C., Puerto Rico, and the Virgin Islands, to draft their own local statutes and otherwise maintain independent systems that generally supplant federal control and responsibility to maintain this benefit system.

financial eligibility. Those unemployment benefit eligibility rules that determine whether an applicant earned sufficient income to satisfy the appropriate unemployment law requirements of substantial past employment.

G

good cause. When applied in the context of a voluntary quit, it is the satisfactory justification for leaving employment usually involving a situation in which the applicant was left with no reasonable alternative but to separate from the employment.

H

hearing. The formal proceeding at which a claimant and employer present documents, testimony, or other evidence from other sources or in other forms before an administrative law judge, or other hearing officer, in support of their arguments, for or against, unemployment compensation eligibility or related issues.

hearsay. A statement offered outside a formal hearing often by a third person who is not a party to the hearing, which one attempts to admit as evidence during the hearing itself, but is often deemed inadmissible.

hostile work environment. An abusive or intolerable work atmosphere in which an employee who wishes to remain employed is left with no reasonable alternative but to voluntarily quit.

I

independent contractor. A self-employed individual who offers his services to others, or the public in general, rather than to just one person or business entity.

insubordination. A manner of treatment or speaking to an employer or other supervisor evidencing disrespect, and/or the failure to submit to the authority of either, which a reasonable employer should not have to accept or tolerate from the employee.

insured work. Work performed under an employer who is statutorily required to participate in the unemployment compensation system. This category includes most employers except those exempt under state law such as religious organizations or governmental employers.

involuntary retirement. Retirement of an employee demanded by or coerced by an employer.

irrelevance. Documentation, testimony, or information from other sources or in other forms which is deemed unimportant relative to the key hearing issues such as eligibility for unemployment compensation, or the calculations for weekly benefit amounts, and thus typically deemed inadmissible.

L

labor dispute. A disagreement between labor and management concerning wages or other terms of employment often culminating in strikes or lockouts.

lag period wages. The income earned by a claimant during the period occurring after the conclusion of his or her prior Base Period and before the commencement of his or her prior Benefit Year.

layoff. Term used by an employer who directs an employee not to return to work due to business downswings, replacement of workers through mechanization, or other reasons not related to alleged misconduct.

leaves of absence. A separation from employment intended to be temporary in nature.

lockout. The act of an employer who refuses to allow employees to return to work, usually occurring during a labor dispute.

P

partially unemployed. The term for an applicant who is currently employed but who still may be eligible for unemployment compensation benefits by virtue of a substantial reduction in income suffered as a result of either a reduction in pay rate, a reduction in work hours, or a combination of both.

purging disqualification. The act of satisfying additional statutory requirements, once disqualified from receiving unemployment benefits, such as working additional hours and/or earning additional income during subsequent employment, which will again render the applicant eligible for benefits.

R

reasonable assurance. A term used to refer to the expectations of an employee, often of an educational institution or firm contracting its employees to work for such an institution, that he or she likely will return to work, usually after a leave for a scheduled vacation period or between scheduled work sessions such as school semester.

rebuttal. Documentation, testimony, or information from other sources or in other forms offered at a formal hearing or to unemployment agency staff which contradicts and thus tends to disprove the documentation, testimony, or other evidence offered by an opponent party.

recall. An offer by an employer, to a former employee, to return to work.

re-employment services. A program in which an applicant may, or is sometimes compelled to participate, in which the applicant is retrained or otherwise prepared for a vocation or other gainful employment, usually distinct from that in which he or she normally works.

referee. The formal title given in certain states to the administrative law judge or other hearing officer who presides at a formal unemployment compensation hearing.

S

seasonal workers. Employees working in vocations that typically suspend operations for extended periods of time at least once during each calendar year. Per applicable state law, select seasonal workers may be ineligible for benefits during shutdown periods despite the apparent "temporary layoff" nature of the separation.

statewide average weekly wage. A measure of the typical amount of wages earned by an employee, in a week, in a particular state. This factor is commonly used in the state to calculate the maximum and minimum weekly unemployment benefits available to claimants.

strike. The act of one or more employees refusing to return to work, often during a labor dispute, and often calculated to apply pressure to motivate employers to offer improved terms of employment.

suitable work. Employment position making optimum use of the particular talents and/or skills possessed by an applicant and offering an appropriate compensation package, work hours, and other terms of employment commensurate with the expectations of the employer.

T

testimony. Oral information offered in a hearing setting by a party to the hearing or other witness.

U

unemployed. The state of holding no employment or having one's work hours and/or wages substantially reduced.

unemployment compensation. Term used under state law to define a public system in which benefits are payable to applicants who where formerly gainfully employed, but separated from work through no fault of their own.

unemployment insurance. Term used under state law to define a public system in which benefits are payable to applicants who where formerly gainfully employed, but separated from work through no fault of their own. This term may also be used by private insurance carriers who offer job loss wage protection benefits by collecting premiums directly from future claimants before a separation from employment.

W

waiting week. A period of time, usually seven days in duration, which must be served by the unemployed or partially unemployed applicant after the initial application for benefits and before he or she will be eligible for unemployment compensation benefits.

weekly benefit amount. The dollar amount of unemployment benefits for which an applicant is eligible on a weekly basis, even if the payments are actually distributed on a bi-weekly or monthly basis.

willful misconduct. Actions or statements made by an employee which exhibit an intentional disregard for a reasonable employer rule or an employer's other interests and/or are contrary to the conduct an employer has a right to expect from the employee.

Appendix A
State Unemployment
Compensation Agencies

This appendix contains the name, address, and telephone number of the central office of each state agency that administers its respective unemployment compensation law. There may also be a local office closer to where you live. Such local offices can be located by looking in the state government listings of your telephone directory, or by calling the central office and asking for the location and phone number of the office closest to you.

Technical questions regarding legal issues are usually best directed to the personnel of the central offices. Most other questions, such as those regarding the application procedure, can usually be answered by a local office as well.

ALABAMA

Department of Industrial Relations
649 Monroe Street
Montgomery, AL 36131
334-242-8467
www.dir.state.al.us

ALASKA

Department of Labor
Employment Security Division
PO Box 25509
Juneau, AK 99802
907-465-5912
www.labor.state.ak.us

ARIZONA

Department of Economic Security
3225 N. Central Ave., Suite 1400
Phoenix, AZ 85012
602-248-9396
www.de.state.az.us

ARKANSAS

Employment Security Department
PO Box 2981
Little Rock, AR 72203
501-682-3253
www.state.ar.us/esd

CALIFORNIA

Employment Development Department
3321 Power Inn Road, Suite 220
Sacramento, CA 95826
916-464-3502
www.edd.cahwnet.gov

COLORADO

Department of Labor & Employment
1515 Arapahoe Street
Tower 2, Suite 400
Denver, CO 80202
800-480-8299
unemploytax.cdle.state.co.us

CONNECTICUT

Department of Labor
200 Folly Brook Blvd. Wethersfield, CT
06109
860-263-6785
www.ctdol.state.ct.us

DELAWARE

Department of Labor
4425 North Market Street
Wilmington, DE 19802
302-761-8446
www.delawareworks.com

DISTRICT OF COLUMBIA

Department of Employment Services
609 H Street NE, Room 362
Washington, DC 20002
202-698-7550
does.ci.washington.dc.us

FLORIDA

Department of Labor and Employment
Security
107 East Madison Street
Tallahassee, FL 32399
800-482-8293
www.fdles.state.fl.us

GEORGIA

Department of Labor
148 International Blvd., Suite 800
Atlanta, GA 30303
404-656-3122
www.dol.state.ga.us

HAWAII

Department of Labor and Industrial
Relations
830 Punchbowl Street,
Room 437
Honolulu, HI 96813
808-586-8913
www.ehawaiigov.org/working/html

IDAHO

Department of Labor
317 Main Street
Boise, ID 83735
208-334-6318
www.doe.state.id.us

ILLINOIS

Department of Employment Security
401 South State Street Chicago, IL 60605
312-793-4880
www.ides.state.il.us

INDIANA

Department of Workforce Development
10 North Senate Avenue
Indianapolis, IN 46204
317-232-7436
www.dwd.state.in.us

IOWA

Workforce Development
1000 East Grand Avenue
Des Moines, IA 50319
515-281-8200
www.state.ia.us/ government/des

KANSAS

Department of Human Resources
401 SW. Topeka Blvd.
Topeka, KS 66603
785-296-5025
www.hr.state.ks.us

KENTUCKY

Division of Unemployment Insurance
PO Box 948
Frankfort, KY 40602
502-564-6838
www.des.state.ky.us

LOUISIANA

Department of Labor
PO Box 98146
Baton Rouge, LA 70804
225-342-2944
www.ldol.state.la.us

MAINE

Department of Labor
PO Box 259
Augusta, ME 04332
207-287-3176
janus.state.me.us/labor

MARYLAND

Department of Labor, Licensing &
Regulation
1100 North Eutaw St., Room 411
Baltimore, MD 21201
800-492-5524
www.dllr.state.md.us/employment

MASSACHUSETTS

Division of Employment & Training
19 Staniford Street
Boston, MA 02114
617-626-6560
www.detma.org

MICHIGAN

Employment Security Division
7310 Woodward Avenue
Detroit, MI 48202
313-876-5131
www.cis.state.mi.us/ua

MINNESOTA

Department of Economic Security
390 North Robert Street
St. Paul, MN 55101
651-296-6141
www.des.state.mn.us

MISSISSIPPI

Employment Security Commission
PO Box 22781
Jackson, MS 39225
601-961-7755
www.mesc.state.ms.us

MISSOURI

Division of Employment Security
PO Box 59
Jefferson City, MO 65104
573-751-3215
www.dolir.state.mo.us

MONTANA

Department of Labor and Industry
PO Box 1728
Helena, MT 59624
406-444-6900
http://dli.state.mt.us

NEBRASKA

Department of Labor
Box 94600, State House Station
Lincoln, NE 68509
402-471-9835
www.dol.state.ne.us

NEVADA

Department of Employment,
Training and Rehabilitation
500 East Third Street
Carson City, NV 89713
775-687-4545
www.state.nv.us/detr

NEW HAMPSHIRE

Department of Employment Security
32 South Main Street
Concord, NH 03301
603-228-4045
www.nhworks.state.nh.us

NEW JERSEY

Department of Labor
PO Box 947
Trenton, NJ 08625
609-292-6400
www.state.nj.us/labor

NEW MEXICO

Department of Labor
PO Box 2281
Albuquerque, NM 87103
505-841-2000
www3.state.nm.us/dol

NEW YORK

Department of Labor
State Campus, Building 12, Rm.542
Albany, NY 12240
800-225-5829
www.labor.state.ny.us

NORTH CAROLINA

Employment Security Commission
PO Box 26504
Raleigh, NC 27611
919-733-7395
www.esc.state.nc.us

NORTH DAKOTA

Job Service of North Dakota
PO Box 5507
Bismarck, ND 58506
800-472-2952
www.state.nd.us/jsnd

OHIO

Department of Job & Family Services
PO Box 923
Columbus, OH 43216
614-466-2319
www.state.oh.us/odjfs

OKLAHOMA

Employment Security Commission
2401 North Lincoln
Will Rogers Memorial Office Bldg.
Oklahoma City, OK 73105
405-557-7226
www.oesc.state.ok.us

OREGON

Employment Department
875 Union Street, NE
Salem, OR 97311
503-947-1488
www.emp.state.or.us

PENNSYLVANIA

Department of Labor and Industry
7th and Forster Streets
Harrisburg, PA 17121
717-787-7679
www.dli.state.pa.us

PUERTO RICO

Department of Labor and Human
Resources
PO Box 1020
San Juan, PR 00919
787-754-5262
www.interempleo.org

RHODE ISLAND

Division of Labor & Training
One Capitol Hill
Providence, RI 02908
401-222-3696
wwww.det.state.ri.us

SOUTH CAROLINA

Employment Security Commission
PO Box 995
Columbia, SC 29202
803-737-3070
www.sces.org

SOUTH DAKOTA

Department of Labor
PO Box 4730
Aberdeen, SD 57402
605-626-2312
www.state.sd.us/dol

TENNESSEE

Department of Employment Security
500 James Robertson Parkway
Davy Crocket Tower, 8th Floor
Nashville, TN 37245
615-741-2486
www.state.tn.us/labor-wfd

TEXAS

Workforce Commission
101 East 15th Street
Austin, TX 78778
512-463-2699
www.twc.state.tx.us

UTAH

Department of Workforce Services
PO Box 45288
Salt Lake City, UT 84145
801-526-9400
www.dws.state.ut.us

VERMONT

Department of Employment Security
PO Box 488
Montpelier, VT 05602
1-877-214-3331
www.det.state.vt.us

VIRGINIA

Employment Commission
PO Box 1358
Richmond, VA 23211
804-371-6325
www.vec.state.va.us

VIRGIN ISLANDS

Employment Security Agency
PO Box 789
St. Croix, U.S. Virgin Islands 00821
340-776-3700
www.gov.vi/vild

WASHINGTON

Employment Security Department
PO Box 9046
Olympia, WA 98507
360-902-9360
www.wa.gov/esd

WEST VIRGINIA

Bureau of Employment Programs
112 California Avenue
Charleston, WV 25305
304-558-2675
www.state.wv.us/bep

WISCONSIN

Department of Workforce Development
PO Box 7942, GEF 1
Madison, WI 53702
608-261-6700
www.dwd.state.wi.us

WYOMING

Department of Employment
PO Box 2760
Casper, WY 82602
307-235-3217
www.wydoe.state.wy.us

APPENDIX B

UNEMPLOYMENT COMPENSATION LAWS (STATE-BY-STATE)

This appendix contains a summary of the unemployment compensation law for each of the fifty states of the United States, the District of Columbia, Puerto Rico, and the Virgin Islands. This appendix attempts to organize each law in a format that is easy to read and understand. The cost of this re-formatting is that, at times, it probably over-simplifies, and therefore, eliminates some of the finer details contained in the statutes.

NOTE: *Unemployment compensation law is an area of the law that is subject to regular legislative changes. Certain portions in nearly every state statute are subject to automatic annual change. Others are changed often, but sporadically.*

Legislative amendments are not the only means by which these laws regularly change. Judicial interpretations of these statutes, which may occur on a daily basis, often alter the way portions of the law are applied in real life in a manner that is not entirely intuitive. Thus, even sections of the law which appear to be understandable, and even crystal clear, may be somewhat deceptive.

Warning: When you find a section of the law that pertains to your particular situation, you are encouraged to contact your local state unemployment office, or to visit your local law library concerning changes, additions, and other details contained in the law. (Local law libraries are typically located in or near law schools and county courthouses.)

One final word of caution is merited. When reading the information contained in this appendix: *Do not panic.* Some state laws are very complex and, even in a simplified form, are difficult to understand. Even in states with laws that are generally well written, individual sections may cause you problems in your endeavor to understand what the legislature was actually trying to say.

In this area of the law, perhaps more than many others, knowledge is power. If, for example, you do not understand fully how to calculate the amount of unemployment benefits for which you should be eligible, it may still help if you at least understand what factors your Weekly Benefit Amount will be based upon, or that, perhaps, there is more than one way to calculate your Weekly Benefit Amount.

Most state unemployment offices are fairly overburdened. States are more regularly turning to less individualized treatment, such as group orientation programs, to handle the mounting numbers of annual claims. As treatment of claimants becomes less personalized, there is a greater likelihood that errors will be made at the earlier levels of the process, and every bit of information you know helps you to keep the employees of these offices in check. Similarly, if you have not kept a sufficient amount of past pay stubs to calculate your exact Weekly Benefit Amount, you should still be able to estimate this rate using the information contained in this appendix, so you will know if the Weekly Benefit Amount calculated by the state unemployment office at least seems to be in the right "ballpark."

Before referring to your particular state, or states of interest, it may help you to first read the explanatory information contained on the following two pages under the SAMPLE STATE heading. This template is provided to help you understand how this appendix divides and summarizes each state's unemployment compensation laws.

NOTE: *The symbol "§" means "section" and "§§" means "sections," as in the section number of a statute. However, all numbers appearing in parentheses are also section numbers of the statutes in that state.*

*** SAMPLE STATE ***

STATUTE:

LAW: This subsection contains the common and/or formal name given to the unemployment compensation law of the relevant state.

CITATION: This subsection contains a citation for the law. It basically directs you where to find a specific unemployment compensation law among all the legislation enacted for the relevant state. The citation often contains a title number, chapter number, paragraph number, and/or a section number where the unemployment compensation law begins. Most unemployment compensation laws follow for many sections past the initial section cited.

Throughout the remaining subsections of this appendix you will see numbers contained in parenthesis, e.g. "(6-706)." These are known as pinpoint citations because they direct you to the exact section of the law where the proposition immediately preceding the parenthetical is located.

Under certain citations you will notice a "(***)" marker. This indicates that a particular proposition is not directly contained in the state statute itself. There can be one of two primary reasons why it is not written directly into the law. Often the propositions marked as such are set to change periodically under the law. Thus, instead of, for example, amending the law every year, the law often provides some agency the authority to periodically change this figure given a list of guidelines. For example, the Department of Labor in many states is given the authority to calculate the statewide maximum Weekly Benefit Amount. Such amount typically is based upon a factor such as the Statewide Average Weekly Wage. The asterisk marker may also indicate another point. Some of the propositions marked as such identify figures which could be calculated using other information contained in the law but which is not in itself written into the law. Either way, the asterisk markers alert the reader that the prior proposition is subject to periodic change. You are encouraged to contact your state unemployment compensation agency for up to date information on these propositions.

If you choose to research the law further, be careful. If a given citation does not contain, for example, a chapter number, then ignore the chapter numbers when searching through the law. Many state laws contain certain numbering systems for mere organizational purposes and others to help a reader actually locate relevant portions. Only the latter numbers, those contained in the official citation provided, will help you to locate particular passages throughout the statute.

BENEFIT CALCULATION:

WEEKLY BENEFIT AMT.: This subsection explains how to calculate the maximum amount of benefits that a claimant will receive for each week he or she is unemployed if he or she is deemed eligible for benefits. Sometimes Weekly Benefit Amounts are included on a schedule or table contained in the law itself. These amounts cannot be summarized in one particular equation. If you are attempting to calculate the Weekly Benefit Amount for a state which uses one of these schedules or tables, you will have to visit your local unemployment office or nearby law library to secure a copy.

PARTIAL EMPLOYMENT: This subsection explains how a claimant's Weekly Benefit Amount, as calculated as described above, is reduced if he or she earns at least some wages during a period of only partial employment. Conversely, it often also explains how much a claimant can earn through partial employment and still receive full benefits.

REDUCTION IN BENEFITS: This subsection provides a list of certain variable amounts which are normally deducted from a claimant's Weekly Benefit Amount, to the extent they are applicable. In certain cases the reduction is not the full value of the variable indicated, but only a portion of the amount associated with that particular variable.

DEPENDENCY BENEFIT: This subsection relates whether the relevant state provides additional benefits for claimants who have dependent children or a dependent spouse.

MIN./MAX. WEEKLY: This subsection contains any maximum and/or minimum weekly benefit rates that apply in a relevant state. In some states the maximum weekly benefit figure includes the Dependency Benefits described above, and in others the Dependency Benefits are added to the maximum amounts indicated. In some states the minimum weekly benefit figure also serves as an eligibility qualification in that if a claimant's Weekly Benefit Amount, as calculated as described above, yields a Weekly Benefit Amount that is lower than the minimum weekly benefit rate contained in this subsection, the claimant will be deemed ineligible for benefits. For details regarding either of these special conditions, consult your local unemployment compensation office or visit a nearby law library.

MAXIMUM TOTAL: This subsection indicates how to calculate the maximum amount of unemployment compensation benefits a claimant is eligible for within his or her entire Benefit Year.

BENEFIT ELIGIBILITY:

GENERALLY: This subsection lists the eligibility requirements which must be met by a claimant before he or she will be granted unemployment compensation benefits. It is self-evident that each claimant also must be deemed "unemployed" or at least "partially unemployed" in every state as well.

SUBSEQUENT APPLICATION: This subsection enlists limitations which the relevant state places upon claimants who have filed for unemployment compensation benefits in the past and are now filing for benefits once again. These limitations essentially place an additional eligibility requirement on those claimants who file for unemployment compensation benefits more than once in their lives.

WAITING WEEK: This subsection indicates whether or not the relevant state requires a claimant to establish a period of time, during which he or she is unemployed, but during which he or she will not receive unemployment compensation benefits, before he or she will actually receive his or her weekly benefit payments.

DISQUALIFICATION: This subsection enlists scenarios which, when applicable, serve to disqualify a claimant from unemployment compensation benefits. The length of a particular disqualification period may be based entirely on a time variable, e.g. such as four weeks, or may conclude upon some affirmative act by a claimant, e.g. the claimant accepts available work and subsequently becomes unemployed. Contact your local unemployment office if you have specific questions regarding how long a particular disqualification lasts.

PURGING DISQUALIFICATION: In certain states, once a claimant is disqualified from benefits, as described above, he or she must perform some act, such as returning to work and earning a certain amount of income, before he or she will ever be deemed eligible for unemployment compensation benefits. This subsection enlists these additional eligibility requirements which must be met by such claimants if they later find themselves unemployed again and subsequently file for benefits.

NOTE: *In addition to the positive acts to purge disqualification included in this appendix, many states also require the passing of statutory time intervals before the Claimant may once again apply for benefits after disqualification. For information on the requisite time intervals, please contact the appropriate state agency listed in Appendix A.*

SPECIAL TREATMENT:

This subsection contains a potpourri of miscellaneous areas of the relevant state unemployment compensation law which call for unique treatment of certain described claimants. Unique treatment may be provided in a variety of forms. For example, certain sections may render seemingly ineligible claimants eligible for benefits while others may require certain types of claimants to calculate their Weekly Benefit Amount in a manner different than that utilized by other individuals. If you feel you fall in one or more of the enlisted categories, you should contact your local unemployment compensation office and request more information about the special treatment afforded to such claimants.

ALABAMA

STATUTE:

LAW: Alabama Unemployment Compensation Law

CITATION: Code of Alabama, Title 25, Chapter 4 (C.A. § 25-4-1)

BENEFIT CALCULATION:

WEEKLY BENEFIT AMT.: Benefit amount is 1/24 of the average of the quarterly wages he or she earned in his or her two highest-paying Base Period quarters. (25-4-72)

PARTIAL EMPLOYMENT: Any wages Claimant receives during the week from partial employment in excess of $15 are deducted from his or her Weekly Benefit Amount. (25-4-72)

REDUCTION IN BENEFITS: Claimant's Weekly Benefit Amount may be reduced if: (i) Claimant receives pension benefits (25-4-78); (ii) Claimant receives retirement pay (25-4-78); (iii) Claimant receives Social Security benefits (25-4-78); (iv) Claimant receives annuity payments (25-4-78); (v) Claimant receives other similar periodic payments in connection with previous work (25-4-78); (vi) Claimant receives a training allowance (25-4-78); (vii) Claimant receives or is seeking benefits for a temporary disability under a workers' compensation law (25-4-78); (viii) Claimant receives dismissal or separation allowance (25-4-78); (ix) Claimant receives wages in lieu of notice (25-4-78); (x) Claimant receives back pay award. (25-4-78)

DEPENDENCY BENEFIT: None.

MIN./MAX. WEEKLY: Minimum weekly benefit is $44.50. (25-4-72) Maximum weekly benefit is $190. (25-4-72)

MAXIMUM TOTAL: Claimant may receive total benefits equaling the lesser of (i) 26 x his or her Weekly Benefit Amount or (ii) 1/3 of his or her Base Period wages. (25-4-74) In times of high unemployment, extended benefits may be available. (25-4-75)

BENEFIT ELIGIBILITY:

GENERALLY: To be eligible for unemployment compensation benefits, Claimant must: (i) File a claim for benefits (25-4-77); (ii) Register for work at a state unemployment office (25-4-77); (iii) Earn Base Period wages of 1 1/2 x wages he or she earns in his or her highest-paying Base Period quarter (25-4-77); (iv) Be physically and mentally able to work and available for work (25-4-77); (v) Be making a reasonable and active effort to secure work. (25-4-77)

SUBSEQUENT APPLICATION: A Claimant who received benefits during a preceding Benefit Year must have worked and earned 8 x his or her Weekly Benefit Amount, as calculated for his or her prior Benefit Year, subsequent to the commencement of such Benefit Year and before the commencement of his or her new Benefit Year. (25-4-77)

WAITING WEEK: None.

DISQUALIFICATION: Claimant may be partially, fully or at least temporarily disqualified from receiving benefits if: (i) Claimant was discharged or suspended for misconduct connected with work (25-4-78); (ii) Claimant voluntarily left most recent work without good cause (25-4-78); (iii) Claimant failed to accept available work or failed to apply for suitable work without good cause (25-4-78); (iv) Claimant had a license or bond required for employment revoked (25-4-78); (v) Claimant separation was caused by a labor dispute (25-4-78); (vi) Claimant was or is self-employed (25-4-78); (vii) Claimant was participating in federal or state public works projects (25-4-78); (viii) Claimant made a fraudulent misrepresentation in connection with his or her benefit claim (25-4-145); (ix) Claimant is receiving or has applied for unemployment benefits from another state or under federal law (25-4-78); (x) Claimant is an illegal alien. (25-4-78)

PURGING DISQUALIFICATION: A Claimant who was discharged in connection with work for (i) committing a dishonest act, a criminal act, or sabotage, (ii) committing an act endangering the safety of others, (iii) the use of illegal drugs after being provided with previous warning, (iv) failing to submit to a drug test after being provided with previous warning concerning drug use, may be eligible for benefits only after receiving remuneration for work subsequent to the disqualifying separation in the amount of 10 x his or her Weekly Benefit Amount. (25-4-78) A Claimant who voluntarily quit without good cause may be eligible for benefits only after receiving remuneration for work subsequent to the disqualifying separation in the amount of 10 x his or her Weekly Benefit Amount. (25-4-78)

SPECIAL TREATMENT:

Claimants in the following categories are afforded distinct treatment under the statute and thus further research may be merited for: (i) Claimants who are on jury duty (25-4-77); (ii) Claimants who take leave-of-absences due to pregnancy (25-4-78); (iii) Claimants who are in approved training programs (25-4-77); (iv) Claimants who are employees of educational institutions when it is between school semesters (25-4-70); (v) Claimants who are professional athletes when it is between sports seasons. (25-4-78)

ALASKA

STATUTE:

LAW: Alaska Employment Security Act

CITATION: Alaska Statutes, Title 23, Section 23.20.005 (A.S. § 23.20.005)

BENEFIT CALCULATION:

WEEKLY BENEFIT AMT.: Benefit amount depends upon a schedule found in the statute which takes Base Period wages into account. (Total Base Period earnings of $1,000 yield the Claimant a Weekly Benefit Amount of 200% of his or her average weekly earnings. Total Base Period earnings of $14,000 yield the Claimant with a Weekly Benefit Amount of 55% of his or her average weekly earnings. Total Base Period earnings of $26,500 yield the Claimant with a Weekly Benefit Amount of 48% of his or her average weekly earnings.) (23.20.350)

PARTIAL EMPLOYMENT: 75% of any wages in a week Claimant receives from partial employment in excess of $50 are deducted from his or her Weekly Benefit Amount. (23.20.360)

REDUCTION IN BENEFITS: Claimant's Weekly Benefit Amount may be reduced if: (i) Claimant receives pension benefits (23.20.362); (ii) Claimant receives retirement pay (23.20.362); (iii) Claimant receives annuity payments (23.20.362); (iv) Claimant receives other similar periodic payments in connection with previous work (23.20.362); (v) Claimant receives severance, termination or dismissal pay (23.20.362); (vi) Claimant receives wages in lieu of notice (23.20.362); (vii) Claimant receives vacation pay (23.20.362); (viii) Claimant receives sick leave pay (23.20.362); (ix) Claimant receives holiday pay. (23.20.362)

DEPENDENCY BENEFIT: Claimant's Weekly Benefit Amount may be increased if: Claimant has one or more dependent children or legal wards ($24 per week for each dependent, not to exceed $72 Dependency Benefits per week). (23.20.350)

MIN./MAX. WEEKLY: Minimum weekly benefit is $44. (23.20.350) Maximum weekly benefit is subject to periodic changes. For 2001, the maximum weekly benefit was $248. (23.20.350)

MAXIMUM TOTAL: Claimant may receive benefits for between 16 and 26 weeks depending upon his or her Earnings Ratio (i.e. the ratio obtained by dividing Claimant's total Base Period wages by the wages paid in his or her highest-paying Base Period quarter). (23.20.350) In times of high unemployment, extended benefits may be available. (23.20.406)

BENEFIT ELIGIBILITY:

GENERALLY: To be eligible for unemployment compensation benefits, Claimant must: (i) File an initial claim for benefits (23.20.375); (ii) Earn Base Period wages of $1,000 which must have been paid in at least two of the quarters of such Base Period (23.20.350); (iii) Be able to work and available for suitable work. (23.20.378)

SUBSEQUENT APPLICATION: A Claimant who received benefits during a preceding Benefit Year must have worked and earned 8 x his or her Weekly Benefit Amount subsequent to the commencement of such Benefit Year and before the commencement of his or her new Benefit Year. (23.20.381)

WAITING WEEK: Claimant must serve 1 Waiting Week before collecting benefits. (23.20.375)

DISQUALIFICATION: Claimant may be partially, fully or at least temporarily disqualified from receiving benefits if: (i) Claimant was discharged for misconduct connected with last work (23.20.379); (ii) Claimant voluntarily left suitable work without good cause (23.20.379); (iii) Claimant failed to apply for or accept suitable work (23.20.379); (iv) Claimant separation was caused by a labor dispute (23.20.383); (v) Claimant knowingly made a false statement, misrepresentation of a material fact or knowingly failed to disclose a material fact in connection with his or her benefit claim (23.20.387); (vi) Claimant is receiving unemployment benefits from another state or under federal law (23.20.362); (vii) Claimant is an illegal alien. (23.20.381)

PURGING DISQUALIFICATION: A Claimant who was discharged for misconduct connected with work, who voluntarily quit without good cause, or who failed to apply for or accept suitable work, may be eligible for benefits only after receiving remuneration for work subsequent to the disqualifying separation in the amount of 8 x his or her Weekly Benefit Amount. (23.20.379) A Claimant who was discharged for committing a felony or theft in connection with work may be eligible for benefits only after receiving remuneration for work subsequent to the disqualifying separation in the amount of 20 x his or her Weekly Benefit Amount. (23.20.379)

SPECIAL TREATMENT:

Claimants in the following categories are afforded distinct treatment under the statute and thus further research may be merited for: (i) Claimants who are on jury duty (23.20.378); (ii) Claimants who are in approved training programs (23.20.382); (iii) Claimants who are on leave for four or fewer weeks pursuant to an employer work schedule (23.20.505); (iv) Claimants who are employees of educational institutions when it is between school semesters (23.20.381); (v) Claimants who are professional athletes when it is between sports seasons. (23.20.381)

ARIZONA

STATUTE:

LAW: Arizona Employment Security Act

CITATION: Arizona Revised Statutes Annotated, Section 23-601 (A.R.S. § 23-601)

BENEFIT CALCULATION:

WEEKLY BENEFIT AMT.: Benefit amounts are calculated as 1/25 of the amount Claimant received during his or her highest-paying quarter during his or her Base Period. (23-778)

PARTIAL EMPLOYMENT: Any wages Claimant receives during the week from partial employment in excess of $30 are deducted from his or her Weekly Benefit Amount. (23-779)

REDUCTION IN BENEFITS: Claimant's Weekly Benefit Amount may be reduced if: (i) Claimant receives pension benefits (23-791); (ii) Claimant receives Social Security benefits (23-791); (iii) Claimant receives retirement pay; (iv) Claimant receives annuity payments (23-791); (v) Claimant receives other similar periodic payments based upon previous work. (23-791)

DEPENDENCY BENEFIT: None.

MIN./MAX. WEEKLY: Minimum weekly benefit is $40. (23-771, 23-779) Maximum weekly benefit is $205. (23-779)

MAXIMUM TOTAL: Claimant may receive total benefits equaling the lesser of (i) 26 x his or her Weekly Benefit Amount or (ii) 1/3 of his or her Base Period earnings. (23-780) In times of high unemployment, extended benefits may be available. (23-634)

BENEFIT ELIGIBILITY:

GENERALLY: To be eligible for unemployment compensation benefits, Claimant must: (i) File a claim for benefits (23-771); (ii) Register for work at a state unemployment office (23-771); (iii) Continue to report to a state unemployment office as required (23-771); (iv) Earn either (a) Base Period wages equal to 1 1/2 x his or her highest-paying Base Period quarter with a minimum of $1,000 in one quarter or (b) Wages in at least two quarters of his or her Base Period and have wages in one Base Period quarter sufficient to qualify Claimant for the maximum Weekly Benefit Amount with total Base Period wages at least equal to the taxable limit (i.e. $7,000) (23-622, 23-771); (v) Be able to work and available for work. (23-771)

SUBSEQUENT APPLICATION: A Claimant who received benefits during a preceding Benefit Year must have worked and earned 8 x his or her Weekly Benefit Amount subsequent to the commencement of such Benefit Year and before the commencement of his or her new Benefit Year. (23-771)

WAITING WEEK: Claimant must serve 1 Waiting Week before collecting benefits. (23-771)

DISQUALIFICATION: Claimant may be partially, fully or at least temporarily disqualified from receiving benefits if: (i) Claimant was discharged for willful or negligent misconduct connected with work (23-775); (ii) Claimant voluntarily left work without good cause (23-775); (iii) Claimant failed to accept or apply for suitable work when so directed by the department (23-776); (iv) Claimant separation was caused by a labor dispute (23-777); (v) Claimant made a false statement or representation of a material fact knowing it to be false or knowingly failed to disclose material facts to obtain benefits (23-778); (vi) Claimant is receiving unemployment benefits from another state or under federal law (23-775); (vii) Claimant is not working during a customary suspension of work operations (23-775); (viii) Claimant is unemployed during customary suspension of all operations, except maintenance work, at the factory, plant or other premises at which he or she is employed (23-775); (ix) Claimant is an illegal alien. (23-781)

PURGING DISQUALIFICATION: A Claimant who was fired for willful or negligent misconduct or who voluntarily quit without good cause may be eligible for benefits after receiving remuneration for work subsequent to the disqualifying separation in the amount of 5 x his or her Weekly Benefit Amount. (23-775)

SPECIAL TREATMENT:

Claimants in the following categories are afforded distinct treatment under the statute and thus further research may be merited for: (i) Claimants who are in approved training programs (23-771.01); (ii) Claimants who are members of the National Guard, other reserve units, or the U.S. Armed Forces (23-622, 23-771); (iii) Claimants who participate in shared work programs (23-763); (iv) Claimants who are employees of educational institutions when it is between school semesters (23-750); (v) Claimants who are professional athletes when it is between sports seasons. (23-781)

ARKANSAS

STATUTE:

LAW: Arkansas Employment Security Law.

CITATION: Arkansas Code of 1987 Annotated, Title 11, Chapter 10, Section 11-10-101 (A.C.A. § 11-10-101)

BENEFIT CALCULATION:

WEEKLY BENEFIT AMT.: Benefit amounts are calculated as 1/26 of Claimant's wages earned during the highest-paying quarter of his or her Base Period. (11-10-502)

PARTIAL EMPLOYMENT: Any wages Claimant receives during the week from partial employment in excess of 40% of his or her Weekly Benefit Amount are deducted from this amount. (11-10-503)

REDUCTION IN BENEFITS: Claimant's Weekly Benefit Amount may be reduced if: (i) Claimant receives pension benefits (11-10-517); (ii) Claimant receives retirement pay (11-10-517); (iii) Claimant receives annuity payments; (iv) Claimant receives other similar periodic payments in connection with previous work (11-10-517); (v) Claimant receives bonus payments (11-10-517); (vi) Claimant receives vacation pay. (11-10-517)

DEPENDENCY BENEFIT: None.

MIN./MAX. WEEKLY: Minimum weekly benefit is calculated as 12% of the Statewide Average Weekly Wage for the preceding calendar year. (11-10-502) For 2001, the minimum weekly benefit was $60. (***) Maximum weekly benefit is calculated as 66 2/3% of the Statewide Average Weekly Wage for the preceding calendar quarter. (11-10-502) For 2001, the maximum weekly benefit was $333. (***)

MAXIMUM TOTAL: Claimant may receive total benefits equaling the lesser of (i) 26 x his or her Weekly Benefit Amount or (ii) 1/3 of his or her Base Period wages. (11-10-504) In times of high unemployment, extended benefits may be available. (11-10-536)

BENEFIT ELIGIBILITY:

GENERALLY: To be eligible for unemployment compensation benefits, Claimant must: (i) File a claim for benefits (11-10-507); (ii) Register for work at a state unemployment office (11-10-507); (iii) Continue to report to a state unemployment office as required (11-10-507); (iv) Earn Base Period wages of at least 27 x his or her Weekly Benefit Amount with such wages being paid in at least two quarters of his or her Base Period (11-10-507); (v) Be physically and mentally able to perform suitable work and available for suitable work (11-10-507); (vi) Act in a manner that a reasonably prudent individual would to secure work (11-10-507); (vii) Participate in reemployment services as required. (11-10-507)

SUBSEQUENT APPLICATION: A Claimant who received benefits during a preceding Benefit Year must have worked and earned 3 x his or her Weekly Benefit Amount subsequent to filing his or her claim for the prior Benefit Year and before the commencement of his or her new Benefit Year. (11-10-507)

WAITING WEEK: Claimant must serve 1 Waiting Week before collecting benefits. (11-10- 507)

DISQUALIFICATION: Claimant may be partially, fully or at least temporarily disqualified from receiving benefits if: (i) Claimant was discharged or suspended for misconduct connected with work (11-10-514); (ii) Claimant voluntarily left work without good cause (11-10-513); (iii) Claimant failed to apply for available suitable work or to accept available suitable work (11-10-515); (iv) Claimant separation was caused by a labor dispute other than a lockout (11-10-508); (v) Claimant willfully made a false statement or misrepresentation of a material fact or willfully failed to disclose a material fact to obtain benefits (11-10-519); (vi) Claimant is receiving federal training or retraining allowances (11-10-517); (vii)Claimant received separation payments (11-10-517); (viii) Claimant is an illegal alien (11-10-511); (ix) Claimant made a false statement or representation in order to obtain benefits. (11-10-517)

PURGING DISQUALIFICATION: A Claimant who voluntarily quit without good cause is not eligible for benefits until after being employed for at least 30 days. (11-10-513) A Claimant who was discharged for misconduct in connection with work in the form of dishonesty, drinking on the job, being under the influence of intoxicants, or for a willful violation of the rules or customs of an employer pertaining to the safety of employees or company property, however, is not eligible for benefits until after being employed for 10 weeks at a wage at least equal to his or her Weekly Benefit Amount. (11-10-514)

SPECIAL TREATMENT:

Claimants in the following categories are afforded distinct treatment under the statute and thus further research may be merited for: (i) Claimants who are on jury duty (11-10-507); (ii) Claimants who are in approved training programs (11-10-518); (iii) Claimants who are attending state vocational school (11-10-507); (iv) Claimants who participate in shared work plans (11-10-602); (v) Claimants who are employees of educational institutions when it is between school semesters (11-10-509); (vi) Claimants who are professional athletes when it is between sports seasons. (11-10-510); (vii) Claimants who are employed in seasonal industries (11-10-506)

CALIFORNIA

STATUTE:

LAW: California Unemployment Insurance Code

CITATION: West's Annotated California Codes, Unemployment Insurance Code, Section 1 (Cal. Un. Ins. Code § 1)

BENEFIT CALCULATION:

WEEKLY BENEFIT AMT.: Benefit amount depends upon a schedule found in the statute which takes Base Period wages into account. (1280) A Claimant who was paid $4,966.99 or more in his or her highest-paying Base Period quarter receives a weekly benefit of 39% of these wages divided by 13. (High-quarter earnings of $450 yield the Claimant a Weekly Benefit Amount of 85% of his or her average weekly wage. High-quarter earnings of $2,500 yield the Claimant a Weekly Benefit Amount of 46% of his or her average weekly wage. High-quarter earnings of $5,533 yield the Claimant a Weekly Benefit Amount of 39% of his or her average weekly wage.) (1280)

PARTIAL EMPLOYMENT: The lesser of (i) Any weekly wages Claimant receives from partial employment in excess of $25 or (ii) Any weekly wages Claimant receives from partial employment in excess of 25% of the amount of wages payable to him or her by reason of such partial employment, are deducted from his or her Weekly Benefit Amount. (1279)

REDUCTION IN BENEFITS: Claimant's Weekly Benefit Amount may be reduced if: (i) Claimant receives pension benefits (1255.3); (ii) Claimant receives retirement pay (1255.3); (iii) Claimant receives Social Security benefits; (iv) Claimant receives annuity payments (1255.3); (v) Claimant receives other payments in connection with previous work (1255.3); (vi) Claimant receives benefits for temporary total disability under a workers' compensation law. (1255.5)

DEPENDENCY BENEFIT: None.

MIN./MAX. WEEKLY: Minimum weekly benefit is $40. (1280) Maximum weekly benefit is $230. (1280)

MAXIMUM TOTAL: Claimant may receive total benefits equaling 26 x his or her Weekly Benefit Amount, but may not receive an amount which exceeds 1/2 of his or her total Base Period wages. (1281) In times of high unemployment, extended benefits may be available. (3552)

BENEFIT ELIGIBILITY:

GENERALLY: To be eligible for unemployment compensation benefits, Claimant must: (i) File a claim for benefits (1253); (ii) Register for work at a state unemployment office (1253); (iii) Continue to report to a state unemployment office as required (1253); (iv) Either have (a) Earned at least $900 in his or her highest-paying Base Period quarter with overall Base Period earnings of at least 1.25 x his or her highest-paying Base Period quarter wages or (b) Earned at least $1,300 in his or her highest-paying Base Period quarter (1281); (v) Be able to work and available for work (1253); (vi) Search for work as directed by employment office. (1253); (vii) Participate in reemployment activities as required by the employment office.

SUBSEQUENT APPLICATION: Any wages used in the calculation of unemployment benefits for Claimant during one Benefit Year may not be used in determining Claimant's benefits in a subsequent Benefit Year. (1277) Claimant must again meet the regular qualifying requirements subsequent to the commencement of his or her prior Benefit Year.

WAITING WEEK: Claimant must serve 1 Waiting Week before collecting benefits. (1253)

DISQUALIFICATION: Claimant may be partially, fully or at least temporarily disqualified from receiving benefits if: (i) Claimant was discharged for misconduct connected with his or her most recent work (1256); (ii) Claimant voluntarily left his or her most recent work without good cause (1256); (iii) Claimant's discharge from most recent work was related to use of intoxicants (1256.5); (iv) Claimant refused to accept suitable work or apply for suitable work when notified that such work exists by an unemployment office (1257); (v) Claimant's absence was due to incarceration in connection with an act to which either Claimant was convicted, entered a guilty plea, or entered a nolo contendere plea (1256.1); (vi) Claimant separation was caused by a labor dispute (1262); (vii) Claimant knowingly made a false statement or failed to disclose a material fact to obtain benefits (1257); (viii) Claimant is receiving unemployment benefits from another state or under federal law (1255); (ix) Claimant is an illegal alien. (1264)

PURGING DISQUALIFICATION: A Claimant who was fired for misconduct connected with work, whose discharge was related to the use of intoxicants, or who voluntarily quit without good cause, may be eligible for benefits after receiving remuneration for work subsequent to the disqualifying separation in the amount of 5 x his or her Weekly Benefit Amount. (1256.5, 1260) A Claimant who enters into a treatment program and is subsequently certified by a physician or program administrator as able to return to work purges intoxicant-related disqualifications. (1256.5)

SPECIAL TREATMENT:

Claimants in the following categories are afforded distinct treatment under the statute and thus further research may be merited for: (i) Claimants who voluntarily leave work while accepting layoffs pursuant to a collective bargaining agreement (1256); (ii) Claimants who are in approved training programs (1267); (iii) Claimants who are on jury duty (1253.7); (iv) Claimants who are serving as witnesses under subpoena (1253.6); (v) Claimants who are students (1253.8); (vi) Claimants who are physically or mentally ill or injured (1253.5); (vii) Claimants who are longshoremen (1253.2); (viii) Claimants who participate in shared work programs (1279.5); (ix) Claimants who are discharged from military service (1253.15); (x) Claimants who are commercial fishermen (1252.1); (xi) Claimants who receive wages due to service in the National Guard or other reserve unit of the Armed Forces (1279); (xii) Claimants who are employees of educational institutions when it is between school semesters (1253.3); (xiii) Claimants who are professional athletes when it is between sports seasons. (1253.4)

COLORADO

STATUTE:

LAW: Colorado Employment Security Act

CITATION: Colorado Revised Statutes Annotated, Title 8, Article 70, Section 8-70-101 (C.R.S.A. § 8-70-101)

BENEFIT CALCULATION:

WEEKLY BENEFIT AMT.: Benefit amount is calculated as 60% of 1/26 x the sum of the wages Claimant received in the two consecutive quarters in his or her Base Period in which he or she received his or her highest wages. (8-73-102)

PARTIAL EMPLOYMENT: Any wages Claimant receives in excess of 25% of his or her Weekly Benefit Amount are deducted from his or her Weekly Benefit Amount. (8-73-102) If the wages Claimant earns through partial employment in a week exceed his or her Weekly Benefit Amount. Claimant is ineligible for benefits. (8-73-107)

REDUCTION IN BENEFITS: Claimant's Weekly Benefit Amount may be reduced if: (i) Claimant receives pension benefits (8-73-110); (ii) Claimant receives retirement pay (8-73-110); (iii) Claimant receives annuity payments; (iv) Claimant receives Social Security payments (8-73-110); (v) Claimant receives other similar periodic payments in connection with previous work (8-73-110); (vi) Claimant receives other payments with respect to a Base Period employer (8-73-110); (vii) Claimant receives benefits for a temporary disability under a workers' compensation law (8-73-110); (viii) Claimant receives sick pay. (8-73-110)

DEPENDENCY BENEFIT: None.

MIN./MAX. WEEKLY: Minimum weekly benefit is $25. (8-73-102) Maximum weekly benefit is re-calculated periodically as 50% of the Statewide Average Weekly Wage. (8-73-102) A Claimant who is entitled to the state maximum Weekly Benefit Amount may, if it is greater, have his or her benefit amount calculated as 50% of 1/52 x the total wages he or she received during his or her Base Period as long as such amount does not exceed 55% of the Statewide Average Weekly Wage. (8-73-102) For 2001, the regular maximum was $307. (***)

MAXIMUM TOTAL: Claimant may receive total benefits equaling the lesser of (i) 26 x his or her Weekly Benefit Amount or (ii) 1/3 of the Wage Credits he or she is entitled in his or her Base Period. (Wage Credits granted in a Base Period equal the lesser of (a) the total wages Claimant received during his or her Base Period or (b) 26 x the current maximum benefit amount.) (8-73-104) In times of high unemployment, extended benefits may also be available. (8-75-103)

BENEFIT ELIGIBILITY:

GENERALLY: To be eligible for unemployment compensation benefits, Claimant must: (i) File a claim for benefits (8-73-107); (ii) Furnish the division with separation information and other reports necessary for its determination (8-73-107); (iii) Register for work at a state unemployment office (8-73-107); (iv) Continue to report to a state unemployment office as required (8-73-107); (v) Earn Base Period wages of at least 40 x his or her Weekly Benefit Amount or $2,500, whichever is greater (8-73-107); (vi) Be able and available for work (8-73-107); (vii) Be actively seeking work. (8-73-107)

SUBSEQUENT APPLICATION: A Claimant who received benefits during a preceding Benefit Year must have worked and earned $2,000 subsequent to the commencement of such Benefit Year and before the commencement of his or her new Benefit Year. (8-73-107)

WAITING WEEK: Claimant must serve 1 Waiting Week before collecting benefits. (8-73-107)

DISQUALIFICATION: Claimant may be partially, fully or at least temporarily disqualified from receiving benefits if: (i) Claimant voluntarily quits (a) because of unmerited dissatisfaction with pay, work hours, working conditions or supervisors who acted reasonably, (b) to accept an inferior job, (c) to get married, (d) to move to a different location as a matter of personal preference, (e) for other non-compelling personal reasons, (f) to retire (8-73-108); (ii) Claimant was discharged for (a) insubordination, deliberately disobeying a reasonable instruction, or refusing or failing to obtain or renew a license necessary to perform a job, (b) the nonpayment of union dues, (c) unacceptable rudeness, insolence, or offensive behavior to a customer, supervisor, or fellow worker, (d) careless or shoddy work, (e) failure to safeguard employer's property, (f) taking unauthorized vacations, refusing to work a different shift or refusing to accept a transfer, (g) sleeping or loafing on the job, (h) excessive tardiness or absenteeism, (i) failure to meet established job performance or other defined standards, (j) violating a statute or company rule which resulted or could have resulted in serious damage to the employer's property or other interests, (k) being incarcerated for the violation of any law, (l) losing a license essential to work, (m) theft, (n) assault or threatened assault upon a supervisor, co-worker or others, (o) willful neglect or damage to an employer's property or interests, (p) consuming intoxicating beverages or controlled substances while at work or at a time when such intoxicants interfere with job performance, (q) failure to go to work due to lack of transportation unless it would be unreasonable to require the worker to move to a job site less accessible or substantially more distant from his home than the site which he had worked, (r) failure to enter and/or complete an approved program to deal with an addiction, (s) commission of repeated acts of agitation against working conditions, pay policies, or company procedures, (t) having non-medically prescribed controlled substances in his or her system, (u) falsification of records or reports, (v) immoral conduct which has an affect on the worker's job status, (w) divulging of confidential information which could have resulted in change to the

[continued on next page]

employer's interests (8-73-108); (iii) Claimant was discharged for gross misconduct evincing willful or wanton disregard for an employer's interests or negligence regarding the same (8-73-108); (iv) Claimant refused suitable work or referral to suitable work (8-73-108); (v) Claimant separation was caused by a labor dispute (8-73-109); (vi) Claimant receives severance allowance, separation bonuses, or wages in lieu of notice; (vii) Claimant receives vacation pay, wages in lieu of notice, severance allowances, or separation bonus (8-73-110); (viii) Claimant made a false representation or failed to disclose a material fact to obtain benefits (8-81-101); (ix) Claimant is receiving unemployment benefits from another state or under federal law (8-73-112); (x) Claimant is an illegal alien. (8-73-107)

PURGING DISQUALIFICATION: N/A

SPECIAL TREATMENT:

Claimants in the following categories are afforded distinct treatment under the statute and thus further research may be merited for: (i) Claimants who separated due to an illness or injury compensable under the Workmen's Compensation Law (8-73-112); (ii) Claimants who are in approved training programs (8-73-113); (iii) Claimants who are on jury duty (8-73-107); (iv) Claimants who receive disability compensation in connection with military service (8-73-110); (v) Claimants who are seasonal workers (8-73-104); (vi) Claimants who participate in internship programs (8-73-107); (vii) Claimants who quit work to attend community college or other occupational, educational, technical or junior college (8-73-108); (viii) Claimants who are employees of educational institutions when it is between school semesters (8-73-107); (ix) Claimants who are professional athletes when it is between sports seasons (8-73-107); (x) Claimants who are hired only as temporary employees or by temporary help contracting firms (8-73-105); (xi) Claimants who are on medical leave.

CONNECTICUT

STATUTE:

LAW: Connecticut Unemployment Compensation Law

CITATION: Connecticut General Statutes Annotated, Title 31, Section 31-222 (C.G.S.A. § 31-222)

BENEFIT CALCULATION:

WEEKLY BENEFIT AMT.: Benefit amounts are calculated as 1/26 x the sum of the wages Claimant earned in his or her two highest-paying Base Period quarters. (31-231a)

PARTIAL EMPLOYMENT: The Weekly Benefit Amount of a Claimant who is Partially Unemployed (i.e. any week in which he or she works less than full-time and earned less than 1 1/2 x his or her Weekly Benefit Amount) will be reduced by 2/3 of the wages he or she earns during such partial employment. (31-229)

REDUCTION IN BENEFITS: Claimant's Weekly Benefit Amount may be reduced if: (i) Claimant receives pension benefits (31-227); (ii) Claimant receives retirement pay (31-227); (iii) Claimant receives Social Security benefits (31-227); (iv) Claimant receives annuity payments (31-227); (v) Claimant receives other similar periodic payments in connection with previous work. (31-227)

DEPENDENCY BENEFIT: Claimant's Weekly Benefit Amount may be increased if: Claimant has a non-working spouse or dependent child ($15 for the spouse and $15 for each child up to 5 dependents as long as the dependency allowance does not exceed 100% of the benefits otherwise payable to Claimant). (31-234)

MIN./MAX. WEEKLY: Minimum weekly benefit is $15. (31-231a) Maximum weekly benefit is re-calculated each year as 60% of the statewide average wage to production and related workers. (31-231a) For 2001, the maximum weekly benefit was $406. (***)

MAXIMUM TOTAL: Claimant may receive total benefits equaling 26 x his or her Weekly Benefit Amount. (31-231b) In times of high unemployment, extended benefits may be available. (31-232d)

BENEFIT ELIGIBILITY:

GENERALLY: To be eligible for unemployment compensation benefits, Claimant must: (i) File a claim for benefits (31-235); (ii) Register for work at a state unemployment office (31-235); (iii) Earn during his or her Base Period wages of at least 40 x his or her Weekly Benefit Amount (31-235); (iv) Be physically and mentally able to work and available for work (31-235); (v) Be making a reasonable effort to find work (31-235); (vi) Participate in reemployment services as required. (31-235)

SUBSEQUENT APPLICATION: A Claimant who received benefits during a preceding Benefit Year must have worked and earned the greater of (a) $300 or (b) 5 x his or her Weekly Benefit Amount subsequent to the commencement of such Benefit Year and before the commencement of his or her new Benefit Year. (31-236)

WAITING WEEK: None.

DISQUALIFICATION: Claimant may be partially, fully or at least temporarily disqualified from receiving benefits if: (i) Claimant was discharged for willful misconduct in the course of employment (31-236); (ii) Claimant was discharged for just cause (31-236); (iii) Claimant was discharged or suspended for an act constituting a felony (31-236); (iv) Claimant was discharged or suspended during a period of imprisonment (31-236); (v) Claimant was discharged for conduct which amounts to larceny of property, service, or currency (31-236); (vi) Claimant was discharged or suspended as a result of drug or alcohol testing mandated by law (31-236); (vii) Claimant voluntarily left work without good cause attributed to employer (31-236); (viii) Claimant failed to apply for or accept suitable work (31-236); (ix) Claimant separation was caused by a labor dispute other than a lockout (31-236); (x) Claimant knowingly made a false statement or misrepresentation or knowingly failed to disclose a material fact in order to obtain benefits (31-273); (xi) Claimant is receiving unemployment benefits from another state or under federal law (31-236); (xii) Claimant receives dismissal, severance, or separation payments, or wages in lieu of notice (31-236); (xiii) Claimant leaves work to attend school (31-236); (xiv) Claimant has voluntarily retired (31-236); (xv) Claimant receives benefits under a workers' compensation law for a temporary disability (31-236); (xvi) Claimant is an illegal alien. (31-227)

PURGING DISQUALIFICATION: A Claimant who was fired for just cause, willful misconduct, due to his or her imprisonment, for failing a drug or alcohol test, participating in an illegal strike, felonious conduct, or larceny, or a Claimant who voluntarily quit without good cause, may be eligible for benefits only after returning to work and receiving remuneration for work subsequent to the disqualifying separation in the amount of 10 x his or her Weekly Benefit Amount. (31-236) A Claimant who failed to accept or apply for suitable work may be eligible for benefits only after returning to work and receiving remuneration for work subsequent to the disqualifying separation in the amount of 6 x his or her Weekly Benefit Amount. (31-236)

SPECIAL TREATMENT:

Claimants in the following categories are afforded distinct treatment under the statute and thus further research may be merited for: (i) Claimants who are construction workers (31-231a); (ii) Claimants who are attending school, college, or a university as a regularly enrolled student (31-235); (iii) Claimants who are in approved training programs (31-236b); (iv) Claimants who leave part-time work to pursue full-time work (31-236); (v) Claimants who receive compensation tied to separation from military service (31-236); (vi) Claimants who are employees of educational institutions when it is between school semesters (31-227); (vii) Claimants who are professional athletes when it is between sports seasons. (31-227)

DELAWARE

STATUTE:

LAW: Delaware Unemployment Compensation Law

CITATION: Delaware Code Annotated, Title 19, Section 3301 (D.C.A. 19 § 3301)

BENEFIT CALCULATION:

WEEKLY BENEFIT AMT.: Benefit amounts are calculated as 1/46 x the sum of the wages Claimant earned in his or her two highest-paying Base Period quarters, but may be reduced to 1/52 of the sum of the wages Claimant earned in his or her two highest-paying Base Period quarters if the state unemployment fund balance drops below a certain level. (3313)

PARTIAL EMPLOYMENT: Any wages Claimant receives from partial employment in excess of the greater of (i) 50% of his or her Weekly Benefit Amount or (ii) $10, are deducted from his or her Weekly Benefit Amount. (3313) The Weekly Benefit Amount, however, never dips below $20. (3313)

REDUCTION IN BENEFITS: Claimant's Weekly Benefit Amount may be reduced if: (i) Claimant receives pension benefits (3313); (ii) Claimant receives retirement pay (3313); (iii) Claimant receives Social Security benefits; (iv) Claimant receives annuity payments (3313); (v) Claimant receives other similar periodic payments in connection with previous work (3313); (vi) Claimant receives sickness disability or workers' compensation benefits. (3313)

DEPENDENCY BENEFIT: None.

MIN./MAX. WEEKLY: Minimum weekly benefit is $20. (3313) Maximum weekly benefit depends upon the state unemployment trust fund balance. (3313) For 2001, the maximum weekly benefit was $315. (3313)

MAXIMUM TOTAL: Claimant may receive total benefits equaling the lesser of (i) 26 x his or her Weekly Benefit Amount or (ii) 50% of his or her total Base Period wages. (3313) In times of high unemployment, extended benefits may be available. (3326)

BENEFIT ELIGIBILITY:

GENERALLY: To be eligible for unemployment compensation benefits, Claimant must: (i) File a claim for benefits (3314); (ii) Register for work at a state unemployment office (3314); (iii) Continue to report to a state unemployment office as required (3314); (iv) Earn Base Period wages of at least 36 x his or her Weekly Benefit Amount (Claimant may be eligible for reduced benefits if he or she has earned at least $720 during his or her Base Period and if the difference between his or her Base Period wages and 36 x his or her Weekly Benefit Amount is not greater than $180.) (3314); (v) Be able to work and available for work; (vi) Be actively seeking work (3314); (vii) Participate in reemployment services as required. (3314)

SUBSEQUENT APPLICATION: Lag Period Wages (i.e. wages paid prior to the filing of a claim, but after the Base Period for such claim) may not be used in a subsequent claim for benefits until Claimant has become newly employed and has earned at least 10 x his or her new Weekly Benefit Amount. (3314)

WAITING WEEK: None.

DISQUALIFICATION: Claimant may be partially, fully or at least temporarily disqualified from receiving benefits if: (i) Claimant was discharged for just cause in connection with employment (3315); (ii) Claimant voluntarily left work without good cause attributable to work (3315); (iii) Claimant refused suitable work or a referral to a job opportunity by a local state unemployment office without good cause (3315); (iv) Claimant separation was due to incarceration (3315); (v) Claimant separation was caused by a labor dispute other than a lockout (3315); (vi) Claimant made a false statement knowing it to be false or knowingly has failed to disclose a material fact to obtain benefits (3315); (vii) Claimant is receiving unemployment benefits from another state or under federal law (3315); (viii) Claimant is unable to work (3315); (ix) Claimant is an illegal alien. (3315)

PURGING DISQUALIFICATION: A Claimant who was fired for just cause, refused suitable work, separated from work due to incarceration, or who voluntarily quit without good cause may be eligible for benefits only after (i) receiving remuneration for work subsequent to the disqualifying separation in the amount of 4 x his or her Weekly Benefit Amount and (ii) working in each of 4 weeks, whether or not consecutive. (3315)

SPECIAL TREATMENT:

Claimants in the following categories are afforded distinct treatment under the statute and thus further research may be merited for: (i) Claimants who are generally seasonal workers (3316); (ii) Claimants who are employed on a temporary or casual basis (3327); (iii) Claimants who are in approved training programs (3315); (iv) Claimants who elect to remain away from work pursuant to a collective bargaining agreement or other employer plan (3315); (v) Claimants who are employees of educational institutions when it is between school semesters (3314); (vi) Claimants who are professional athletes when it is between sports seasons (3315); (vii) Claimants who leave work due to experience with domestic violence.

DISTRICT OF COLUMBIA

STATUTE:

LAW: District of Columbia Unemployment Compensation Act

CITATION: D.C. Code, Title 46, Section 101 (D.C.C. § 46-101)

BENEFIT CALCULATION:

WEEKLY BENEFIT AMT.: Benefit amounts are calculated as 1/26 x the wages Claimant earned in his or her highest-paying Base Period quarter. (46-108)

PARTIAL EMPLOYMENT: A Claimant who is only partially employed will receive weekly benefits as follows: (i) $20 will be added to his or her Weekly Benefit Amount and (ii) 80% of any earnings payable to him or her from such employment will be subtracted from the resulting sum. (46-108)

REDUCTION IN BENEFITS: Claimant's Weekly Benefit Amount may be reduced if: (i) Claimant receives pension benefits (46-108); (ii) Claimant receives retirement pay (46-108); (iii) Claimant receives Social Security benefits (46-108); (iv) Claimant receives annuity payments. (46-108)

DEPENDENCY BENEFIT: Claimant's Weekly Benefit Amount may be increased if: Claimant has one or more dependent relatives ($5 for each per week, not to exceed $20 per week). (46-108)

MIN./MAX. WEEKLY: Minimum weekly benefit is $50. (***) Maximum weekly benefit is calculated as 50% of the Statewide Average Weekly Wage. (46-108) For 2001, the maximum weekly benefit was $309. (***)

MAXIMUM TOTAL: Claimant may receive total benefits equaling the lesser of (i) 26 x his or her Weekly Benefit Amount or (ii) 50% of his or her total Base Period wages. (46-108) In times of high unemployment, extended benefits may be available. (46-108)

BENEFIT ELIGIBILITY:

GENERALLY: To be eligible for unemployment compensation benefits, Claimant must: (i) File a claim for benefits (46-110); (ii) Register for work at a state unemployment compensation office (46-110); (iii) Inquire for work with the frequency required by the Director (46-110); (iv) Make at least 2 contacts for new work in the week (46-110); (v) Earn (a) at least $1,300 in a single quarter of his or her Base Period, (b) at least $1,950 in not less than two quarters of his or her Base Period, and (c) total Base Period wages of at least 1 1/2 x his or her highest-paying Base Period quarter (Claimant may be eligible for reduced benefits even if he or she fails to meet requirement "(c)," as long as such deficit does not exceed $70.) (46-108); (vi) Be physically able to work and available for work. (46-110)

SUBSEQUENT APPLICATION: Lag Period Wages (i.e. wages paid prior to the filing of a claim, but after the Base Period for such claim) may not be used in a subsequent claim for benefits unless Claimant has earned at least 10 x his or her Weekly Benefit Amount calculated for the prior Benefit Year. (46-108)

WAITING WEEK: Claimant must serve 1 Waiting Week before collecting benefits. (46- 110)

DISQUALIFICATION: Claimant may be partially, fully or at least temporarily disqualified from receiving benefits if: (i) Claimant was discharged for misconduct or gross misconduct occurring in most recent work (46-111); (ii) Claimant voluntarily left his or her most recent work without good cause connected with work (46-111); (iii) Claimant failed to apply for or accept suitable work (46-111); (iv) Claimant separation was caused by a labor dispute other than a lockout (46-111); (v) Claimant made a false statement or representation knowing it to be false or knowingly failed to disclose material facts to obtain benefits (46-120); (vi) Claimant is receiving unemployment benefits from another state or under federal law (46-111); (vii) Claimant failed to attend a training, retraining, or job counseling course when required (46-111); (viii) Claimant is an illegal alien. (46-110)

PURGING DISQUALIFICATION: A Claimant who was fired for gross misconduct, failed to apply for or accept suitable work, or who voluntarily quit without good cause, may be eligible for benefits only after (i) receiving remuneration for work subsequent to the disqualifying separation in the amount of 10 x his or her Weekly Benefit Amount and (ii) working in each of 10 weeks, whether or not consecutive. (46-111) A Claimant who was fired for misconduct may be eligible for benefits only after (i) receiving remuneration for work subsequent to the disqualifying separation in the amount of 8 x his or her Weekly Benefit Amount and (ii) working in each of 8 weeks. (46-111)

SPECIAL TREATMENT:

Claimants in the following categories are afforded distinct treatment under the statute and thus further research may be merited for: (i) Claimants who are in approved training programs (46-111); (ii) Claimants who are or recently were pregnant (46-111); (iii) Claimants who are employees of educational institutions when it is between school semesters (46-110); (iv) Claimants who are professional athletes when it is between sports seasons. (46-110)

FLORIDA

STATUTE:

LAW: Florida Unemployment Compensation Law

CITATION: West's Florida Statutes Annotated, Chapter 443, Section 443.011 (F.S. § 443.011)

BENEFIT CALCULATION:

WEEKLY BENEFIT AMT.: Benefit amounts are calculated as 1/26 x the wages Claimant earned in his or her highest-paying Base Period quarter. (443.111)

PARTIAL EMPLOYMENT: Any wages Claimant receives from partial employment in excess of an amount equal to 8 x the federal minimum hourly wage shall be deducted from his or her Weekly Benefit Amount. (443.111)

REDUCTION IN BENEFITS: Claimant's Weekly Benefit Amount may be reduced if: (i) Claimant receives pension benefits (443.101); (ii) Claimant receives retirement pay (443.101); (iii) Claimant receives annuity payments (443.101); (iv) Claimant receives temporary total or permanent total disability payments under a workers' compensation law or other disability benefit program (443.101); (v) Claimant receives wages in lieu of notice (443.101); (vi) Claimant receives social security benefits. (443.101)

DEPENDENCY BENEFIT: None.

MIN./MAX. WEEKLY: Minimum weekly benefit is $32. (443.111) Maximum weekly benefit is $288. (443.111)

MAXIMUM TOTAL: Claimant may receive total benefits equaling 25% of the total wages he or she earned during his or her Base Period. (443.111) The maximum total, however, cannot exceed $7,150. (443.111) In times of high unemployment, extended benefits may be available. (443.111)

BENEFIT ELIGIBILITY:

GENERALLY: To be eligible for unemployment compensation benefits, Claimant must: (i) File a claim for benefits (443.091); (ii) Register for work at a state unemployment office (443.091); (iii) Continue to report to a state unemployment office as required (443.091); (iv) Earn during his or her entire Base Period an amount equal to at least 1 1/2 x the amount he or she earned during his or her highest-paying Base Period quarter (443.091); (v) Earn at least $3,400 during his or her Base Period (443.091); (vi) Be able to work and available for work (443.091); (vii) Must participate in reemployment services whenever he or she has been determined to be likely to exhaust regular benefits (443.091); (viii) Earn wage credits in two or more calendar quarters of his or her Base Period. (443.111)

SUBSEQUENT APPLICATION: A Claimant who received benefits during a preceding Benefit Year must have worked and earned 3 x his or her Weekly Benefit Amount for the current Benefit Year subsequent to the commencement of such Benefit Year and before the commencement of his or her new Benefit Year. (443.091)

WAITING WEEK: Claimant must serve 1 Waiting Week before collecting benefits. (443.091)

DISQUALIFICATION: Claimant may be partially, fully or at least temporarily disqualified from receiving benefits if: (i) Claimant was discharged or suspended for misconduct connected with work (443.101); (ii) Claimant was discharged for misconduct consisting of drug use evidenced by a positive confirmed drug test (443.101); (iii) Claimant voluntarily left work without good cause (443.101); (iv) Claimant failed without good cause to apply for available suitable work or to accept suitable work or to return to self-employment when directed (443.101); (v) Claimant separation was caused by a labor dispute other than a lockout (443.101); (vi) Claimant made a false statement or fraudulent representation to receive benefits (443.101); (vii) Claimant is receiving unemployment benefits from another state or under federal law (443.101); (viii) Claimant is an inmate working as part of a correctional work program or work release program (443.036); (ix) Claimant voluntarily takes a leave of absence (443.101); (x) Claimant was discharged for a violation of criminal law which is punishable by imprisonment (443.101); (xi) Claimant was discharged for dishonest acts in connection with work (443.101); (xii) Claimant is an illegal alien. (443.101)

PURGING DISQUALIFICATION: A Claimant who was fired for misconduct, the violation of a criminal law or a dishonest act, or who failed to apply for or accept suitable work, or who voluntarily quit without good cause, may be eligible for benefits only after receiving remuneration for work subsequent to the disqualifying separation in the amount of 17 x his or her Weekly Benefit Amount. (443.101)

SPECIAL TREATMENT:

Claimants in the following categories are afforded distinct treatment under the statute and thus further research may be merited for: (i) Claimants who are in approved training programs (443.091); (ii) Claimants who participate in short-time systems (i.e. shared work programs) (443.036); (iii) Claimants who are on jury duty (443.091); (iv) Claimants who voluntarily quit to accept recall (443.101); (v) Claimants who are employed by temporary help firms (443.101); (vi) Claimants who are employees of educational institutions when it is between school semesters (443.091); (vii) Claimants who are professional athletes when it is between sports seasons. (443.091)

GEORGIA

STATUTE:

LAW: Georgia Employment Security Law

CITATION: Official Code of Georgia Annotated, Title 34, Chapter 8, Section 1 (C.G.A. § 34-8-1)

BENEFIT CALCULATION:

WEEKLY BENEFIT AMT.: Benefit amounts are calculated as follows: (i) If Claimant's total Base Period wages are at least 150% x the amount of wages Claimant received during his or her highest-paying Base Period quarter, Claimant's Weekly Benefit Amount will be computed by dividing the sum of the total Base Period wages that he or she received in his or her two highest-paying Base Period quarters by 48 (34-8-193); (ii) If Claimant's total Base Period wages are less than 150% x the amount of wages Claimant received during his or her highest-paying Base Period quarter, Claimant's Weekly Benefit Amount will be computed by dividing the wages he or she received in his or her highest-paying Base Period quarter by 24. (34-8-193)

PARTIAL EMPLOYMENT: Any wages Claimant receives from partial employment in excess of $30 are deducted from his or her Weekly Benefit Amount. (34-8-30)

REDUCTION IN BENEFITS: Claimant's Weekly Benefit Amount may be reduced if: (i) Claimant receives pension benefits (34-8-193); (ii) Claimant receives retirement pay (34-8-193); (iii) Claimant receives annuity payments (34-8-193); (iv) Claimant receives other similar periodic payments based on previous work (34-8-193); (v) Claimant receives wages in lieu of notice (34-8-194); (vi) Claimant receives terminal leave pay, severance pay, separation pay or dismissal payments. (34-8-194)

DEPENDENCY BENEFIT: None.

MIN./MAX. WEEKLY: Minimum weekly benefit in 2001 is $39. (34-8-193) Maximum weekly benefit in 2001 was $284. (34-8-193)

MAXIMUM TOTAL: Claimant may receive total benefits equaling the lesser of (i) 26 x his or her Weekly Benefit Amount or (ii) 1/4 x his or her Base Period wages. (34-8-193) In times of high unemployment, extended benefits may be available. (34-8-197)

BENEFIT ELIGIBILITY:

GENERALLY: To be eligible for unemployment compensation benefits, Claimant must: (i) File a claim for benefits (34-8-195); (ii) Register for work at a state unemployment office (34-8-195); (iii) Continue to report to a state unemployment office as required (34-8-195); (iv) Continue to report his or her deductible earnings (34-8-195); (v) Earn wages during at least two quarters of his or her Base Period (34-8-193); (vi) Earn total Base Period wages (a) amounting to at least 150% x his or her highest-paying Base Period quarter or (b) amounting to at least 40 x his or her Weekly Benefit Amount (34-8-193); (vii) Be able to work and available for work (34-8-195); (viii) Be actively seeking work (34-8-195); (ix) Participate in reemployment services if so required. (34-8-195)

SUBSEQUENT APPLICATION: A Claimant who received benefits during a preceding Benefit Year must have worked and earned 10 x his or her Weekly Benefit Amount subsequent to the commencement of such Benefit Year and before the commencement of his or her new Benefit Year. (34-8-194)

WAITING WEEK: None.

DISQUALIFICATION: Claimant may be partially, fully or at least temporarily disqualified from receiving benefits if: (i) Claimant was discharged or suspended from most recent employer for failure to obey orders, rules, or instructions or for failure to discharge duties of employment (34-8-194); (ii) Claimant was discharged from most recent employer for intentional conduct which results in the physical assault upon or bodily injury to the employer, fellow employees, customers, patients, bystanders, or product consumers (34-8-194); (iii) Claimant was discharged from most recent employer for intentional conduct which included theft of property, goods or money valued at $100 or less (34-8-194); (iv) Claimant was discharged from most recent employer for intentional conduct on premises of employer or while on the job that resulted in property loss or damages amounting to $2000 or more or theft of property, goods, or money valued at over $100, or for sabotage or embezzlement (34-8-194); (v) Claimant was discharged or suspended from most recent employer for the violation of an employer's drug-free workplace policy (34-8-194); (vi) Claimant voluntarily left most recent work without good cause (34-8-194); (vii) Claimant voluntarily separated from approved training or was ousted from such program due to his or her own failure to abide by the rules of the training facility (34-8-194); (viii) Claimant failed to apply for or accept available suitable work without good cause (34-8-194); (ix) Claimant separation was caused by a labor dispute other than a lockout (34-8-194); (x) Claimant knowingly made a false statement or misrepresentation or knowingly failed to disclose a material fact in order to obtain benefits (34-8-255); (xi) Claimant is receiving unemployment benefits from another state or under federal law (34-8-194); (xii) Claimant is receiving temporary partial or temporary total disability benefits under workers' compensation law (34-8-194); (xiii) Claimant is on vacation or leave of absence at his or her own request, pursuant to an employment contract or collective bargaining agreement, or pursuant to an established employer custom or practice (34-8-195); (xiv) Claimant is an illegal alien. (34-8-196)

[continued on next page]

PURGING DISQUALIFICATION: A Claimant who failed to apply for or accept suitable work without good cause, voluntarily left work without good cause, or who was discharged or suspended for failure to obey orders, rules, or instructions or for failure to discharge duties of employment, or a Claimant who was discharged for the violation of a drug-free workplace policy, may be eligible for benefits only after receiving remuneration for work subsequent to the disqualifying separation in the amount of 10 x his or her Weekly Benefit Amount. (34-8-194) A Claimant who was discharged for intentional conduct that resulted in physical assault or bodily injury or the theft of property, goods or money valued at $100 or less, may be eligible for benefits only after receiving remuneration for work subsequent to the disqualifying separation in the amount of 12 x his or her Weekly Benefit Amount. (34-8-194) A Claimant who was discharged for intentional conduct that resulted in property loss or damages of $2,000 or more or the theft of property, goods, or money valued at over $100, or for sabotage or embezzlement, may be eligible for benefits only after receiving remuneration for work subsequent to the disqualifying separation in the amount of 16 x his or her Weekly Benefit Amount. (34-8-194)

SPECIAL TREATMENT:

Claimants in the following categories are afforded distinct treatment under the statute and thus further research may be merited for: (i) Claimants who are in approved training programs (34-8-195); (ii) Claimants who entered the Armed Forces during a national emergency (34-8-193); (iii) Claimants who were laid off with a scheduled return to work date (34-8-195); (iv) Claimants who refuse temporary or intermittent assignments (34-8-195); (v) Claimants who separate from employment pursuant to a labor-management contract or agreement or an established employer plan, program, policy, layoff or recall that permits him or her to do so because of lack of work (34-8-195); (vi) Claimants who are employees of educational institutions when it is between school semesters (34-8-196); (vii) Claimants who are professional athletes when it is between sports seasons. (34-8-196)

HAWAII

STATUTE:

LAW: Hawaii Employment Security Law

CITATION: Hawaii Revised Statutes Annotated, Title 21, Chapter 383, Section 1 (H.R.S. § 21-383-1)

BENEFIT CALCULATION:

WEEKLY BENEFIT AMT.: Benefit amounts are calculated as 1/21 x the wages Claimant earned in his or her highest-paying Base Period quarter. (21-383-22)

PARTIAL EMPLOYMENT: Any wages Claimant receives from partial employment in excess of $50 are deducted from his or her Weekly Benefit Amount. (21-383-23)

REDUCTION IN BENEFITS: Claimant's Weekly Benefit Amount may be reduced if: (i) Claimant receives pension benefits (21-383-23.5); (ii) Claimant receives retirement pay (21-383-23.5); (iii) Claimant receives Social Security benefits (21-383-23.5); (iv) Claimant receives annuity payments (21-383-23.5); (v) Claimant receives other similar periodic payments under a plan maintained or contributed to by a Base Period or chargeable employer. (21-383-23.5)

DEPENDENCY BENEFIT: None.

MIN./MAX. WEEKLY: Minimum weekly benefit of $5. (21-383-22) Maximum weekly benefit is calculated annually as 70% of the Statewide Average Weekly Wage. (21-383-22) For 2001, the maximum weekly benefit was $383. (***)

MAXIMUM TOTAL: Claimant may receive total benefits equaling 26 x his or her Weekly Benefit Amount. (21-383-24) In times of high unemployment, extended benefits may be available. (21-383-170) In the event of a disaster, additional benefits may be available amounting up to 13 x Claimant's normal Weekly Benefit Amount. (21-385-1)

BENEFIT ELIGIBILITY:

GENERALLY: To be eligible for unemployment compensation benefits, Claimant must: (i) File a claim for benefits (21-383-29); (ii) Register for work in a state unemployment office (21-383-29); (iii) Continue to report to a state unemployment office as required (21-383-29); (iv) Earn during his or her Base Period, wages at least equaling 26 x his or her Weekly Benefit Amount (21-383-29); (v) Earn wages during at least 2 quarters of his or her Base Period (21-383-29); (vi) Be able to work and available for work (21-383-29); (vii) Participate in reemployment services as required. (21-383-29)

SUBSEQUENT APPLICATION: To qualify for a second Benefit Year, Claimant must, prior to the beginning of the prior Benefit Year, earn wages equal to at least 5 x the Weekly Benefit Amount calculated for the succeeding Benefit Year. (21-383-29)

WAITING WEEK: Claimant must serve 1 Waiting Week before collecting benefits. (21- 383-29)

DISQUALIFICATION: Claimant may be partially, fully or at least temporarily disqualified from receiving benefits if: (i) Claimant was discharged or suspended for misconduct connected with work (21-383-30); (ii) Claimant voluntarily left work without good cause (21-383-30); (iii) Claimant failed to apply for or accept available suitable work without good cause (21-383-30); (iv) Claimant separation was caused by a labor dispute (21-383-30); (v) Claimant knowingly made a false statement or representation of a material fact or knowingly failed to disclose a material fact in order to obtain benefits (21-383-30); (vi) Claimant is receiving unemployment benefits from another state or under federal law (21-383-30); (vii) Claimant is an illegal alien. (21-383-29)

PURGING DISQUALIFICATION: A Claimant who was discharged for misconduct, failed to accept or apply for suitable work, or who voluntarily quit, may be eligible for benefits only after receiving remuneration for work subsequent to the disqualifying separation in the amount of 5 x his or her Weekly Benefit Amount. (21-383-30)

SPECIAL TREATMENT:

Claimants in the following categories are afforded distinct treatment under the statute and thus further research may be merited for: (i) Claimants who are in approved training programs (21-383-29.5); (ii) Claimants who are enrolled in vocational training courses (21-383-29); (iii) Claimants who are ill or disabled (21-383-29); (iv) Claimants who are owner-employees of a corporation and are subsequently unemployed (21-383-30); (v) Claimants who are employees of educational institutions when it is between school semesters (21-383-29); (vi) Claimants who are professional athletes when it is between sports seasons. (21-383-29)

IDAHO

STATUTE:

LAW: Idaho Employment Security Law

CITATION: Idaho Code, Title 72, Section 72-1301 (I.C. § 72-1301)

BENEFIT CALCULATION:

WEEKLY BENEFIT AMT.: Benefit amounts are calculated as 1/26 x the wages Claimant earned in his or her highest-paying Base Period quarter. (72-1367)

PARTIAL EMPLOYMENT: Any wages Claimant receives from partial employment in excess of an amount equal to 1/2 x his or her Weekly Benefit Amount are deducted from his or her Weekly Benefit Amount. (72-1367)

REDUCTION IN BENEFITS: Claimant's Weekly Benefit Amount may be reduced if: (i) Claimant receives pension benefits (72-1312); (ii) Claimant receives retirement pay (72-1312); (iii) Claimant receives Social Security benefits (72-1312); (iv) Claimant receives annuity payments (72-1312); (v) Claimant receives other similar periodic payments based upon previous work. (72-1312)

DEPENDENCY BENEFIT: None.

MIN./MAX. WEEKLY: Minimum weekly benefit in 2001 was $51. (72-1367) Maximum weekly benefit is calculated annually as 60% of the Statewide Average Weekly Wage. (72-1367) For 2001, the maximum weekly benefit was $296. (***)

MAXIMUM TOTAL: Claimant may receive total benefits equaling between 10 and 26 x his or her Weekly Benefit Amount depending upon the ratio of his or her total Base Period wages to the wages he or she received during his or her highest-paying Base Period quarter. (72-1367) In times of high unemployment, extended benefits may be available. (72-1367A)

BENEFIT ELIGIBILITY:

GENERALLY: To be eligible for unemployment compensation benefits, Claimant must: (i) File a claim for benefits and provide all information necessary to make the eligibility determination (72-1366); (ii) Register for work at a state unemployment office (72-1366); (iii) Continue to report to a state unemployment office as required (72-1366); (iv) Earn at least an amount equal to 50% x the state minimum wage x 520 (approximately $1326) in wages during his or her highest-paying Base Period quarter (72-1367); (v) Earn total Base Period wages at least equal to 1 1/4 x the wages he or she received during his or her highest-paying Base Period quarter (72-1367); (vi) Be able to work and available for work (72-1366); (vii) Be seeking work (72-1366); (viii) Participate in reemployment services under a worker profiling system. (72-1366)

SUBSEQUENT APPLICATION: To qualify for benefits in a successive Benefit Year, Claimant must have earned 6 x his or her Weekly Benefit Amount subsequent to the commencement of his or her prior Benefit Year and before the commencement of his or her new Benefit Year. (72-1366)

WAITING WEEK: Claimant must serve 1 Waiting Week before collecting benefits. (72- 1329)

DISQUALIFICATION: Claimant may be partially, fully or at least temporarily disqualified from receiving benefits if: (i) Claimant was discharged for misconduct connected with work (72-1366); (ii) Claimant voluntarily left work without good cause connected with employment (72-1366); (iii) Claimant voluntarily left work to marry, perform customary duties of maintaining a household, or to leave a locale to live with a spouse (72-1366); (iv) Claimant failed without good cause to apply for or accept suitable work (72-1366); (v) Claimant separation was caused by a labor dispute (72-1366); (vi) Claimant willfully made a false statement or representation or willfully failed to report a material fact to obtain benefits (72-1366); (vii) Claimant is receiving unemployment benefits from another state or under federal law (72-1366); (viii) Claimant is attending school during customary work hours (72-1312); (ix) Claimant is self-employed (72-1366); (x) Claimant is an illegal alien. (72-1366)

PURGING DISQUALIFICATION: A Claimant who was discharged for misconduct, failed to apply for or accept suitable work, or who voluntarily quit, may be eligible for benefits only after receiving remuneration for work subsequent to the disqualifying separation in the amount of 12 x his or her Weekly Benefit Amount. (72-1366)

SPECIAL TREATMENT:

Claimants in the following categories are afforded distinct treatment under the statute and thus further research may be merited for: (i) Claimants who are in approved training programs (72-1366); (ii) Claimants who are ill or disabled (72-1366); (iii) Claimants who are employees of educational institutions when it is between school semesters (72-1366); (iv) Claimants who are professional athletes when it is between sports seasons (72-1366); (v) Claimants who work or worked for staffing services. (72-1366)

ILLINOIS

STATUTE:

LAW: Illinois Unemployment Insurance Act

CITATION: West's Smith-Hurd Illinois Compiled Statutes Annotated, Chapter 820, Paragraph 405/100 (820 I.L.C.S. 405/100)

BENEFIT CALCULATION:

WEEKLY BENEFIT AMT.: Benefit amounts are calculated as 49.5% of Claimant's prior average weekly wage (i.e. the sum of the wages he or she received in his or her two highest-paying Base Period quarters x 1/26). (405/401)

PARTIAL EMPLOYMENT: Any wages Claimant receives from partial employment in excess of an amount equal to 50% of his or her Weekly Benefit Amount are deducted from Claimant's Weekly Benefit Amount. (405/402)

REDUCTION IN BENEFITS: Claimant's Weekly Benefit Amount may be reduced if: (i) Claimant receives retirement pay (405/611); (ii) Claimant receives pension benefits (405/611); (iii) Claimant receives annuity payments; (iv) Claimant receives Social Security benefits (405/611); (v) Claimant receives temporary disability benefits under a workers' compensation act (405/606); (vi) Claimant is unable to work or unavailable for work (405/403); (vii) Claimant receives holiday or vacation day. (405/403)

DEPENDENCY BENEFIT: The Weekly Benefit Amount for an individual with a nonworking spouse is increased by 9% of his or her prior average weekly wage, but cannot exceed 58.5% of the Statewide Average Weekly Wage. (405/401) The Weekly Benefit Amount for an individual with one or more dependent children is increased by 16% of his or her average weekly wage, but cannot exceed 65.5% of the Statewide Average Weekly Wage. (405/401)

MIN./MAX. WEEKLY: Minimum weekly benefit of $51. (405/401) Maximum weekly benefit is generally calculated annually as 49.5% of the Statewide Average Weekly Wage although modifications are sometimes made to reflect trends in this average. (405/401) For 2001, the maximum weekly benefit was $475. (***)

MAXIMUM TOTAL: Claimant may receive total benefits equaling the lesser of (i) 26 x his or her Weekly Benefit Amount plus any dependents' allowances or (ii) the sum of all wages he or she received during his or her Base Period. (405/403) In times of high unemployment, extended benefits may be available. (405/409)

BENEFIT ELIGIBILITY:

GENERALLY: To be eligible for unemployment compensation benefits, Claimant must: (i) File a claim for benefits (405/500); (ii) Register for work at a state unemployment office (405/500); (iii) Continue to report to a state unemployment office as required (405/500); (iv) Earn $1,600 in wages during his or her Base Period (405/500); (v) Earn at least $440 in wages in Base Period quarters other than his or her highest-paying Base Period quarter (405/500); (vi) Be able to work and available for work (405/500); (vii) Be actively seeking work (405/500); (viii) Participate in reemployment services if required by the employment office. (405/500)

WAITING WEEK: Claimant must serve 1 Waiting Week before collecting benefits. (405/500)

SUBSEQUENT APPLICATION: A Claimant who received benefits during a preceding Benefit Year must have worked and earned 3 x his or her current Weekly Benefit Amount subsequent to the commencement of such Benefit Year and before the commencement of his or her new Benefit Year. (405/607)

DISQUALIFICATION: Claimant may be partially, fully or at least temporarily disqualified from receiving benefits if: (i) Claimant was discharged for misconduct connected with work (405/602); (ii) Claimant was discharged for felony or theft in connection with work (405/602); (iii) Claimant voluntarily left work without good cause (405/601); (iv) Claimant failed without good cause either to apply for or accept suitable work (405/603); (v) Claimant separation was caused by a labor dispute other than a lockout (405/604); (vi) Claimant knowingly made a false statement or failed to disclose a material fact in order to obtain benefits (405/901); (vii) Claimant is receiving unemployment benefits from another state or under federal law (405/605); (viii) Claimant's principal occupation is that of a student in attendance at or on vacation from a public or private school (405/500); (ix) Claimant is an illegal alien. (405/614)

PURGING DISQUALIFICATION: A Claimant who was discharged for misconduct, failed to accept or apply for suitable work, or who voluntarily quit may be eligible for benefits only after earning remuneration for work subsequent to the disqualifying separation in an amount at least equal to his or her Weekly Benefit Amount in each of four calendar weeks. (405/601, 405/602, 405/603)

SPECIAL TREATMENT:

Claimants in the following categories are afforded distinct treatment under the statute and thus further research may be merited for: (i) Claimants who are in approved training programs (405/500); (ii) Claimants who are discharged from military service (405/406); (iii) Claimants who leave work to accept other jobs (405/601); (iv) Claimants who are employees of educational institutions when it is between school semesters (405/612); (v) Claimants who are professional athletes when it is between sports seasons. (405/613)

INDIANA

STATUTE:
LAW: Indiana Employment Security Law
CITATION: West's Annotated Indiana Code, Title 22, Article 4, Chapter 1, Section 1 (I.C. § 22-4-1-1)

BENEFIT CALCULATION:
WEEKLY BENEFIT AMT.: Benefit amounts are calculated as the sum of 5% of the first $2,000 the Claimant earned in his or her highest-paying Base Period quarter and 4% of the remaining Wage Credits (i.e. remuneration paid for employment by employer, however, beginning in 2001, Wage Credits cannot exceed $7,300 per quarter) he or she earned in his or her highest-paying Base Period quarter. (22-4-12-2)

PARTIAL EMPLOYMENT: When reducing unemployment compensation benefits to only partial benefits, any wages from partial employment that Claimant receives from other than his or her Base Period employer in excess of the greater of (i) an amount equal to 20% of his or her Weekly Benefit Amount or (ii) $3, will be disregarded. (22-4-5-1)

REDUCTION IN BENEFITS: Claimant's Weekly Benefit Amount may be reduced if: (i) Claimant receives retirement pay (22-4-15-4); (ii) Claimant receives Social Security benefits (22-4-15-4); (iii) Claimant receives dismissal pay (22-4-5-2); (iv) Claimant receives holiday or vacation pay (22-4-5-2); (v) Claimant receives annuity payments (22-4-15-4); (vi) Claimant receives sick pay (22-4-5-2); (vii) Claimant receives pay for idle time. (22-4-5-2)

DEPENDENCY BENEFIT: Claimant's Weekly Benefit Amount may be increased if Claimant has one or more dependent children. (22-4-12-3)

MIN./MAX. WEEKLY: Maximum weekly benefit in 2001 was $288. (22-4-12-2) Minimum weekly benefit is $50. (22-4-12-2)

MAXIMUM TOTAL: Claimant may receive total benefits equaling the lesser of (i) 26 x his or her Weekly Benefit Amount or (ii) 28% of Claimant's Wage Credits. (22-4-12-4) In times of high unemployment, extended benefits may be available. (22-4-14-6) In the event of a disaster, additional unemployment benefits may also be available. (22-4-12-4)

BENEFIT ELIGIBILITY:
GENERALLY: To be eligible for unemployment compensation benefits, Claimant must: (i) File a claim for benefits (22-4-14-1); (ii) Register for work at a state unemployment office (22-4-14-2); (iii) Continue to report to a state unemployment office as required (22-4-14-2); (iv) Earn $1,650 in Wage Credits in the last 2 calendar quarters of his or her Base Period (if he or she received unemployment benefits in former years, such amount must be earned subsequent to the end of his or her prior Base Period) (22-4-14-5); (v) Earn at least $2,750 in Wage Credits in his or her entire Base Period (if he or she received unemployment benefits in former years, such amount must be earned subsequent to the end of his or her prior Base Period) (22-4-14-5); (vi) Earn Wage Credits at least equal to 1.25 x the amount he or she earned in his or her highest-paying calendar quarter (if he or she received unemployment benefits in former years, such amount must be earned subsequent to the end of his or her prior Base Period) (22-4-14-5); (vii) Be physically and mentally able to work and available for work (22-4-14-3); (viii) Make an effort to secure work (22-4-14-3); (ix) Participate in reemployment services as required. (22-4-14-3)

WAITING WEEK: Claimant must serve 1 Waiting Week before collecting benefits. (22-14-14-4)

SUBSEQUENT APPLICATION: A Claimant who received benefits during a preceding Benefit Year must have worked and earned an amount at least equal to his or her Weekly Benefit Amount in each of 8 weeks subsequent to the commencement of such Benefit Year and before the commencement of his or her new Benefit Year. (22-4-14-5)

DISQUALIFICATION: Claimant may be partially, fully or at least temporarily disqualified from receiving benefits if: (i) Claimant was discharged for good cause (22-4-15-1); (ii) Claimant voluntarily left most recent work without good cause (22-4-15-1); (iii) Claimant failed to apply for or accept suitable work (22-4-15-2); (iv) Claimant separation was caused by a labor dispute (22-4-15-3); (v) Claimant knowingly failed to disclose earnings or has falsified as to any fact in connection with filing which affects the eligibility, duration, or amount of benefits to which he or she may be entitled (22-4-16-1); (vi) Claimant is receiving unemployment benefits from another state or under federal law (22-4-15-5); (vii) Claimant is working on public works or assistance projects (22-4-14-3); (viii) Claimant is in full-time military service or in civilian service as a conscientious objector (22-4-14-3); (ix) Claimant is an illegal alien (22-4-14-9); (x) Claimant fails to return to customary self-employment when directed by employment office (22-4-15-2)

PURGING DISQUALIFICATION: A Claimant who was discharged for just cause, failed to apply for or accept suitable work, failed to return to customary self-employment when directed, or who voluntarily left work without good cause, may be eligible for benefits only after earning remuneration for work equal to at least his or her Weekly Benefit Amount in each of 8 weeks. (22-4-15-1)

SPECIAL TREATMENT:
Claimants in the following categories are afforded distinct treatment under the statute and thus further research may be merited for: (i) Claimants who are in approved training programs (22-4-15-1; 22-4-14-3); (ii) Claimants who are attending school (22-4-14-3); (iii) Claimants who voluntarily leave employment to accept a better job (22-4-15-1); (iv) Claimants who are simultaneously employed by two or more employers (22-4-15-1); (v) Claimants who are physically disabled (22-4-15-1); (vi) Claimants who left work to enter the Armed Forces (22-4-15-1); (vii) Claimants who left work due to compulsory retirement (22-4-15-1); (viii) Claimants who are employed on a seasonal basis (22-4-14-11); (ix) Claimants who are employees of educational institutions when it is between school semesters (22-4-14-7); (x) Claimants who are professional athletes when it is between sports seasons. (22-4-14-8)

IOWA

STATUTE:
LAW: Iowa Employment Security Law

CITATION: Iowa Code Annotated, Section 96.1 (I.C.A. § 96.1)

BENEFIT CALCULATION:
WEEKLY BENEFIT AMT.: Benefit amounts are calculated to be between 1/23 and 1/19 x the wages Claimant earned in his or her highest-paying Base Period quarter depending upon whether Claimant has 0, 1, 2, 3, or 4 or more dependents. (96.3)

PARTIAL EMPLOYMENT: Any wages from partial employment that Claimant receives in excess of 1/4 of his or her Weekly Benefit Amount are deducted from his or her Weekly Benefit Amount. (96.3)

REDUCTION IN BENEFITS: Claimant's Weekly Benefit Amount may be reduced if: (i) Claimant receives pension benefits (96.5); (ii) Claimant receives retirement pay (96.5); (iii) Claimant receives annuity payments (96.5); (iv) Claimant receives Social Security benefits (96.5); (v) Claimant receives other periodic payments under a plan maintained or contributed to by a Base Period or chargeable employer (96.5); (vi) Claimant receives or is entitled to wages in lieu of notice (96.5); (vii) Claimant receives or is entitled to separation allowance, severance pay or dismissal pay (96.5); (viii) Claimant receives or is entitled to compensation for a temporary disability under a workers' compensation law (96.5); (ix) Claimant receives vacation pay, a vacation pay allowance, or pay in lieu of a vacation. (96.5)

DEPENDENCY BENEFIT: Claimant's Weekly Benefit Amount may be increased if Claimant has dependents (as the number of dependents which Claimant claims increases from 0 to 4 or more, the Claimant is entitled to a greater fraction of the wages he or she earned in his or her highest-paying Base Period quarter). (96.3)

MIN./MAX. WEEKLY: Minimum weekly benefit is $51. (96.3, 96.4) Maximum weekly benefit is calculated as 53%, 55%, 57%, 60% or 65% of the Statewide Average Weekly Wage depending upon whether Claimant has 0, 1, 2, 3, or 4 or more dependents, respectively. (96.3) Currently the maximum weekly benefit is determined using the Statewide Average Weekly Wage computed for the calendar year 1981. For 2001, the maximum weekly benefit is $347. (***)

MAXIMUM TOTAL: Claimant may receive total benefits equaling the lesser of (i) the total of his or her Wage Credits (i.e. Claimant's account is credited with 1/3 (1/2 if he or she separates from employment because his or her employer was going out of business) of wages paid to him or her during his or her Base Period), or (ii) an amount equal to 26 x his or her Weekly Benefit Amount. (96.3) In times of high unemployment, extended benefits may be available. (96.29)

BENEFIT ELIGIBILITY:
GENERALLY: To be eligible for unemployment compensation benefits, Claimant must: (i) File a claim for benefits (96.4); (ii) Register for work at a state unemployment office (96.4); (iii) Continue to report to a state unemployment office as required (96.4); (iv) Earn during his or her Base Period, wages at least equaling 1 1/4 x the amount he or she earned in his or her highest-paying Base Period quarter (96.4); (v) Earn wages at least equal to 3.5% of the statewide average annual wage during his or her highest-paying Base Period quarter (96.4); (vi) Earn wages in one of his or her Base Period quarters equal to at least 1/2 x the amount he or she earned in his or her highest-paying Base Period quarter (96.4); (vii) Be able to work and available for work (96.4); (viii) Be earnestly and actively seeking work (96.4); (ix) Participate in reemployment services as required. (96.4)

SUBSEQUENT APPLICATION: To qualify for a second Benefit Year, Claimant must, during or subsequent to the former Benefit Year, earn at least $250 in wages. (96.4)

WAITING WEEK: None.

DISQUALIFICATION: Claimant may be partially, fully or at least temporarily disqualified from receiving benefits if: (i) Claimant was discharged for misconduct connected with work or gross misconduct (96.5); (ii) Claimant voluntarily left work without good cause (96.5); (iii) Claimant failed to accept suitable work or apply for available suitable work without good cause (96.5); (iv) Claimant separation was caused by a labor dispute (96.5); (v) Claimant willfully and knowingly made a false statement or misrepresentation or willfully and knowingly failed to disclose a material fact in order to obtain benefits (96.5); (vi) Claimant is receiving unemployment benefits from another state or under federal law (96.5); (vii) Claimant is an illegal alien (96.5); (viii) Claimant was an employee of a temporary employment firm and failed to promptly notify firm of completion of former assignment. (96.5)

PURGING DISQUALIFICATION: A Claimant who was discharged for misconduct connected with work, failed to apply for or accept suitable work, or who voluntarily quit, may be eligible for benefits only after receiving remuneration for work subsequent to the disqualifying separation in the amount of 10 x his or her Weekly Benefit Amount. (96.5)

SPECIAL TREATMENT:
Claimants in the following categories are afforded distinct treatment under the statute and thus further research may be merited for: (i) Claimants who are in approved training programs (96.4); (ii) Claimants who enter shared work programs (96.40); (iii) Claimants who voluntarily leave in lieu of exercising a right to "bump" or oust another less senior employee (96.5); (iv) Claimants who are pregnant (96.5); (v) Claimants who leave for a better job (96.5); (vi) Claimants who leave work to care for an immediate family member who is injured or ill (96.5); (vii) Claimants who are ill or injured (96.5); (viii) Claimants who are employees of educational institutions when it is between school semesters (96.4); (ix) Claimants who are professional athletes when it is between sports seasons. (96.5)

KANSAS

STATUTE:

LAW: Kansas Employment Security Law

CITATION: Kansas Statutes Annotated, Section 44-701 (K.S.A. § 44-701)

BENEFIT CALCULATION:

WEEKLY BENEFIT AMT.: Benefit amounts are calculated as 4.25% x the wages Claimant earned in his or her highest-paying Base Period quarter. (44-704)

PARTIAL EMPLOYMENT: Any wages Claimant receives from partial employment in excess of 25% of his or her Weekly Benefit Amount are deducted from his or her Weekly Benefit Amount. (44-705)

REDUCTION IN BENEFITS: Claimant's Weekly Benefit Amount may be reduced if: (i) Claimant receives pension benefits (44-706); (ii) Claimant receives retirement pay (44-706); (iii) Claimant receives annuity payments (44-706); (iv) Claimant receives other similar periodic payments based upon previous work under a Base Period employer (44-706); (v) Claimant receives holiday or vacation pay (44-705); (vi) Claimant receives severance pay. (44-705)

DEPENDENCY BENEFIT: None.

MIN./MAX. WEEKLY: The minimum weekly benefit is calculated as 25% of the maximum weekly benefit. (44-704) Minimum weekly benefit in 2001 was $83. (***) Maximum weekly benefit is calculated annually as 60% of the Statewide Average Weekly Wage. (44-704) For 2001, the maximum weekly benefit was $333. (***)

MAXIMUM TOTAL: Claimant may receive total benefits equaling the lesser of (i) 26 x his or her Weekly Benefit Amount or (ii) 1/3 x his or her total Base Period wages. (44-704) In times of high unemployment, extended benefits may be available. (44-704(a))

BENEFIT ELIGIBILITY:

GENERALLY: To be eligible for unemployment compensation benefits, Claimant must: (i) File a claim for benefits (44-705); (ii) Register for work at a state unemployment office (44-705); (iii) Continue to report to a state unemployment office as required (44-705); (iv) Earn during his or her Base Period, wages at least equaling 30 x his or her Weekly Benefit Amount (44-705); (v) Earn wages during at least 2 quarters of his or her Base Period (44-705); (vi) Be able to perform the duties of his or her customary occupation or other occupations for which he or she is reasonably fitted and available for work as demonstrated by Claimant's pursuit of the full course of action most reasonably calculated to result in reemployment (44-705); (vii) Participate in reemployment services as required. (44-705)

SUBSEQUENT APPLICATION: The wages Claimant earned between the end of his or her prior Base Period and the day he or she filed a valid initial claim may not be used by Claimant for benefit purposes for a subsequent Benefit Year unless he or she has worked and earned 8 x his or her current Weekly Benefit Amount subsequent to the commencement of his or her prior Benefit Year and before the commencement of his or her new Benefit Year. (44-705)

WAITING WEEK: Claimant must serve 1 Waiting Week before collecting benefits. (44- 705)

DISQUALIFICATION: Claimant may be partially, fully or at least temporarily disqualified from receiving benefits if: (i) Claimant was discharged for misconduct connected with work or gross misconduct connected with work (44-706); (ii) Claimant voluntarily left work without good cause (44-706); (iii) Claimant failed to apply for or accept suitable work (44-706); (iv) Claimant separation was caused by a labor dispute (44-706); (v) Claimant knowingly made a false statement or representation or has knowingly failed to disclose material information to obtain benefits (44-706); (vi) Claimant is receiving unemployment benefits from another state or under federal law (44-706); (vii) Claimant received temporary total disability or permanent total disability benefits under a workers' compensation law (44-706); (viii) Claimant is an illegal alien (44-706); (ix) Claimant failed to request an additional assignment after completing a temporary assignment. (44-706)

PURGING DISQUALIFICATION: Claimant who was discharged for misconduct, failed to accept or apply for suitable work, failed to request an additional assignment after completing a temporary assignment, or who voluntarily quit, may be eligible for benefits only after receiving remuneration for work subsequent to the disqualifying separation in the amount of 3 x his or her Weekly Benefit Amount. (44-706) A Claimant who was discharged for gross misconduct, may be eligible for benefits only after receiving remuneration for work subsequent to the disqualifying separation in the amount of 8 x his or her Weekly Benefit Amount. (44-706)

SPECIAL TREATMENT:

Claimants in the following categories are afforded distinct treatment under the statute and thus further research may be merited for: (i) Claimants who are in approved training programs (44-706); (ii) Claimants who elect to enter a shared work program (44-757); (iii) Claimants who receive back pay awards or settlements (44-706); (iv) Claimants who are attending school (44-709); (v) Claimants registered for and attending school (44-706); (vi) Claimants who leave work to enter the Armed Forces (44-706); (vii) Claimants who leave work after completing a temporary job assignment (44-706); (viii) Claimants who leave temporary work to return to a regular employer (44-706); (ix) Claimants who leave work to accept better jobs. (44-706); (x) Claimants who are employees of educational institutions when it is between school semesters (44-706); (xi) Claimants who are professional athletes when it is between sports seasons. (44-706)

KENTUCKY

STATUTE:

LAW: Kentucky Unemployment Insurance Law

CITATION: Baldwin's Kentucky Revised Statutes Annotated, Chapter 341, Section 001 (K.R.S.A. § 341.005)

BENEFIT CALCULATION:

WEEKLY BENEFIT AMT.: Benefit amounts are calculated as 1.185% x the wages Claimant earned during his or her Base Period. (341.380)

PARTIAL EMPLOYMENT: 80% of the wages Claimant receives from partial employment are deducted from his or her Weekly Benefit Amount. (341.390)

REDUCTION IN BENEFITS: Claimant's Weekly Benefit Amount may be reduced if: (i) Claimant receives pension benefits (341.390); (ii) Claimant receives retirement pay (341.390); (iii) Claimant receives annuity payments (341.390); (iv) Claimant receives other similar periodic payments based upon previous work under a Base Period or chargeable employer (341.390); (v) Claimant receives remuneration in lieu of notice of termination. (341.390)

DEPENDENCY BENEFIT: None.

MIN./MAX. WEEKLY: Minimum weekly benefit is $39. (341.380) Maximum weekly benefit is calculated annually as 55% of the Statewide Average Weekly Wage. (341.380) For 2001, the maximum weekly benefit was $329. (***) The maximum weekly benefit rate may be subject to adjustments depending upon the current balance in the state unemployment compensation trust fund. (341.380)

MAXIMUM TOTAL: Claimant may receive total benefits equaling the lesser of (i) 26 x his or her Weekly Benefit Amount or (ii) 1/3 x his or her total Base Period wages. (341.380) Claimant's maximum total cannot, however, drop below an amount equal to 15 x his or her Weekly Benefit Amount. In times of high unemployment, extended benefits may be available. (341.710)

BENEFIT ELIGIBILITY:

GENERALLY: To be eligible for unemployment compensation benefits, Claimant must: (i) File a claim for benefits (341.350); (ii) Register for work at a state unemployment office (341.350); (iii) Earn at least $750 during his or her highest-paying Base Period quarter (341.350); (iv) Earn during his or her entire Base Period, wages at least equaling 1 1/2 x the amount of wages he or she earned in his or her highest-paying Base Period quarter (341.350); (v) Earn during the last 6 months of his or her Base Period wages at least equaling 8 x his or her Weekly Benefit Amount (341.350); (vi) Earn at least $750 during his or her Base Period outside of his or her highest-paying Base Period quarter (341.350); (vii) Be physically and mentally able to work and available for work (341.350); (viii) Make a reasonable effort to find work (341.350); (ix) Participate in reemployment services as required. (341.350)

SUBSEQUENT APPLICATION: N/A

WAITING WEEK: None.

DISQUALIFICATION: Claimant may be partially, fully or at least temporarily disqualified from receiving benefits if: (i) Claimant was discharged for misconduct or dishonesty connected with most recent work or any work which occurred after the first day of Claimant's Base Period and which last preceded his or her most recent work (341.370); (ii) Claimant voluntarily left work without good cause his or her most recent work or any other suitable work which occurred after the first day of Claimant's Base Period and which last preceded his or her most recent work (341.370); (iii) Claimant failed to apply for or accept suitable work (341.370); (iv) Claimant separation was caused by a labor dispute other than a lockout (341.360); (v) Claimant knowingly made a false statement to obtain benefits (341.370); (vi) Claimant is receiving unemployment benefits from another state or under federal law (341.360); (vii) Claimant is an illegal alien. (341.360)

PURGING DISQUALIFICATION: A Claimant who was discharged for misconduct or dishonesty, failed to accept or apply for suitable work, or who voluntarily quit, may be eligible for benefits only after working in each of 10 weeks, whether or not consecutive, and receiving remuneration for such work in the amount of 10 x his or her Weekly Benefit Amount. (341.370)

SPECIAL TREATMENT:

Claimants in the following categories are afforded distinct treatment under the statute and thus further research may be merited for: (i) Claimants who are in approved training programs (341.350); (ii) Claimants who separated from work pursuant to a labor-management contract or an established employer plan or policy which permits the employer to close a plant or facility for vacation or maintenance (341.370); (iii) Claimants who are employees of educational institutions when it is between school semesters (341.360); (iv) Claimants who are professional athletes when it is between sports seasons. (341.360)

LOUISIANA

STATUTE:

LAW: Louisiana Employment Security Law

CITATION: West's Louisiana Revised Statutes Annotated, Section 23:1471 (L.R.S.A. § 23:1471)

BENEFIT CALCULATION:

WEEKLY BENEFIT AMT.: Benefit amounts are calculated as 1/25 x the average of Claimant's Base Period wages, if Base Period wages are at least $1,200. (23:1592) Weekly Benefit Amount calculation is subject to changes based upon unemployment trust fund balance. (23:1592)

PARTIAL EMPLOYMENT: Any wages Claimant receives from partial employment in excess of the lesser of (i) 50% of his or her Weekly Benefit Amount or (ii) $50, are deducted from his or her Weekly Benefit Amount. (23:1593)

REDUCTION IN BENEFITS: Claimant's Weekly Benefit Amount may be reduced if: (i) Claimant receives pension benefits (23:1601); (ii) Claimant receives retirement pay (23:1601); (iii) Claimant receives annuity payments (23:1601); (iv) Claimant receives other similar periodic payments based upon previous work (23:1601); (v) Claimant receives wages in lieu of notice of termination (23:1601); (vi) Claimant receives temporary total, temporary partial or total and permanent disability under workers' compensation law. (23:1601)

DEPENDENCY BENEFIT: None.

MIN./MAX. WEEKLY: Minimum weekly benefit is $10. (23:1592) Maximum weekly benefit is calculated annually as 66 2/3% of the Statewide Average Weekly Wage. (23:1592) The maximum weekly benefit was subject to modification depending on other factors such as the balance in the state unemployment compensation trust fund. (23:1592) For 2001, the maximum weekly benefit was $258. (23:1592)

MAXIMUM TOTAL: Claimant may receive total benefits equaling the lesser of (i) 26 x his or her Weekly Benefit Amount or (ii) 27% x his or her total Base Period wages. (23:1595) In times of high unemployment, extended benefits may be available. (23:1613)

BENEFIT ELIGIBILITY:

GENERALLY: To be eligible for unemployment compensation benefits, Claimant must: (i) File a claim for benefits (23:1600); (ii) Register for work at a state unemployment office (23:1600); (iii) Continue to report to a state unemployment office as required (23:1600); (iv) Earn during his or her entire Base Period, wages at least equaling 1 1/2 x the amount he or she earned in his or her highest-paying Base Period quarter (23:1600); (v) Be able to work and available for work (23:1600); (vi) Be actively searching for work. (23:1600)

SUBSEQUENT APPLICATION: A Claimant who received benefits during a preceding Benefit Year must have worked and earned the lesser of (i) 3/13 of the wages paid to him or her during his or her highest-paying Benefit Period quarter or (ii) 6 x his or her new Weekly Benefit Amount, subsequent to the commencement of such prior Benefit Year and before the commencement of his or her new Benefit Year. (23:1601)

WAITING WEEK: Claimant must serve 1 Waiting Week before collecting benefits. (23:1600)

DISQUALIFICATION: Claimant may be partially, fully or at least temporarily disqualified from receiving benefits if: (i) Claimant was discharged by a Base Period or subsequent employer for misconduct connected with work (23:1601); (ii) Claimant was discharged for use of illegal or non-prescribed drugs or other controlled substances (23:1601); (iii) Claimant left work from a Base Period or subsequent employer without good cause attributable to a substantial change made to the employment by the employer (23:1601); (iv) Claimant failed to accept or apply for available, suitable work, or return to customary self-employment without good cause (23:1601); (v) Claimant separation was caused by a labor dispute (23:1601); (vi) Claimant made a false statement or representation knowing it to be false or knowingly failed to disclose a material fact in order to obtain benefits (23:1601); (vii) Claimant is receiving unemployment benefits from another state or under federal law (23:1601); (viii) Claimant is an illegal alien. (23:1600)

PURGING DISQUALIFICATION: A Claimant who was discharged for misconduct or illegal drug use, failed to accept or apply for suitable work, or who quit without good cause, may be eligible for benefits only after receiving remuneration for work subsequent to the disqualifying separation in the amount of 10 x his or her Weekly Benefit Amount. (23:1601)

SPECIAL TREATMENT:

Claimants in the following categories are afforded distinct treatment under the statute and thus further research may be merited for: (i) Claimants who are in approved training programs (23: 1602); (ii) Claimants who participate in shared work programs (23:1750); (iii) Claimants who are attending school (23:1602); (iv) Claimants who are enrolled in school when it is between successive academic terms (23:1602); (v) Claimants who quit part-time or interim employment to preserve concurrent full-time jobs (23:1601); (vi) Claimants who receive vacation pay, a vacation pay allowance, or pay in lieu of a vacation (23:1601); (vii) Claimants who receive dismissal pay or severance pay (23:1601); (viii) Claimants who are employees of educational institutions when it is between school semesters (23:1600); (ix) Claimants who are professional athletes when it is between sports seasons. (23:1600)

MAINE

STATUTE:

LAW: Maine Employment Security Law

CITATION: Maine Revised Statutes Annotated, Title 26, Section 1041 (26 M.R.S.A. § 1041)

BENEFIT CALCULATION:

WEEKLY BENEFIT AMT.: Benefit amounts are calculated as 1/22 x the average of wages Claimant earned in his or her highest-paying Base Period quarter. (1191)

PARTIAL EMPLOYMENT: Any wages Claimant receives from partial employment in excess of $25 are deducted from his or her Weekly Benefit Amount. (1191)

REDUCTION IN BENEFITS: Claimant's Weekly Benefit Amount may be reduced if: (i) Claimant receives pension benefits (1193); (ii) Claimant receives retirement pay (1193); (iii) Claimant receives annuity payments (1193); (iv) Claimant receives other similar periodic payments based upon previous work under a Base Period or chargeable employer (1193); (v) Claimant receives vacation or holiday pay (1193); (vi) Claimant receives dismissal wages (1193); (vii) Claimant receives wages in lieu of notice, or terminal pay. (1193)

DEPENDENCY BENEFIT: Claimant's Weekly Benefit Amount may be increased if: Claimant has one or more dependent children ($10 for each dependent, up to 50% of Claimant's Weekly Benefit Amount). (1191)

MIN./MAX. WEEKLY: Minimum weekly benefit in 2001 was $47. (1191) Maximum weekly benefit is calculated annually as 52% of the Statewide Average Weekly Wage, although other limitations may apply. (1191) For 2001, the maximum weekly benefit was $272. (***)

MAXIMUM TOTAL: Claimant may receive total benefits equaling the lesser of (i) 26 x his or her Weekly Benefit Amount or (ii) 33 1/3% x his or her total Base Period wages. (1191) The maximum total for which a Claimant may be eligible, however, may not drop below $300. (1191) In times of high unemployment, extended benefits may be available. (1195)

BENEFIT ELIGIBILITY:

GENERALLY: To be eligible for unemployment compensation benefits, Claimant must: (i) File a claim for benefits (1192); (ii) Register for work at a state unemployment office (1192); (iii) Continue to report to a state unemployment office as required (1192); (iv) Earn during each of 2 different Base Period quarters, wages at least equaling 2 x the Statewide Average Weekly Wage (1192); (v) Earn during his or her entire Base Period, wages equal to at least 6 x the Statewide Average Weekly Wage (1192); (vi) Be able to work and available for full-time work at his usual or customary trade, occupation, profession, or business or in such other trade, occupation, profession, or business for which prior training or experience shows him to be fitted or qualified (1192); (vii) Be actively seeking work (1192); (viii) Participate in reemployment services as required. (1192)

SUBSEQUENT APPLICATION: A Claimant who received benefits during a preceding Benefit Year must have worked and earned 8 x his or her Weekly Benefit Amount subsequent to the commencement of such Benefit Year and before the commencement of his or her new Benefit Year. (1192)

WAITING WEEK: Claimant must serve 1 Waiting Week before collecting benefits. (1192)

DISQUALIFICATION: Claimant may be partially, fully or at least temporarily disqualified from receiving benefits if: (i) Claimant was discharged or suspended for misconduct connected with work (1193); (ii) Claimant was discharged for the conviction of a felony or misdemeanor connected with work (1193); (iii) Claimant was discharged due to absence from work for more than two days due to incarceration for the conviction of a criminal offense (1193); (iv) Claimant voluntarily left work without good cause (1193); (v) Claimant refused to accept an offer for or a referral to suitable work (1193); (vi) Claimant's employer is unable to contact Claimant at his or her last-known address for the purpose of recall (1193); (vii) Claimant separation was caused by a labor dispute unless such separation was caused by a lockout or strike caused by certain actions of an employer (1193); (viii) Claimant made a false statement or representation knowing it to be false or knowingly failed to disclose a material fact in order to obtain benefits (1193); (ix) Claimant is receiving unemployment benefits from another state or under federal law (1193); (x) Claimant retired (1193); (xi) Claimant is an illegal alien. (1192)

PURGING DISQUALIFICATION: A Claimant who was discharged or suspended for misconduct, was discharged for being absent from work due to incarceration, or who voluntarily quit, may be eligible for benefits only after receiving remuneration for work subsequent to the disqualifying separation in the amount of 4 x his or her Weekly Benefit Amount. (1193) A Claimant who was discharged for the conviction of a felony or misdemeanor in connection with work may be eligible for benefits only after receiving remuneration for work subsequent to the disqualifying separation in the amount of the greater of (i) $600 or (ii) 8 x his or her Weekly Benefit Amount. (1193) A Claimant who separates from work during a labor dispute, may be eligible for benefits only after (i) working for 5 full weeks subsequent to the disqualifying separation or (ii) earning remuneration for work subsequent to the disqualifying separation of at least 8 x his or her Weekly Benefit Amount. (1193) A Claimant who refuses to accept an offer for or referral to suitable work, or is unavailable for recall, may be eligible for benefits only after receiving remuneration for work

[continued on next page]

subsequent to the disqualifying separation of at least 8 x his or her Weekly Benefit Amount. (1193) A Claimant who retires may be eligible for benefits only after receiving remuneration for work subsequent to the disqualifying separation in the amount of 6 x his or her Weekly Benefit Amount. (1193)

SPECIAL TREATMENT:

Claimants in the following categories are afforded distinct treatment under the statute and thus further research may be merited for: (i) Claimants who are in approved training programs (1192); (ii) Claimants who are dislocated workers (1191); (iii) Claimants who are on jury duty (1192); (iv) Claimants who have certain parental obligations or have immediate family members who need special care (1192); (v) Claimants who are members of the national guard (1191); (vi) Claimants who are firemen or emergency medical service personnel (1191); (vii) Claimants who are elected members of the Legislature (1191); (viii) Claimants who are handicapped (1192); (ix) Claimants who separate from work while relocating with a spouse (1193); (x) Claimants who are employees of educational institutions when it is between school semesters (1192); (xi) Claimants who are professional athletes when it is between sports seasons (1192); (xii) Claimants who are participating in approved activities to prepare and establish self-employment business. (1197)

MARYLAND

STATUTE:

LAW: Maryland Unemployment Insurance Law

CITATION: A.C.M. Labor and Employment § 8-101 (Lab. 8-101)

BENEFIT CALCULATION:

WEEKLY BENEFIT AMT.: Benefit amounts are included on a schedule and depend upon the total Base Period wages earned by Claimant and the amount of wages he or she earned in his or her highest-paying Base Period quarter. (A high-quarter wage of $576 is paired with a Weekly Benefit Amount of $25. A high-quarter wage of $2,952 is paired with a Weekly Benefit Amount of $124. A high-quarter wage of $5,304 is paired with a Weekly Benefit Amount of $222.) (8-803)

PARTIAL EMPLOYMENT: Any wages Claimant receives from partial employment in excess of $70 are deducted from his or her Weekly Benefit Amount. (8-803)

REDUCTION IN BENEFITS: Claimant's Weekly Benefit Amount may be reduced if: (i) Claimant receives pension benefits (8-1008); (ii) Claimant receives retirement pay (8-1008); (iii) Claimant receives annuity payments (8-1008); (iv) Claimant receives insurance fund retirement pay (8-1008); (v) Claimant receives other similar lump sum or periodic payments based upon previous work under a Base Period employer (8-1008); (vi) Claimant receives dismissal pay (8-1009); (vii) Claimant receives wages in lieu of notice. (8-1009)

DEPENDENCY BENEFIT: Claimant's Weekly Benefit Amount may be increased if: Claimant has dependent children ($8 for each dependent child under 16 years old, up to 5 children). (8-804)

MIN./MAX. WEEKLY: Minimum weekly benefit is $25. (8-803) Maximum weekly benefit is $280. (8-803)

MAXIMUM TOTAL: Claimant may receive total benefits equaling 26 x his or her Weekly Benefit Amount. (8-808) In times of high unemployment, extended benefits may be available. (8-1104)

BENEFIT ELIGIBILITY:

GENERALLY: To be eligible for unemployment compensation benefits, Claimant must: (i) Register for work at a state unemployment office (8-902); (ii) Continue to report to a state unemployment office as required (8-902); (iii) Earn during his or her entire Base Period, wages at least equaling 1 1/2 x the upper limit of the highest-quarterly Base Period earnings as included on a schedule in the law for Claimant's Weekly Benefit Amount (8-802); (iv) Earn wages during at least 2 quarters of his or her Base Period (8-802); (v) Earn wages during his or her highest-paying Base Period quarter of at least $576.01 (8-802); (vi) Be able to work and available for work (8-802); (vii) Be actively seeking work (8-802); (viii) File a claim for benefits.

SUBSEQUENT APPLICATION: A Claimant who received benefits during a preceding Benefit Year must have worked and earned 10 x his or her Weekly Benefit Amount, as calculated for the latter Benefit Year, subsequent to the commencement of the former Benefit Year and before the commencement of his or her new Benefit Year. (8-910)

WAITING WEEK: None.

DISQUALIFICATION: Claimant may be partially, fully or at least temporarily disqualified from receiving benefits if: (i) Claimant was discharged or suspended for misconduct connected with work (8-1003); (ii) Claimant was discharged for gross misconduct (i.e. repeated violations or deliberate and willful disregard of employer's interests) (8-1002); (iii) Claimant was discharged or suspended for aggravated misconduct (i.e. exhibiting actual malice and a deliberate disregard for an employer's interests) (8-1002.1); (iv) Claimant voluntarily left work without good cause (8-1001); (v) Claimant failed, without good cause, to apply for or accept suitable work or return to self-employment when directed (8-1005); (vi) Claimant separation was caused by a labor dispute other than a lockout (8-1004); (vii) Claimant knowingly made a false statement or representation, or knowingly failed to disclose a material fact in order to obtain benefits (8-809); (viii) Claimant is receiving unemployment benefits from another state or under federal law (8-1006); (ix) Claimant is an illegal alien. (8-905)

PURGING DISQUALIFICATION: A Claimant who voluntarily quit, except under certain conditions, may be eligible for benefits only after receiving remuneration for work subsequent to the disqualifying separation in the amount of 15 x his or her Weekly Benefit Amount. (8-1001) A Claimant who was discharged for refusing to apply for or accept suitable work, may be eligible for benefits only after the passing of 5 to 10 weeks or after receiving remuneration for work subsequent to the disqualifying separation in the amount of 10 x his or her Weekly Benefit Amount. (8-1005) A Claimant who was discharged or suspended for gross misconduct may be eligible for benefits only after receiving remuneration for work subsequent to the disqualifying separation in the amount of 20 x his or her Weekly Benefit Amount. (8-1002) A Claimant who was discharged or suspended for aggravated misconduct, such as physical assault or causing severe property loss, may be eligible for benefits only after receiving remuneration for work subsequent to the disqualifying separation in the amount of 30 x his or her Weekly Benefit Amount. (8-1002.1)

SPECIAL TREATMENT:

Claimants in the following categories are afforded distinct treatment under the statute and thus further research may be merited for: (i) Claimants who are in approved training programs (8-903); (ii) Claimants who elect to enter a shared work program (8-1207); (iii) Claimants who are on jury duty (8-907); (iv) Claimants who are disabled (8-907); (v) Claimants who are over 60 years old and furloughed temporarily (8-907); (vi) Claimants who are members of the Armed Forces or National Guard (8-906); (vii) Claimants who work for firms that close their plants for a vacation, to take inventory, or for other purposes (8-904); (viii) Claimants who receive holiday or vacation pay and are expected to return to work (8-1007); (ix) Claimants who are employees of educational institutions when it is between school semesters (8-909); (x) Claimants who are professional athletes when it is between sports seasons (8-908); (xi) Claimants who are in approved self-employment assistance programs. (8-1604)

MASSACHUSETTS

STATUTE:

LAW: Massachusetts Employment and Training Law

CITATION: Massachusetts General Laws Annotated, Chapter 151A, Section 1 (M.G.L.A. § 151A-1)

BENEFIT CALCULATION:

WEEKLY BENEFIT AMT.: For a Claimant whose average weekly wage during his or her Base Period is $66 or less, his or her Weekly Benefit Amount will range from $14 to $34, depending upon the wages he or she earned in his or her highest-paying Base Period quarter. (151A-29) For a Claimant whose average weekly wage during his or her Base Period is over $66, his or her Weekly Benefit Amount will equal 50% x the average weekly wage that Claimant received during his or her Base Period. (151A-29)

PARTIAL EMPLOYMENT: Any wages Claimant receives from partial employment in excess of 1/3 of his or her Weekly Benefit Amount are deducted from his or her Weekly Benefit Amount. (151A-29) In no case, however, shall the sum of the amount of any earnings disregarded and his or her weekly benefit be greater than or equal to his or her average weekly wage. (151A-29)

REDUCTION IN BENEFITS: Claimant's Weekly Benefit Amount may be reduced if: (i) Claimant receives pension benefits (151A-29); (ii) Claimant receives retirement pay (151A-29); (iii) Claimant receives annuity payments (151A-29); (iv) Claimant receives other similar periodic payments based upon previous work. (151A-29)

DEPENDENCY BENEFIT: Claimant's Weekly Benefit Amount may be increased if: Claimant has one or more dependent children under the age of 18 or dependent children over the age of 18 which are either mentally or physically incapacitated or full-time students under 24 years of age ($25 for each dependent, not to exceed an amount equal to 50% of Claimant's Weekly Benefit Amount). (151A-29)

MIN./MAX. WEEKLY: Minimum weekly benefit is $27. (151A-29) Maximum weekly benefit is calculated annually as 57 1/2% of the Statewide Average Weekly Wage. (151A-29) For 2001, the maximum weekly benefit was $512. (***)

MAXIMUM TOTAL: Claimant may receive total benefits equaling the lesser of (i) 30 x his or her Weekly Benefit Amount or (ii) 36% of his or her total Base Period wages. (151A-30) Dependency Benefits are then added to this figure. (151A-30) In times of high unemployment, extended benefits may be available. (151A-30A)

BENEFIT ELIGIBILITY:

GENERALLY: To be eligible for unemployment compensation benefits, Claimant must: (i) Register for work at a state unemployment office (151A-24); (ii) Continue to give the state unemployment office notice of unemployment (151A-24); (iii) Furnish the state unemployment office with information regarding any remuneration for work received during weeks of partial unemployment (151A-24); (iv) Earn during his or her Base Period, wages at least equal to $2,400 (this figure changes when the minimum wage changes) (151A-24); (v) Earn wages during his or her entire Base Period amounting to at least 30 x his or her Weekly Benefit Amount (151A-24); (vi) Be capable of working and available for work (151A-24); (vii) Be actively seeking work. (151A-24)

SUBSEQUENT APPLICATION: A Claimant who received benefits during a preceding Benefit Year must have worked and earned 3 x his or her Weekly Benefit Amount subsequent to the commencement of such Benefit Year and before the commencement of his or her new Benefit Year. (151A-31)

WAITING WEEK: Claimant must serve 1 Waiting Week before collecting benefits. (151A-23)

DISQUALIFICATION: Claimant may be partially, fully or at least temporarily disqualified from receiving benefits if: (i) Claimant was discharged for deliberate misconduct in willful disregard of his or her employer's interests or for a knowing violation of a reasonable and uniformly enforced rule or policy (151A-25); (ii) Claimant was suspended for disciplinary reasons for a violation of established rules or regulations (151A-25); (iii) Claimant was convicted of a felony or misdemeanor (151A-25); (iv) Claimant voluntarily left work without good cause (151A-25); (v) Claimant fails, without good cause, to apply for suitable work or to accept suitable employment (151A-25); (vi) Claimant separation was caused by a labor dispute other than a lockout (151A-25); (vii) Claimant is receiving unemployment benefits from another state or under federal law (151A-26); (viii) Claimant received or is about to receive benefits for total disability under any workers' compensation law (151A-25); (ix) Claimant fails without good cause to comply with registration or other filing requirements (151A-25); (x) Claimant is an illegal alien (151A-25); (xi) Claimant has an outstanding default or arrest warrant.

PURGING DISQUALIFICATION: A Claimant who was discharged for deliberate misconduct or a knowing violation of a firm rule or policy, who voluntarily quit without good cause, or who is convicted of a felony or misdemeanor, may be eligible for benefits only after working for 8 weeks in each of which he or she has earned an amount equivalent to or in excess of his or her Weekly Benefit Amount. (151A-25)

SPECIAL TREATMENT:

Claimants in the following categories are afforded distinct treatment under the statute and thus further research may be merited for: (i) Claimants who are in approved industrial retraining or other vocational training programs (151A-24, 151A-30); (ii) Claimants who participate in worksharing plans (151A-29D); (iii) Claimants who are ill or disabled (151A-24); (iv) Claimants who are not recalled after the end of a labor dispute (151A-25); (v) Claimants who leave work to accept new full-time employment (151A-25); (vi) Claimants who have pension or retirement programs which require them to leave (151A-25); (vii) Claimants who have seasonal employment (151A-24A); (viii) Claimants who are employees of educational institutions when it is between school semesters (151A-28A); (ix) Claimants who are professional athletes when it is between sports seasons (151A-25); (x) Claimants who knowingly make false or misleading statements in order to maintain, obtain or increase benefits. (151A-47)

MICHIGAN

STATUTE:

LAW: Michigan Employment Security Act

CITATION: Michigan Compiled Laws Annotated, Section 421.1 (M.C.L.A. § 421.1)

BENEFIT CALCULATION:

WEEKLY BENEFIT AMT.: Benefit amounts are calculated as 4.1% x the wages Claimant earned in his or her highest-paying Base Period quarter. (421.27)

PARTIAL EMPLOYMENT: $.50 of each $1 Claimant receives from partial employment is deducted from his or her Weekly Benefit Amount. (421.27) A Claimant who receives such remuneration may not receive benefits plus such remuneration which in total exceed 1 1/2 x his or her Weekly Benefit Amount. (421.27) For each $1 of total benefits plus such remuneration that exceed 1 1/2 x his or her Weekly Benefit Amount, his or her benefits will be reduced by $1. (421.27)

REDUCTION IN BENEFITS: Claimant's Weekly Benefit Amount may be reduced if: (i) Claimant receives pension benefits; (ii) Claimant receives retirement pay; (iii) Claimant receives annuity payments; (iv) Claimant receives other similar payments based upon previous work. (421.27)

DEPENDENCY BENEFIT: Claimant's Weekly Benefit Amount may be increased if: Claimant has one or more dependent children or relatives or a dependent spouse ($6 for each dependent, up to 5 dependents). (421.27)

MIN./MAX. WEEKLY: Minimum weekly benefit in 2001 was $88. (421.27, 421.46) For 2001, the maximum weekly benefit was $300. (421.27)

MAXIMUM TOTAL: Claimant may receive total benefits equal to the product of the number of eligible weeks of Claimant x the Claimant's Weekly Benefit Amount. (421.27) The number of eligible weeks of Claimant is calculated as 40% of Claimant's Base Period wages divided by Claimant's Weekly Benefit Amount. (421.27) The number of eligible weeks for a Claimant may not exceed 26 nor be less than 14. (421.27) In times of high unemployment, extended benefits may be available. (421.64)

BENEFIT ELIGIBILITY:

GENERALLY: To be eligible for unemployment compensation benefits, Claimant must: (i) File a claim for benefits (421.28); (ii) Register for work at a state unemployment office (421.28); (iii) Continue to report to a state unemployment office as required (421.28); (iv) Earn (a) during his or her entire Base Period, wages at least equaling 1.5 x the wages he or she earned in his or her highest-paying Base Period quarter, OR (b) during 2 or more quarters of his or her Base Period wages which total at least 20 x the Statewide Average Weekly Wage (421.46); (v) Earn at least 20 Credit Weeks (i.e. at least 20 weeks each in which Claimant receives remuneration greater than or equal to 20 x the state minimum hourly wage) during the 52 calendar weeks before he or she files for benefits (Under certain conditions, Claimant may qualify with 14 Credit Weeks and Base Period wages in excess of 20 x the Statewide Average Weekly Wage.) (421.46, 421.50); (vi) Earn at least an amount equal to the state minimum hourly wage x 388.06 in one calendar quarter of his or her Base Period (421.46); (vii) Be able to work and available for suitable full-time work (421.28); (viii) Be seeking work (421.28); (ix) Participate in reemployment services as required. (421.28)

SUBSEQUENT APPLICATION: A Claimant who received benefits during a preceding Benefit Year must have worked and earned an amount equal to at least 5 x his or her Weekly Benefit Amount, as calculated for the subsequent Benefit Year, subsequent to the commencement of the former Benefit Year and before the commencement of his or her new Benefit Year. (421.46)

WAITING WEEK: None.

DISQUALIFICATION: Claimant may be partially, fully or at least temporarily disqualified from receiving benefits if: (i) Claimant was discharged for misconduct connected with work, for intoxication while at work, for theft or willful destruction of property connected with work, for participation in certain strikes, wildcat strikes, or strikes in violation of a collective bargaining agreement, or for an act of assault and battery connected with work (421.29); (ii) Claimant is on disciplinary layoff or suspension based upon misconduct directly or indirectly connected with work, or for participation in certain wildcat strikes or strikes in violation of a collective bargaining agreement (421.29); (iii) Claimant lost his or her job because he or she was absent from work as a result of his or her incarceration following a conviction (421.29); (iv) Claimant was discharged for illegally ingesting, injecting, inhaling, or possessing a controlled substance on the premises of his or her employer or for refusing to be tested for drugs (421.29); (v) Claimant voluntarily left work without good cause attributable to the employer (421.29); (vi) Claimant failed to apply for or accept suitable work or to return to customary self-employment without good cause (421.29); (vii) Claimant separation was caused by a labor dispute other than a lockout (421.29); (viii) Claimant was an employee of a temporary help firm and did not give notice to such firm when he or she completed his or her former assignment (421.29); (ix) Claimant violated a collective bargaining agreement, curtailed work, or restricted production (421.29); (x) Claimant intentionally made false statements or misrepresentations or concealed information to obtain benefits (421.62); (xi) Claimant is receiving unemployment benefits from another state or under federal law (421.29); (xii) Claimant is an illegal alien. (421.27)

[continued on next page]

PURGING DISQUALIFICATION: A Claimant who was discharged for participation in certain strikes, who was absent from work as a result of his or her incarceration, who completed a former assignment for a temporary help firm and failed to notify such firm, or a Claimant who failed to apply for or accept suitable work or who failed to return to customary self-employment, may be eligible for benefits only after completing 6 Requalification Weeks (i.e. 6 weeks in which Claimant either (i) earns or receives remuneration in an amount equal to at least 1/13 of the minimum amount needed in a calendar quarter of the Base Period for such Claimant to qualify for benefits, or (ii) otherwise meets all the requirements of the act to be eligible for benefits if the individual were not disqualified). (421.29) A Claimant who was discharged for misconduct, intoxication while at work, or who voluntarily left work without good cause, may be eligible for benefits only after he or she earns the lesser of (i) an amount equal to 7 times his or her Weekly Benefit Amount, or (ii) an amount equal to at least 40 x the state minimum hourly wage times 7. (421.29) A Claimant who was discharged for assault and battery connected with work, for theft or the willful destruction of property connected with work, for illegally ingesting controlled substances, for failing to submit to drug testing, or for a violation of a collective bargaining agreement, curtailing work, or restricting production, may be eligible for benefits only after completing 13 Requalification Weeks. (421.29)

SPECIAL TREATMENT:

Claimants in the following categories are afforded distinct treatment under the statute and thus further research may be merited for: (i) Claimants who are in approved training programs (421.28); (ii) Claimants who receive termination, separation, severance, or dismissal payments (421.50); (iii) Claimants who are enrolled in and attending school (421.28); (iv) Claimants who are seamen employed on an American vessel (421.43); (v) Claimants who work for firms in which they or their immediate family own a 50% or more proprietary interest (421.26); (vi) Claimants who are seasonal employees (421.27); (vii) Claimants who leave work for permanent full-time work with another employer (421.29); (viii) Claimants who are employees of educational institutions when it is between school semesters (421.27); (ix) Claimants who are professional athletes when it is between sports seasons. (421.27)

MINNESOTA

STATUTE:

LAW: Minnesota Jobs and Training Law

CITATION: Minnesota Statutes Annotated, Section 268.001 (M.S.A. § 268.001)

BENEFIT CALCULATION:

WEEKLY BENEFIT AMT.: Benefit amounts are calculated as the greater of (i) 50% of the Claimant's average weekly wage during his or her Base Period, to a maximum of 66 2/3% of the statewide Average Weekly Wage or (ii) 50% of the Claimant's average weekly wage during his or her highest-paying Base Period quarter to a maximum of the higher of $331 or 50% of the statewide Average Weekly Wage. (268.07)

PARTIAL EMPLOYMENT: Any earnings Claimant receives from partial employment that are the greater of (i) $50 or (ii) 25% of his or her earnings in other work are deducted from his or her Weekly Benefit Amount. (268.07)

REDUCTION IN BENEFITS: Claimant's Weekly Benefit Amount may be reduced if: (i) Claimant receives pension payments (268.085); (ii) Claimant receives retirement pay (268.085); (iii) Claimant receives annuity payments (268.085); (iv) Claimant receives Social Security benefits (268.085); (v) Claimant receives holiday pay or sick pay (268.085); (vi) Claimant receives a vacation allowance (268.085); (vii) Claimant receives back pay (268.085); (viii) Claimant receives severance (268.085); (ix) Claimant receives workers' compensation benefits (268.085); (x) Claimant receives national guard or U.S. Military Reserve pay. (268.085)

DEPENDENCY BENEFIT: None.

MIN./MAX. WEEKLY: Minimum weekly benefit is $38. (268.07) Maximum weekly benefit is calculated as the greater of (i) 66 2/3% of the Statewide Average Weekly Wage and (ii) $331. (268.07) For 2001, the maximum weekly benefit was $452. (***)

MAXIMUM TOTAL: Claimant may receive total benefits equaling the lesser of (i) 26 x his or her Weekly Benefit Amount or (ii) 1/3 x the amount he or she earned during his or her entire Base Period. (268.07) In times of high unemployment, extended benefits may be available. (268.115) Additional benefit payments may also be available where Claimant's last employer was fairly large and such employer significantly reduced operations resulting in a substantial workforce reduction. (268.125)

BENEFIT ELIGIBILITY:

GENERALLY: To be eligible for unemployment compensation benefits, Claimant must: (i) File an application for benefits (268.085); (ii) Earn at least $250 in wage credits in quarters of his or her Base Period other than in his or her highest paying Base Period quarter (268.07); (iii) Earn wages of at least $1,000 during his or her highest-paying Base Period quarter (268.07); (iv) Be able to work and available for work (268.085); (v) Be actively seeking work (268.085); (vi) Participate in reemployment services as required (268.085); (vii) File a continued request for benefits. (268.085)

SUBSEQUENT APPLICATION: A Claimant who received benefits during a preceding Benefit Year must have worked and earned an amount equal to 8 x his or her Weekly Benefit Amount, as calculated for the latter Benefit Year, subsequent to the commencement of his or her first Benefit Year and before the commencement of his or her new Benefit Year. (268.07)

WAITING WEEK: Claimant must serve 1 Waiting Week before collecting benefits. (268.085)

DISQUALIFICATION: Claimant may be partially, fully or at least temporarily disqualified from receiving benefits if: (i) Claimant was discharged for misconduct or aggravated misconduct connected with work or for misconduct which interferes with, or adversely affects, employment (268.095); (ii) Claimant is on disciplinary suspension for 30 days or less resulting from Claimant's misconduct (268.095); (iii) Claimant voluntarily left work without good cause (268.095); (iv) Claimant failed to apply for or accept suitable work (268.095); (v) Claimant separation was caused by a labor dispute except for a lockout or dismissal during negotiations (268.095); (vi) Claimant knowingly and willfully misrepresented or misstated a material fact or knowingly and willfully failed to disclose a material fact in order to obtain benefits (268.182); (vii) Claimant is receiving unemployment benefits from another state or under federal law (268.18); (viii) Claimant is an illegal alien (268.085); (ix) Claimant is on a voluntary leave of absence whether paid or not. (268.085)

PURGING DISQUALIFICATION: A Claimant who was discharged for misconduct, refused to accept or apply for suitable work, or who voluntarily quit, may be eligible for benefits only after four calendar weeks have elapsed and he or she has received remuneration for work subsequent to the disqualifying separation in the amount of 8 x his or her Weekly Benefit Amount. (268.085)

SPECIAL TREATMENT:

Claimants in the following categories are afforded distinct treatment under the statute and thus further research may be merited for: (i) Claimants who are in approved training programs (268.095); (ii) Claimants who participate in a shared work plan (268.135); (iii) Claimants who are enrolled in school when it is between successive academic terms (268.085); (iv) Claimants who are members of the National Guard or other reserve unit (268.085); (v) Claimants who are fire fighters (268.07); (vi) Claimants who are ambulance service personnel (268.07); (vii) Claimants who are on jury duty (268.085); (viii) Claimants who are separated from employment due to illness or chemical dependency (268.095); (ix) Claimants who leave part-time employment while still maintaining other full-time employment (268.095); (x) Claimants who quit to accept employment offering substantially better conditions or higher wages (268.095); (xi) Claimants who were formerly employed by a firm in which they or their family members owned or controlled at least a 25% interest (268.07); (xii) Claimants who are employees of educational institutions when it is between school semesters (268.085); (xiii) Claimants who are professional athletes when it is between sports seasons (268.085); (xiv) Claimants who work in any capacity for 32 hours per week or more, regardless of earnings (268.085); (xv) Claimants who work in the recreational or tourist industry (268.085); (xvi) Claimants working for employers during a vacation period assigned by the employer under (a) a uniform vacation shut down or (b) collective bargaining agreement. (268.085)

MISSISSIPPI

STATUTE:

LAW: Mississippi Employment Security Law

CITATION: Mississippi Code 1972 Annotated, Title 71, Section 71-5-11 (M.C. § 71-5-11)

BENEFIT CALCULATION:

WEEKLY BENEFIT AMT.: Benefit amounts are calculated as 1/26 x the wages Claimant earned in his or her highest-paying Base Period quarter. (61-5-503)

PARTIAL EMPLOYMENT: Any wages Claimant receives from partial employment in excess of $40 are deducted from his or her Weekly Benefit Amount. (71-5-505)

REDUCTION IN BENEFITS: Claimant's Weekly Benefit Amount may be reduced if: Claimant receives pension benefits or retirement plan payments. (71-5-513)

DEPENDENCY BENEFIT: None.

MIN./MAX. WEEKLY: Minimum weekly benefit is $30. (71-5-503) Maximum weekly benefit is calculated annually as 60% of the Statewide Average Weekly Wage, not to exceed $200 in 2001. (71-5-503)

MAXIMUM TOTAL: Claimant may receive total benefits equaling the lesser of (i) 26 x his or her Weekly Benefit Amount or (ii) 1/3 x his or her total Base Period wages. (71-5-507) In times of high unemployment, extended benefits may be available. (71-5-541)

BENEFIT ELIGIBILITY:

GENERALLY: To be eligible for unemployment compensation benefits, Claimant must: (i) File a claim for benefits (71-5-511); (ii) Register for work at a state unemployment office (71-5-511); (iii) Continue to report to a state unemployment office as required (71-5-511); (iv) Earn during his or her Base Period, wages at least equaling 40 x his or her Weekly Benefit Amount (71-5-511); (v) Earn during his or her highest-paying Base Period quarter wages equaling at least 26 x the minimum Weekly Benefit Amount (71-5-511); (vi) Earn wages during at least 2 quarters of his or her Base Period (71-5-511); (vii) Be able to work and available for work (71-5-511); (viii) Participate in reemployment services as required. (71-5-511)

SUBSEQUENT APPLICATION: A Claimant who received benefits during a preceding Benefit Year must have worked and earned 8 x his or her prior Weekly Benefit Amount subsequent to the commencement of such Benefit Year and before the commencement of his or her new Benefit Year. (71-5-511)

WAITING WEEK: Claimant must serve 1 Waiting Week before collecting benefits. (71-5- 511)

DISQUALIFICATION: Claimant may be partially, fully or at least temporarily disqualified from receiving benefits if: (i) Claimant was discharged for misconduct connected with work (71-5-513); (ii) Claimant voluntarily left work without good cause (71-5-513); (iii) Claimant failed, without good cause, to either apply for available, suitable work or to accept suitable work or to return to customary self-employment when directed (71-5-513); (iv) Claimant separation was caused by a labor dispute other than a lock-out (71-5-513); (v) Claimant willfully made a false statement, false representation of fact, or willfully failed to disclose a material fact for the purpose of obtaining benefits (71-5-513); (vi) Claimant is receiving unemployment benefits from another state or under federal law (71-5-513); (vii) Claimant receives back pay or other compensation allocable to a working week (71-5-513); (viii) Claimant is an illegal alien. (71-5-511)

PURGING DISQUALIFICATION: A Claimant who was discharged for misconduct, or who voluntarily quit without good cause, may be eligible for benefits only after receiving remuneration for work subsequent to the disqualifying separation in the amount of 8 x his or her Weekly Benefit Amount. (71-5-513)

SPECIAL TREATMENT:

Claimants in the following categories are afforded distinct treatment under the statute and thus further research may be merited for: (i) Claimants who are in approved training programs (71-5-513); (ii) Claimants who worked in the cotton gin industry (71-5-509); (iii) Claimants who leave work due to pregnancy (71-5-513); (iv) Claimants who are members of military reserve units (71-5-507; 71-5-505); (v) Claimants who are employees of educational institutions when it is between school semesters (71-5-511); (vi) Claimants who are professional athletes when it is between sports seasons. (71-5-511)

Missouri

STATUTE:

LAW: Missouri Employment Security Law

CITATION: Vernon's Annotated Missouri Statutes, Chapter 288, Section 288.010 (A.M.S. § 288.010)

BENEFIT CALCULATION:

WEEKLY BENEFIT AMT.: Benefit amounts are calculated as 4.0% of the wages Claimant earned in his or her highest-paying Base Period quarter. (288.038)

PARTIAL EMPLOYMENT: Any wages Claimant receives from partial employment in excess of $20 are deducted from his or her Weekly Benefit Amount. (288.060)

REDUCTION IN BENEFITS: Claimant's Weekly Benefit Amount may be reduced if: (i) Claimant receives pension payments (288.040); (ii) Claimant receives retirement pay (288.040); (iii) Claimant receives an annuity (288.040); (iv) Claimant receives other similar periodic payments based on his or her previous work (288.040); (v) Claimant receives workers' compensation for temporary partial disability. (288.040)

DEPENDENCY BENEFIT: None.

MIN./MAX. WEEKLY: Minimum weekly benefit is $40. (288.030, 288.038) Maximum weekly benefit. (288.038) For 2001 the maximum weekly benefit was $250. (288.038)

MAXIMUM TOTAL: Claimant may receive total benefits equaling the lesser of (i) 26 x his or her Weekly Benefit Amount or (ii) 33 1/3% of his or her Base Period Wage Credits (i.e. 33 1/3% of the lesser of the amount of (a) the wages he or she earned during his or her entire Base Period or (b) an amount equal to 26 x his or her Weekly Benefit Amount). (288.06) In times of high unemployment, extended benefits may be available. (288.062)

BENEFIT ELIGIBILITY:

GENERALLY: To be eligible for unemployment compensation benefits, Claimant must: (i) File a claim for benefits (288.040); (ii) Register for work at a state unemployment office (288.040); (iii) Continue to report to a state unemployment office as required (288.040); (iv) Earn (a) at least $1000 in wages during at least one quarter of his or her Base Period and earn during his or her entire Base Period wages equal to at least 1 1/2 x the wages he or she earned during his or her highest-paying Base Period quarter OR (b) wages in at least two quarters of his or her Base Period and earn during his or her entire Base Period wages equal to at least 1 1/2 x the maximum taxable wage base (i.e. $8,500) taxable to any one employer (288.030, 288.036); (v) Be able to work and available for work (288.040); (vi) Be actively and earnestly seeking work (288.040); (vii) Participate in reemployment services as required. (288.040)

SUBSEQUENT APPLICATION: A Claimant who received benefits during a preceding Benefit Year must have worked and earned 5 x his or her Weekly Benefit Amount in wages in insured work or 10 x his or her Weekly Benefit Amount in non-covered work subsequent to the end of his or her previous Base Period. (288.06)

WAITING WEEK: Claimant must serve 1 Waiting Week before collecting benefits. (288.040)

DISQUALIFICATION: Claimant may be partially, fully or at least temporarily disqualified from receiving benefits if: (i) Claimant was discharged or suspended for misconduct connected with work (288.040); (ii) Claimant voluntarily left work without good cause (288.050); (iii) Claimant failed to apply for available, suitable work, or to accept suitable work (288.050); (iv) Claimant separation was caused by a labor dispute (288.040); (v) Claimant willfully failed to disclose a material fact or made a false statement or representation in order to obtain benefits (288.380); (vi) Claimant is receiving unemployment benefits from another state or under federal law (288.040); (vii) Claimant is an illegal alien. (288.040)

PURGING DISQUALIFICATION: A Claimant who was discharged for misconduct may be eligible for benefits only after receiving remuneration for work subsequent to the disqualifying separation in the amount of 8 x his or her Weekly Benefit Amount. (288.050) A Claimant who voluntarily left work without good cause may be eligible for benefits only after receiving remuneration for work subsequent to the disqualifying separation in the amount of 10 x his or her Weekly Benefit Amount. (288.050)

SPECIAL TREATMENT:

Claimants in the following categories are afforded distinct treatment under the statute and thus further research may be merited for: (i) Claimants who are in approved training or retraining programs (288.040); (ii) Claimants who participate in shared work programs (288.500); (iii) Claimants who are on jury duty (288.040); (iv) Claimants who are substitute teachers (288.040); (v) Claimants who are pregnant or who were recently pregnant (288.050); (vi) Claimants who receive termination or severance pay (288.060); (vii) Claimants who quit to accept higher paying jobs (288.050); (viii) Claimants who quit temporary work to return to regular employment (288.050); (ix) Claimants who retire pursuant to a labor-management agreement (288.050); (x) Claimants who are employees of educational institutions when it is between school semesters (288.040); (xi) Claimants who are professional athletes when it is between sports seasons. (288.040)

MONTANA

STATUTE:

LAW: Montana Unemployment Insurance Law

CITATION: Montana Code Annotated, Title 39, Chapter 51, Section 39-51-101 (M.C.A. § 39-51-101)

BENEFIT CALCULATION:

WEEKLY BENEFIT AMT.: Benefit amounts are calculated as either 1% of the total wages Claimant received during his or her entire Base Period or 1.9% of the total wages he or she received in his or her two highest-paying Base Period quarters. (39-51-2201)

PARTIAL EMPLOYMENT: 50% of the wages a Claimant earns in excess of 1/4 x his or her Weekly Benefit Amount are deducted from his or her Weekly Benefit Amount. (39-51-2202)

REDUCTION IN BENEFITS: Claimant's Weekly Benefit Amount may be reduced if: (i) Claimant receives pension benefits (39-51-2203); (ii) Claimant receives retirement pay (39-51-2203); (iii) Claimant receives annuity pay (39-51-2203); (iv) Claimant receives other similar periodic payments based upon previous work. (39-51-2203)

DEPENDENCY BENEFIT: None.

MIN./MAX. WEEKLY: Minimum weekly benefit is calculated as 15% of the Statewide Average Weekly Wage. (39-51-2201) Minimum weekly benefit in 2001 was $68. (***) Maximum weekly benefit is calculated annually as 60% of the Statewide Average Weekly Wage. (39-51-2201) The maximum weekly benefit in 2001 was $286. (***)

MAXIMUM TOTAL: Claimant may receive total benefits equaling the product of his or her Weekly Benefit Amount times the number of full weeks of benefits to which he or she is entitled. (39-51-2204) The number of weeks of benefits to which a Claimant is entitled (between 8 and 26) can be found on a schedule included in the law and depends upon the ratio of Claimant's total Base Period earnings to the amount of wages Claimant earned in his or her highest-paying Base Period quarter. (39-51-2204) In times of high unemployment, extended benefits may be available. (39-51-2508)

BENEFIT ELIGIBILITY:

GENERALLY: To be eligible for unemployment compensation benefits, Claimant must: (i) File a claim for benefits (39-51-2104); (ii) Continue to report to a state unemployment office as required (39-51-2104); (iii) Earn (a) the greater of total Base Period wages of at least 1 1/2 x the wages he or she earned in his or her highest-paying Base Period quarter or total Base Period wages of at least 7% of the statewide average annual wage OR (b) total Base Period wages of at least 50% of the statewide average annual wage (39-51-2105); (iv) Be able to work and available for work (39-51-2104); (v) Seek work (39-51-2104); (vi) Participate in reemployment services as required. (39-51-2104)

SUBSEQUENT APPLICATION: A Claimant who received benefits during a preceding Benefit Year must have worked and earned the lesser of (i) 6 x his or her Weekly Benefit Amount or (ii) 3/13 x the wages he or she earned in his or her highest-paying Base Period quarter in his or her second Benefit Year, subsequent to the commencement of his or her initial separation in his or her previous Benefit Year and before the commencement of his or her new Benefit Year. (39-51-2107)

WAITING WEEK: Claimant must serve 1 Waiting Week before collecting benefits. (39-51- 2104)

DISQUALIFICATION: Claimant may be partially, fully or at least temporarily disqualified from receiving benefits if: (i) Claimant was discharged for misconduct connected with work or affecting the individual's employment (39-51-2303); (ii) Claimant was discharged for gross misconduct connected with work or committed on his or her employer's premises (39-51-2303); (iii) Claimant voluntarily left work without good cause attributable to employment (39-51-2302); (iv) Claimant failed without good cause either to apply for available, suitable work or to accept an offer of suitable work which the individual is physically able and mentally qualified to perform, or Claimant failed to return to customary self-employment (39-51-2304); (v) Claimant separation was caused by a strike (39-51-2305); (vi) Claimant made a false statement or representation knowing it to be false or knowingly failed to disclose a material fact in order to obtain benefits (39-51-3201); (vii) Claimant is receiving unemployment benefits from another state or under federal law (39-51-2306); (viii) Claimant received payments under any state or federal workers' compensation law, occupational disease law, or under the Social Security disability law (39-51-2306); (ix) Claimant is an illegal alien. (39-51-2110)

PURGING DISQUALIFICATION: A Claimant who was discharged for misconduct, may be eligible for benefits only after receiving remuneration for work subsequent to the disqualifying separation in the amount of 8 x his or her Weekly Benefit Amount. (39-51-2303) A Claimant who voluntarily quits without good cause or who fails to apply for or accept suitable work, may be eligible for benefits only after receiving remuneration for work subsequent to the disqualifying separation in the amount of 6 x his or her Weekly Benefit Amount. (39-51-2302)

SPECIAL TREATMENT:

Claimants in the following categories are afforded distinct treatment under the statute and thus further research may be merited for: (i) Claimants who are in approved training programs (39-51-2307); (ii) Claimants who are ill or disabled (39-51-2303); (iii) Claimants who are students (39-51-2307); (iv) Claimants who are employees of educational institutions when it is between school semesters (39-51-2108); (v) Claimants who are professional athletes when it is between sports seasons. (39-51-2109)

NEBRASKA

STATUTE:

LAW: Nebraska Employment Security Law

CITATION: Revised Statutes of Nebraska, Chapter 48, Section 48-601 (R.S.N. § 48-601)

BENEFIT CALCULATION:

WEEKLY BENEFIT AMT.: Benefit amounts are calculated as 1/2 x the average weekly wages the Claimant earned in his or her highest-paying Base Period quarter. (48-624)

PARTIAL EMPLOYMENT: If Claimant receives wages in a week from partial employment which in sum are less than 1/2 x his or her Weekly Benefit Amount, he or she will receive his or her full Weekly Benefit Amount. (48-625) If Claimant earns wages from partial employment during a week which in sum are greater or equal to 1/2 x his or her Weekly Benefit Amount but less than his or her full weekly Benefit Amount, Claimant will receive 1/2 of his or her Weekly Benefit Amount. (48-625) If Claimant receives remuneration in any week which is greater than or equal to his or her Weekly Benefit Amount, however, he or she will not be eligible for benefits. (48-625)

REDUCTION IN BENEFITS: Claimant's Weekly Benefit Amount may be reduced if: (i) Claimant receives pension benefits (48-628); (ii) Claimant receives retirement pay (48-628); (iii) Claimant receives annuity pay (48-628); (iv) Claimant receives other similar periodic payments under a plan maintained or contributed to by a Base Period or chargeable employer (48-628); (v) Claimant receives wages in lieu of notice, dismissal or separation payments (48-628); (vi) Claimant receives temporary partial disability payments under a workers' compensation act or other disability pay from his or her employer (48-628); (vii) Claimant receives Social Security benefits (48-628); (viii) Claimant receives a bonus based on prior service. (48-628)

DEPENDENCY BENEFIT: None.

MIN./MAX. WEEKLY: Minimum weekly benefit is $36. (48-624) Maximum weekly benefit is $214 and is calculated as 1/2 x the Statewide Average Weekly Wage. (48-624)

MAXIMUM TOTAL: Claimant may receive total benefits equaling the lesser of (i) 26 x his or her Weekly Benefit Amount or (ii) 1/3 x his or her Base Period wages. (48-628) In times of high unemployment, extended benefits may be available. (48-628.03)

BENEFIT ELIGIBILITY:

GENERALLY: To be eligible for unemployment compensation benefits, Claimant must: (i) File a claim for benefits (48-627); (ii) Register for work at a state unemployment office (48-627); (iii) Continue to report to a state unemployment office as required (48-627); (iv) Earn during his or her entire Base Period, wages at least equaling $1,200 of which at least $400 was paid in each of two quarters of his or her Base Period (48-627); (v) Be able to work and available for work (48-627); (vi) Participate in reemployment services as required. (48-627)

SUBSEQUENT APPLICATION: A Claimant who received benefits during a preceding Benefit Year must have worked for at least 4 weeks subsequent to his or her filing a claim in his or her previous Benefit Year. (48-627)

WAITING WEEK: Claimant must serve 1 Waiting Week before collecting benefits. (48- 627)

DISQUALIFICATION: Claimant may be partially, fully or at least temporarily disqualified from receiving benefits if: (i) Claimant was discharged for misconduct connected with work or gross, flagrant, and willful misconduct or misconduct that was unlawful (48-628); (ii) Claimant voluntarily left work without good cause (48-628); (iii) Claimant voluntarily left work to secure permanent, full-time work (48-628); (iv) Claimant failed to apply for or accept suitable work or to return to customary self-employment (48-628); (v) Claimant separation was caused by a labor dispute (48-628); (vi) Claimant willfully failed to disclose amounts earned during any week with respect to which benefits are claimed or willfully failed to disclose or falsified as to any fact which would have disqualified or rendered him or her ineligible for benefits (48-663.01); (vii) Claimant is receiving unemployment benefits from another state or under federal law (48-628); (viii) Claimant is a full-time student attending school (48-628); (ix) Claimant is an illegal alien (48-628); (x) Claimant accepts work as a temporary employee and does not contact the temporary placement firm upon completion of an assignment for reassignment (48-628); (xi) Claimant is on a leave of absence. (48-628)

PURGING DISQUALIFICATION: Purging disqualification based upon merely the passage of time. (48-628)

SPECIAL TREATMENT:

Claimants in the following categories are afforded distinct treatment under the statute and thus further research may be merited for: (i) Claimants who are in approved training programs (48-628); (ii) Claimants who receive disability compensation in connection with military service (48-628); (iii) Claimants who are on vacation without pay (48-627); (iv) Claimants who are employees of educational institutions when it is between school semesters (48-628); (v) Claimants who are professional athletes when it is between sports seasons. (48-628)

Nevada

Statute:

Law: Nevada Unemployment Compensation Law

Citation: Nevada Revised Statutes Annotated, Chapter 612, Section 612.010 (N.R.S.A. § 612.010)

Benefit Calculation:

Weekly Benefit Amt.: Benefit amounts are calculated as 1/25 x the wages Claimant earned in his or her highest-paying Base Period quarter. (612.340)

Partial Employment: 75% of the wages Claimant receives from partial employment are deducted from his or her Weekly Benefit Amount. (612.350)

Reduction in Benefits: Claimant's Weekly Benefit Amount may be reduced if: (i) Claimant receives pension benefits (612.375); (ii) Claimant receives retirement pay (612.375); (iii) Claimant receives annuity payments (612.375); (iv) Claimant receives Social Security payments (612.375); (v) Claimant receives other similar periodic payments based upon previous work. (612.375)

Dependency Benefit: None.

Min./Max. Weekly: Minimum weekly benefit is $16. (612.340) Maximum weekly benefit is calculated annually as 50% of the Statewide Average Weekly Wage. (612.34) For 2001, the maximum weekly benefit was $301. (***)

Maximum Total: Claimant may receive total benefits equaling the lesser of (i) 26 x his or her Weekly Benefit Amount or (ii) 1/3 x his or her total Base Period wages. (612.355) In times of high unemployment, extended benefits may be available. (612.3774)

Benefit Eligibility:

Generally: To be eligible for unemployment compensation benefits, Claimant must: (i) File a claim for benefits (612.375); (ii) Register for work at a state unemployment office (612.375); (iii) Continue to report to a state unemployment office as required (612.375); (iv) Earn (a) during his or her entire Base Period, wages of at least 1 1/2 x the wages he or she earned in his or her highest-paying Base Period quarter OR (b) wages in each of at least three of the four Base Period quarters (612.375); (v) Be able to work and available for work (612.375); (vi) Participate in reemployment services as required. (612.375)

Subsequent Application: A Claimant who received benefits during a preceding Benefit Year must have worked and earned 3 x his or her Weekly Benefit Amount, for the prior year, subsequent to the commencement of such Benefit Year and before the commencement of his or her new Benefit Year. (612.375)

Waiting Week: None.

Disqualification: Claimant may be partially, fully or at least temporarily disqualified from receiving benefits if: (i) Claimant was discharged by most recent employer, or next to last employer, for misconduct connected with work (612.385); (ii) Claimant was discharged for the commission of assault, arson, sabotage, grand larceny, embezzlement, or wanton destruction of property in connection with work, if such act is admitted in writing, admitted under oath in a hearing, or if Claimant was convicted in a court of law for committing such act (612.383); (iii) Claimant voluntarily left most recent or next to most recent work without good cause or to seek other work (612.380); (iv) Claimant failed, without good cause, to apply for available, suitable work or to accept suitable work (612.390); (v) Claimant separation was caused by a labor dispute (612.395); (vi) Claimant made a false statement or representation, knowing it to be false, or knowingly failed to disclose a material fact in order to obtain or increase any benefit or other payment (612.445); (vii) Claimant is receiving unemployment benefits from another state or under federal law (612.400); (viii) Claimant receives wages in lieu of notice, severance pay, vacation pay, or Claimant is on a paid vacation (612.420, 612.425, 612.430); (ix) Claimant was discharged or left employment while incarcerated in a custodial or penal institution due to a transfer or release (612.376); (x) Claimant is an illegal alien. (612.448)

Purging Disqualification: A Claimant who was discharged for misconduct may be eligible for benefits only after receiving remuneration at least equal to his or her Weekly Benefit Amount in each of 15 weeks subsequent to the disqualifying separation. (612.385) A Claimant who voluntarily quit without good cause may be eligible for benefits only after receiving remuneration at least equal to his or her Weekly Benefit Amount in each of 10 weeks. (612.380) A Claimant who voluntarily quit to seek better work, may be eligible for benefits only after he or she either secures better work or receives remuneration at least equal to his or her Weekly Benefit Amount in each of 10 weeks. (612.380) A Claimant who separates while incarcerated due to transfer or release from the institution may be eligible for benefits only after receiving remuneration at least equal to his or her Weekly Benefit Amount in each of 10 weeks. (612.376) A Claimant who fails to accept or apply for suitable work, may be eligible for benefits only after receiving remuneration at least equal to his or her Weekly Benefit Amount in each of up to 15 weeks as determined by the circumstances of each case. (612.390)

Special Treatment:

Claimants in the following categories are afforded distinct treatment under the statute and thus further research may be merited for: (i) Claimants who are in approved training programs (612.375); (ii) Claimants who are ill or disabled (612.375); (iii) Claimants who come very close but do not satisfy wage requirements for benefits (612.375); (v) Claimants who are employees of educational institutions when it is between school semesters (612.434); (vi) Claimants who are professional athletes when it is between sports seasons. (612.436)

New Hampshire

Statute:

Law: New Hampshire Unemployment Compensation Law

Citation: New Hampshire Revised Statutes, Chapter 282-A, Section 282-A:1 (N.H.R.S.A § 282-A:1)

Benefit Calculation:

Weekly Benefit Amt.: Benefit amounts depend upon a schedule which considers Claimant's annual earnings. (Annual earnings of $2,800 are paired with a Weekly Benefit Amount of $32. Annual earnings of $12,900 are paired with a Weekly Benefit Amount of $136. Annual earnings of $25,500 are paired with a Weekly Benefit Amount of $246.) (282-A:25)

Partial Employment: Any wages Claimant receives from partial employment in excess of 30% of his or her Weekly Benefit Amount are deducted from his or her Weekly Benefit Amount. (282-A:14)

Reduction in Benefits: Claimant's Weekly Benefit Amount may be reduced if: (i) Claimant receives pension benefits (282-A:28); (ii) Claimant receives retirement pay (282-A:28); (iii) Claimant receives annuity payments (282-A:28); (iv) Claimant receives other similar periodic payments in connection with previous work (282-A:28); (v) Claimant receives compensation for temporary partial disability under the workers' compensation law (282-A:14); (vi) Claimant receives payments in lieu of notice of termination (282-A:14); (vii) Claimant receives sick pay (282-A:14); (viii) Claimant receives a separation allowance (282-A:14); (ix) Claimant receives accrued leave pay (282-A:14); (x) Claimant receives payments upon discharge from military service. (282-A:14)

Dependency Benefit: None

Min./Max. Weekly: Minimum weekly benefit in 2001 was $32. (282-A:25) Maximum weekly benefit for 2001 was $331. (282-A:25)

Maximum Total: Claimant may receive total benefits equaling between $832 and $5,928 in 1996 according to a schedule which considers his or her annual earnings. (282-A:27) In times of high unemployment, extended benefits may be available. (282-A:31)

Benefit Eligibility:

Generally: To be eligible for unemployment compensation benefits, Claimant must: (i) File a claim for benefits (282-A:31); (ii) Register for employment at a state unemployment office and be classified in accordance with his or her experience and abilities (282-A:31); (iii) Continue to report to a state unemployment office as required (282-A:31); (iv) Have annual earnings of at least $2,800 (282-A:25); (v) Earn wages of at least $1,200 in each of 2 quarters of his or her Base Period (282-A:25); (vi) Be ready, willing, and able to accept and perform suitable work on all shifts and during all hours for which there is a market for the services which he or she offers (282-A:31); (vii) Be available for permanent full-time work (282-A:31); (viii) Seek permanent, full-time work for which he or she is qualified (282-A:31); (ix) Expose himself or herself to the labor market to the extent commensurate with the economic conditions and the efforts of a reasonable prudent person seeking work (282-A:31); (x) Participate in reemployment services as required. (282-A:31)

Subsequent Application: N/A

Waiting Week: None.

Disqualification: Claimant may be partially, fully or at least temporarily disqualified from receiving benefits if: (i) Claimant was discharged for misconduct connected with work (282-A:32); (ii) Claimant was discharged for arson, sabotage, committing a felony or dishonesty (282-A:35); (iii) Claimant was discharged for being intoxicated or abusing controlled substances (282-A:34); (iv) Claimant voluntarily left work without good cause (282-A:32); (v) Claimant failed, without good cause, either to apply for available, suitable work or to accept suitable work when offered to him or her, or failed, without good cause, to return to his or her customary self-employment (282-A:32); (vi) Claimant left self-employment or closed his or her business (282-A:32); (vii) Claimant separation was caused by a labor dispute other than a lockout (282-A:36); (viii) Claimant willfully made a false statement or representation or knowingly failed to disclose a material fact in order to obtain benefits (282-A:163); (ix) Claimant is receiving unemployment benefits from another state or under federal law (282-A:37, 282-A:38); (x) Claimant is on disciplinary layoff status (282-A:40); (xi) Claimant is unavailable for work outside the home (282-A:39); (xii) Claimant is an illegal alien (282-A:41); (xiii) Claimant is an employee of an educational institution and it is between school semesters. (282-A:31)

Purging Disqualification: A Claimant who was discharged for misconduct, who voluntarily quit without good cause, who failed to apply for or accept suitable work, who failed to return to customary self-employment, or who left self-employment, closed a business, or refuses to return to self-employment, may be eligible for benefits only after earning remuneration of at least 120% of his or her Weekly Benefit Amount in each of 5 consecutive weeks subsequent to the disqualifying separation. (282-A:32)

Special Treatment:

Claimants in the following categories are afforded distinct treatment under the statute and thus further research may be merited for: (i) Claimants who are in approved training programs (282-A:31); (ii) Claimants who quit to seek better full-time work (282-A:32); (iii) Claimants who are unable to work during the hours of the "third shift" because they must care for children (282-A:32); (iv) Claimants who are employees of educational institutions when it is between school semesters (282-A:31); (v) Claimants who establish a Supplemental Unemployment Plan through their employers, unions, or other agents (282-A:3-a, 282-A:14); (vi) Claimants who accept employment not deemed "suitable." (282-A:32)

New Jersey

Statute:

Law: New Jersey Unemployment Compensation Law

Citation: New Jersey Statutes Annotated, Title 43, Chapter 31, Section 43:21-1 (N.J.S.A. § 43:21-1)

Benefit Calculation:

Weekly Benefit Amt.: Benefit amounts are calculated as 60% of the Claimant's average weekly wage. (43:21-3)

Partial Employment: Any wages Claimant receives from partial employment in excess of the greater of (i) 20% of his or her Weekly Benefit Amount or (ii) $5, are deducted from his or her Weekly Benefit Amount. (43:21-3)

Reduction in Benefits: Claimant's Weekly Benefit Amount may be reduced if: (i) Claimant receives pension benefits; (ii) Claimant receives retirement pay; (iii) Claimant receives annuity payments; (iv) Claimant receives other similar periodic payments based upon previous work. (43:21-5a)

Dependency Benefit: Claimant's Weekly Benefit Amount may be increased if: Claimant has one or more dependent children or an unemployed dependent spouse (increased by 7% of Claimant's Weekly Benefit Amount for the first dependent and 4% of his or her Weekly Benefit Amount for each of the next two dependents). (43:21-3)

Min./Max. Weekly: Minimum weekly benefit is $61. (43:21-3, 43:21-4) Maximum weekly benefit is calculated annually as 56 2/3% of the Statewide Average Weekly Wage. (43:21-3) For 2001, the maximum weekly benefit was $429. (***)

Maximum Total: Claimant may receive total benefits equaling the lesser of (i) 26 x his or her Weekly Benefit Amount or (ii) 3/4 of the number of Base Weeks Claimant has during his or her Base Period x his or her Weekly Benefit Amount. (43:21-3) (A Base Week is a calendar week during Claimant's Base Period in which he or she earned remuneration greater than or equal to 20 x the state hourly minimum wage. In 2001 this amounted to approximately $103 per week. (43:21-19)) In times of high unemployment, extended benefits may be available. (43:21-24.13)

Benefit Eligibility:

Generally: To be eligible for unemployment compensation benefits, Claimant must: (i) File a claim for benefits (43:21-4); (ii) Continue to report to a state unemployment office as required (43:21-4); (iii) Either (a) earn remuneration equal to at least 20 x the state minimum hourly wage in each of 20 weeks during his or her Base Period (in 2001 this amounted to approximately $103 per week), or (d) earn remuneration of at least 1,000 x the minimum hourly wage during his or her Base Period (in 2001 this amounted to approximately $5,200) (43:21-4); (iv) Be able to work and available for work (43:21-4); (v) Be actively seeking work; (vi) Participate in reemployment services as required. (43:21-4)

Subsequent Application: A Claimant who received benefits during a preceding Benefit Year must have worked for at least 4 weeks and earned 6 x his or her previous Weekly Benefit Amount subsequent to the commencement of such Benefit Year and before the commencement of his or her new Benefit Year. (43:21-4)

Waiting Week: Claimant must serve 1 Waiting Week before collecting benefits. (43:21-4)

Disqualification: Claimant may be partially, fully or at least temporarily disqualified from receiving benefits if: (i) Claimant was discharged or suspended for misconduct connected with work (43:21-5); (ii) Claimant was discharged for gross misconduct connected with work because of the commission of an act punishable as a crime (43:21-5); (iii) Claimant voluntarily left work without good cause attributable to such work (43:21-5); (iv) Claimant failed, without good cause, either to apply for available, suitable work or to accept suitable work or to return to customary self-employment when so directed (43:21-5); (v) Claimant separation was caused by a labor dispute (43:21-5); (vi) Claimant illegally received or attempted to receive benefits (43:21-5); (vii) Claimant is receiving unemployment benefits from another state or under federal law (43:21-5); (viii) Claimant receives pay in lieu of notice; (ix) Claimant receives disability benefits (43:21-4); (x) Claimant is an illegal alien. (43:21-4)

Purging Disqualification: A Claimant who was discharged for gross misconduct or who voluntarily quit without good cause, may be eligible for benefits only after being employed for 4 weeks and receiving remuneration for work subsequent to the disqualifying separation in the amount of 6 x his or her Weekly Benefit Amount. (43:21-5)

Special Treatment:

Claimants in the following categories are afforded distinct treatment under the statute and thus further research may be merited for: (i) Claimants who are in approved training programs (43:21-4); (ii) Claimants who are attending school (43:21-5); (iii) Claimants who are enrolled in school when it is between successive academic terms (43:21-5); (iv) Claimants who are on vacation without pay (43:21-4); (v) Claimants who are agricultural workers (43:21-4); (vi) Claimants who are officers of a corporation or who own an equitable or debt interest of a corporation of at least 5% (43:21-19); (vii) Claimants who are on jury duty (43:21-4); (viii) Claimants who are attending funerals of immediate family members (43:21-4); (ix) Claimants who receive lump sum payments in lieu of a pension, retirement, or annuity payments (43:21-5a); (x) Claimants who participate in self-employment assistance activities (43:21-4); (xi) Claimants who suffer from an illness or accident not compensable under the workers' compensation law resulting in total disability and rendering Claimant unable to perform work (43:21-4); (xii) Claimants who are employees of educational institutions when it is between school semesters (43:21-4); (xiii) Claimants who are professional athletes when it is between sports seasons (43:21-4); (ix) Claimants who leave work while escaping domestic violence. (43:21-5)

NEW MEXICO

STATUTE:

LAW: New Mexico Unemployment Compensation Law

CITATION: New Mexico Statutes 1978 Annotated, Chapter 51, Section 51-1-1 (N.M.S.A. § 51-1-1)

BENEFIT CALCULATION:

WEEKLY BENEFIT AMT.: Benefit amounts are calculated as 1/26 x the wages Claimant earned in his or her highest-paying Base Period quarter. (51-1-4)

PARTIAL EMPLOYMENT: Any wages Claimant receives from partial employment in excess of 1/5 x of his or her Weekly Benefit Amount are deducted from his or her Weekly Benefit Amount. (51-1-4)

REDUCTION IN BENEFITS: Claimant's Weekly Benefit Amount may be reduced if: (i) Claimant receives pension benefits (51-1-4); (ii) Claimant receives retirement benefits (51-1-4); (iii) Claimant receives annuity payments (51-1-4); (iv) Claimant receives other similar periodic payments based on previous work (51-1-4); (v) Claimant receives wages in lieu of notice (51-1-4); (vi) Claimant receives back pay for loss of employment; (vii) Claimant receives vacation pay for a period where he or she has a return-to-work date. (51-1-4)

DEPENDENCY BENEFIT: None.

MIN./MAX. WEEKLY: Minimum weekly benefit is calculated annually as 10% of the Statewide Average Weekly Wage. (51-1-4) Minimum weekly benefit in 2001 was $50. (***) Maximum weekly benefit is calculated annually as 50% of the Statewide Average Weekly Wage. (51-1-4) Maximum weekly benefit in 2001 was $267. (***)

MAXIMUM TOTAL: Claimant may receive total benefits equaling the lesser of (i) 26 x his or her Weekly Benefit Amount or (ii) 60% of his or her total Base Period wages. (51-1-4) In times of high unemployment, extended benefits may be available. (51-1-48.1)

BENEFIT ELIGIBILITY:

GENERALLY: To be eligible for unemployment compensation benefits, Claimant must: (i) File a claim for benefits (51-1-5); (ii) Register for work at a state unemployment office (51-1-5); (iii) Continue to report to a state unemployment office as required (51-1-5); (iv) Earn wages in at least two quarters of his or her Base Period. (51-1-5); (v) Be able to work and available for work (51-1-5); (vi) Be actively seeking permanent and substantially full-time work in accordance with the terms and conditions and hours common in the occupation or business in which Claimant is seeking work (51-1-5); (vii) Participate in reemployment services as required. (51-1-5)

SUBSEQUENT APPLICATION: A Claimant who received benefits during a preceding Benefit Year must have worked and earned 5 x his or her Weekly Benefit Amount subsequent to the commencement of such Benefit Year and before the commencement of his or her new Benefit Year. (51-1-5)

WAITING WEEK: Claimant must serve 1 Waiting Week before collecting benefits. (51-1- 5)

DISQUALIFICATION: Claimant may be partially, fully or at least temporarily disqualified from receiving benefits if: (i) Claimant was discharged from his or her last employer for misconduct connected with work (51-1-7); (ii) Claimant voluntarily left last employer without good cause (51-1-7); (iii) Claimant failed, without good cause, either to apply for available, suitable work or to accept suitable work when offered (51-1-7); (iv) Claimant separation was caused by a labor dispute (51-1-7); (v) Claimant is receiving unemployment benefits from another state or under federal law (51-1-7); (vi) Claimant is a full-time student (51-1-5); (vii) Claimant is an illegal alien (51-1-5); (vii) Claimant made false statements or representations knowing them to be false or knowingly failed to disclose a material fact in application for benefits. (51-1-38)

PURGING DISQUALIFICATION: A Claimant who was discharged for misconduct, who voluntarily quit without good cause, or who failed to apply for or accept suitable work, may be eligible for benefits only after receiving remuneration for work subsequent to the disqualifying separation in the amount of 5 x his or her Weekly Benefit Amount. (51-1-7)

SPECIAL TREATMENT:

Claimants in the following categories are afforded distinct treatment under the statute and thus further research may be merited for: (i) Claimants who are in approved training programs (51-1-5); (ii) Claimants who are on jury duty (51-1-5); (iii) Claimants who suffer illness or injuries compensable under state workers' compensation law or occupational disease disablement law (51-1-6); (iv) Claimants who are employed by ski area operators (51-1-5); (v) Claimants who are employees of educational institutions when it is between school semesters (51-1-5); (vi) Claimants who are professional athletes when it is between sports seasons. (51-1-5)

NEW YORK

STATUTE:

LAW: New York Unemployment Insurance Law

CITATION: McKinney's Consolidated Laws of New York Annotated, Labor Law, Section 500 (N.Y. Labor § 500)

BENEFIT CALCULATION:

WEEKLY BENEFIT AMT.: Benefit amounts are calculated as 1/26 x income Claimant earned in his or her highest-paying Base Period quarter, unless these quarterly earnings are less than or equal to $3575 in which case the weekly Benefit Amount will equal 1/25 x these quarterly earnings. (590)

PARTIAL EMPLOYMENT: Claimant's weekly Benefit Amount will be reduced by 1/4 for each day during a week that the Claimant works. In 2001, if a Claimant earns over $405 in any week, regardless of the number of days worked by the Claimant, the Claimant will not be eligible for benefits during that week. (523)

REDUCTION IN BENEFITS: Claimant's Weekly Benefit Amount may be reduced if: (i) Claimant receives pension benefits (600); (ii) Claimant receives retirement pay; (iii) Claimant receives annuity payments (600); (iv) Claimant receives other similar periodic payments based upon previous work (600); (v) Claimant receives workers compensation benefits. (591)

DEPENDENCY BENEFIT: None.

MIN./MAX. WEEKLY: Minimum weekly benefit is $40. (590) Maximum weekly benefit in 2001 was $405 and is calculated as 1/2 x the Statewide Average weekly wage. (590)

MAXIMUM TOTAL: Claimant may receive a total of 26 weeks of benefits. (590) In times of high unemployment, extended benefits may be available. (601)

BENEFIT ELIGIBILITY:

GENERALLY: To be eligible for unemployment compensation benefits, Claimant must: (i) File a claim for benefits in a week in which Claimant has at least one Effective Day (527, 596); (ii) Register as totally unemployed (596; 591); (iii) Continue to report to a state unemployment office as required (596); (iv) Earn wages during at least two calendar quarters of his or her Base Period (527); (v) Earn during his or her Base Period wages at least equaling 1 1/2 x the amount of wages he or she earned in his or her highest-paying Base Period quarter (527); (vi) Earn at least $1600 during his or her highest-paying Base Period quarter (527); (vii) Be capable of work and ready, willing and able to work (591); (viii) Participate in reemployment services as required (591); (ix) Wait until the expiration of any previously established Benefit Year.

SUBSEQUENT APPLICATION: A Claimant who received benefits during a preceding Benefit Year must have worked and earned at least 5 x his or her weekly Benefit Amount prior to the commencement of his or her new benefit year but Claimant may not use remuneration used to establish original claim to also establish the subsequent claim for benefits. (527)

WAITING WEEK: Claimant must serve a period of 4 Effective Days either wholly within the week in which he or she established his or her valid original claim or partly within such week and partly within his or her Benefit Year initiated by the claim before collecting benefits. (An Effective Day is a full day of total unemployment provided the day falls within a week in which Claimant had 4 or more days of total unemployment. Only those days of total unemployment in excess of 3 days within a week are deemed Effective Days. No Effective Day will be deemed to occur, however, in a week in which a worker is paid remuneration in excess of the maximum Weekly Benefit Amount. (523) (590)

DISQUALIFICATION: Claimant may be partially, fully or at least temporarily disqualified from receiving benefits if: (i) Claimant was discharged for misconduct connected with work (593); (ii) Claimant was discharged for committing a felony in connection with work to which he or she has signed a statement admitting that he or she has committed such act or been duly convicted (593); (iii) Claimant voluntarily left last employer without good cause (593); (iv) Claimant refused to accept work without good cause for which he or she is reasonably fitted by training or experience (593); (v) Claimant separation was caused by an industrial controversy (e.g. strike or lockout) (592); (vi) Claimant willfully made a false statement or representation to obtain benefits (594); (vii) Claimant is receiving unemployment benefits from another state or under federal law (592); (viii) Claimant is on a paid vacation or a paid holiday (591); (ix) Claimant is an illegal alien. (590)

PURGING DISQUALIFICATION: A Claimant who was discharged for misconduct, refused to accept suitable work, or who voluntarily quit, may be eligible for benefits only after working and receiving remuneration subsequent to the disqualifying separation in the amount of 5 x his or her Weekly Benefit Amount. (593)

SPECIAL TREATMENT:

Claimants in the following categories are afforded distinct treatment under the statute and thus further research may be merited for: (i) Claimants who are enrolled in approved training programs, self-employed assistance programs, or taking a course in basic education skills (599, 591); (ii) Claimants who participate in shared work programs (602); (iii) Claimants who are college students (511); (iv) Claimants who voluntarily leave work while accepting layoffs pursuant to labor-management contracts or written employer plans (593); (v) Claimants who have received workers' compensation benefits (527); (vi) Claimants who have received volunteer fire fighters' benefits (527); (vii) Claimants who are on jury duty (591); (viii) Claimants who are or are training to become self-employed (591-a); (ix) Claimants who are employees of educational institutions when it is between school semesters (590); (x) Claimants who are professional athletes when it is between sports seasons (590); (xi) Claimants who are only seeking part-time employment (596); (xii) Claimants who voluntarily choose or customarily work part-time (596); (xiii) Claimants who leave work while escaping domestic violence. (596)

NORTH CAROLINA

STATUTE:

LAW: North Carolina Employment Security Law

CITATION: General Statutes of North Carolina, Chapter 96, Section 96-1 (G.S.N.C. § 96-1)

BENEFIT CALCULATION:

WEEKLY BENEFIT AMT.: Benefit amounts are calculated as 1/26 x the wages Claimant earned in his or her highest-paying Base Period quarter. (96-12)

PARTIAL EMPLOYMENT: Any wages Claimant receives from partial employment in excess of 10% of the average weekly wage he or she received in his or her highest-paying Base Period quarter are deducted from his or her Weekly Benefit Amount. (96-12)

REDUCTION IN BENEFITS: Claimant's Weekly Benefit Amount may be reduced if: (i) Claimant receives pension benefits (96-14); (ii) Claimant receives retirement pay (96-14); (iii) Claimant receives annuity payments (96-14); (iv) Claimant receives other similar periodic payments based upon previous work under a Base Period employer (96-14); (v) Claimant receives a back pay award. (96-14)

DEPENDENCY BENEFIT: None.

MIN./MAX. WEEKLY: Minimum weekly benefit is $15. (96-12) Maximum weekly benefit is calculated annually as 66 2/3% of the Statewide Average Weekly Wage. (96-12) For 2001, the maximum weekly benefit was $396. (***)

MAXIMUM TOTAL: Claimant may receive total benefits equaling between 13 and 26 x his or her Weekly Benefit Amount. Claimant's total benefits are determined by (i) dividing his or her entire Base Period wages by the amount of wages he or she received in his or her highest-paying Base Period quarter and (ii) multiplying this amount by 8 2/3 and then (iii) multiplying this product by his or her Weekly Benefit Amount. (96-12) In times of high unemployment, extended benefits may be available. (96-12.01)

BENEFIT ELIGIBILITY:

GENERALLY: To be eligible for unemployment compensation benefits, Claimant must: (i) File a claim for benefits (96-13); (ii) Register for work at a state unemployment office (96-13); (iii) Continue to report to a state unemployment office as required (96-13); (iv) Have a Weekly Benefit Amount, as calculated above, which is greater or equal to $15 (96-12); (v) Earn during his or her entire Base Period an amount equal to at least 6 x the Statewide Average Weekly Wage (approximately $3,564 in 2001) (96-8); (vi) Earn during his or her entire Base Period wages equaling at least 1 1/2 x the amount he or she earned in his or her highest-paying Base Period quarter (96-8); (vii) Earn during his or her highest-paying Base Period quarter an amount equal to at least 1.5 x the Statewide Average Weekly Wage (approximately $594 in 2001) (96-8); (viii) Be able to work and available for work (96-13); (ix) Be actively seeking work (96-13); (x) Participate in reemployment services as required. (96-13)

SUBSEQUENT APPLICATION: A Claimant who received benefits during a preceding Benefit Year must have worked and earned at least 6 x the Statewide Average Weekly Wage subsequent to the commencement of the prior Benefit Year, and before the commencement of his or her new Benefit Year, and must have been paid wages in at least 2 quarters of his or her new Base Period. (96-12)

WAITING WEEK: Claimant must serve 1 Waiting Week before collecting benefits. (96-13)

DISQUALIFICATION: Claimant may be partially, fully or at least temporarily disqualified from receiving benefits if: (i) Claimant was discharged for misconduct connected with work (i.e. willful or wanton disregard of his or her employer's interests or a deliberate violation or disregard of the standards of behavior which an employer has a right to expect) (96-14); (ii) Claimant was discharged for substantial fault connected with work, but not rising to level of misconduct (e.g. an act or omission of Claimant over which he or she had reasonable control and which violated a reasonable requirement of his or her employment) (96-14); (iii) Claimant was discharged due to revocation, suspension or loss of license, permit, bond, certificate, or surety necessary to such employment (96-14); (iv) Claimant tests positive for a controlled substance (96-13); (v) Claimant was discharged for reporting to work significantly impaired by alcohol, illegal drugs, consuming alcohol or illegal drugs on his or her employer's premises, or being convicted in court for manufacturing, selling, or distributing controlled substances while in the employ of his or her employer (96-14); (vi) Claimant placed on bona fide disciplinary suspension (96-13); (vii) Claimant voluntarily left work without good cause (96-14); (viii) Claimant failed without good cause to apply for available, suitable work, to accept suitable work, or to return to customary self-employment (96-14); (ix) Claimant failed to attend or quit a vocational school or training course without good cause or separated from such course because of misconduct (96-14); (x) Claimant separation was caused by a labor dispute (96-14); (xi) Claimant is receiving unemployment benefits from another state or under federal law (96-14); (xii) Claimant is receiving or applying for temporary-total or permanent-total disability benefits (96-13); (xiii) Claimant received wages in lieu of notice (96-8); (xiv) Claimant received vacation pay (96-8); (xv) Claimant is receiving terminal leave pay, severance pay, separation pay, or dismissal pay (96- 8); (xvi) Claimant separated from work subsequent to his or her voluntarily selling a 5% or more ownership share of a corporation, a partnership interest in a partnership, or an ownership interest in a sole proprietorship, which employed Claimant (96-14); (xvii) Claimant is an illegal alien (96-13); (xviii) Claimant made a misrepresentation to obtain or increase benefits. (96-15)

[continued on next page]

PURGING DISQUALIFICATION: A Claimant who was discharged for misconduct, for substantial fault connected with work, for failing to accept or apply for employment, for having his or her license, permit, bond, certificate or surety expire, or a Claimant who failed to attend, discontinued, or separated from a vocational school or training course without good cause, or a Claimant who voluntarily quit, may be eligible for benefits only after returning to work for at least 5 weeks and receiving remuneration for work subsequent to the disqualifying separation in the amount of 10 x his or her Weekly Benefit Amount. (96-14)

SPECIAL TREATMENT:

Claimants in the following categories are afforded distinct treatment under the statute and thus further research may be merited for: (i) Claimants who are in approved vocational school or training programs (96-13); (ii) Claimants who are students (96-13); (iii) Claimants who quit to accompany their spouse to a new geographic location (96-14); (v) Claimants who are on vacation (96-13); (vi) Claimants who are employees of educational institutions when it is between school semesters (96-13); (vii) Claimants who are professional athletes when it is between sports seasons (96-13); (viii) Claimants who fail to return when recalled within 4 weeks of layoff (96-14); (ix) Claimants who separate from work while escaping domestic violence. (96-14)

NORTH DAKOTA

STATUTE:

LAW: North Dakota Unemployment Compensation Law

CITATION: North Dakota Century Code Annotated, Title 52, Chapter 52-01, Section 52-01-01 (N.D.C.C. § 52-01-01)

BENEFIT CALCULATION:

WEEKLY BENEFIT AMT.: Benefit amounts are calculated as 1/65 x the sum of (i) the total wages Claimant earned during his or her two highest-paying Base Period quarters and (ii) 1/2 x the wages he or she earned in his or her third highest-paying Base Period quarter. (52-06-04)

PARTIAL EMPLOYMENT: Any wages Claimant receives in partial employment in excess of 60% of his or her Weekly Benefit Amount are deducted from his or her Weekly Benefit Amount. (52-06-06)

REDUCTION IN BENEFITS: Claimant's Weekly Benefit Amount may be reduced if: (i) Claimant receives pension benefits (52-06-02); (ii) Claimant receives retirement pay (52-06-02); (iii) Claimant receives annuity payments; (iv) Claimant receives Social Security benefits (52-06-02); (v) Claimant receives other similar periodic payments based upon previous work. (52-06-02)

DEPENDENCY BENEFIT: None.

MIN./MAX. WEEKLY: Minimum weekly benefit is $43. (52-06-04) Maximum weekly benefit is calculated as 60% of the Statewide Average Weekly Wage. (52-06-04) For 2001, the maximum weekly benefit was $290. (52-06-04) The maximum weekly benefit is subject to change depending upon the balance in the state unemployment compensation trust fund. (52-06-04)

MAXIMUM TOTAL: Claimant may receive total benefits equaling between 12 and 26 x his or her Weekly Benefit Amount. (52-06-04) Such amount depends upon the ratio between his or her total Base Period wages and the wages he or she earned in his or her highest-paying Base Period quarter. (52-06-04) The higher the ratio, the more benefits he or she may receive. (52-06-04) In times of high unemployment, extended benefits may be available. (52-07.1-05)

BENEFIT ELIGIBILITY:

GENERALLY: To be eligible for unemployment compensation benefits, Claimant must: (i) File a claim for benefits (52-06-01); (ii) Register for work at a state unemployment compensation office (52-06-01); (iii) Continue to report to a state unemployment office as required (52-06-01); (iv) Earn during his or her entire Base Period, wages at least equaling 1 1/2 x the amount of wages he or she earned in his or her highest-paying Base Period quarter (52-06-04); (v) Earn wages during at least 2 calendar quarters of his or her Base Period (52-06-04); (vi) Have a Weekly Benefit Amount, as calculated above, which amounts to at least $43 (52-06-04); (vii) Be able to work and available for suitable work (52-06-01); (viii) Be actively seeking work (52-06-01); (ix) Participate in reemployment services as required. (52-06-01)

SUBSEQUENT APPLICATION: Wages earned after the end of a previous Base Period and before the filing of a valid new claim cannot be used for benefit purposes in a subsequent Benefit Year until Claimant earns remuneration greater than or equal to 10 x his or her Weekly Benefit Amount. (52-06-04)

WAITING WEEK: Claimant must serve 1 Waiting Week before collecting benefits. (52-06-01)

DISQUALIFICATION: Claimant may be partially, fully or at least temporarily disqualified from receiving benefits if: (i) Claimant was discharged or suspended from most recent work for misconduct connected with work or gross misconduct (52-06-02); (ii) Claimant is on disciplinary suspension (52-06-02); (iii) Claimant voluntarily left his or her most recent employment without good cause attributable to his or her employer (52-06-02); (iv) Claimant failed to apply for or accept suitable employment or to return to his or her customary self-employment (52-06-02); (v) Claimant separation was caused by a labor dispute (52-06-02); (vi) Claimant made a false statement for the purposes of obtaining benefits to which he or she was not lawfully entitled (52-06-02); (vii) Claimant is receiving unemployment benefits from another state or under federal law (52-06-02); (viii) Claimant is an illegal alien (52-06-02); (ix) Claimant previously placed by a temporary help firm who fails to notify firm when assignment complete. (52-06-02)

PURGING DISQUALIFICATION: A Claimant who was discharged for misconduct, who failed to accept or apply for suitable work, or who failed to return to suitable self-employment, may be eligible for benefits only after receiving remuneration for work subsequent to the disqualifying separation in the amount of 10 x his or her Weekly Benefit Amount. (52-06-02) A Claimant who voluntarily left work, may be eligible for benefits only after receiving remuneration for work subsequent to the disqualifying separation in the amount of 8 x his or her Weekly Benefit Amount. (52-06-02)

SPECIAL TREATMENT:

Claimants in the following categories are afforded distinct treatment under the statute and thus further research may be merited for: (i) Claimants who are in approved training programs (52-06-02); (ii) Claimants who have ownership interests or who have relatives who have ownership interests in partnerships or corporations which employ them (52-06-04); (iii) Claimants who are attending school (52-06-02); (iv) Claimants who are ill or disabled (52-06-01); (v) Claimants who are employees of educational institutions when it is between school semesters (52-06-02); (vi) Claimants who are professional athletes when it is between sports seasons (52-06-02); (vii) Claimants who voluntarily quit employment to return to work for a prior employer who previously placed him or her on layoff status (52-06-02); (viii) Claimants who are participating in shared-work programs. (52-06.1-03)

OHIO

STATUTE:

LAW: Ohio Unemployment Compensation Act

CITATION: Baldwin's Ohio Revised Code Annotated, Title 41, Section 4141.01 (O.R.C.A. § 4141.01)

BENEFIT CALCULATION:

WEEKLY BENEFIT AMT.: Benefit amount calculated as 50% of Claimant's average weekly wage. (4141.30)

PARTIAL EMPLOYMENT: Any wages Claimant receives from partial employment in excess of 20% of his or her Weekly Benefit Amount are deducted from his or her Weekly Benefit Amount. (4141.30)

REDUCTION IN BENEFITS: Claimant's Weekly Benefit Amount may be reduced if: (i) Claimant receives pension benefits (4141.31); (ii) Claimant receives retirement pay (4141.31); (iii) Claimant receives annuity payments (4141.31); (iv) Claimant receives other periodic payments based upon previous work (4141.31); (v) Claimant receives termination or other separation pay (4141.31); (vi) Claimant receives vacation pay (4141.31); (vii) Claimant receives payments in lieu of notice (4141.31); (viii) Claimant receives disability or other payments under workers' compensation law. (4141.31)

DEPENDENCY BENEFIT: Claimant's maximum Weekly Benefit Amount may be increased if he or she has 1, 2, or 3 or more dependent children or a dependent spouse. (4141.30)

MIN./MAX. WEEKLY: The minimum Weekly Benefit Amount is $68. (***) Maximum weekly benefits are calculated annually and are based upon increases in the Statewide Average Weekly Wage and whether or not Claimant has dependents. (4141.30) The maximum Weekly Benefit Amount for a Claimant who has no dependents can be no more than 50% of the Statewide Average Weekly Wage, the maximum Weekly Benefit Amount for a Claimant with 1 or two dependents can be no more than 60% of the Statewide Average Weekly Wage, and for a Claimant with 3 or more dependents, the maximum Weekly Benefit Amount can be no more than 66 2/3% of the Statewide Average Weekly Wage. (4141.30) For 2001, the maximum Weekly Benefit Amount for a Claimant with no dependents was $303, for a Claimant with 1 or 2 dependents was $367, and for a Claimant who has 3 or more dependents the maximum weekly benefit was $407. (***)

MAXIMUM TOTAL: Claimant may receive total benefits equaling the lesser of (i) 26 x his or her Weekly Benefit Amount or (ii) an amount equal to the sum of (a) 20 x his or her Weekly Benefit Amount for the 1st 20 Base Period weeks in which he or she worked and (b) 1 x his or her Weekly Benefit Amount for each additional week in which Claimant worked beyond the 1st 20 qualifying weeks in his or her Base Period. (4141.30) In times of high unemployment, extended benefits may be available. (4141.301)

BENEFIT ELIGIBILITY:

GENERALLY: To be eligible for unemployment compensation benefits, Claimant must: (i) File a claim for benefits (4141.29); (ii) Register at a state unemployment office (4141.29); (iii) Continue to report to a state unemployment office as required (4141.29); (iv) Work for 20 weeks in his or her Base Period and earn remuneration in each of such weeks greater than or equal to 27.5% of the Statewide Average Weekly Wage (4141.29; 4101.01); (v) Be able to work and available for suitable work (4141.29); (vi) Be unable to obtain suitable work (4141.29); (vii) Be actively seeking suitable work either in a locality where Claimant earned Base Period wages or in a locality where work suitable for Claimant is normally performed (4141.29); (viii) Participate in reemployment services as required. (4141.29)

SUBSEQUENT APPLICATION: A Claimant who received benefits during a preceding Benefit Year must have worked for at least 6 weeks and earned in employment an amount equal to at least 3 x his or her average weekly wage subsequent to the commencement of such Benefit Year and before the commencement of his or her new Benefit Year. (4141.01)

WAITING WEEK: Claimant must serve 1 Waiting Week before collecting benefits. (4141.29)

DISQUALIFICATION: Claimant may be partially, fully or at least temporarily disqualified from receiving benefits if: (i) Claimant was discharged for just cause in connection with work (4141.29); (ii) Claimant is on disciplinary layoff for misconduct connected with work (4141.29); (iii) Claimant separation was due to dishonesty in connection with his or her most recent or any Base Period employment (4141.29); (iv) Claimant separation was due to commitment to correctional institution (4141.29); (v) Claimant voluntarily left work without just cause (4141.29); (vi) Claimant voluntarily left work to fulfill domestic obligations (4141.29); (vii) Claimant refused without good cause to accept suitable work (4141.29); (viii) Claimant refused to investigate a referral to suitable work (4141.29); (ix) Claimant separation was caused by a labor dispute other than a lockout (4141.29); (x) Claimant knowingly made a false statement or representation or knowingly failed to report any material fact with the object of obtaining benefits to which he or she is not entitled (4141.29); (xi) Claimant is receiving unemployment benefits from another state or under federal law (4141.31); (xii) Claimant is an illegal alien (4141.29); (xiii) Claimant failed to contact temporary help firm to inquire about another work assignment at the conclusion of the former assignment. (4141.29)

[continued on next page]

PURGING DISQUALIFICATION: N/A

SPECIAL TREATMENT:

Claimants in the following categories are afforded distinct treatment under the statute and thus further research may be merited for: (i) Claimants who are in vocational training programs (4141.29); (ii) Claimants who are attending school (4141.29); (iii) Claimants who quit to accept other employment or recall to a former employer (4141.29); (iv) Claimants who separate from work due to lack of work pursuant to a labor-management contract or employer policy which permits such separation (4141.29); (v) Claimants who were former members of the Armed Forces and receive allowances for their prior service (4141.311); (vi) Claimants who receive payments due to National Guard or other Armed Forces reserve affiliations (4141.31); (vii) Claimants who were formerly members of the Armed Forces and subsequently receive disability pensions (4141.312); (viii) Claimants who separate from employment to join the Armed Forces of the United States (4141.29); (ix) Claimants who have seasonal employment (4141.33); (x) Claimants who are employees of educational institutions when it is between school semesters (4141.29); (xi) Claimants who are professional athletes when it is between sports seasons. (4141.33)

OKLAHOMA

STATUTE:

LAW: Oklahoma Employment Security Act

CITATION: Oklahoma Statutes Annotated, Title 40, Section 1-101 (40 O.S.A. § 1- 101)

BENEFIT CALCULATION:

WEEKLY BENEFIT AMT.: Benefit amounts are calculated as 1/23 x the wages Claimant earned in his or her highest-paying Base Period quarter. (2-104)

PARTIAL EMPLOYMENT: Any wages Claimant receives from partial employment in excess of $100 a week are deducted from his or her Weekly Benefit Amount. (2-105)

REDUCTION IN BENEFITS: Claimant's Weekly Benefit Amount may be reduced if: (i) Claimant receives pension benefits (2-411); (ii) Claimant receives retirement pay (2-411); (iii) Claimant receives annuity payments (2-411); (iv) Claimant receives other similar periodic payments based upon previous work. (2-411)

DEPENDENCY BENEFIT: None.

MIN./MAX. WEEKLY: Minimum weekly benefit is $16. (2-104) Maximum weekly benefit is calculated annually as the greater of (i) $197 or (ii) between 50% and 60% of the Statewide Average Weekly Wage depending upon the current balance in the state unemployment compensation fund. (2-104) For 1996, the maximum weekly benefit was $247. (***)

MAXIMUM TOTAL: Claimant may receive total benefits equaling the lesser of (i) 26 x his or her Weekly Benefit Amount; (ii) Between 20% of the Statewide Average Annual Wage for the second preceding calendar quarter (depending on the balance of the unemployment compensation fund); (iii) Between 40% and 50% of the Claimant's wages earned while working in covered employment during his or her Base Period (depending on the conditional factor in place during the calendar year in which the individual files for benefits). (12-106)

BENEFIT ELIGIBILITY:

GENERALLY: To be eligible for unemployment compensation benefits, Claimant must: (i) Personally appear at employment office and file a written claim for benefits including information necessary for the commission to make a determination of eligibility (2-203); (ii) Register for work at a state unemployment office (2-204); (iii) Continue to report to a state unemployment office as required (2-204); (iv) Earn during his or her entire Base Period wages of at least $1,500 (2-207); (v) Earn during his or her entire Base Period wages at least equal to 1 1/2 x the amount of wages he or she earned in his or her highest-paying Base Period quarter (2-207); (vi) Be able to perform work duties in keeping with his or her education, training, and experience (2-205A); (vii) Be available to seek and accept work at any time and not be engaged in any activity that would normally restrict seeking or accepting such work (2-205); (viii) Participate in reemployment services as required. (2-204)

SUBSEQUENT APPLICATION: A Claimant who received benefits during a preceding Benefit Year must have worked and earned 10 x his or her Weekly Benefit Amount subsequent to the commencement of such Benefit Year and before the commencement of his or her new Benefit Year. (2-109)

WAITING WEEK: Claimant must serve 1 Waiting Week before collecting benefits. (2-206)

DISQUALIFICATION: Claimant may be partially, fully or at least temporarily disqualified from receiving benefits if: (i) Claimant was discharged for misconduct connected with his or her last work (2-406); (ii) Claimant voluntarily left his or her last work without good cause connected with work (2-404); (iii) Claimant failed to diligently search for suitable work at a pay rate generally available in the area and in keeping with Claimant's prior experience, education, and training (2-417); (iv) Claimant failed to apply for work with employers who could reasonably be expected to have work available within that geographic area (2-417); (v) Claimant failed to present himself or herself as an applicant for employment in a manner designed to encourage favorable employment consideration (2-417); (vi) Claimant failed to accept an offer of work from an employer or former employer (2-418); (vii) Claimant failed to apply for or accept work when so directed (2-418); (viii) Claimant failed to accept employment pursuant to a hiring hall agreement (2-418); (ix) Claimant separation was caused by a labor dispute other than a lockout (2-410); (x) Claimant made a false statement or representation or failed to disclose a material fact in order to obtain benefits (2-402); (xi) Claimant is receiving unemployment benefits from another state or under federal law (2-412); (xii) Claimant is an inmate in a correctional facility (2-413); (xiii) Claimant is an illegal alien. (2-208)

PURGING DISQUALIFICATION: A Claimant who was discharged for misconduct, who voluntarily quit, who failed to accept an offer of suitable work from an employer, including a former employer, or when so directed to accept an offer, diligently search for suitable employment, present himself or herself at interviews in a manner to encourage favorable employment decisions, apply for employment, or accept employment pursuant to a hiring hall agreement, may be eligible for benefits only after receiving remuneration for work subsequent to the disqualifying separation in the amount of 10 x his or her Weekly Benefit Amount. (2-404, 2-406, 2-417, 2-418)

SPECIAL TREATMENT:

Claimants in the following categories are afforded distinct treatment under the statute and thus further research may be merited for: (i) Claimants who are in approved training programs (2-108); (ii) Claimants who receive sick leave pay (1-218); (iii) Claimants who receive pay for accident disability (1-218); (iv) Claimants who are working for temporary help firms (2-404A); (v) Claimants who are employees of educational institutions when it is between school semesters (2-209); (vi) Claimants who are professional athletes when it is between sports seasons (2-415); (vi) Women who are pregnant. (2-414)

OREGON

STATUTE:

LAW: Oregon Employment Department Law

CITATION: Oregon Revised Statutes, Annotated, Chapter 657, Section 657.005 (O.R.S. § 657.005)

BENEFIT CALCULATION:

WEEKLY BENEFIT AMT.: Benefit amounts are calculated as 1.25% of the wages Claimant received in his or her entire Base Period. (657.150)

PARTIAL EMPLOYMENT: Any wages Claimant receives from partial employment in excess of the greater of (i) 10 x the minimum hourly wage or (ii) 1/3 x his or her Weekly Benefit Amount are deducted from his or her Weekly Benefit Amount. (657.150)

REDUCTION IN BENEFITS: Claimant's Weekly Benefit Amount may be reduced if: (i) Claimant receives pension benefits (657.205); (ii) Claimant receives retirement pay (657.205); (iii) Claimant receives annuity payments (657.205); (iv) Claimant receives other similar periodic payments based upon previous work (657.205); (v) Claimant receives vacation pay (657.150); (vi) Claimant receives holiday pay. (657.150)

DEPENDENCY BENEFIT: None.

MIN./MAX. WEEKLY: The minimum weekly benefit is calculated annually as 15% of the Statewide Average Weekly Wage. (657.150) Minimum weekly benefit in 2001 was $93. (***) Maximum weekly benefit is calculated annually as 64% of the Statewide Average Weekly Wage. (657.150) For 2001, the maximum weekly benefit was $400. (***)

MAXIMUM TOTAL: Claimant may receive total benefits equaling the lesser of (i) 26 x his or her Weekly Benefit Amount or (ii) 1/3 x his or her total Base Period wages. (657.150) In times of high unemployment, extended benefits may be available. (657.325)

BENEFIT ELIGIBILITY:

GENERALLY: To be eligible for unemployment compensation benefits, Claimant must: (i) File a claim for benefits (657.155); (ii) Register for work at a state unemployment office (657.155); (iii) Continue to report to a state unemployment office as required (657.155); (iv) Work for at least 18 weeks during his or her entire Base Period and earn at least $1,000 during his or her entire Base Period (657.150); (v) Be able to work and available for work (657.155); (vi) Be actively seeking and unable to obtain work (657.155); (vii) Participate in reemployment services as required. (657.156)

SUBSEQUENT APPLICATION: A Claimant who received benefits during a preceding Benefit Year must have worked and earned 6 x his or her Weekly Benefit Amount subsequent to the commencement of such Benefit Year and before the commencement of his or her new Benefit Year. (657.150)

WAITING WEEK: Claimant must serve 1 Waiting Week before collecting benefits. (657.155)

DISQUALIFICATION: Claimant may be partially, fully or at least temporarily disqualified from receiving benefits if: (i) Claimant was discharged or suspended for misconduct connected with work (657.176); (ii) Claimant committed a felony or theft in connection with work (657.176); (iii) Claimant voluntarily left work without good cause (657.176); (iv) Claimant voluntarily left work without good cause prior to the known date of a discharge for other than misconduct or a good cause for voluntarily leaving work (657.176); (v) Claimant failed to apply for available, suitable work or accept suitable work without good cause (657.176); (vi) Claimant separation was caused by a labor dispute except a lockout or a separation motivated by an employer's breach of a collective bargaining agreement by unilaterally modifying employee wages (657.176, 657.200)); (vii) Claimant willfully made a false statement or misrepresentation, or willfully failed to report a material fact in order to obtain benefits (657.215); (viii) Claimant is receiving unemployment benefits from another state or under federal law (657.210); (ix) Claimant is an illegal alien (657.184); (x) Claimant discharged or suspended for being absent or tardy twice because of the unlawful use of controlled substances or as a result of the inappropriate consumption of alcohol. (657.176)

PURGING DISQUALIFICATION: A Claimant who was discharged or suspended for misconduct or for being absent or tardy twice for the inappropriate or unlawful use of alcohol or controlled substances, failed to accept or apply for suitable work, or who voluntarily quit, may be eligible for benefits only after receiving remuneration for work subsequent to the disqualifying separation in the amount of 4 x his or her Weekly Benefit Amount subsequent to the week in which the disqualifying act occurred. (657.176)

SPECIAL TREATMENT:

Claimants in the following categories are afforded distinct treatment under the statute and thus further research may be merited for: (i) Claimants who are in approved training programs or enrolled in programs to obtain basic educational skills (657.155); (ii) Claimants who participate in shared work plans (657.380); (iii) Claimants who are dislocated workers (657.340); (iv) Claimants who leave, during the major part of a week, the general geographic area in which they are or were employed (657.155); (v) Claimants who receive payments for service in a reserve component of the Armed Forces of the United States (657.150); (vi) Claimants who are employees of educational institutions when it is between school semesters (657.221); (vii) Claimants who are professional athletes when it is between sports seasons (657.186); (viii) Claimants who choose to become self-employed (657.158); (ix) Claimants who are discharged for the use of alcohol or other controlled substances. (657.176)

PENNSYLVANIA

STATUTE:

LAW: Pennsylvania Unemployment Compensation Law

CITATION: Purdon's Pennsylvania Statutes Annotated, Title 43, Section 751 (43 P.S § 751)

BENEFIT CALCULATION:

WEEKLY BENEFIT AMT.: Benefit amounts are based upon a schedule contained in the law which considers the amount of wages Claimant earned in his or her highest-paying Base Period quarter and the total wages he or she received throughout his or her entire Base Period. (804) Weekly Benefit Amount, however, may not drop below 50% of Claimant's full time weekly wage. (804)

PARTIAL EMPLOYMENT: Any wages Claimant receives from partial employment in excess of the greater of (i) 40% of his or her Weekly Benefit Amount or (ii) $6, are deducted from his or her Weekly Benefit Amount. (804)

REDUCTION IN BENEFITS: Claimant's Weekly Benefit Amount may be reduced if: (i) Claimant receives pension benefits (804); (ii) Claimant receives retirement pay (804); (iii) Claimant receives Social Security benefits (804); (iv) Claimant receives annuity payments (804); (v) Claimant receives other similar payments under a plan maintained or contributed by a Base Period or chargeable employer (804); (vi) Claimant receives vacation pay (804); (vii) State unemployment compensation trust fund dips below a specified amount. (804)

DEPENDENCY BENEFIT: Claimant's Weekly Benefit Amount may be increased if: Claimant has either a dependent child or dependent spouse ($5 for the first dependent, $3 for one additional dependent). (804)

MIN./MAX. WEEKLY: Minimum weekly benefit is $35. (804) Maximum weekly benefit is re-calculated each year as 66 2/3% of the Statewide Average Weekly Wage. (804) For 2001, the maximum weekly benefit was $430. (***)

MAXIMUM TOTAL: Claimant who has 18 or more Credit Weeks (i.e. weeks in Claimant's Base Period in which he or she received at least $50 in remuneration) may receive total benefits equaling 26 x his or her Weekly Benefit Amount. (804) Claimant who has 16 or 17 Credit Weeks may receive total benefits equaling 16 x his or her Weekly Benefit Amount. (804) In times of high unemployment, extended benefits may be available. (813)

BENEFIT ELIGIBILITY:

GENERALLY: To be eligible for unemployment compensation benefits, Claimant must: (i) File a claim for compensation and valid application for benefits (801); (ii) Register for work at a state unemployment office (801); (iii) Continue to report to a state unemployment office as required (801); (iv) Earn $1,320 in Base Period wages, with $800 of this amount earned during his or her highest-paying Base Period quarter wages and at least 20% of this amount received in other quarters besides the highest-paying Base Period quarter (801, 804); (v) Be able to work and available for suitable work (801); (vi) Have 16 or more Credit Weeks during his or her Base Period (804); (vii) Participate in reemployment services as required. (802)

SUBSEQUENT APPLICATION: A Claimant who received benefits during a preceding Benefit Year must have worked and earned 6 x his or her Weekly Benefit Amount, as calculated for the prior Benefit Year, subsequent to the commencement of such Benefit Year and before the commencement of his or her new Benefit Year. (753)

WAITING WEEK: Claimant must serve 1 Waiting Week before collecting benefits. (801)

DISQUALIFICATION: Claimant may be partially, fully or at least temporarily disqualified from receiving benefits if: (i) Claimant was discharged or suspended for willful misconduct connected with work (802); (ii) Claimant voluntarily left work without a necessitous or compelling reason (802); (iii) Claimant failed, without good cause, either to apply for suitable work or to accept suitable work when offered to him or her (802); (iv) Claimant separation was caused by a labor dispute other than a lockout (802); (v) Claimant is self-employed (802); (vi) Claimant failed to accept an offer of suitable full-time work in order to pursue seasonal or part-time employment (802); (vii) Claimant is receiving unemployment benefits from another state or under federal law (802); (viii) Claimant is an illegal alien (802.3); (ix) Claimant makes a false statement knowing it to be false or knowingly fails to disclose a material fact to obtain or increase benefits (801); (x) Claimant is incarcerated after a conviction. (802.6)

PURGING DISQUALIFICATION: A Claimant who was fired for willful misconduct, voluntarily quit without a necessitous and compelling reason, or was engaged in self-employment, may be eligible for benefits only after receiving remuneration for work subsequent to the disqualifying separation in the amount of 6 x his or her Weekly Benefit Amount. (801)

SPECIAL TREATMENT:

Claimants in the following categories are afforded distinct treatment under the statute and thus further research may be merited for: (i) Claimants who voluntarily leave work while accepting layoffs pursuant to labor-management contracts or established employer plans, programs, or policies (801); (ii) Claimants who are in approved training programs (801); (iii) Claimants who work for employers who freeze or can fruits or vegetables (802.5); (iv) Claimants who leave work due to a disability (802); (v) Claimants who are or formerly were officers of a corporation (802.4); (vi) Claimants who are employees of educational institutions when it is between school semesters (802.1); (vii) Claimants who are professional athletes when it is between sports seasons (802.4); (viii) Claimant's participating in approved self-employment training programs. (920.4)

PUERTO RICO

STATUTE:

LAW: Puerto Rico Employment Security Act

CITATION: Laws of Puerto Rico Annotated, Title 29, Section 701 (L.P.R.A. § 701)

BENEFIT CALCULATION:

WEEKLY BENEFIT AMT.: Weekly Benefit Amounts are contained in a schedule in the law which considers both Claimant's total Base Period earnings and the amount of wages Claimant earned in his or her highest-paying Base Period quarter. (Usually this amounts to between 1/11 and 1/26 x the wages Claimant received in his or her highest-paying Base Period quarter.) (703)

PARTIAL EMPLOYMENT: Any wages Claimant receives from partial employment in excess of an amount equal to his or her Weekly Benefit Amount are deducted from his or her Weekly Benefit Amount. (703)

REDUCTION IN BENEFITS: Claimant's Weekly Benefit Amount may be reduced if: (i) Claimant receives pension benefits; (ii) Claimant receives Social Security payments. (704)

DEPENDENCY BENEFIT: None.

MIN./MAX. WEEKLY: Minimum weekly benefit is $7. (703, ***) Maximum weekly benefit is calculated annually as 50% of the Statewide Average Weekly Wage. (703) For 2001, the maximum weekly benefit was $133. (***)

MAXIMUM TOTAL: Claimant may receive total benefits equaling 26 x his or her Weekly Benefit Amount. (703) In times of high unemployment, extended benefits may be available. (716a)

BENEFIT ELIGIBILITY:

GENERALLY: To be eligible for unemployment compensation benefits, Claimant must: (i) File a notice of unemployment (704); (ii) File a claim for benefits (704); (iii) Register for work at a state unemployment office (704); (iv) Earn $280 during his or her entire Base Period (703,***); (v) Earn at least $75 in at least one quarter of his or her Base Period (703,***); (vi) Earn wages during at least 2 quarters of his or her Base Period (703); (vii) Be able to work and available for suitable work (704); (viii) File notice of unemployment and register for work. (704)

SUBSEQUENT APPLICATION: A Claimant who received benefits during a preceding Benefit Year must have worked and earned the greater of (i) $50 or (ii) 3 x his or her Weekly Benefit Amount, as calculated for the preceding Benefit Year, subsequent to the commencement of such Benefit Year and before the commencement of his or her new Benefit Year. (703)

WAITING WEEK: Claimant must serve 1 Waiting Week before collecting benefits. (704)

DISQUALIFICATION: Claimant may be partially, fully or at least temporarily disqualified from receiving benefits if: (i) Claimant was discharged or suspended for misconduct connected with work (704); (ii) Claimant voluntarily left suitable work without good cause (704); (iii) Claimant failed, without good cause, either to apply for available, suitable work, or accept suitable work (704); (iv) Claimant separation was caused by a labor dispute (704); (v) Claimant made a false statement or representation of a material fact knowing it to be false or knowingly concealed a material fact for the purpose of increasing benefits (704); (vi) Claimant is receiving unemployment benefits from another state or under federal law (704); (vii) Claimant is an illegal alien. (704)

PURGING DISQUALIFICATION: A Claimant who was discharged or suspended for misconduct, failed to accept or apply for suitable work, or who voluntarily quit, may be eligible for benefits only after working for at least 4 weeks and receiving remuneration for work subsequent to the disqualifying separation in the amount of 10 x his or her Weekly Benefit Amount. (704)

SPECIAL TREATMENT:

Claimants in the following categories are afforded distinct treatment under the statute and thus further research may be merited for: (i) Claimants who are in approved training programs (704); (ii) Claimants who are agricultural workers (703); (iii) Claimants who receive payments for accrued vacation or sick leave (704); (iv) Claimants who are employees of educational institutions when it is between school semesters (704); (v) Claimants who are professional athletes when it is between sports seasons. (704)

RHODE ISLAND

STATUTE:

LAW: Rhode Island Employment Security Act

CITATION: General Laws of Rhode Island, Section 28-42-1 (G.L.R.I. § 28-42-1)

BENEFIT CALCULATION:

WEEKLY BENEFIT AMT.: Benefit amounts are calculated as 4.62% of the wages Claimant earned in his or her highest-paying Base Period quarter. (28-44-6)

PARTIAL EMPLOYMENT: Any wages Claimant earns from partial employment in excess of 1/5 x his or her Weekly Benefit Amount are deducted from his or her Weekly Benefit Amount. (28-42-3, 28-44-7) Claimant is ineligible for partial benefits if he or she earns remuneration in a week which is equal to or exceeds his or her Weekly Benefit Amount. (28-44-7)

REDUCTION IN BENEFITS: Claimant's Weekly Benefit Amount may be reduced if: (i) Claimant receives pension benefits (28-44-19.1); (ii) Claimant receives retirement pay (28-44-19.1); (iii) Claimant receives annuity payments (28-44-19.1); (iv) Claimant receives other similar periodic payments based upon previous work (28-44-19.1); (v) Claimant receives temporary partial disability payments under a workers' compensation law (28-44-19); (vi) Claimant is receiving unemployment benefits from another state or under federal law. (28-44-19)

DEPENDENCY BENEFIT: Claimant's Weekly Benefit Amount may be increased if Claimant has dependent children who are either under the age of 18 or incapable of earning wages because of a mental or physical incapacity (increased by the greater of (i) $10 or (ii) 5% of his or her Weekly Benefit Amount for up to 5 dependents). (28-44-6)

MIN./MAX. WEEKLY: Minimum weekly benefit is $56. (28-44-6, 28-44-11) Maximum weekly benefit is calculated as 67% of the Statewide Average Weekly Wage. (28-44-6) For 2001, the maximum weekly benefit was $415. (***)

MAXIMUM TOTAL: Claimant may receive total benefits, exclusive of dependency allowances, equaling the lesser of (i) 26 x his or her Weekly Benefit Amount or (ii) 36% of his or her total Base Period wages. (28-44-9) In times of high unemployment, extended benefits may be available. (28-44-62)

BENEFIT ELIGIBILITY:

GENERALLY: To be eligible for unemployment compensation benefits, Claimant must: (i) File a claim for benefits (28-44-12); (ii) Register for work at a state unemployment office (28-44-12); (iii) Report whenever duly called for work through a state unemployment office (28-44-12); (iv) Make an active, independent search for suitable work (28-44-12); (v) Earn (a) during at least one quarter of his or her Base Period, wages at least equaling 200 x the minimum hourly wage, and during his or her entire Base Period wages of at least 1 1/2 x the amount of wages he or she earned in his or her highest-paying Base Period quarter, and during his or her entire Base Period wages of at least 400 x the minimum hourly wage, OR (b) during his or her entire Base Period wages of at least 1200 x the minimum hourly wage (28-44-11); (vi) Be physically able to work and available for work (28-44-12); (vii) Participate in reemployment services as required. (28-44-12)

SUBSEQUENT APPLICATION: A Claimant who received benefits during a preceding Benefit Year must have worked and earned 80 x the minimum hourly wage subsequent to the commencement of such Benefit Year and before the commencement of his or her new Benefit Year. (28-44-11)

WAITING WEEK: Claimant must serve 7 consecutive day waiting period before collecting benefits. (28-44-14)

DISQUALIFICATION: Claimant may be partially, fully or at least temporarily disqualified from receiving benefits if: (i) Claimant was discharged for proved misconduct connected with work (28-44-18); (ii) Claimant voluntarily left work without good cause (28-44-17); (iii) Claimant failed to apply for or accept suitable work (28-44-20); (iv) Claimant separation was caused by a labor dispute other than a lockout (28-44-16); (v) Claimant was convicted in a court of competent jurisdiction of knowingly or fraudulently misrepresenting a material fact, with intent thereby to defraud the employment security fund (28-44-24); (vi) Claimant is on paid vacation (28-44-21); (vii) Claimant is an illegal alien. (28-44-67)

PURGING DISQUALIFICATION: A Claimant who was discharged for proved misconduct, failed to apply for or accept suitable work, or who voluntarily quit, may be eligible for benefits only after working for at least 8 weeks and receiving remuneration in each such week equal to at least 20 x the minimum hourly wage. (28-44-17, 28-44-18, 28-44-20)

SPECIAL TREATMENT:

Claimants in the following categories are afforded distinct treatment under the statute and thus further research may be merited for: (i) Claimants who are in approved basic education or vocational training programs (28-44-60); (ii) Claimants who receive holiday pay (28-44-61); (iii) Claimants who receive worksharing benefits (28-44-69); (iv) Claimants who are discharged under circumstances prompting the National Labor Relations Board or the state labor relations board to issue a complaint against his or her employer for unfair labor practices (28-44-18); (v) Claimants who retire (28-44-18); (vi) Claimants who enter entrepreneurial training assistance programs (28-44-70); (vii) Claimants who are employees of educational institutions when it is between school semesters (28-44-68); (viii) Claimants who are professional athletes when it is between sports seasons (28-44-66); (ix) Claimants who leave work while escaping from domestic abuse. (28-44-17.1)

SOUTH CAROLINA

STATUTE:

LAW: South Carolina Employment Security Law

CITATION: Code of Laws of South Carolina, Title 41, Section 41-27-10 (C.L.S.C. § 41-27-10)

BENEFIT CALCULATION:

WEEKLY BENEFIT AMT.: Benefit amounts are calculated as 50% of Claimant's average weekly wage. (41-35-40)

PARTIAL EMPLOYMENT: Any wages Claimant earns from partial employment in excess of 1/4 x his or her Weekly Benefit Amount are deducted from his or her Weekly Benefit Amount. (41-35-60)

REDUCTION IN BENEFITS: Claimant's Weekly Benefit Amount may be reduced if: (i) Claimant receives pension benefits (41-27-370); (ii) Claimant receives retirement pay (41-27-370); (iii) Claimant receives annuity payments (41-27-370); (iv) Claimant receives other similar periodic payments based upon previous work (41-27-370); (v) Claimant receives pay for service as a juror. (41-35-115)

DEPENDENCY BENEFIT: None.

MIN./MAX. WEEKLY: Minimum weekly benefit is $20. (41-35-40) Maximum weekly benefit is calculated annually as 66 2/3% of the Statewide Average Weekly Wage. (41-35-40) For 2001, the maximum weekly benefit was $268. (***)

MAXIMUM TOTAL: Claimant may receive total benefits equaling the lesser of (i) 26 x his or her Weekly Benefit Amount or (ii) 1/3 x his or her total Base Period wages. (41-35-50) In times of high unemployment, extended benefits may be available. (41-35-420)

BENEFIT ELIGIBILITY:

GENERALLY: To be eligible for unemployment compensation benefits, Claimant must: (i) File a claim for benefits (41-35-110); (ii) Register for work at a state unemployment office (41-35-110); (iii) Continue to report to a state unemployment office as required (41-35-110); (iv) Earn at least $540 during his or her highest-paying Base Period quarter (41-27-310); (v) Earn at least $900 during his or her entire Base Period (41-27-310); (vi) Earn during his or her entire Base Period wages at least equal to 1 1/2 x the wages he or she earned in his or her highest-paying Base Period quarter (41-27-310); (vii) Be able to work and available for work at his or her usual trade, occupation, or business or in such other trade, occupation, or business as his or her prior training or experience shows him or her to be fitted or qualified (41-35-110); (viii) Be available for work either at a locality in which he or she earned wages during his or her Benefit Period, or if he or she moved, then at an alternative locality where he or she can reasonably expect to find work (41-35-110); (ix) Be actively seeking work (41-35-110); (x) Participate in reemployment services as required. (41-35-110)

SUBSEQUENT APPLICATION: A Claimant who received benefits during a preceding Benefit Year must have worked and earned, in the employ of a single employer, 8 x his or her Weekly Benefit Amount, as calculated for the preceding Benefit Year, subsequent to the commencement of such Benefit Year and before the commencement of his or her new Benefit Year. (41-35-50)

WAITING WEEK: Claimant must serve 1 Waiting Week before collecting benefits. (41-35- 110)

DISQUALIFICATION: Claimant may be partially, fully or at least temporarily disqualified from receiving benefits if: (i) Claimant was discharged for cause connected with his or her most recent work (41-35-120); (ii) Claimant voluntarily left his or her most recent work without good cause (41-35-120); (iii) Claimant failed, without good cause, either to apply for available, suitable work, to accept available suitable work, or to return to his or her customary self-employment (41-35-120); (iv) Claimant separation was caused by a labor dispute (41-35-120); (v) Claimant knowingly made a false statement or knowingly failed to disclose a material fact in order to obtain benefits (41-41-20); (vi) Claimant is receiving unemployment benefits from another state or under federal law (41-35-120); (vii) Claimant voluntarily retired from his or her most recent employment (41-35-120); (viii) Claimant is an illegal alien. (41-35-67)

PURGING DISQUALIFICATION: A Claimant who failed to apply for or accept suitable work, who voluntarily quit, or who voluntarily retired, may be eligible for benefits only after receiving remuneration for work subsequent to the disqualifying separation in the amount of 8 x his or her Weekly Benefit Amount. (41-35-110)

SPECIAL TREATMENT:

Claimants in the following categories are afforded distinct treatment under the statute and thus further research may be merited for: (i) Claimants who are in approved training programs (41-35-110); (ii) Claimants who are on vacations (41-35-20); (iii) Claimants who are or were formerly self-employed (35-110); (iv) Claimants who have volunteered, enlisted, or been drafted into the Armed Forces (41-35-100); (v) Claimants who are members of the National Guard or other military reserve units (41-27-380); (vi) Claimants who are employees of educational institutions when it is between school semesters (41-35-20); (vii) Claimants who are professional athletes when it is between sports seasons. (41-35-66)

SOUTH DAKOTA

STATUTE:

LAW: South Dakota Employment Security Law

CITATION: South Dakota Codified Laws, Title 61, Chapter 61-1, Section 61-1-1 (S.D.C.L. § 61-1-1)

BENEFIT CALCULATION:

WEEKLY BENEFIT AMT.: Benefit amounts are calculated as 1/26 x wages Claimant earned in his or her highest-paying Base Period quarter. (61-6-6)

PARTIAL EMPLOYMENT: Claimant's Weekly Benefit Amount is reduced by 75% of the amount of wages he or she earns from partial employment in excess of $25 and reduces to $0 if such wages equal or exceed his or her Weekly Benefit Amount. (61-6-1)

REDUCTION IN BENEFITS: Claimant's Weekly Benefit Amount may be reduced if: (i) Claimant receives pension benefits (61-6-2); (ii) Claimant receives retirement pay (61-6-20); (iii) Claimant receives annuity payments (61-6-20); (iv) Claimant receives Social Security benefits (61-6-20); (v) Claimant receives wages in lieu of notice (61-6-20); (vi) Claimant receives vacation or holiday pay; (vii) Claimant receives severance, dismissal, or termination pay (61-6-20); (viii) Claimant receives disability pension payments (61-6-20); (ix) Claimant receives wages for a temporary-partial disability under a workers' compensation law. (61-6-20)

DEPENDENCY BENEFIT: None.

MIN./MAX. WEEKLY: Minimum weekly benefit is $28. (61-6-6, 61-6-7) Maximum weekly benefit is calculated annually as 50% of the Statewide Average Weekly Wage. (61-6-6) For 2001, the maximum weekly benefit was $234. (***)

MAXIMUM TOTAL: Claimant may receive total benefits equaling the lesser of (i) 26 x his or her Weekly Benefit Amount or (ii) 1/3 x his or her total Base Period wages. (61-6-8) In times of high unemployment, extended benefits may be available. (61-6-37)

BENEFIT ELIGIBILITY:

GENERALLY: To be eligible for unemployment compensation benefits, Claimant must: (i) File a claim for benefits (61-6-2); (ii) Register for work at a state unemployment office (61-6-2); (iii) Continue to report to a state unemployment office as required (61-6-2); (iv) Earn at least $728 during his or her highest-paying Base Period quarter (61-6-7); (v) Earn wages during his or her Base Period outside of his or her highest-paying Base Period quarter at least equal to 20 x his or her Weekly Benefit Amount (61-6-7); (vi) Be able to work and available for work. (61-6-2)

SUBSEQUENT APPLICATION: In order to apply the income Claimant earned during the lag period before his or her prior claim was established (i.e. the income he or she earned after his or her prior Base Period ended and before he or she filed a claim for benefits for the prior Benefit Year) to his or her new benefit claim, Claimant must have worked and earned 4 x his or her Weekly Benefit Amount, subsequent to the commencement of the prior Benefit Year and before the commencement of his or her new Benefit Year. (61-6-9)

WAITING WEEK: Claimant must serve 1 Waiting Week before collecting benefits. (61-6- 2)

DISQUALIFICATION: Claimant may be partially, fully or at least temporarily disqualified from receiving benefits if: (i) Claimant was discharged or suspended for misconduct from most recent work (61-6-14); (ii) Claimant was discharged when transferred or released from a custodial or penal institution (61-6-1.10); (iii) Claimant voluntarily left most recent work without good cause (61-6-13); (iv) Claimant failed, without good cause, either to apply for available, suitable work or to accept suitable work (61-6-15); (v) Claimant separation was caused by a labor dispute, unless he or she was subject to a lockout (61-6-19); (vi) Claimant willfully or fraudulently misrepresented any fact to secure or increase benefits (61-6-22); (vii) Claimant is receiving unemployment benefits from another state or under federal law (61-6-21); (viii) Claimant is principally occupied as a student (61-6-15.2); (ix) Claimant is an illegal alien. (61-6-1.5)

PURGING DISQUALIFICATION: A Claimant who was discharged or suspended for misconduct, discharged due to transfer or release from a custodial or penal institution, or a Claimant who refused suitable work or voluntarily quit, may be eligible for benefits only after working for at least 6 weeks, subsequent to the disqualifying separation, during each of which he or she received remuneration for work at least equal to his or her Weekly Benefit Amount. (61-6-1.10, 61-6-13, 61-6-14)

SPECIAL TREATMENT:

Claimants in the following categories are afforded distinct treatment under the statute and thus further research may be merited for: (i) Claimants who are in approved training programs (61-6-15.1); (ii) Claimants who are employed by secondary or elementary schools operated by the federal government (61-6-1.9); (iii) Claimants who receive disability payments connected with military service (61-6-20); (iv) Claimants who are employees of educational institutions when it is between school semesters (61-6-1.2); (v) Claimants who are professional athletes when it is between sports seasons. (61-6-1.4)

TENNESSEE

STATUTE:

LAW: Tennessee Employment Security Law

CITATION: Tennessee Code Annotated, Title 50, Section 50-7-101 (T.C.A. § 50-7- 101)

BENEFIT CALCULATION:

WEEKLY BENEFIT AMT.: Benefit amounts depend upon a Benefit Table contained in the law which takes into account the average total wages for work paid to Claimant during his or her Base Period and the wages he or she receives in his or her two highest-paying Base Period quarters. (A Claimant who receives $780 during his or her two highest-paying Base Period quarters receives a Weekly Benefit Amount of $30. From there, each increase of $26 in such two highest-paying Base Period quarters draws an additional $1 increase in his or her Weekly Benefit Amount.) (50-7-301)

PARTIAL EMPLOYMENT: Any wages Claimant receives from partial employment in excess of the greater of $50 or 25% of his or her Weekly Benefit Amount are deducted from his or her Weekly Benefit Amount. (50-7-301)

REDUCTION IN BENEFITS: Claimant's Weekly Benefit Amount may be reduced if: (i) Claimant receives pension benefits (50-7-303); (ii) Claimant receives retirement pay (50-7-303); (iii) Claimant receives annuity payments (50-7-303); (iv) Claimant receives Social Security benefits (50-7-303); (v) Claimant receives other similar periodic payments based upon previous work (50-7-303); (vi) Claimant receives vacation pay. (50-7-303)

DEPENDENCY BENEFIT: None.

MIN./MAX. WEEKLY: Minimum weekly benefit is $30. (50-7-301) Maximum weekly benefit is modified periodically. (50-7-301) For 2001, the maximum weekly benefit was $255. (50-7-301) For 1998, the maximum weekly benefit was $255. (50-7-301)

MAXIMUM TOTAL: Claimant may receive total benefits equaling the lesser of (i) 26 x his or her Weekly Benefit Amount or (ii) 1/4 x his or her total Base Period wages. (50-7-301) In times of high unemployment, extended benefits may be available. (50-7-305)

BENEFIT ELIGIBILITY:

GENERALLY: To be eligible for unemployment compensation benefits, Claimant must: (i) File a claim for benefits (50-7-302); (ii) Register for work at a state unemployment office (50-7-302); (iii) Continue to report to a state unemployment office as required (50-7-302); (iv) Earn wages during his or her Base Period, excluding wages earned during his or her highest-paying Base Period quarter, of at least 6 x his or her Weekly Benefit Amount or $900 (50-7-301); (v) Earn during his or her two highest-paying Base Period quarters wages of at least $780.01 (50-7-301); (vi) Earn during his or her entire Base Period wages equaling at least 40 x his or her Weekly Benefit Amount (50-7-301); (vii) Be able to work and available for work (50-7-302); (viii) Make reasonable efforts to secure work (50-7-302); (ix) Participate in reemployment services as required. (50-7-302)

SUBSEQUENT APPLICATION: In order for Claimant to count wages he or she earned before the establishment of a prior Benefit Year for purposes of eligibility for a new Benefit Year, he or she must earn wages subsequent to the establishment of the prior Benefit Year of at least 5 x his or her Weekly Benefit Amount as calculated for the current Benefit Year. (50-7-302)

WAITING WEEK: Claimant must serve 1 Waiting Week before collecting benefits. (50-7- 302)

DISQUALIFICATION: Claimant may be partially, fully or at least temporarily disqualified from receiving benefits if: (i) Claimant was discharged for misconduct in connection with his or her most recent work (50-7-303); (ii) Claimant voluntarily left his or her most recent work without good cause connected with such work (50-7-303); (iii) Claimant left his or her most recent work either to avoid taking a drug or alcohol screening test or after receiving a positive result to a drug or alcohol screening test (50-7-302); (iv) Claimant failed to apply for available, suitable work, to accept suitable work when offered, or to return to his or her customary self-employment (50-7-303); (v) Claimant separation was caused by a labor dispute other than a lockout (50-7-303); (vi) Claimant made a false or fraudulent representation or intentionally withheld material information for purposes of obtaining benefits (50-7-303); (vii) Claimant is seeking or receiving unemployment benefits from another state or under federal law (50-7-303); (viii) Claimant receives wages in lieu of notice (50-7-303); (ix) Claimant receives temporary partial disability benefits under a workers' compensation law (50-7-303); (x) Claimant is an illegal alien. (50-7-302)

PURGING DISQUALIFICATION: A Claimant who was discharged for misconduct, failed to apply for or accept suitable work or to return to customary self-employment, who voluntarily quit, or who separated from work during a labor dispute, may be eligible for benefits only after receiving remuneration for work subsequent to the disqualifying separation in the amount of 10 x his or her Weekly Benefit Amount. (50-7-303)

SPECIAL TREATMENT:

Claimants in the following categories are afforded distinct treatment under the statute and thus further research may be merited for: (i) Claimants who are in approved training programs (50-7-302); (ii) Claimants who are in the National Guard (50-7-301); (iii) Claimants who are ill or disabled (50-7-302); (iv) Claimants who voluntarily leave work while their employer has insufficient work pursuant to labor-management contracts or established employer plans (50-7-303); (v) Claimants who are employed by firms which close down during vacation periods (50-7-302); (vi) Claimants who are pregnant (50-7-303); (vii) Claimants who voluntarily leave work to join the Armed Forces (50-7-303); (viii) Claimants who are employees of educational institutions when it is between school semesters (50-7-302); (ix) Claimants who are professional athletes when it is between sports seasons (50-7-302); (x) Claimants who are students. (50-7-302)

TEXAS

STATUTE:

LAW: Texas Unemployment Compensation Act

CITATION: Vernon's Texas Codes Annotated, Labor Code 201.001 (T.C.A. Labor Code § 201.001)

BENEFIT CALCULATION:

WEEKLY BENEFIT AMT.: Benefit amounts are calculated as 1/25 x the wages Claimant earned in his or her highest-paying Base Period quarter. (207.002)

PARTIAL EMPLOYMENT: Any wages Claimant receives from partial employment in excess of the greater of (i) 25% of his or her Weekly Benefit Amount or (ii) $5, are deducted from his or her Weekly Benefit Amount. (207.003)

REDUCTION IN BENEFITS: Claimant's Weekly Benefit Amount may be reduced if: (i) Claimant receives pension benefits (207.050); (ii) Claimant receives retirement pay (207.050); (iii) Claimant receives annuity payment (207.050); (iv) Claimant receives other similar periodic payments based upon previous work. (207.050)

DEPENDENCY BENEFIT: None.

MIN./MAX. WEEKLY: Minimum weekly benefit is calculated as 7.6% of the Statewide Average Weekly Wage for state manufacturing production workers (207.002,***) and was $51 for 2001. (***) Maximum weekly benefit is calculated as 47.6% of the Statewide Average Weekly Wage for state manufacturing production workers (207.002,***) and was $319 for 2001. (***)

MAXIMUM TOTAL: Claimant may receive total benefits equaling the lesser of (i) 26 x his or her Weekly Benefit Amount or (ii) 27% of his or her total Base Period wages. (207.005) In times of high unemployment, extended benefits may be available. (209.041)

BENEFIT ELIGIBILITY:

GENERALLY: To be eligible for unemployment compensation benefits, Claimant must: (i) File a claim for benefits (207.021); (ii) Register for work at a state unemployment office (207.021); (iii) Continue to report to a state unemployment office as required (207.021); (iv) Earn wages during at least two quarters of his or her Base Period (207.021); (v) Earn wages of at least 37 x his or her Weekly Benefit Amount during his or her entire Base Period (207.021); (vi) Be able to work and available for work (207.021); (vii) Participate in reemployment services as required. (207.021)

SUBSEQUENT APPLICATION: A Claimant who received benefits during a preceding Benefit Year must have worked and earned 6 x his or her Weekly Benefit Amount, subsequent to the commencement of such Benefit Year and before the commencement of his or her new Benefit Year. (207.021) Wages used by Claimant to qualify for unemployment benefits in a prior Benefit Year may not be used again to qualify Claimant for benefits in a succeeding Benefit Year. (207.004)

WAITING WEEK: Claimant must serve 7 consecutive day waiting period before collecting benefits. (207.021)

DISQUALIFICATION: Claimant may be partially, fully or at least temporarily disqualified from receiving benefits if: (i) Claimant was discharged for misconduct connected with last work (207.044); (ii) Claimant voluntarily left work without good cause connected with work (207.045); (iii) Claimant left most recent work to attend an educational institution (207.052); (iv) Claimant failed, without good cause, to apply for available, suitable work, accept suitable work, or to return to customary self-employment (207.047); (v) Claimant separation was caused by a labor dispute (207.048); (vi) Claimant willfully failed to disclose or misrepresented a material fact in order to obtain benefits (214.003); (vii) Claimant is a partner in a partnership or a corporate officer and controlling shareholder of a corporation involved in the sale of the partnership or corporation (207.051); (viii) Claimant is an employee of a temporary help firm who fails to contact the firm for reassignment after completion of a prior assignment (207.045); (ix) Claimant receives wages in lieu of notice (207.049); (x) Claimant receives workers' compensation benefits for a temporary partial disability, temporary total disability, or total permanent disability (207.049); (xi) Claimant is an illegal alien. (207.043)

PURGING DISQUALIFICATION: A Claimant who was discharged for misconduct, failed to accept or apply for suitable work or to return to customary self-employment, or who voluntarily quit, may be eligible for benefits only after either (i) working for 6 weeks or (ii) receiving remuneration for work subsequent to the disqualifying separation in the amount of 6 x his or her Weekly Benefit Amount. (207.044, 207.045, 207.047)

SPECIAL TREATMENT:

Claimants in the following categories are afforded distinct treatment under the statute and thus further research may be merited for: (i) Claimants who are in approved training programs (207.022); (ii) Claimants who are participating in shared work plans (215.041); (iii) Claimants who are pregnant or who were recently pregnant (207.025); (iv) Claimants who leave work to move to a new location with their spouse (207.045); (v) Claimants who leave work to care for an ill minor child (207.045); (vi) Claimants who leave one job to accept another which is expected to pay more (207.045); (vii) Claimants who were members of the Armed Forces but who did not reenlist (207.045); (viii) Claimants who left their last work or were discharged because they refused to provide services to an individual infected with a communicable disease (207.053); (ix) Claimants who are employees of educational institutions when it is between school semesters (207.041); (x) Claimants who are professional athletes when it is between sports seasons. (207.042)

UTAH

STATUTE:

LAW: Utah Employment Security Act

CITATION: Utah Code Annotated, Title 35A, Chapter 4, Section 35A-4-101 (U.C.A. § 35A-4-101)

BENEFIT CALCULATION:

WEEKLY BENEFIT AMT.: Benefit amounts are calculated as 1/26 x the wages Claimant received in his or her highest-paying Base Period quarter. (35A-4-401)

PARTIAL EMPLOYMENT: Any wages Claimant receives from partial employment in excess of 30% of his or her Weekly Benefit Amount, are deducted from his or her Weekly Benefit Amount. (35A-4-401)

REDUCTION IN BENEFITS: Claimant's Weekly Benefit Amount may be reduced if: (i) Claimant receives pension benefits (35A-4-401); (ii) Claimant receives retirement pay (35A-4-401); (iii) Claimant receives Social Security payments (35A-4-401); (iv) Claimant receives wages in lieu of notice (35A-4-405); (v) Claimant receives termination leave, separation pay, or dismissal pay (35A-4-405); (vi) Claimant receives vacation pay (35A-4-405); (vii) Claimant receives disability pay. (35A-4-401)

DEPENDENCY BENEFIT: None.

MIN./MAX. WEEKLY: Maximum weekly benefit is calculated annually as 60% of the insured Statewide Average Weekly Wage. (35A-4-401) For 2001, the maximum weekly benefit was $355. (***) Minimum weekly benefit was $23 in 2001. (***)

MAXIMUM TOTAL: Claimant may receive total benefits equaling between 10 and 26 x his or her Weekly Benefit Amount. The actual amount within this range is determined by taking 27% of Claimant's total Base Period wages, and dividing this amount by Claimant's Weekly Benefit Amount. (35A-4-401) In times of high unemployment, extended benefits may be available. (35A-4-402)

BENEFIT ELIGIBILITY:

GENERALLY: To be eligible for unemployment compensation benefits, Claimant must: (i) File a claim for benefits (35A-4-403); (ii) Register for work at a state unemployment office (35A-4-403); (iii) Furnish the division with separation and other reports containing any information required (35A-4-403); (iv) Continue to report to a state unemployment office as required (35A-4-403); (v) Either (a) earn during his or her entire Base Period wages at least equal to 1 1/2 x the wages he or she earned in his or her highest-paying Base Period quarter OR (b) work for at least 20 weeks in insured work during his or her Base Period and earn wages of at least 5% of the Monetary Base Period Wage requirement (i.e. 5 % of the 8% of the statewide average annual wage for the preceding fiscal year) each week provided that total Base Period wages were not less than the Monetary Base Period Wage requirement (35A-4-202, 35A-4-403); (vi) Be able to work and available for work each and every week with respect to which benefits are claimed (35A-4-403); (vii) Act in good faith in an active effort to secure employment. (35A-4-403)

SUBSEQUENT APPLICATION: A Claimant who received benefits during a preceding Benefit Year must have worked and earned 6 x his or her Weekly Benefit Amount, as calculated for the preceding Benefit Year, subsequent to the commencement of such Benefit Year and before the commencement of his or her new Benefit Year. (35A-4-403)

WAITING WEEK: Claimant must serve 1 Waiting Week before collecting benefits. (35A- 4-403)

DISQUALIFICATION: Claimant may be partially, fully or at least temporarily disqualified from receiving benefits if: (i) Claimant was discharged for just cause due to an act or omission which is deliberate, willful or wanton and adverse to his or her employer's rightful interests (35A-4-405); (ii) Claimant was discharged for dishonesty constituting a crime or any felony or certain misdemeanors in connection with work (35A-4-405); (iii) Claimant voluntarily left work without good cause (35A-4-405); (iv) Claimant failed without good cause to accept or apply for suitable work (35A-4-405); (v) Claimant separation was caused by a work stoppage that exists because of a strike at the factory at which he or she was last employed (35A-4-405); (vi) Claimant willfully made a false statement or representation or knowingly failed to report a material fact in order to obtain benefits (35A-4-405); (vii) Claimant is receiving unemployment benefits from another state or under federal law (35A-4-405); (viii) Claimant is an illegal alien. (35A-4-405)

PURGING DISQUALIFICATION: A Claimant who was discharged due to an act or omission adverse to his or her employer's interests, because he or she failed to apply for or accept suitable work, or who voluntarily quit, may be eligible for benefits only after receiving remuneration for work subsequent to the disqualifying separation in the amount of 6 x his or her Weekly Benefit Amount. (35A-4-405)

SPECIAL TREATMENT:

Claimants in the following categories are afforded distinct treatment under the statute and thus further research may be merited for: (i) Claimants who are in approved training programs (35A-4-403); (ii) Claimants who are attending school or in school, during school vacations (35A-4-205); (iii) Claimants who suffer from sickness or injury compensated under a workers' compensation or occupational disease law (35A-4-404); (iv) Claimants who are employees of educational institutions when it is between school semesters (35A-4-405); (v) Claimants who are professional athletes when it is between sports seasons. (35-A-405)

VERMONT

STATUTE:

LAW: Vermont Unemployment Compensation Law

CITATION: Vermont Statutes Annotated, Title 21, Section 1301 (21 V.S.A. § 1301)

BENEFIT CALCULATION:

WEEKLY BENEFIT AMT.: Benefit amounts are calculated by dividing the wages Claimant received during his or her two highest-paying Base Period quarters by 45. (1338)

PARTIAL EMPLOYMENT: Any wages Claimant receives from partial employment in excess of the greater of (i) 30 x his or her Weekly Benefit Amount or (ii) $40, are deducted from his or her Weekly Benefit Amount. (1338a, 1339)

REDUCTION IN BENEFITS: Claimant's Weekly Benefit Amount may be reduced if: (i) Claimant receives pension benefits (1344); (ii) Claimant receives retirement pay (1344); (iii) Claimant receives annuity payments (1344); (iv) Claimant receives other similar periodic payments based upon previous work (1344).

DEPENDENCY BENEFIT: None.

MIN./MAX. WEEKLY: Maximum weekly benefit is calculated annually and is based upon changes in the Statewide Average Weekly Wage. (1338) For 2001, the maximum weekly benefit was $312. (***) Minimum weekly benefit is $31. (***)

MAXIMUM TOTAL: Claimant may receive total benefits equaling 26 x his or her Weekly Benefit Amount. (1340) In times of high unemployment, extended benefits may be available. (1423)

BENEFIT ELIGIBILITY:

GENERALLY: To be eligible for unemployment compensation benefits, Claimant must: (i) File a claim for benefits (1343); (ii) Register for work at a state unemployment office (1343); (iii) Continue to report to a state unemployment office as required (1343); (iv) Earn at least $1,000 during his or her highest-paying Base Period quarter (this amount is subject to upward adjustments based upon changes in the state minimum wage) (1338); (v) Earn during his or her Base Period, outside of his or her highest-paying Base Period quarter, an amount equal to at least 40% of the wages he or she earned during his or her highest-paying Base Period quarter (1338); (vi) Be able to work and available for work (1343); (vii) Make such other efforts to secure suitable work as the commissioner may reasonably direct under the circumstances (1343); (viii) Participate in re-employment services as required. (1343)

SUBSEQUENT APPLICATION: A Claimant who received benefits during a preceding Benefit Year must have worked and earned, 4 x his or her Weekly Benefit Amount, as calculated for the preceding Benefit Year, subsequent to the commencement of such Benefit Year and before the commencement of his or her new Benefit Year. (1338)

WAITING WEEK: Claimant must serve 1 Waiting Week before collecting benefits. (1343)

DISQUALIFICATION: Claimant may be partially, fully or at least temporarily disqualified from receiving benefits if: (i) Claimant was discharged from last employer for misconduct connected with work (1344); (ii) Claimant was discharged from last employer for gross misconduct connected with work (1344); (iii) Claimant is unable to perform work duties without good cause attributable to his or her employer due to his or her conviction for a felony, misdemeanor, or due to an action or order of a judge or court in any criminal or civil matter (1344); (iv) Claimant voluntarily left last employer without good cause (1344); (v) Claimant failed, without good cause, to apply for available, suitable work, to accept suitable work when offered him, or to return to customary self-employment (1344); (vi) Claimant made an untrue or displayed an unreasonable lack of interest or acted in a manner calculated to preclude an offer of work during a job interview (1344); (vii) Claimant separation was caused by a labor dispute other than a lockout (1344); (viii) Claimant intentionally misrepresented or failed to disclose a material fact with respect to his or her claim for benefits (1347); (ix) Claimant is receiving unemployment benefits from another state or under federal law (1344); (x) Claimant receives vacation or holiday pay (1344); (xi) Claimant receives wages in lieu of notice (1344); (xii) Claimant receives a back pay award or settlement (1344); (xiii) Claimant receives temporary partial disability or temporary total disability benefits under a workers' compensation law (1344); (xiv) Claimant is an illegal alien. (1343)

PURGING DISQUALIFICATION: A Claimant who was discharged for gross misconduct, failed to accept or apply for suitable work or return to customary self-employment, who made untrue statements or calculated statements to preclude an employment offer during an interview, who displayed an unreasonable lack of interest during an interview, or who voluntarily quit, may be eligible for benefits only after receiving remuneration for work subsequent to the disqualifying separation in excess of 6 x his or her Weekly Benefit Amount. (1344)

SPECIAL TREATMENT:

Claimants in the following categories are afforded distinct treatment under the statute and thus further research may be merited for: (i) Claimants who are in approved training programs (1343); (ii) Claimants who are ill or disabled (1343); (iii) Claimants who receive cash severance payments (1344); (iv) Claimants who participate in short-time compensation programs (1457); (v) Claimants who are employees of educational institutions when it is between school semesters (1343); (vi) Claimants who are professional athletes when it is between sports seasons (1343); (vii) Claimants who are self-employed. (1343)

VIRGIN ISLANDS

STATUTE:

LAW: Virgin Islands Unemployment Insurance Law

CITATION: Virgin Islands Code Annotated, Title 24, Section 301 (24 V.I.C. § 301)

BENEFIT CALCULATION:

WEEKLY BENEFIT AMT.: Benefit amounts are calculated as (i) 1/26 x the wages he or she earned in his or her highest-paying Base Period quarter if he or she earned during his or her entire Base Period wages of at least 1 1/2 x the wages he or she earned in his or her highest-paying Base Period quarter, OR (ii) 1/26 x the wages he or she earned in his or her highest-paying Base Period quarter, minus $1, if the result of the original Weekly Benefit Amount calculation, when multiplied by 39, equals of exceeds the sum of all wages he or she earned during his or her entire Base Period. (303)

PARTIAL EMPLOYMENT: 75% of any and all wages Claimant receives during a week from partial employment in excess of $15 are deducted from his or her Weekly Benefit Amount. (303)

REDUCTION IN BENEFITS: Claimant's Weekly Benefit Amount may be reduced if: (i) Claimant receives pension benefits (304); (ii) Claimant receives retirement pay (304); (iii) Claimant receives annuity payments (304); (iv) Claimant receives other similar periodic payments based upon previous work. (304)

DEPENDENCY BENEFIT: None.

MIN./MAX. WEEKLY: Maximum weekly benefit is calculated annually as 50% of the average weekly wage in the Virgin Islands. (303) For 2001, the maximum weekly benefit was $312. (***) Minimum weekly benefit is $33. (***)

MAXIMUM TOTAL: Claimant may receive total benefits equaling the lesser of (i) 26 x his or her Weekly Benefit Amount or (ii) 1/3 x his or her total Base Period wages. (303) In times of high unemployment, extended benefits may be available. (315)

BENEFIT ELIGIBILITY:

GENERALLY: To be eligible for unemployment compensation benefits, Claimant must: (i) File a notice of his or her unemployment at a state unemployment office (304); (ii) Register for work at a state unemployment office (304); (iii) Earn at least $858 during his or her highest-paying Base Period quarter (303); (iv) Earn either (a) during his or her entire Base Period, wages at least equal to 1 1/2 x the wages he or she earned in his or her highest-paying Base Period quarter or (b) sufficient wages during his or her Base Period such that 1/26 x the wages he or she earned in his or her highest-paying Base Period quarter, minus $1, multiplied by 39, equals or exceeds the amount of Base Period wages Claimant earned during his or her entire Base Period (303); (v) Be able to work and available for suitable work (304); (vi) Make reasonable efforts to seek suitable work (304); (vii) Participate in reemployment services as required. (304)

SUBSEQUENT APPLICATION: A Claimant who received benefits during a preceding Benefit Year must have worked and earned wages subsequent to the commencement of his or her prior Benefit Year and before the commencement of his or her new Benefit Year, equal to the lesser of (i) 6 x his or her Weekly Benefit Amount or (ii) 3/13 x the wages he or she earned in his or her highest-paying Base Period quarter. (303)

WAITING WEEK: Claimant must serve 1 Waiting Week before collecting benefits. (304)

DISQUALIFICATION: Claimant may be partially, fully or at least temporarily disqualified from receiving benefits if: (i) Claimant was discharged or suspended from most recent work for misconduct connected with work (304); (ii) Claimant voluntarily left most recent work without good cause (304); (iii) Claimant failed, without good cause, to apply for available, suitable work or to accept suitable work (304); (iv) Claimant separation was caused by a labor dispute (304); (v) Claimant has, with intent to defraud by obtaining benefits not due, made a false statement or misrepresentation of a mater of fact, knowing it to be false or knowingly failed to disclose a material fact (313); (vi) Claimant is receiving unemployment benefits from another state or under federal law (304); (vii) Claimant is an illegal alien. (304)

PURGING DISQUALIFICATION: A Claimant who was discharged or suspended for misconduct, failed to apply for or accept suitable work, or who voluntarily quit, may be eligible for benefits only after working for at least 4 weeks, whether or not consecutive, and receiving remuneration for work subsequent to the disqualifying separation in the amount of 4 x his or her Weekly Benefit Amount. (304)

SPECIAL TREATMENT:

Claimants in the following categories are afforded distinct treatment under the statute and thus further research may be merited for: (i) Claimants who are in approved training programs (304); (ii) Claimants who are pregnant or who were recently pregnant (304); (iii) Claimants who are employees of educational institutions when it is between school semesters (304); (iv) Claimants who are professional athletes when it is between sports seasons. (304)

VIRGINIA

STATUTE:

LAW: Virginia Unemployment Compensation Act

CITATION: Code of Virginia 1950, Title 60.2, Section 60.2-100 (C.V. § 60.2-100)

BENEFIT CALCULATION:

WEEKLY BENEFIT AMT.: Benefit amounts are included on a Benefit Table contained in the law which takes into account the total amount of wages Claimant receives during his or her two highest-paying Base Period quarters. (A Claimant who receives $3,250 during his or her two highest-paying Base Period quarters receives a Weekly Benefit Amount of $65. From there, each increase of $50 in such two highest-paying Base Period quarters draws an additional $1 increase in his or her Weekly Benefit Amount.) (60.2-602)

PARTIAL EMPLOYMENT: Any wages Claimant receives from partial employment in excess of $25 are deducted from his or her Weekly Benefit Amount. (60.2-603)

REDUCTION IN BENEFITS: Claimant's Weekly Benefit Amount may be reduced if: (i) Claimant receives pension benefits (60.2-604); (ii) Claimant receives retirement pay (60.2-604); (iii) Claimant receives annuity payments (60.2-604); (iv) Claimant receives other similar periodic payments based upon previous work. (60.2-604)

DEPENDENCY BENEFIT: None.

MIN./MAX. WEEKLY: Minimum weekly benefit is $50. (60.2-602) The maximum weekly benefit is $368. (60.2-602)

MAXIMUM TOTAL: Claimant may receive total benefits equaling between 12 and 26 x his or her Weekly Benefit Amount depending upon the sum of the wages he or she received during his or her two highest-paying Base Period quarters. (60.2-607) In times of high unemployment, extended benefits may be available. (60.2-611)

BENEFIT ELIGIBILITY:

GENERALLY: To be eligible for unemployment compensation benefits, Claimant must: (i) File a claim for benefits (60.2-612); (ii) Register for work at a state unemployment office (60.2-612); (iii) Continue to report to a state unemployment office as required (60.2-612); (iv) Earn between $2,800 and $8,800.01 during his or her two highest-paying Base Period quarters, depending upon his or her Weekly Benefit Amount (60.2-612); (v) Earn wages during at least two of his or her Base Period quarters (60.2-612); (vi) Be able to work and available for work (60.2-612); (vii) Be actively seeking but unable to obtain work; (60.2-612); (viii) Participate in reemployment services as required. (60.2-612)

SUBSEQUENT APPLICATION: A Claimant who received benefits during a preceding Benefit Year must have worked either (i) for at least 30 days or (ii) for 240 hours, and must subsequently become totally or partially separated from such employment. (60.2-614)

WAITING WEEK: Claimant must serve 1 Waiting Week before collecting benefits. (60.2-613)

DISQUALIFICATION: Claimant may be partially, fully or at least temporarily disqualified from receiving benefits if: (i) Claimant was discharged for misconduct connected with work (60.2-618); (ii) Claimant separated from work as a result of an unlawful act resulting in a conviction which leads to imprisonment or confinement in jail (60.2-618); (iii) Claimant voluntarily left work without good cause (60.2-618); (iv) Claimant failed, without good cause, either to apply for available, suitable work or to accept suitable work (60.2-618); (v) Claimant tests positive for a non-prescribed controlled substance, in connection with an offer of suitable work, if such test is required as a condition of employment (60.2-618); (vi) Claimant separation was caused by a labor dispute (60.2-612); (vii) Claimant made a false statement or representation knowing it to be false or knowingly failed to disclose a material fact in order to obtain benefits (60.2-618); (viii) Claimant is receiving unemployment benefits from another state or under federal law (60.2-612); (ix) Claimant is on a paid vacation (60.2-612); (x) Claimant is an illegal alien (60.2-617); (xi) Claimant made a false or misleading statement concerning past criminal convictions in a written job application. (60.2-618)

PURGING DISQUALIFICATION: A Claimant who was discharged for misconduct, failed to accept or apply for suitable work, who voluntarily quit, who was imprisoned or confined to jail, or who tested positive for a non-prescribed controlled substance, may be eligible for benefits only after working for 30 days or for 240 hours, and subsequently must become totally or partially separated from such employment. (60.2-618)

SPECIAL TREATMENT:

Claimants in the following categories are afforded distinct treatment under the statute and thus further research may be merited for: (i) Claimants who are in approved training programs (60.2-613); (ii) Claimants who leave their labor market during a major portion of an unemployed week (60.2-612); (iii) Claimants who leave work pursuant to a policy based upon seniority (60.2-618); (iv) Claimants who voluntarily leave their normal geographic area of employment to accompany their spouse to a new location (60.2-618); (v) Claimants who are employees of educational institutions when it is between school semesters (60.2-615); (vi) Claimants who are professional athletes when it is between sports seasons (60.2-616); (vii) Claimants who are students. (60.2-612)

WASHINGTON

STATUTE:

LAW: Washington Employment Security Act

CITATION: West's Revised Code of Washington Annotated, Title 50, Chapter 50.01, Section 50.01.005 (R.C.W.A. § 50.01.005)

BENEFIT CALCULATION:

WEEKLY BENEFIT AMT.: Benefit amounts are calculated as 1/25 x the average quarterly wages Claimant received during his or her two highest-paying Base Period quarters. (50.20.120)

PARTIAL EMPLOYMENT: Claimant's Weekly Benefit Amount will be reduced by 75% of the amount of wages Claimant earns from partial employment, to the extent that such wages exceed $5. (50.20.130)

REDUCTION IN BENEFITS: Claimant's Weekly Benefit Amount may be reduced if: (i) Claimant receives pension benefits (50.04.323); (ii) Claimant receives retirement pay (50.04.323); (iii) Claimant receives annuity payments (50.04.323); (iv) Claimant receives other similar periodic payments based upon previous work. (50.04.323)

DEPENDENCY BENEFIT: None.

MIN./MAX. WEEKLY: Minimum weekly benefit is calculated annually as 15% of the Statewide Average Weekly Wage. (50.20.120) Minimum weekly benefit for 2001 was $106. (***) Maximum weekly benefit is calculated annually as 70% of the Statewide Average Weekly Wage. (50.20.120) For 2001, the maximum weekly benefit was $496. (***)

MAXIMUM TOTAL: Claimant may receive total benefits equaling the lesser of (i) 30 x his or her Weekly Benefit Amount or (ii) 1/3 x his or her total Base Period wages. (50.20.120) In times of high unemployment, extended benefits may be available. (50.22.020)

BENEFIT ELIGIBILITY:

GENERALLY: To be eligible for unemployment compensation benefits, Claimant must: (i) File a claim for benefits and an application for an initial determination regarding benefits (50.20.010); (ii) Register for work at a state unemployment compensation office (50.20.010); (iii) Continue to report to a state unemployment office as required (50.20.010); (iv) Earn wages in at least 680 hours of work during his or her Base Period (50.04.030); (v) Be able to work and available for work in any trade, occupation, profession, or business for which he or she is reasonably fitted (50.20.010); (vi) Be ready, able, and willing, immediately to accept any suitable work (50.20.010); (vii) Be actively seeking work (50.20.010); (viii) Participate in reemployment services as required. (50.20.010)

SUBSEQUENT APPLICATION: Claimant may not use wages he or she earned prior to the establishment of a prior Benefit Year for eligibility purposes unless he or she worked and earned wages (i) since his or her last separation from employment immediately before he or she applied for an initial determination in the prior Benefit Year if he or she was unemployed at the time of such application, or (ii) since the initial separation in the prior Benefit Year if he or she was employed at the time of filing the application for determination for the prior Benefit Year, an amount equal to at least 6 x his or her Weekly Benefit Amount. (50.04.030)

WAITING WEEK: Claimant must serve 1 Waiting Week before collecting benefits. (50.20.020)

DISQUALIFICATION: Claimant may be partially, fully or at least temporarily disqualified from receiving benefits if: (i) Claimant was discharged or suspended for misconduct connected with work (50.20.060); (ii) Claimant was discharged for the commission of a felony or gross misdemeanor connected with work of which he or she was convicted or admitted (50.20.065); (iii) Claimant voluntarily left work without good cause (50.20.050); (iv) Claimant failed, without good cause, either to apply for available, suitable work, to accept suitable work, or to return to customary self-employment (50.20.080); (v) Claimant separation was caused by a labor dispute (50.20.090); (vi) Claimant knowingly made a false statement or representation involving a material fact or knowingly failed to report a material fact in order to obtain benefits (50.20.070); (vii) Claimant receives industrial insurance disability benefits (50.20.085); (viii) Claimant is a full-time student (50.20.095); (ix) Claimant is an illegal alien (50.20.098); (x) Claimant failed to attend a job search workshop or training course. (50.20.044)

PURGING DISQUALIFICATION: A Claimant who was discharged or suspended for misconduct, who failed to apply for or accept suitable work or return to customary self-employment, or who voluntarily quit, may be eligible for benefits only after the passing of 7 calendar weeks and after Claimant received remuneration for work subsequent to the disqualifying separation in the amount of 7 x his or her Weekly Benefit Amount. (50.20.050, 50.20.060, 50.20.080)

SPECIAL TREATMENT:

Claimants in the following categories are afforded distinct treatment under the statute and thus further research may be merited for: (i) Claimants who are in approved training programs (50.20.118); (ii) Claimants who are timber workers or employed in rural natural resources impact areas (50.22.090); (iii) Claimants who participate in shared work plans (50.60.090); (iv) Claimants who are discharged by employers who were forced to garnish their wages (50.20.045); (v) Claimants who are alcoholics (50.20.060); (vi) Claimants who voluntarily quit to accept another job offer (50.20.050); (vii) Claimants who are ill or disabled (50.20.050); (viii) Claimants who voluntarily quit to perform domestic responsibilities (50.20.050); (ix) Claimants who were formerly aerospace workers (50.20.042); (x) Claimants who leave employment to relocate with a spouse (50.20.050); (xi) Claimants who are employees of educational institutions when it is between school semesters (50.44.050); (xii) Claimants who are professional athletes when it is between sports seasons. (50.20.113)

WEST VIRGINIA

STATUTE:

LAW: West Virginia Unemployment Compensation Law

CITATION: West Virginia Code, Chapter 21A, Article 1, Section 21A-1-1 (W.V.C. § 21A-1-1)

BENEFIT CALCULATION:

WEEKLY BENEFIT AMT.: Benefit amounts are contained in a Benefit Table in the law which takes into account the wages Claimant earned during his or her Base Period. (Benefit Table pairs $2,200 of total Base Period wages with a Weekly Benefit Amount of $24. From there, with each increase of $150 in Base Period wages, Claimant's Weekly Benefit Amount increases by approximately $1.60) (21A-6-10)

PARTIAL EMPLOYMENT: Claimant may earn up to $60 through partial employment and still receive his or her full Weekly Benefit Amount. (21A-6-11)

REDUCTION IN BENEFITS: Claimant's Weekly Benefit Amount may be reduced if: (i) Claimant receives pension benefits (21A-6-3); (ii) Claimant receives annuity payments (21A-6-3); (iii) Claimant receives Social Security payments (21A-6-3); (iv) Claimant receives retirement pay (21A-6-3); (v) Claimant receives payments from a trust fund contributed to by a Base Period and/or chargeable employer. (21A-6-3)

DEPENDENCY BENEFIT: None.

MIN./MAX. WEEKLY: Minimum weekly benefit is $24. (21A-6-10) Maximum weekly benefit is calculated as 66 2/3% of the Statewide Average Weekly Wage. (21A-6-10) For 2001, the maximum weekly benefit was $338. (21A-6-10)

MAXIMUM TOTAL: Claimant may receive total benefits equaling 26 x his or her Weekly Benefit Amount. (21A-6-10) In times of high unemployment, extended benefits may be available. (21A-6A-3)

BENEFIT ELIGIBILITY:

GENERALLY: To be eligible for unemployment compensation benefits, Claimant must: (i) File a claim for benefits (21A-6-1); (ii) Register for work at a state unemployment office (21A-6-1); (iii) Continue to report to a state unemployment office as required (21A-6-1); (iv) Earn at least $2,200 during his or her entire Base Period (21A-6-1); (v) Earn wages during more than one quarter of his or her Base Period (21A-6-1); (vi) Be able to work and available for full-time work for which he or she is fitted for by prior training or experience (21A-6-1); (vii) Do what a reasonably prudent person would do in his or her circumstances to seek work (21A-6-1); (viii) Participate in reemployment services as required. (21A-6-1)

SUBSEQUENT APPLICATION: A Claimant who received benefits during a preceding Benefit Year must have worked and earned 8 x his or her Weekly Benefit Amount, as calculated for the prior Benefit Year, subsequent to the commencement of the prior Benefit Year and before the commencement of his or her new Benefit Year. (21A-6-1b)

WAITING WEEK: Claimant must serve 1 Waiting Week before collecting benefits. (21A- 6-1)

DISQUALIFICATION: Claimant may be partially, fully or at least temporarily disqualified from receiving benefits if: (i) Claimant was discharged for misconduct from most recent work or from his or her last thirty-day employing unit (21A-6-3); (ii) Claimant was discharged for gross misconduct (i.e. discharged for the willful destruction of employer's property, an assault on his or her employer or fellow employees at work or during the course of employment, being under the influence of a controlled substance at work, committing theft, arson, larceny, fraud, or embezzlement in connection with work, or for any acts of misconduct where Claimant received prior written warning that termination of employment may result from such acts) from most recent work or from his or her last thirty-day employing unit (21A-6-3); (iii) Claimant voluntarily left most recent work without good cause involving fault on part of employer (21A-6-3); (iv) Claimant voluntarily left work to marry or perform marital, parental or familial duties (21A-6-3); (v) Claimant failed, without good cause, to apply for suitable work, or to return to customary self-employment (21A-6-3); (vi) Claimant separation was caused by a labor dispute (21A-6-3); (vii) Claimant made a false statement knowing it to be false or knowingly failed to disclose a material fact in order to obtain benefits (21A-6-3); (viii) Claimant is receiving unemployment benefits from another state or under federal law (21A-6-3); (ix) Claimant receives wages in lieu of notice (21A-6-3); (x) Claimant receives temporary total disability payments under the workmen's compensation act (21A-6-3); (xi) Claimant quit to attend school (21A-6-3); (xii) Claimant requested and was granted a vacation which caused his or her employer to suspend operations (21A-6-3); (xiii) Claimant is an illegal alien. (21A-6-3)

PURGING DISQUALIFICATION: A Claimant who voluntarily quit may be eligible for benefits only after he or she returns to employment and works for at least 30 days. (21A-6-3) A Claimant who was discharged for gross misconduct may be eligible for benefits only after a 7 week disqualification period passes and after he or she returns to employment and works for at least 30 days. (21A-6-3)

SPECIAL TREATMENT:

Claimants in the following categories are afforded distinct treatment under the statute and thus further research may be merited for: (i) Claimants who are in approved vocational training programs (21A-6-4); (ii) Claimants who are members of the National Guard or other Armed Forces reserve unit who are engaged in inactive duty for training (21A-6-4a); (iii) Claimants who return to their last previous employer preceding the employer from which they separate (21A-6-3); (iv) Claimants who work in seasonal employment (e.g. food processing or canning) (21A-6-1a); (v) Claimants who are employees of educational institutions when it is between school semesters (21A-6-15); (vi) Claimants who are professional athletes when it is between sports seasons. (21A-6-3)

WISCONSIN

STATUTE:

LAW: Wisconsin Unemployment Insurance and Reserves Act

CITATION: West's Wisconsin Statutes Annotated, Section 108.01 (W.S.A. § 108.01)

BENEFIT CALCULATION:

WEEKLY BENEFIT AMT.: Benefit amounts are calculated as 4% of the wages Claimant received during his or her highest-paying Base Period quarter. (108.05)

PARTIAL EMPLOYMENT: Claimant may earn from partial employment wages equaling up to $30 and still receive his or her full Weekly Benefit Amount, but his or her Weekly Benefit Amount will be reduced by 67% of any wages in excess of this amount. (108.05) Claimant is ineligible for benefits in any week in which his or her partial benefits dip below $5 and may otherwise be rendered ineligible despite this calculation if the Claimant continues to work for his or her regular employer. (108.05)

REDUCTION IN BENEFITS: Claimant's Weekly Benefit Amount may be reduced if: (i) Claimant receives pension benefits (108.05); (ii) Claimant receives retirement pay (108.05); (iii) Claimant receives annuity payments (108.05); (iv) Claimant receives other similar payments, whether periodic or not, based upon previous work (108.05); (v) Claimant receives Social Security payments (108.05); (vi) Claimant receives holiday, vacation, termination, sick, or back pay. (108.05)

DEPENDENCY BENEFIT: None.

MIN./MAX. WEEKLY: Minimum weekly benefit is calculated every 6 months as 15% of the maximum weekly benefit. (108.05) For 2001, the minimum weekly benefit was $46. (108.05) Maximum weekly benefit is calculated each 6 months as 66 2/3% of the Statewide Average Weekly Wages. (108.05) For 2001, the maximum weekly benefit was $313. (108.05)

MAXIMUM TOTAL: Claimant may receive total benefits equaling the lesser of (i) 26 x his or her Weekly Benefit Amount or (ii) 40% of his or her total Base Period wages. (108.06) In times of high unemployment, extended or supplemental benefits may be available. (108.141, 108.142) Disaster unemployment assistance may also be available. (108.145)

BENEFIT ELIGIBILITY:

GENERALLY: To be eligible for unemployment compensation benefits, Claimant must: (i) Register for work at a state unemployment office (108.04); (ii) Answer all questions regarding eligibility for benefits asked by the department (108.04); (iii) Earn wages of at least 30 x his or her Weekly Benefit Amount during his or her entire Base Period (108.04); (iv) Earn in sum during all but his or her highest-paying Base Period quarter an amount at least equal to 4 x his or her Weekly Benefit Amount (108.04); (v) Earn at least $1,150 in his or her highest-paying Base Period quarter (108.05); (vi) Be able to work and available for work (108.04); (vii) Seek suitable work during each week he or she is unemployed. (108.04)

SUBSEQUENT APPLICATION: A Claimant who received benefits during a preceding Benefit Year must have worked and earned, 8 x his or her Weekly Benefit Amount, as calculated for the new Benefit Year, subsequent to the commencement of his or her prior Benefit Year. (108.04)

WAITING WEEK: None.

DISQUALIFICATION: Claimant may be partially, fully or at least temporarily disqualified from receiving benefits if: (i) Claimant was discharged for misconduct connected with work (108.04); (ii) Claimant suspended for good cause connected with work (108.04); (iii) Claimant voluntarily left work without good cause (108.04); (iv) Claimant failed to accept or return to suitable work without good cause (108.04); (v) Claimant separation was caused by a labor dispute other than a lockout (108.04); (vi) Claimant files a fraudulent claim for benefits, fails to provide sufficient information, fails to comply with a request to provide relevant information, conceals any part of his or her wages earned, conceals his or her refusal of a job offer, or conceals any other material fact (108.04); (vii) Claimant is receiving unemployment benefits from another state or under federal law (108.04); (viii) Claimant is on a voluntary leave of absence for a finite period (108.04); (ix) Claimant has a license which is necessary for his or her employment and it is either suspended, revoked, or not renewed due to employee fault (108.04); (x) Claimant is unable to work or unavailable for work (108.04); (xi) Claimant is on family or medical leave under the federal Family and Medical Leave Act of 1993 (108.04); (xii) Claimant voluntarily requests an indefinite reduction in his or her working hours (108.04); (xiii) Claimant is an illegal alien. (108.04)

PURGING DISQUALIFICATION: A Claimant who was discharged for misconduct, may be eligible for benefits only after 7 weeks have elapsed since the discharge and he or she has received remuneration for work subsequent to the disqualifying separation in the amount of 14 x his or her Weekly Benefit Amount. (108.04) A Claimant who voluntarily quits or fails to accept or return to suitable work, may be eligible for benefits only after 4 weeks have elapsed since the separation and he or she has received remuneration for work subsequent to the disqualifying separation in the amount of 4 x his or her Weekly Benefit Amount. (108.04)

[continued on next page]

SPECIAL TREATMENT:

Claimants in the following categories are afforded distinct treatment under the statute and thus further research may be merited for: (i) Claimants who are in vocational training or basic education programs (108.04); (ii) Claimants who apply for benefits while working for the same employer who paid them 80% of their Base Period wages (108.05); (iii) Claimants who quit part-time positions but who are otherwise eligible because of the loss of a full-time position (108.04); (iv) Claimants who stop working for a labor organization and subsequently are discharged by their employer (108.04); (v) Claimants who work for more than one employer and quit from only one of these positions (108.04); (vi) Claimants who quit to return to a permanent residence (108.04); (vii) Claimants who quit current employment to accept an employment recall (108.04); (viii) Claimants who leave or are discharged for reaching the age of compulsory retirement in a firm (108.04); (ix) Claimants who are self-employed (108.04); (x) Claimants who own or who have immediate family members who own a substantial interest in the partnership, limited liability company, or corporation by which they are or were employed (108.04); (xi) Claimants who quit due to health problems affecting members of their immediate family (108.04); (xii) Claimants who quit to accept other employment (108.04); (xiii) Claimants who are volunteer fire fighters or volunteer emergency medical technicians (108.05); (xiv) Claimants who receive temporary total disability payments or temporary partial disability payments (108.04); (xv) Claimants who are employees of educational institutions, governmental units or nonprofit organizations when it is between school semesters (108.04); (xvi) Claimants who are professional athletes when it is between sports seasons (108.04); (xvii) Claimants who leave work while escaping domestic violence. (108.04)

WYOMING

STATUTE:

LAW: Wyoming Employment Security Law

CITATION: Wyoming Statutes Annotated, Title 27, Chapter 3, Section 27-3-101 (W.S.A. § 27-3-101)

BENEFIT CALCULATION:

WEEKLY BENEFIT AMT.: Benefit amounts are calculated as 4% of the wages Claimant received during his or her highest-paying Base Period quarter. (27-3-303) Claimants Weekly Benefit Amount may be modified depending on the unemployment trust fund balance. (27-3-303)

PARTIAL EMPLOYMENT: Any wages Claimant receives from partial employment in excess of 50% of his or her Weekly Benefit Amount are deducted from his or her Weekly Benefit Amount. (27-3-303)

REDUCTION IN BENEFITS: Claimant's Weekly Benefit Amount may be reduced if: (i) Claimant receives pension benefits (27-3-313); (ii) Claimant receives retirement pay (27-3-313); (iii) Claimant receives annuity payments (27-3-313); (iv) Claimant receives other payments from any former employer or any trust or fund contributed by a former employer (27-3-313); (v) Claimant receives severance or termination pay (27-3-313); (vi) Claimant receives earned vacation pay (27-3-313); (vii) Claimant receives sick pay.

DEPENDENCY BENEFIT: None.

MIN./MAX. WEEKLY: Minimum weekly benefit is calculated as 4% of the amount a Claimant must earn in his or her highest-paying Base Period quarter to qualify for benefits (see calculation below) (27-3-303). For 2001, the minimum weekly benefit was $20 (***). Maximum weekly benefit is calculated annually as 55% of the Statewide Average Weekly Wage, but cannot exceed $200 (27-3-303). For 2001, the maximum weekly benefit was $283. (***)

MAXIMUM TOTAL: Claimant may receive total benefits equaling the lesser of (i) 26 x his or her Weekly Benefit Amount or (ii) 30% of his or her total Base Period wages. (27-3-304) In times of high unemployment, extended benefits may be available. (27-3-317)

BENEFIT ELIGIBILITY:

GENERALLY: To be eligible for unemployment compensation benefits, Claimant must: (i) File a claim for benefits (27-3-306); (ii) Register for work at a state unemployment office (27-3-306); (iii) Continue to report to a state unemployment office as required (27-3-306); (iv) Earn during his or her entire Base Period wages in an amount at least equal to 8% of the statewide average annual wage (which was approximately $1,750 in 1996) (27-3-306); (v) Earn during his or her entire Base Period wages which are at least 1.4 x the amount of wages he or she received in his or her highest-paying Base Period quarter (27-3-306); (vi) Be able to work and available for work (27-3-306); (vii) Be actively seeking work (27-3-306); (viii) Participate in reemployment services as required. (27-3-306)

SUBSEQUENT APPLICATION: A Claimant who received benefits during a preceding Benefit Year must have worked and earned 8 x his or her Weekly Benefit Amount subsequent to the commencement of such Benefit Year and before the commencement of his or her new Benefit Year. (27-3-306)

WAITING WEEK: Claimant must serve 1 Waiting Week before collecting benefits. (27-3-306)

DISQUALIFICATION: Claimant may be partially, fully or at least temporarily disqualified from receiving benefits if: (i) Claimant was discharged for misconduct connected with most recent work (27-3-311); (ii) Claimant voluntarily left most recent work without good cause attributable directly to his or her employment (27-3-311); (iii) Claimant failed, without good cause, to apply for available, suitable work, or to accept suitable work (27-3-311); (iv) Claimant who was unemployed for at least 4 weeks failed to apply for or accept available work, other than his or her customary occupation, which offered at least 50% of the compensation of his or her previous work in his or her customary occupation (27-3-311); (v) Claimant who was unemployed for at least 4 weeks and a member of a labor organization failed to apply for or accept suitable nonunion work in his or her customary occupation (27-3-311); (vi) Claimant separation was caused by a labor dispute (27-3-313); (vii) Claimant knowingly files a claim for benefits which contains a false statement or misrepresentation of a material fact, or failed to disclose a material fact in order to obtain benefits (27-3-311); (viii) Claimant committed fraud in connection with a claim for benefits (27-3-702); (ix) Claimant is receiving unemployment benefits from another state or under federal law (27-3-313); (x) Claimant is self-employed in an independently established trade or business for more than 3 days or earns from self-employment an amount which exceeds his or her Weekly Benefit Amount (27-3-313); (xi) Claimant is an illegal alien. (27-3-309)

[continued on next page]

PURGING DISQUALIFICATION: A Claimant who was discharged for misconduct, voluntarily quit work, failed to apply for or accept suitable work, failed to apply for or accept available work offering at least 50% of the compensation of his or her previous work after 4 weeks of unemployment, or failed to apply for or accept suitable nonunion work after 12 weeks of unemployment, may be eligible for benefits only after working for 12 weeks, whether consecutive or not, and receiving remuneration for work subsequent to the disqualifying separation in the amount of 12 x his or her Weekly Benefit Amount. (27-3-311)

SPECIAL TREATMENT:

Claimants in the following categories are afforded distinct treatment under the statute and thus further research may be merited for: (i) Claimants who are in approved training programs (27-3-307); (ii) Claimants who have suffered from illness or injury for which they were compensated under the state workers' compensation act (27-3-310); (iii) Claimants who formerly held positions as corporate officers (27-3-306); (iv) Claimants who are employees of educational institutions when it is between school semesters (27-3-308); (v) Claimants who are professional athletes when it is between sports seasons (27-3-308); (vi) Claimants who separate from employment while escaping from domestic violence. (27-3-311)

Appendix C
Case Study Examples
Defining Terms

There are certain words and phrases common to nearly every state unemployment compensation law. Some of these are particularly ambiguous and open to a variety of interpretations. Where such ambiguity in statutory terminology exists, attorneys and legal scholars turn to court decisions to aid in their interpretations. That is, where legislation is unclear, people typically look toward interpretations provided by judges on what a certain word or phrase means.

This appendix contains a discussion of five of the least understandable phrases found in nearly every state unemployment compensation statute. After explaining where the phrase is normally found in the law, this appendix dissects the key concepts contained in each phrase, and attempts to define these concepts through a series of questions and answers. Finally, case study examples, modeled loosely after the facts in actual court cases, are provided to help explain the issues more clearly.

List of Questions

Question 1: Willful Misconduct

What does *willful misconduct in connection with work* mean?

In nearly every state, if an employee is discharged for *willful misconduct in connection with work,* he or she will be disqualified from collecting unemployment compensation benefits. Sometimes state laws use similar phrases, such as *just cause in connection with employment* or *misconduct occurring in most recent work,* but these and other similar phrases are roughly interpreted in a similar manner.

Basically, these phrases all mean that if an employer contests a discharged employee's eligibility for benefits, the employer must demonstrate three distinct points:

1.   That the act which resulted in the discharge was *willfully* performed by the employee.

2.   That the willful act should be construed as *misconduct* under the law.

3.   That the willful misconduct was *sufficiently connected to the employee's work* experience that the employer was justified in discharging the employee for committing the particular act.

The following series of questions and answers should help you to understand more clearly how these key concepts are typically interpreted by interviewers at state unemployment offices, administrative law judges, unemployment compensation review boards, and courts of law. Case study examples are also provided to help define the issues more clearly.

QUESTION: When is employee misconduct *willful?*

ANSWER 1:   An employee who *deliberately disregards* a reasonable request by his or her employer willfully fails to perform his or her duties.

Case Study Example:

Facts: Eileen Emploi had been employed by Request Co., Ltd., for approximately three years as an assembly line supervisor. In this capacity, she always worked a forty hour work week. Due to machine breakdowns, production at Request Co., Ltd., fell behind two days. Eileen's boss asked her to supervise the other laborers for some additional hours this week to try to bring production up to pace. Eileen refused to put in the overtime because she had already worked a full work week. Request Co., Ltd., fired Eileen for refusing to work.

📖 Eileen is not eligible for unemployment compensation benefits because she deliberately disregarded her employer's reasonable request to work overtime. (See *Dorisma v. Florida Unemployment Appeals Comm'n*, 544 So.2d 1110 (Fla.App. 3 Dist. 1989).)

ANSWER 2:   An employee who acts with *recurring carelessness* despite repeated warnings, willfully fails to perform his or her duties.

Case Study Example:

Facts: Jeni Jobster had been employed by Oil Inc., for the last seventeen years as a pumper. During the last six years of her employment she had been given five warnings and placed on suspension three times for careless errors. Yesterday, while goofing around, Jeni accidentally allowed two tanks containing different types of waste oil to mix causing Oil Inc., over $12,000 in damages. This is the second time she has made this mistake in the past two months. Oil Inc., discharged Jeni.

📖 Jeni is not eligible for unemployment compensation benefits because she caused her employer significant financial loss by failing to pay sufficient attention to her job duties despite repeated warnings by her employer. (See *Simmons v. Unemployment Compensation Bd. of Review*, 565 A.2d 829 (Pa.Cmwlth. 1989).)

ANSWER 3:   An employee who has a *compelling reason* to disregard an employer's instructions does not wilfully fail to perform his or her duties.

Case Study Example:

Facts: Elliott Eveready had been employed on a work crew for Revolving Company for less than a year, on a work schedule that was constantly changing. One day Elliott's supervisor told Elliott he and the rest of the crew would be working on a very important project the next day during the 9:00 a.m. to 5:00 p.m. shift. When Elliott woke up the following day he had a stomach ache so he telephoned his employer to take sick leave. Without Elliott, the remaining crew members were unable to complete the important project. This is the fourth time Elliott was absent for work in the last three months. Revolving Company discharged Elliott for failing to report to work.

Elliott may be eligible for unemployment benefits because his illness provided him a compelling reason to fail to report to work. (See *Cargill, Inc. v. Hill,* 503 So.2d 1340 (Fla.App. 1 Dist. 1987).)

ANSWER 4:   An employee who accidentally fails to perform a duty of his or her employment, lacks the proper skills to complete a duty, or who is otherwise *unable to satisfactorily complete an assignment*, does not willfully fail to perform his or her duties.

Case Study Example:

Facts: Max Machinist was recently employed by Red Tape Inc., to help manufacture specialty gears and other machine parts. While Max performed his machining responsibilities satisfactorily, he encountered significant difficulties filling out the paperwork associated with different products since he could not read very well. Red Tape Inc., discharged Max when his failure to complete a form properly resulted in a product being shipped to Pittsburgh, Peru, instead of Pittsburgh, Pennsylvania.

📖 Max may be eligible for unemployment benefits because his poor performance was due to his inability to fulfill his job duties not his failure to apply himself. (See *Lewis v. Unemployment Appeals Comm'n.*, 498 So.2d 608 (Fla.App. 5 Dist. 1986).)

QUESTION: When does an act or omission by an employee constitute *misconduct*?

ANSWER 1:   When an employee *fails to abide by an established workplace rule*, he or she commits an act of misconduct.

Case Study Example:

Facts: Dawn Druggedowt drove a forklift at Kaboom Co., a nuclear power plant. As a condition of being hired, Dawn was required to sign a form provided by Kaboom Co., in which she consented to regular drug testing and was made aware of company policy to discharge those who refused to submit to such tests when asked. One day when Dawn's supervisor noticed she had been driving the forklift in a rather reckless manner, the supervisor asked her to submit to a drug test. The supervisor warned her that she would be discharged unless she agreed to the test. Dawn remembered signing the consent form, but refused to take the test. Kaboom Co., discharged Dawn.

📖 Dawn is not eligible for unemployment compensation benefits because she refused to abide by an established policy of which she had knowledge. (See *Moore v. Unemployment Compensation Bd. of Review*, 578 A.2d 606 (Pa.Cmwlth. 1990).)

ANSWER 2:   When an employee fails to abide by the *standards of behavior that an employer has a right to expect*, he or she commits an act of misconduct.

Case Study Example:

Facts: Monroe Motersikel had been hired by Delivery Incorporated to deliver groceries all over the city. While delivering the groceries on his own motorscooter, Monroe had to wear the well-known company uniform, a roadrunner bird outfit. On Monroe's second day of work, Delivery Incorporated received over thirty telephone complaints that a guy wearing a roadrunner bird outfit and driving a motorscooter had driven recklessly, causing three automobile accidents, and consistently had disobeyed a litany of other traffic laws. Monroe was the only delivery person who had worked on the day in question. Delivery Incorporated discharged Monroe when he completed his daily route.

📖 Monroe is not eligible for unemployment benefits because he was discharged for committing a variety of acts which reflected very poorly on his employer and of which he should have known his employer would disapprove. (See *Trinh Trung Do v. Amoco Oil Co.*, 510 So.2d 1063 (Fla.App. 4 Dist. 1987).)

ANSWER 3: Where an *employer tolerates* the regular violation of a workplace rule, the employee who fails to abide by it does not commit an act of misconduct.

Case Study Example:

Facts: Maria Maskara worked as a receptionist for Anon Ltd., a company which distributes cosmetics for women on a door-to-door basis. After working there for about a year, Maria realized that she rarely received telephone calls during her final hour of work. Maria began skipping her lunch hour and leaving work an hour early. Her immediate supervisor had witnessed this practice a few times, but had not confronted Maria on this issue. On her final day at work Maria failed to direct an extremely important call to her supervisor's office because she had left work early. Maria was fired.

📖 Maria may be eligible for unemployment compensation benefits because her employer had acquiesced to her leaving work an hour early each day, and had therefore relinquished its right to complain that this act violated company policy. (See *Avon Products, Inc. v. Wilson*, 513 A.2d 1315 (Del.Supr. 1986).)

ANSWER 4: When a *workplace rule is unreasonable*, an employee who fails to abide by it does not commit an act of misconduct.

Case Study Example:

Facts: Buffy Bupher was employed by Scrubber Co., to wash and wax stadium floors. Because the company had a reputation for its detailed work, each employee was forced to use a toothbrush to complete his or her assignment, making it a very physically demanding job. After working a full day and putting in six hours of overtime, Buffy's boss informed him that he would have to stay for at least an additional four hours because a relief worker had just called in sick. Buffy, claiming he was too exhausted to continue working, went home and was promptly discharged by Scrubber Co.

📖 Buffy may be eligible for unemployment benefits because he was discharged for refusing to put in additional overtime hours which were unreasonable considering he had already worked additional hours on the day in question and his job was very physically demanding. (See *Nelson v. Star Tribune*, 445 N.W.2d 864 (Minn.App. 1989).)

QUESTION: When is an act of willful misconduct by an employee sufficiently *connected with work?*

ANSWER 1: When employee misconduct *occurs on his or her employer's premises or during work*, the act is sufficiently connected with work.

Case Study Example:

Facts: Scott Soused was fired from his job at the Just Meat, Ltd., meat processing facility after three years of service. Scott had been caught drinking alcohol during his afternoon break, contrary to the established rule of the company prohibiting the consumption of alcohol on the job. Scott argued that he was on a break and had a right to do what he wanted. The management of Just Meat, Ltd., responded that since all employees take their paid fifteen minute breaks on company property, employees are subject to company rules during their break-time.

📖 Scott is not eligible for unemployment benefits because he failed to abide by company policy when on company property during a paid break period. (See *Longmont Turkey Processors v. Industrial Claim Appeals Office*, 765 P.2d 1073 (Colo.App. 1988).)

ANSWER 2:   When employee misconduct *affects his or her ability to do his or her job*, the act is sufficiently connected with work.

Case Study Example:

Facts: Andy Alkohall was employed as a drug and alcohol rehabilitation counselor for the Just Say Not Now Clinic. One Friday evening after leaving work Andy was pulled over by a policeman claiming Andy had been swerving all over the road. Tests revealed that Andy had been driving under the influence of alcohol and several other controlled substances. The local newspaper reported this fact in its next edition. The Just Say Not Now Clinic discharged Andy for his misbehavior.

📖*:* Andy is not eligible for benefits because the negative publicity received for Andy's indiscretion would have rendered him ineffective as a drug and alcohol counselor. (See *Feagin v. Everett*, 652 S.W.2d 839 (Ark.App. 1983).)

ANSWER 3:   When employee misconduct is more of a *personal or private nature*, then the act is not sufficiently "connected with work."

Case Study Example:

Facts: Arthur Autobus worked as a mechanic for Moral Authority Bus Lines. One day when he was off duty, Arthur took part in a barroom brawl. When the police arrived to break up the altercation, they arrested Arthur along with fourteen other drunken men and placed them in jail for the night. Arthur was released the next day on his own recognizance. When Arthur's supervisor heard about the event he disapproved of Arthur's conduct and fired him.

📖 Arthur may be eligible for unemployment benefits because his inappropriate behavior can in no way be connected with his employment at Moral Authority Bus Lines. (See *Southeastern Pennsylvania Transp. Auth.*, 506 A.2d 974 (Pa.Cmwlth. 1986).)

QUESTION 2:
QUIT WITHOUT GOOD CAUSE

What does *voluntarily quit work without good cause* mean?

In nearly every state, if you *voluntarily quit work without good cause*, you will be disqualified from collecting unemployment compensation benefits. Sometimes state laws include a similar but slightly different phrase such as "voluntarily left work without a necessitous and compelling reason," but this and other similar phrases are roughly interpreted in a similar manner.

Basically, an employee filing a claim for benefits after quitting work must demonstrate at least one of two points:

1. That he or she did not quit voluntarily, but was in essence forced to leave by the employer. In such a case, the employee's separation generally will be judged upon the willful misconduct grounds discussed in the prior subsection. Under these circumstances, the employer must demonstrate that it discharged the employee for willful misconduct.

2. That he or she quit for good cause.

The following series of questions and answers should help you to understand more clearly how these key concepts are typically interpreted by interviewers at state unemployment offices, administrative law judges, unemployment compensation review boards, and courts of law. Case study examples are also provided to help define the issues more clearly.

QUESTION: When does an employee quit *voluntarily*?

ANSWER 1:   When an employee leaves an employer merely because he is trying to improve his conditions of employment, or merely feels it is in his *best interest* to quit, he quits voluntarily.

Case Study Example:

Facts: After graduating from law school, Adrienne Atorknee secured a part-time position as a law clerk in the law offices of Scheister & Scheister, in Alexandria, Virginia. After six months of service in this capacity, Adrienne concluded that her income was insufficient to cover the costs associated with living in the Washington area. Despite her constant requests, however, the managing partner of Scheister & Scheister failed to provide her with the full-time position she desperately needed to make ends meet. Adrienne quit her position at the firm to take the bar examination in New Jersey to hopefully secure employment in that state.

📖 Adrienne is not eligible for unemployment compensation benefits because she voluntarily left Scheister & Scheister to try to improve her income. (See *Gopstein v. District of Columbia Dept. of Employment Servs.*, 479 A.2d 1278 (D.C.App. 1984).)

ANSWER 2: When an employee is *compelled to resign* by his or her employer, he or she does not leave voluntarily.

Case Study Example:

Facts: Matthew Managin had worked as bank manager for the Last National Bank in San Francisco for over three years. When the longstanding president of the bank recently retired at age sixty-five, a fellow bank manager, Mr. Meenie, was promoted to the position of bank president. After just three weeks it was clear that Matthew and Mr. Meenie did not get along well. Besides obvious personality clashes, the new president also sent Matthew three memos harshly criticizing his work. After an additional week of work and two more critical memos, Matthew, was given the option of submitting a letter of resignation or being fired. He opted for the less embarrassing and traumatic option of resigning rather than being fired.

📖 Matthew may be eligible for unemployment benefits because he was compelled to leave the bank and did not do so voluntarily. (See *Dobbins v. Everett*, 620 S.W.2d 309 (Ark.App. 1981).)

QUESTION: When does an employee quit for *good cause?*

ANSWER 1: When an employee is motivated to quit by a cause that would have induced any *reasonably prudent person under the circumstances* to quit, he or she quits for good cause.

Case Study Example:

> *Facts:* Rachel Resepshunist had served as the secretary for Loco Co., for over five years. Since being hired, she answered telephone calls and typed memos and formal proposals for two salesmen. She typically worked from 9:00 a.m. to 5:00 p.m. Last February, the officers of Loco Co., decided to market their unique line of novelty items internationally, and hired twelve new salesmen. Unfortunately for Rachel, however, the company failed to budget additional funds for secretarial services. Rachel's schedule, subsequently, became very hectic. She began putting in ten hour workdays and was scheduled for sporadic night work to answer incoming calls from around the world. Feeling very stressed, Rachel began seeing a psychiatrist who warned her that if she did not slow down she may have a nervous breakdown. Rachel notified her immediate supervisor of the severity of her condition on at least three occasions. Her supervisor apologized but stated that the company was slightly over-extended and could not afford to hire help for Rachel. Rachel left her job at Loco Co.

> 📖 Rachel may be eligible for unemployment benefits because a reasonable person in her condition would quit if his or her employer failed to respond to such complaints. (See *Lofton v. Review Bd. of the Indiana Employment Sec. Div.*, 499 N.E.2d 801 (Ind.App. 3 Dist. 1986).)

ANSWER 2: An employee has good cause to voluntarily leave work only if he or she does so in good faith with a *genuine desire to work and be self-supporting.*

Case Study Example:

> *Facts:* Selma Stop was hired as a sales associate for Piggy, Inc., in December of last year, after being unemployed for almost two years. About two weeks after she started work, the company pres-

ident approached her and made several sexually suggestive statements to her. Selma, embarrassed, pretended not to hear the comments and returned to work. Over the course of the next few weeks Selma was subjected to offensive patting, occasional groping, and even kissing by the president on at least three occasions. On each of these occasions Selma withdrew, but because she sincerely needed the income her job provided, never otherwise objected to the treatment. Finally, frustrated, Selma approached the vice-president of Piggy, Inc., and discussed her problem. While the vice-president severely disapproved of the president's behavior, she reluctantly explained that she could not really do anything to help Selma. Selma quit her job.

📖 Selma may be eligible for unemployment benefits because she did everything in her power to preserve her employment, and quit only after she reasonably concluded that her particular problem was impossible to resolve. (See *McEwen v. Everett*, 637 S.W.2d 617 (Ark.App. 1982).)

ANSWER 3: When an employer's *demands on an employee are unreasonable and unfair*, an employee who voluntarily quits does so for good cause.

Case Study Example:

Facts: Kristin Klothing had worked as a full-time seamstress for eleven years for the Montgomery Sword Co., when she was notified that her position would be modified and she would now act as a sales clerk. While the position paid her same hourly rate, she would work only a part-time basis, somewhere between twenty and twenty-nine hours a week. Without being provided any alternative, Kristin quit Montgomery Sword Co., and filed for unemployment benefits.

📖 Kristin may be eligible for unemployment benefits because her employer made unreasonable and unfair modifications in her employment duties, and substantially reduced the number of hours she would be able to work. (See *Mshar v. Review Bd. of Indiana Employment Sec. Div.*, 445 N.E.2d 1376 (Ind.App. 1983).)

ANSWER 4:   When an employee has viable *options available* other than quitting employment, his or her voluntary termination before exploring those options does not constitute good cause.

Case Study Example:

> *Facts:* Harvey Hardlyware had been working for Hammers 'R Us for five weeks when he decided to leave his employment. When he first accepted the position at Hammers 'R Us, he thought he had been hired for a sales position. Despite this, Harvey had been patiently working on the loading dock for the past five weeks, hoping that he would be moved to the sales floor in the near future. Harvey never mentioned his dissatisfaction with his employment to his manager at Hammers 'R Us, or the fact that working on the docks aggravated his pre-existing back condition, because it was clear that the dock was very understaffed and could not spare any workers. After a particularly grueling day at work, Harvey left and never returned.
>
> Harvey is not eligible for unemployment benefits because he should have discussed with his manager the possibility of a reassignment to another position before leaving the company. (See *Ellis v. Northwest Fruit & Produce*, 654 P.2d 914 (Idaho 1982).)

QUESTION 3: SUITABLE WORK

What does *failure, without good cause, to accept or apply for suitable work* mean?

In nearly every state, if an employee *fails, without good cause, to accept or apply for suitable work*, he or she will be disqualified from collecting unemployment compensation benefits. Thus, an employee who is receiving benefits and either rejects work or fails to apply for a potential position, must demonstrate at least one of two distinct points in order to remain eligible for benefits:

1. That he or she had good cause to reject the employment.

2. That the job refused was not suitable for him or her.

The following series of questions and answers should help you to understand more clearly how these key concepts are typically interpreted by interviewers at state unemployment offices, administrative law judges, unemployment compensation review boards, and courts of law. Case study examples are also provided to help define the issues more clearly.

QUESTION: When does an employee have *good cause* to fail to accept or apply for suitable work?

ANSWER 1:   An employee has good cause to fail to accept an offer of suitable work if a *reasonably prudent person would have rejected the terms and/or conditions* of such offer.

Case Study Example:

> *Facts:* Danny Ductwirk held a job with the Blowinaire Co., for five years before he was terminated. Soon after he was found eligible for unemployment benefits at a rather tumultuous hearing, his former employer mailed him a letter offering him another position with the firm. The position required him to perform tasks similar to those required at his former job, at a rate of pay roughly comparable to that received for his prior job. Blowinaire Co., placed a number of conditions on the offer of employment, including that Danny admit that the acts which resulted in his original dismissal constituted misconduct, and agree to accept a suspension without pay for the period between his former and new employment. Such an acceptance would, arguably, disqualify Danny from receiving unemployment benefits during this interim period. Danny refused the offer.

> 📖 Danny is eligible for continued benefits because a reasonably prudent person would reject an offer which forces him or her to relinquish rights for which he or she had successfully fought. (See *Johnson v. Virginia Employment Comm'n*, 382 S.E.2d 476 (Va.App. 1989).)

ANSWER 2:   An employee has good cause to fail to accept an offer of suitable work only if he or she does so in good faith with a *genuine desire to work and be self-supporting*.

Case Study Example:

Facts: Carmine Ciddies was an unemployed bookkeeper who had signed up with the state unemployment office and two other local employment agencies in an effort to secure work. Approximately two months after being laid off from his last job, the unemployment compensation office referred him to Badtyme Co., which was searching for an accounting clerk. Carmine's interview went very well and he was excited when the firm mailed him a letter offering him a position with a wage and benefit package roughly comparable to what he had been provided by his last employer. Under the terms of the offer, however, the position at Badtyme Co., required Carmine to work evenings on the weekends. While this did not excite him, he was more than willing to accommodate Badtyme Co., if he could find a reliable person to watch his children. After one month of feverishly searching for affordable child-care in vain, he reluctantly declined the offer.

📖 Carmine is eligible for continued unemployment benefits because he actively sought work and did all he could to overcome an obstacle limiting his ability to accept an otherwise suitable job offer. (See *Trexler v. Unemployment Compensation Bd. of Review*, 365 A.2d 1341 (Pa.Cmwlth. 1976).)

ANSWER 3:   An employee does not have good cause to fail to accept an offer of suitable work if he or she does so merely because the employment would have subjected him or her to *uncomfortable or moderately stressful working conditions*.

Case Study Example:

Facts: After being unemployed for two months, Jon Jalopee was offered employment by Shipit Inc., a trucking company for which he had worked one year ago. He refused the offer for two reasons. First, he claimed that Shipit Inc., typically scheduled its drivers to work unusually long days which averaged about ten hours. Second, he complained that Shipit Inc., pressured drivers to drive all the way back to the home terminal each night to return their trucks. Jon explained that these were the same two reasons that prompted him to quit the firm originally. ***Decision:*** Jon is not eligible for benefits because, while the working conditions imposed on employees by Shipit Inc. were definitely a source of stress and pressure on employees, the firm did not require such employees to participate in any real dangerous or unlawful conduct. See *Kranstover v. Bergen's Greenhouse*, 404 N.W.2d 842 (Minn.App. 1987).

QUESTION: When is work really *suitable* for a particular employee?

ANSWER 1: Work is suitable for a particular employee only where performing the duties of the occupation will not impose excessive risks upon his or her *health, safety, or morals*.

Case Study Example:

Facts: Jim Jriver had worked as a truck driver for fifteen years for Bee Lines, Inc., until the company closed down at the beginning of last year. Trying to make the best of the situation, Jim decided to take advantage of his temporary free time by undergoing the back surgery his doctor had been recommending for several years. Three months after the surgery, the minor back discomfort he had felt before the surgery had grown into a very sharp pain, which he experienced each time he sat for more than an hour. In the meantime, Jim received a phone call from the president of Bee Lines, Inc., calling him back to work. Jim declined the position one week after filing for unemployment benefits.

Jim may be eligible for benefits because truck driving is no longer suitable work for him as he can no longer sit in the cab of a truck for the extended periods of time. (See *Genetin v. Unemployment Compensation Bd. of Review*, 451 A.2d 1353 (Pa. 1982).)

ANSWER 2: Work is suitable for a particular employee only where the number of *work hours, wages, and work duties* associated with such employment are compatible with his or her skills, experience, and other qualifications.

Case Study Example:

Facts: Harlene Hamer was offered a position as maintenance supervisor for the Maintainen Company, which she rejected as not being suitable employment. While she had never been a supervisor of maintenance, she was well qualified for the position because she had worked in maintenance departments for ten years. Harlene did not complain about the wages offered, but explained that her reluctance to accept the position was at least in part because, unlike her former employer, the Maintainen Company did not provide employees with health insurance, or paid vacations and holidays. Her biggest complaint, was that they wanted to hire her on a six month temporary basis, upon the expiration of which they stated they would interview her again for a permanent position.

📖 Harlene is not eligible for unemployment benefits because most of the terms offered to her are substantially similar to the terms of employment of her prior employer. (See *Roberson v. Director of Labor,* 775 S.W.2d 82 (Ark.App. 1989).)

ANSWER 3:   Work is suitable where the employee is expected to travel only a *reasonable commuting distance* for such employment.

Case Study Example:

Facts: Bryan Breephs was offered a position as a ladies' undergarment inspector for Undies, Inc. While he had only inspected mens' undergarments in the past, he felt up to the challenge. When he received the written offer from the company, however, he discovered that Undies, Inc., wanted him to work in their factory in the city, not in the factory in his suburb where he had been interviewed. Bryan declined the offer because he did not want to travel the fifteen miles back and forth to work each day.

📖 Bryan is not eligible for unemployment benefits because Undies, Inc., did not expect him to drive an unreasonable distance to work. (See *Roberson v. Director of Labor,* 775 S.W.2d 82 (Ark.App. 1989).)

ANSWER 4:   Work is not suitable where the particular employee's *prospects of obtaining superior work in a reasonable amount of time* are reasonably good.

Case Study Example:

> **Facts:** After being unemployed for only one week, Paul Professeder was offered a part-time tutoring position with Skool High School. He declined the offer because he feared that, if he accepted it, he would have a difficult time searching for a full-time position between his hours of employment. As a tutor, he was expected to work an unpredictable number of hours at different times of the day. As such, his weekly pay check was unpredictable as well.
>
> 📖 Paul may be eligible for unemployment benefits because he has only been unemployed for one week and, generally, claimants must be provided a reasonable opportunity to seek an employment position commensurate with their work skills and normal salary levels. (See *Simpson v. Unemployment Compensation Bd. of Review*, 522 A.2d 110 (Pa.Cmwlth. 1987).)

QUESTION 4: ABLE AND AVAILABLE FOR WORK

What does *able and available for work* mean?

In nearly every state, you will only be deemed eligible for benefits if you can prove that you hold yourself out to the labor market as being *able and available for work*. Thus, you must demonstrate two points to establish a valid claim for benefits:

1. That you are able to work.

2. That you have made yourself available to employers who would consider hiring you.

The following series of questions and answers should help you to understand more clearly how these key concepts are typically interpreted by interviewers at state unemployment offices, administrative law judges, unemployment compensation review boards, and courts of law. Case study examples are also provided to help define the issues more clearly.

QUESTION: When is an employee *able* to work?

ANSWER: An employee who is too *mentally or physically ill* to perform any significant purposeful activity is not able to work.

Case Study Example:

Facts: Caitlyn Corrier had been employed by Getitgivit Ltd., a local package delivery company, for almost three years. By the beginning of her second year of employment, she regularly suffered from bouts of dizziness during her morning delivery route. Over time her illness grew worse, until she began suffering from several extended blackouts on a daily basis. Caitlyn visited several doctors concerning her illness and attempted to treat her dizzy spells with bottled oxygen, all to no avail. Caitlyn subsequently left her job, pursuant to her doctor's instructions, and filed for unemployment benefits.

▭ Caitlyn is not eligible for benefits because she is incapable of securing substantial employment given her propensity towards suffering from extended, recurring, and unpredictable spells of unconsciousness. (See *McCurdy v. Unemployment Compensation Bd. of Review*, 442 A.2d 1230 (Pa.Cmwlth 1982).)

QUESTION: When is an employee *available* for work?

ANSWER 1: An employee who is *ready, willing, and able to accept employment* by a reasonable number of employers in the community is available for work.

Case Study Example:

Facts: Frank Fircrakir was hired over two years ago for a receptionist position at Dinomite Unlimited, a firm which manufactures explosives for use in mining and for other industrial applications. Dinomite conducts random quality assurance tests on its products throughout the day. After Frank's first year of service, he began to feel very anxious throughout much of the day, in fear that at any moment Dinomite would ignite one of its products, causing the entire Dinomite building to shake violently. As his condition worsened, he agreed to see a psychologist. After a battery of tests, the psychologist warned Frank that if he did not leave the stressful environment of Dinomite soon, he would be on his way to a severe emotional breakdown. Frank quit his job to look for employment elsewhere.

📖 Frank may be eligible for benefits because he is still qualified and prepared to work as a receptionist in a less stressful environment. (See *Kuna v. Unemployment Compensation Bd. of Review*, 512 A.2d 772 (Pa.Cmwlth. 1986).)

ANSWER 2: An employee who places *reasonable restrictions* on his or her availability for work is still available for work.

Case Study Example:

Facts: Mary Migreat worked as a seasonal agricultural worker just outside of San Francisco, California. When the harvesting season was over in the fall, Mary returned to her permanent residence in the Rio Grande Valley area of Texas, where she filed for benefits and began vigorously searching for work. Before leaving California, and since returning to Texas, she never investigated work available in California.

📖 Mary may be eligible for unemployment benefits, despite the fact that she restricted her labor market area to the Rio Grande Valley, because she is still available for employment by more than a minimal number of employers in the community. (See *Rios v. Employment Dev. Dept.*, 231 Cal.Rptr. 732 (Cal.App. 1 Dist. 1986).)

QUESTION 5:
REASONABLE ASSURANCE OF RETURNING TO WORK

When does an employee have a *reasonable assurance of returning to work?*

Nearly every state statute declares certain employees ineligible for benefits, despite the fact that they are not currently working, when they have a *reasonable assurance of returning to work* in the near future. Certain employees of educational institutions or educational service agencies are typically prohibited from receiving unemployment benefits during extended vacation periods, or between two academic terms, as long as they have such an assurance. It should be noted that certain states only apply this provision to a limited number of such employees, such as "nonprofessional" employees, choosing not to treat "professional" employees who work for educational institutions different from other employees in general. One other group of employees often fall within this reasonable assurance concept: those employees who are compensated for participating in sports or other athletic events are often forbidden to collect benefits between succeeding seasons.

Thus, in a state that broadly applies this provision to all employees of an educational institution, if the administration of a school can demonstrate that a particular teacher was provided with a reasonable assurance that he or she would be re-employed after the summer break, then the teacher would be deemed ineligible for benefits during the break. Similarly, if a sports franchise can show that a player was provided with a reasonable assurance that he or she would play in the following season, he or she would be ineligible for benefits during the hiatus.

The following series of answers should help you to understand more clearly how this key concept typically is interpreted by interviewers at state unemployment offices, administrative law judges, unemployment compensation review boards, and courts of law. Case study examples are also provided to help define the issue more clearly.

ANSWER 1: If an employer provides an employee with a *written, verbal, or implied agreement* to return to work, even if such employer fails to guarantee that the employee will be given the position, the employee has a reasonable assurance of being re-employed.

Case Study Example:

> *Facts:* Sharon Shubstitute has filled in as an instructor on an "as needed" basis for Komonin Elementary School for the past three years. At the end of the last semester Sharon received the same letter she always received at that time of year from the school board. The letter stated that the school board intended to hire her for the upcoming school year in the same capacity as she had worked during the prior three years, asked Sharon to return a form expressing her interest in returning, and further asked her to provide a list of names of any other teachers in the community who she thinks might consider also joining the Komonin team. Finally, the letter contained a disclaimer explaining that those who are employed on an "as needed" basis are given "no assurance of employment" since the nature of the job is only to fill in for absent teachers. Over the last three years, Sharon has worked an average of three days a week. Sharon applied for unemployment benefits over the summer.
>
> 📖 Sharon is not eligible for benefits because the sum of the circumstances surrounding her separation, including the stated intention of the board, the fact that the board anticipated the need for additional teachers, and the fact that Sharon had worked a relatively steady schedule over the last three years, suggest that it is very likely that she will be re-employed by Komonin in the upcoming semester. (See *Board of Educ. v. California Unemployment Ins. Appeals Bd.*, 206 Cal.Rptr. 788 (Cal.App. 2 Dist. 1984).)

ANSWER 2: If an employer makes hiring an employee *contingent on several factors*, the employee will not have a reasonable assurance of being re-employed.

Case Study Example:

> *Facts:* Michael Mathmann served as an arithmetic tutor for the Seeya Private School for Boys for the last two semesters of the school year. Over summer recess Michael asked the chairwoman of

the arithmetic department if he would be re-employed when school resumed after Labor Day, and was told that if enrollment were high enough, she would not object to rehiring him. Not feeling very assured, Michael then approached the principal of the school with the same question. The principal explained that there was no real way of knowing how many students would request Michael as a tutor next semester, so he could not give him a firm commitment. Michael applied for unemployment benefits.

📖 Michael may be eligible for benefits because the decision to re-employ him was contingent upon the number of students registering for arithmetic, the number of students in need of tutors in this subject, and the number of students who specifically requested Michael as a tutor next semester. (See *Redmond v. Employment Div.*, 675 P.2d 1126 (Or.App. 1984).)

ANSWER 3:   The mere fact that an employee has been *employed by an employer for many years* does not in itself always provide him or her with a reasonable assurance of being re-employed.

Case Study Example:

Facts: Richie Reeden taught foreign students to speak English for the past four years at Adios Junior College. After the conclusion of the fall semester he was approached by the head of the English department, as she had done each of his four prior years, and asked if he would be available to teach during the next semester. He said that he would. Richie was never really told, however, whether there would be an adequate number of students enrolled in the next semester to justify rehiring him after the school break. In fact, his questions concerning enrollment always went unanswered. Richie applied for unemployment benefits.

📖 Richie may be eligible for benefits because, under the circumstances, his past employment was not an adequate predictor of his future employment security. (See *Matter of Jama*, 467 N.Y.S.2d 82 (A.D. 3 Dept. 1983).)

APPENDIX D
SAMPLE FORMS

This appendix contains a representative sampling of the forms a claimant may encounter during the unemployment compensation benefit application process. While, the actual information requested on the application in your state may vary slightly, you should be prepared to answer the questions included on the appropriate forms, included herein, during the respective stages of the application process.

NOTE: *Many states now permit claimants to apply for benefits directly over the Internet. The majority of states allow the claimant to file at least the initial application by telephone. For further information concerning application options, please contact your state agency at the telephone numbers or web addresses included in Appendix A.*

TABLE OF FORMS

Employment Development Department

State of California

UNEMPLOYMENT INSURANCE APPLICATION

PRE APPLICATION QUESTIONS MUST BE COMPLETED

A. Were you in the military during the last 18 months? ☐ Yes ☐ No
B. Did you work for an agency of the federal government during the last 18 months? ☐ Yes ☐ No
C. Did you work in a state other than California during the last 18 months? ☐ Yes ☐ No
D. Have you applied for unemployment insurance benefits in another state during the last 12 months? ☐ Yes ☐ No
E. Did your employer or union give you a claim form for unemployment insurance benefits? ☐ Yes ☐ No

If you answered NO to all of the above questions (A through E) proceed.
If you answered YES to any of the above questions (A through E) do not complete this form, call 1 (800) 300-5616.

PLEASE ANSWER ALL QUESTIONS ON EACH PAGE

If a question is not answered it may delay or prevent the filing of your claim, or cause benefits to be denied.

- **Please complete this form with blue or black ink only.**
- **Please print or type information.**

The answers you give to the questions on the application must be true and correct. You may be subject to penalties if you make a false statement or withhold information.

This application will take you approximately 30 minutes to complete.

1. What is your Social Security Number?	1. __ __ __ - __ __ - __ __ __ __
2. List any other Social Security Numbers you have used.	2. a) __ __ __ - __ __ - __ __ __ __ b) __ __ __ - __ __ - __ __ __ __
3. What is your name?	3. Last _____ First _____ Middle Initial: ___
4. List any other names you have used.	4. _____ _____
5. What is your birth date?	5. __ __/__ __/__ __ __ __ (mm/dd/yyyy)
6. What is your gender?	6. ☐ Male ☐ Female
7. a) Would you prefer your written material in English or Spanish? b) What is your preferred spoken language?	7. a) ☐ English ☐ Spanish b) _____
8. List the names of employers you worked for in the last 18 months. a) _____ c) _____ b) _____ d) _____	
9. What is your telephone number?	9. (__ __ __) __ __ __-__ __ __ __

UNEMPLOYMENT INSURANCE APPLICATION

Social Security Number: __ __ __ - __ __ - __ __ __ __

10. What is your **mailing** address? Include your city, state, and ZIP code.	10. Street: _____ City: _____ State: __ __ ZIP Code __ __ __ __ __
11. If you do not live in California, what is the name of the County in which you live?	11. _____

12. What is the highest grade of school you have completed? Check only one box.

☐ Did not complete High School ☐ High School Diploma or GED ☐ Some college or vocational school
☐ Associate of Arts ☐ Bachelor of Arts or Science ☐ Masters or Doctorate

13. Are you a Veteran?	13. ☐ No ☐ Yes
14. In the last 18 months, which employer did you work for the longest?	14. _____
a) How long did you work for that employer?	a) Years __ __ Months __ __
b) What type of business did that employer operate? (Please be **specific.** For example, software manufacturing, legal services, retail furniture sales, road construction.)	b) _____
c) What kind of work did you do for that employer?	c) _____

Please provide information on your **very last employer**. This is the employer you last worked for regardless of the length of time you worked at that job, the type of work you did for that employer or whether or not you have been paid.

Reminder: To file a claim, individuals must be out of work (for any reason), or working less than full time. You must provide information on the last employer you worked for as an employee. Do not include self-employment unless you have elective coverage.

15. a) What is the last date you actually worked for your **very last employer**?	15. a) __ __/__ __/__ __ __ __ (mm/dd/yyyy)
b) What are your gross wages for your last week of work? For unemployment insurance purposes, a week begins on Sunday and ends the following Saturday.	b) $ __ __ __ __ . __ __
c) What is the complete name of your **very last employer?**	c) Name _____
d) What is the mailing address of this employer?	d) Street: _____ City _____ State: __ __ ZIP Code: __ __ __ __ __
e) What is the telephone number of this employer?	e) (__ __ __) __ __ __-__ __ __ __
f) Why are you no longer working for your **very last employer**? Check one box. (Lack of work includes temporary layoff, or on call status)	f) ☐ Laid off, lack of work ☐ Fired ☐ Quit ☐ Strike or lockout ☐ Still working part time

Briefly explain in your own words the reason you are no longer working for your **very last employer**, within the space provided. Please do not include any attachments. _____

_____

UNEMPLOYMENT INSURANCE APPLICATION

Social Security Number: __ __ __ - __ __ - __ __ __ __

16. Do you expect to return to work for any former employer?	16. ☐ Yes ☐ No
17. Are you currently self-employed, or do you plan to become self-employed? (Self-employment means you have your own business or work as an independent contractor.) If yes explain: _____ _____	17. ☐ Yes ☐ No
18. Are you now, or have you been in the last 18 months an officer of a corporation or union or the sole or major stockholder of a corporation? If yes explain: _____ _____	18. ☐ Yes ☐ No
19. Are you currently attending, or do you plan on attending school or training? If yes: a) What is the starting date of the school or training? b) What is the ending date of the current session? c) What is the name of the school? d) What is the telephone number of the school? e) What are the days and hours you are attending, or plan to attend, school?	19. ☐ Yes ☐ No a) __ __/__ __/__ __ __ __ (mm/dd/yyyy) b) __ __/__ __/__ __ __ __ (mm/dd/yyyy) c) _____ d) (__ __ __) __ __ __-__ __ __ __ e) _____ _____
20. What is your usual occupation?	20. _____
21. Are you available for immediate full-time work in your usual occupation? If no: a) Are you available for immediate part-time work in your usual occupation? If no: b) Please explain why you are not available for work:	21. ☐ Yes ☐ No a) ☐ Yes ☐ No b) _____ _____
22. Are you receiving, or will you receive within the next 52 weeks, a pension other than Social Security or Railroad Retirement, which is based on your own work or wages? If yes: a) How are you receiving your pension payments? b) Did you pay into your pension or retirement? c) Did any of the employers you worked for in the last 18 months pay into the pension fund? d) What is the name of the company paying into the pension? e) Who pays the pension check to you?	22. ☐ Yes ☐ No a) ☐ Monthly ☐ Annually ☐ Lump sum b) ☐ Yes ☐ No c) ☐ Yes ☐ No ☐ Unsure d) _____ e) _____

UNEMPLOYMENT INSURANCE APPLICATION

Social Security Number: __ __ __ - __ __ - __ __ __ __

23. Are you receiving, or do you expect to receive, Workers' Compensation? If yes: a) Who is the insurance carrier? b) What is the insurance carrier's telephone number? c) What is the case number, if known? d) What are the dates of your claim, if known?	23. ☐ Yes ☐ No a) _____ b) (__ __ __) __ __ __-__ __ __ __ c) _____ d) from: __ __/__ __/__ __ __ __ (mm/dd/yyyy) to: __ __/__ __/__ __ __ __ (mm/dd/yyyy)

24. Have you received or do you expect to receive any payments from your last employer, other than your regular salary? (for example, holiday pay, vacation pay, severance, in-lieu-of-notice pay, etc.)

If yes: **Example:** Vacation Pay $600.00   10/07/2001   10/20/2001

Type of Payment	Amount	From (mm/dd/yyyy)	To (mm/dd/yyyy)

25. Are you a member of a union? If yes: a) What is your union name and local number? b) Through what date are your dues paid? c) Does your union look for work for you? d) Does your union control your hiring? e) Are you registered with your union as out of work?	25. ☐ Yes ☐ No a) _____ b) __ __/__ __/__ __ __ __ mm/dd/yyyy c) ☐ Yes ☐ No d) ☐ Yes ☐ No e) ☐ Yes ☐ No
26. Do you have a date to start work? If yes: a) What date will you start work?	26. ☐ Yes ☐ No a) __ __/__ __/__ __ __ __ mm/dd/yyyy
27. Are you an employee of a school, educational institution, or a training facility? If yes: a) Are you returning to work in the next school session?	27. ☐ Yes ☐ No a) ☐ Yes ☐ No
28. Is your usual work seasonal? If yes: a) When does the season usually begin? b) When does the season usually end? c) What other work related skills do you have?	28. ☐ Yes ☐ No a) __ __/__ __/__ __ __ __ mm/dd/yyyy b) __ __/__ __/__ __ __ __ mm/dd/yyyy c) _____ _____

UNEMPLOYMENT INSURANCE APPLICATION

Social Security Number: __ __ __ - __ __ - __ __ __ __

29. Are you a U. S. citizen or national? If no: a) Are you registered with INS and authorized to work in the United States? If yes: b) What is your Alien Registration Number? c) What is the expiration date of your work authorization? d) Were you legally entitled to work in the United States for the last 19 months? e) What is the title and number of the INS document you have?	29. ☐ Yes ☐ No a) ☐ Yes ☐ No b) __ __ __ __ __ __ __ __ __ __ __ c) __ __/__ __/__ __ __ __ (mm/dd/yyyy) d) ☐ Yes ☐ No e) Check one box:

☐ Green Card (I-151)   ☐ Employment Authorization Card (I-688A)
☐ Resident Alien Card (I-551)   ☐ Temporary Resident Card (I-688)
☐ Permanent Resident Card (I-551)   ☐ Employment Authorized (I-688B)
☐ Employment Authorization Card (I-766)   ☐ Arrival/Departure Record (I-94)
☐ Stamp on Visa (That states: "Processed for I-551 Temporary Evidence of Lawful Admission of Permanent Residence valid until mmddyyyy, Employment Authorized.")

THE FOLLOWING TWO QUESTIONS ARE OPTIONAL:

30. What race or ethnic group do you identify with? Check one box.

☐ White	☐ Black not Hispanic	☐ Hispanic
☐ American Indian/Alaskan Native	☐ Asian	☐ Chinese
☐ Cambodia	☐ Filipino	☐ Guamanian
☐ Other Pacific Islander	☐ Asian Indian	☐ Japanese
☐ Korean	☐ Laotian	☐ Samoan
☐ Vietnamese	☐ Hawaiian	☐ I choose not to answer

31. Do you have a disability? (A disability is a physical or mental impairment that substantially limits one or more life activities, such as caring for oneself, performing manual tasks, walking, seeing, hearing, speaking, breathing, learning, or working.)	31. ☐ Yes ☐ No ☐ I choose not to answer

YOU MAY SUBMIT THE COMPLETED APPLICATION:

-   By mail to the following address:
 	
    EDD
    P.O. Box 419000
    Sacramento, CA 95841-9000
	- By FAX to the following telephone number:
	
	    1-866-215-9159

UA 1554 WR
(Rev. 2-2001)

PLEASE PRINT CLEARLY —
DO NOT WRITE IN SHADED AREAS

Authorized by
MCL 421.1, et seq.

B.O. No. _____

State of Michigan
Department of Consumer & Industry Services
UNEMPLOYMENT AGENCY

APPLICATION FOR UNEMPLOYMENT BENEFITS

Completion of this form is required to qualify for benefits.

☐ Check this box if your name or address has changed since your last claim.

1. SOCIAL SECURITY NUMBER   CK DIGIT

2. ADDITIONAL SOCIAL SECURITY NUMBER   CK DIGIT

3. LAST NAME

4. FIRST NAME

5. MI

6. BIRTH DATE

7. MAILING ADDRESS

8. CITY

9. STATE

10. ZIP CODE

11. COUNTY

12. AREA CODE and TELEPHONE NUMBER
( )

13. YEARS OF SCHOOL COMPLETED

14. SEX   ☐ MALE   ☐ FEMALE

15. ADDITIONAL NAME WORKED UNDER (INCLUDE MAIDEN NAME)

16. **TO CLAIM A PERSON AS A DEPENDENT:** YOU MUST HAVE PROVIDED MORE THAN HALF THE COST OF HIS OR HER SUPPORT FOR AT LEAST 90 DAYS IMMEDIATELY BEFORE FILING YOUR CLAIM. IF THE RELATIONSHIP HAS EXISTED LESS THAN 90 DAYS, THE PERSON MUST HAVE RECEIVED MORE THAN HALF THE COST OF HIS OR HER SUPPORT FROM YOU FOR THE DURATION OF THE MARITAL OR PARENTAL RELATIONSHIP. YOU CAN CLAIM YOUR HUSBAND OR WIFE, CHILD, ADOPTED CHILD, STEPCHILD, OR GRANDCHILD, OR ORPHANED BROTHER OR SISTER IF UNDER THE AGE OF 18 YEARS, OR 22 IF ENROLLED FULL-TIME IN SCHOOL, OR IF THE BROTHER OR SISTER IS UNABLE TO ENGAGE IN EMPLOYMENT BECAUSE OF A PHYSICAL OR MENTAL INFIRMITY. YOUR LEGAL FATHER OR MOTHER, IF THAT PARENT IS OVER 65 OR IS PERMANENTLY DISABLED. VERIFICATION OF DEPENDENTS MAY BE REQUIRED. ENTER THE TOTAL NUMBER OF DEPENDENTS YOU ARE CLAIMING IN THE BOX TO THE RIGHT. ONLY ONE PERSON MAY CLAIM OR RECEIVE A DEPENDENCY ALLOWANCE FOR THE SAME INDIVIDUAL.

No. of DEPENDENTS
(DO NOT CLAIM YOURSELF)

17. ENTER YOUR DRIVER LICENSE OR STATE ID NUMBER

18. STATE   ☐ Michigan   ☐ Other _____

19. DO YOU WANT FEDERAL AND STATE TAXES WITHHELD?
☐ YES   ☐ NO
IF "YES," NUMBER OF TAX EXEMPTIONS

20. ARE YOU WORKING FULL-TIME THIS WEEK? .... ☐ YES   ☐ NO

21. ARE YOU A CITIZEN OR NATIONAL OF THE UNITED STATES?
☐ YES   ☐ NO

22. IF YOU ARE NOT A CITIZEN OR NATIONAL, ARE YOU IN SATISFACTORY IMMIGRATION STATUS? .... ☐ YES   ☐ NO
WHAT IS YOUR ALIEN REGISTRATION NUMBER AND EXPIRATION DATE?
/

23. *(Optional)* ARE YOU HISPANIC OR LATINO? .... ☐ YES   ☐ NO

24. *(Optional)* IN ADDITION TO ITEM 23, ARE YOU:
Please check one:
☐ White
☐ Asian
☐ Black or African American
☐ Pacific Islander or Native Hawaiian
☐ Native American Indian or Alaskan Native

25. ARE YOU ATTENDING A SCHOOL OR COLLEGE? ... ☐ YES   ☐ NO
CIRCLE DAYS YOU ATTEND: M T W T F
HOURS: FROM _____ TO _____ AM / FROM _____ TO _____ PM

26.

27. DID YOU PERFORM SERVICES AS A PROFESSIONAL ATHLETE IN THE PAST 18 MONTHS? .... ☐ YES   ☐ NO

28. DID YOU EARN AT LEAST A GROSS OF $1,500 WITH ALL EMPLOYERS SINCE FILING YOUR LAST NEW CLAIM? .... ☐ YES   ☐ NO
IF "NO," ENTER YOUR GROSS EARNINGS WITH ALL EMPLOYERS SINCE FILING YOUR LAST NEW CLAIM. $ _____ *(Approximate)*

29. IF YOU RECEIVE OR APPLIED FOR RETIREMENT BENEFITS:
RETIREMENT EFFECTIVE DATE _____
MONTHLY AMOUNT: $ _____
RECEIPT DATE OF FIRST RETIREMENT CHECK: _____
EMPLOYER: _____
REQUEST FORM UA 1554-2 WR IF YOU ARE RECEIVING OR WILL RECEIVE RETIREMENT BENEFITS FROM MORE THAN ONE EMPLOYER.

Continue with Item 31 on the Reverse Side.

— DO NOT WRITE IN THIS AREA — FOR AGENCY USE ONLY

30.
FIPS CITY CODE

FIPS COUNTY CODE

FILING DATE

BYB DATE

OCCUPATION CODE

WAIVER
☐ RSW   ☐ SWW   ☐ JAW
WAIVER DATE:

PROFILE

CERT METHOD
If Other Than "T"

CLAIM TYPE
☐ NEW   ☐ TC

PROCESS TYPE
☐ I - UI   ☐ F - UCFE   ☐ C - CO-MINGLE   ☐ X - UCX

IB/CWC

PRESERVATION OF BENEFIT ENTITLEMENT

COUNTER DENIAL

UCFE
☐ FULL-TIME
☐ PART-TIME
☐ SF8COPY
☐ SF50

GROSS EARNINGS AFTER BYB
(PAY ADJ. TYPE I)
EFFECTIVE W/E DATE _____
AMOUNT $ _____

DOCUMENT USED IN LIEU OF D.L.:

SSN VERIFIED:
☐ SS CARD
☐ WDB

262

UA 1554 WR Reverse Side (Rev. 2-2001)

SOCIAL SECURITY NUMBER | CK DIGIT

LIST EACH EMPLOYER YOU WORKED FOR DURING THE LAST 18 MONTHS, BEGINNING WITH YOUR LAST EMPLOYER. INCLUDE ANY WORK PERFORMED FOR FEDERAL, STATE, OR LOCAL GOVERNMENT, AND ANY WORK PERFORMED IN OTHER STATES. DO NOT WRITE IN SHADED AREAS. PLEASE PRINT CLEARLY. IF MILITARY, REQUEST FORM UCX 970.

LAST

31. EMPLOYER NAME

32. FIRST DAY WORKED | 33. LAST DAY WORKED | EMPLOYER ACCOUNT NUMBER | MULTI-UNIT | CHECK DIGIT

34. PAYROLL ADDRESS

35. CITY | 36. STATE | 37. ZIP CODE | 38. COUNTY/STATE WORKED IN | FIPS CNTY | 39. AREA CODE and TELEPHONE NO. ( )

40. REASON FOR SEPARATION (Enter the reason number in the box)

(1) LAID OFF/LACK OF WORK
(2) FIRED
(3) QUIT
(4) RETIRED (Voluntarily)
(5) RETIRED (Involuntarily)
(6) LABOR DISPUTE ☐ Strike ☐ Lockout
(7) OTHER (Explain in Item 41)
(8) STILL EMPLOYED FULL-TIME
(9) FIRED FOR ANY OF THE FOLLOWING:
☐ WILDCAT STRIKE
☐ IMPRISONMENT
☐ DRUGS ☐ THEFT
☐ ASSAULT AND BATTERY
☐ WILLFUL DESTRUCTION

41. EXPLAIN THE REASON FOR YOUR SEPARATION.

42. JOB TITLE

43a. DO YOU EXPECT TO RETURN TO WORK FOR THIS EMPLOYER? ☐ YES ☐ NO IF YES, GIVE DATE

43b. ARE YOU REQUIRED TO OBTAIN EMPLOYMENT THROUGH A UNION HIRING HALL? ☐ YES ☐ NO

43c. DID YOU HAVE ANY OTHER LAYOFFS OR SEPARATIONS FROM THIS EMPLOYER DURING THE PAST 18 MONTHS? ☐ YES ☐ NO
IF "YES," WHAT WERE YOUR GROSS EARNINGS WITH THIS EMPLOYER SINCE THAT LAYOFF OR SEPARATION?
$ _____ (Approximate)
IF "NO," WHAT WERE YOUR GROSS EARNINGS WITH THIS EMPLOYER IN THE PAST 18 MONTHS?
$ _____ (Approximate)

NEXT TO

31. EMPLOYER NAME

32. FIRST DAY WORKED | 33. LAST DAY WORKED | EMPLOYER ACCOUNT NUMBER | MULTI-UNIT | CHECK DIGIT

34. PAYROLL ADDRESS

35. CITY | 36. STATE | 37. ZIP CODE | 38. COUNTY/STATE WORKED IN | 39. AREA CODE and TELEPHONE NO. ( )

40. REASON FOR SEPARATION (Enter the reason number in the box)

(1) LAID OFF/LACK OF WORK
(2) FIRED
(3) QUIT
(4) RETIRED (Voluntarily)
(5) RETIRED (Involuntarily)
(6) LABOR DISPUTE ☐ Strike ☐ Lockout
(7) OTHER (Explain in Item 41)
(8) STILL EMPLOYED FULL-TIME
(9) FIRED FOR ANY OF THE FOLLOWING:
☐ WILDCAT STRIKE
☐ IMPRISONMENT
☐ DRUGS ☐ THEFT
☐ ASSAULT AND BATTERY
☐ WILLFUL DESTRUCTION

41. EXPLAIN THE REASON FOR YOUR SEPARATION.

42. JOB TITLE

43a. DO YOU EXPECT TO RETURN TO WORK FOR THIS EMPLOYER? ☐ YES ☐ NO IF YES, GIVE DATE

43b. ARE YOU REQUIRED TO OBTAIN EMPLOYMENT THROUGH A UNION HIRING HALL? ☐ YES ☐ NO

44. CHECK BOX IF YOU HAVE OR WILL RECEIVE ANY OF THE FOLLOWING PAYMENTS FOR ANY PERIOD AFTER YOUR LAST DAY OF WORK:
☐ VACATION ☐ HOLIDAY ☐ BONUS ☐ PAYMENT IN LIEU OF NOTICE ☐ DISABILITY COMPENSATION ☐ OTHER
GROSS AMOUNT $ _____ PERIOD COVERED: from _____ to _____

45. DID YOU WORK IN FAMILY EMPLOYMENT AS DEFINED BELOW? _____ ☐ YES ☐ NO
DEFINITION: EMPLOYMENT IN A BUSINESS OR CORPORATION IN WHICH THE MAJORITY INTEREST IS OWNED BY YOU ALONE, OR BY YOU TOGETHER WITH YOUR SON, DAUGHTER OR SPOUSE, OR BY ONE, OR ANY COMBINATION OF THESE INDIVIDUALS; OR BY YOUR MOTHER AND/OR FATHER IF YOU ARE UNDER THE AGE OF 18.
IF YOU WERE EMPLOYED UNDER THE CONDITIONS STATED ABOVE DURING THE LAST 18 MONTHS, PLEASE GIVE THE NAME(S) OF THE BUSINESS(ES): _____

NOTE: IF YOU HAD MORE THAN 2 EMPLOYERS DURING THE PAST 18 MONTHS, ASK FOR FORM UA 1554-2 WR.

STOP – DO NOT WRITE BELOW THIS SPACE UNTIL INSTRUCTED TO DO SO.

46. PLACE A CHECK MARK FOR EACH INFORMATION BOOKLET YOU RECEIVE: ☐ CLAIMANT 1900 HANDBOOK; ☐ MARVIN 1921 BOOKLET; ☐ TRA 1628 PAMPHLET; ☐ NAFTA INFORMATION. I VERIFY BY MY INITIALS THAT I RECEIVED EACH OF THE BOOKLETS CHECKED. _____

47. DID YOU RECEIVE A MICHIGAN TALENT BANK APPLICATION AND REGISTERING FOR WORK WITH MICHIGAN TALENT BANK CARD, FORM UA 1002, WITH INSTRUCTIONS TO REPORT TO A MICHIGAN WORKS! AGENCY LOCATION WITHIN 5 DAYS? _____ ☐ YES ☐ NO

48. YOUR CERTIFICATION: I HEREBY APPLY FOR A DETERMINATION OF MY UNEMPLOYMENT BENEFIT RIGHTS. I DECLARE THAT I AM A CITIZEN OF THE UNITED STATES OR I AM IN SATISFACTORY IMMIGRATION STATUS. I CERTIFY THAT ALL OF THE INFORMATION SUBMITTED BY ME ON THIS FORM IS TRUE AND CORRECT TO THE BEST OF MY KNOWLEDGE AND BELIEF. **I UNDERSTAND THAT THE LAW PROVIDES PENALTIES OF FINE, AND/ OR IMPRISONMENT, AND/OR COMMUNITY SERVICE FOR FALSE STATEMENTS TO SECURE BENEFITS.**
(DO NOT SIGN UNTIL INSTRUCTED) CLAIMANT'S SIGNATURE: _____ DATE: _____

CLAIMS TAKER'S INITIALS: _____ DATE D/E _____ INITIALS _____

263

UC INITIAL AND REOPENED CLAIM INSTRUCTIONS

This application is being provided for your use in filing an initial application for Unemployment Compensation. Please complete ALL information. The Department can determine if the claim is initial or reopened and process the application accordingly. Please answer ALL questions that apply to you.

When completed, mail or fax the form to the office that handles your county of residence. If you reside in New Jersey or Delaware, please mail or fax your application to the Scranton UC Service Center. If you reside in Puerto Rico or any other state, please mail or fax your application to the Lancaster UC Service Center. **NOTE:** You can mail up to 5 pages in one envelope with one $.34 stamp. If you mail 6 pages (all of the pages of the application), the cost is $.55. Mail only the pages that have your answers on them. Do not mail instructions or blank pages.

If you live in this county:	Mail/Fax your application to this office:
Berks, Bucks, Lehigh, Northampton	Allentown UC Service Center 160 W. Hamilton St., Ste 500 Allentown, PA 18101-1994 FAX: (610) 821-6281
Bedford, Blair, Cambria, Cameron, Centre, Clarion, Clearfield, Elk, Forest, Fulton, Huntingdon, Jefferson, McKean, Potter, Somerset, Warren	Altoona UC Service Center 1101 Green Ave. Altoona, PA 16601-3483 FAX: (814) 941-6801
Crawford, Erie, Venango	Erie UC Service Center 1316 State St. Erie, PA 16501-1978 FAX: (814) 871-4570
Adams, Cumberland, Dauphin, Franklin, Juniata, Lancaster, Lebanon, Mifflin, Perry, York	Lancaster UC Service Center 60 W. Walnut St. Lancaster, PA 17603-3015 FAX: (717) 299-7557
Chester, Delaware, Montgomery, Philadelphia	Philadelphia UC Service Center 2901 Grant Ave. Philadelphia, PA 19114-1069 FAX: (215) 560-6981
Bradford, Carbon, Clinton, Columbia, Lackawanna, Luzerne, Lycoming, Monroe, Montour, Northumberland, Pike, Schuylkill, Snyder, Sullivan, Susquehanna, Tioga, Union, Wayne, Wyoming	Scranton UC Service Center 30 Stauffer Industrial Park Taylor, PA 18517-9625 FAX: (570) 562-4873
Armstrong, Fayette, Indiana, Westmoreland	Indiana UC Service Center 630 Kolter Rd. Indiana, PA 15701 FAX: (724) 599-1068
Allegheny, Beaver, Butler, Greene, Lawrence, Mercer, Washington	Duquesne UC Service Center 14 N. Linden St. Duquesne, PA 15110 FAX: (412) 267-1475

IMPORTANT INFORMATION

If you are filing an initial claim, you will receive three separate mailings:

1. An official Notice of Financial Determination
2. A Claim Confirmation Letter
3. An Unemployment Compensation Handbook

You should receive all three of these mailings within 10 working days after you mail or FAX your application. If you do not receive these mailings, try to contact your UC Service Center by telephone. If you continue to have problems contacting the UC Service Center, you can send an Email to uciclaims@state.pa.us and place the words "Initial Claim Tracer" in the subject of the Email. Include your home telephone number in the Email.

When you receive the Notice of Financial Determination, please review it carefully. If any of the information on your financial determination is incorrect, follow the instructions on the reverse side of the form for filing an appeal.

The Claim Confirmation Letter will contain your **confidential** Personal Identification Number (PIN). **PLEASE SAVE IT.** Staff working in the UC Service Center will not know what your PIN number is. Your PIN will not change from year to year unless you personally change it using the PA Teleclaims (PAT) system. The Claim Confirmation Letter will also instruct you when to file your weekly claims using the Internet or by calling our automated telephone system (PAT).

Each new claim is in effect for 52 weeks but you will only receive either 16 or 26 times your weekly benefit rate during that period, depending on the number of credit weeks in the base year period of your claim. You are encouraged to accept every offer of full or part-time work during the period to guarantee benefits are available for the maximum period possible.

If you return to work, and subsequently become laid off, **YOU MUST CALL THE UC SERVICE CENTER TO REOPEN YOUR CLAIM WITHIN SEVEN (7) CALENDAR DAYS OF YOUR LAST DAY OF WORK.**

Filing your weekly claims using PA Teleclaims (PAT)
Detailed information on how to use the PAT is found at:
http://www.dli.state.pa.us/landi/cwp/view.asp?a=152&Q=53770

When you file a new claim, you have **an unpaid waiting week**. You are required to **CLAIM THAT WAITING WEEK TO GET PROPER CREDIT**. Claim your waiting week and the first payable week together unless you returned to work following the waiting week. If you returned to work after your waiting week, claim the second week and sign for the waiting week and then decline the second week because you returned to work.

If you work during a week you are claiming benefits, know your **GROSS EARNINGS, HOLIDAY PAY AND/OR VACATION PAY AMOUNTS BEFORE CLAIMING THE WEEK**. If you refused work or were not available for work when work was available, enter the amount of earnings you **COULD** have earned. Use the star (*) on your telephone pad to indicate a decimal point. (Example: $150.31 = 150*31)

DO NOT HANG UP BEFORE PAT INFORMS YOU THAT YOUR ANSWERS ARE SAVED. If you do, nothing is recorded and you can call PAT and try again. If PAT does not process your claim or you feel you have made a mistake, call the UC Service Center immediately. The UC Service Center has the ability to "reset" your weeks on PAT so you can try again.

APPLICATION FOR UC BENEFITS
CLAIMANT INFORMATION – Page 1

Social Security Number _____ PA Drivers License Number_____

First Name _____ MI _____ Last Name _____

Other Last Name (if used within the last 2 years)_____

Mailing Address: (if this is a PO Box, please also provide a residence address below)

    Street _____

    City _____ State _____

    Zip Code (include the + 4, if known) _____

Residence Address: (if different from the mailing address)

    Street _____

    City _____ State _____

    Zip Code (include the + 4, if known) _____

    NOTE: If you do not reside in the continental U. S., please provide the following:

        Non-US Postal Code _____

        Country _____

Birth date _____ Gender (male or female)_____

Home Telephone Number   (_____)_____

County within State of Residence   _____

Township or borough of Residence   _____

Home FAX Number   _____

Home E- mail address   _____

Highest Grade of School Completed   _____

UC- 42(I) Rev 01/ 11/ 2001

Claimant Name _____ Social Security Number _____

APPLICATION FOR UC BENEFITS (cont'd)
CLAIMANT INFORMATION – Page 2

Do you have any dependents?   **Y**   **N**

If YES, based on PA UC Law you may claim allowance of up to a maximum of $ 8.00 a week for dependents if you wholly or chiefly support them. A dependent can be a legally married spouse who lives with you, or children under the age of 18, or children over 18 who are unable to accept gainful employment due to a physical or mental infirmity.

Do you consider yourself the main support of the dependents you are claiming for UC purposes?   **Y**   **N**

How many dependents do you wish to claim?   _____

Are you claiming your spouse as a dependent?   **Y**   **N**

What is your spouse's name?   _____

Provide the name(s) of the children you are claiming as dependents?   _____

_____

==

Did you ever serve over 180 days in active duty for the U. S. Military?   **Y**   **N**

If **YES**, have you been classified as a disabled veteran?   **Y**   **N**

If **YES**, what is the percentage of the disability?   _____ %

What type of work are you seeking?   _____

Would you like to speak to a CareerLink Representative about employment services?   **Y**   **N**

==

Do you consider yourself to have a disability?   **Y**   **N**

Out of the following categories, how do you describe yourself?
_____ White, Not Hispanic   _____ American Indian / Alaskan Native
_____ Black, Not Hispanic   _____ Asian
_____ Hispanic   _____ Hawaiian/ Pacific Islander

APPLICATION FOR BENEFITS (cont'd)
CLAIMANT INFORMATION – Page 3

During the last 2 years, have you served on active duty in the U.S. Military?	Y	N
During the last 2 years, have you worked in a state other than Pennsylvania?	Y	N
During the last 2 years, have you worked as a civilian for the Federal Government?	Y	N
During the last 2 years, have you worked for a college, university or school?	Y	N
During the last 2 years, have you worked for any local or state government?	Y	N
In the next year are you or will you receive any type of pension including social security or lump sum payments?	Y	N
Are there any conditions under which you may not be able and available for work?	Y	N
UC is a taxable benefit. Do you want 10% of your gross weekly benefit amount withheld for Federal Income Tax?	Y	N
Are you a citizen of the United States?	Y	N
Have you ever received or been approved for Worker's Compensation or other accident or disability payments during the past 18 months?	Y	N
Do you get your jobs through a union hiring hall?	Y	N
Are you engaged in self-employment, working on a commission basis, or operating a farm?	Y	N
Are you working full-time or part-time for any other employer including the Reserves or National Guard?	Y	N
Are you the parent or spouse of your last employer?	Y	N
Did you own stock and serve as an officer for the company where you were last employed?	Y	N
Did you cross the PA state line to commute to work?	Y	N

Claimant Name _____ Social Security Number _____

APPLICATION FOR BENEFITS
EMPLOYER INFORMATION

Name of Employer _____

    Street _____

    City _____ State _____

    Zip Code (include the +4, if known) _____

Employer Telephone Number (_____) _____

    Fax Number (_____) _____

    Email _____

Contact Person (Supervisor or Manager where you worked) _____

    Title of Contact Person _____

PA UI Employer Account Number (if known) _____

    Plant Number or Branch _____

    Potential TRA (if the employer is TAA certified, enter yes) _____

Your First Day of Work for this employer _____

Your Last Day of Work for this employer _____

Did you earn gross wages of **$2,652.00** during the above period of employment
with this employer?   **Y**   **N**

What was your reason for separation from this employer? (or enter STILL EMPLOYED if still working
for this employer) _____

Were you told by your employer that you would be recalled to your job?   **Y**   **N**

    If yes, what is your date of recall? _____

What is your badge or timecard number? (if you have one) _____

Is this employer your separating employer?   **Y**   **N**

UC- 42(I) Rev 01/ 11/ 2001

Claimant Name _____ Social Security Number _____

APPLICATION FOR UC BENEFITS - INITIAL CLAIM
ADDITIONAL INFORMATION

If you served in active duty for the U S Military during the last 2 years, please complete the following questions:

Did you file a claim in another state since your most recent separation
from active military service?   **Y**   **N**

     If **YES**, in what state did you file your claim? _____

     If **YES**, when did you file your claim? _____

Did you apply for or do you receive:

     a subsistence allowance?   **Y**   **N**

     widow/orphan education assistance?   **Y**   **N**

FEDERAL MILITARY APPLICANTS NEED TO INCLUDE A COPY OF YOUR MEMBER- 4 COPY OF YOUR DD- 214 WHEN YOU RETURN YOUR APPLICATION.

If you worked for the federal government in the last two years, please complete the following questions:

Where was your last duty station? _____

Did you work for another employer in PA since your separation
from the Federal Government?   **Y**   **N**

     If **YES**, which city? _____

Is the Federal Agency Payroll office and address based on SF- 8?   **Y**   **N**

     If **NO**, was an SF- 8 issued? _____

What was your position / title? _____

Did you work full or part- time? _____

Was the work Permanent or Intermittent? _____

FEDERAL CIVILIAN APPLICANTS NEED TO INCLUDE COPIES OF YOUR PAYSTUBS FOR THE PAST 18 MONTHS WHEN YOU RETURN YOUR APPLICATION

UC- 42(I) Rev 01/ 11/ 2001

Claimant Name _____ Social Security Number _____

If you worked in any other state (besides PA) in the last 2 years, please complete the following questions:

In what state(s) were you employed?
_____
_____
_____
_____
_____

Do you want to file against another state instead of PA?   **Y**   **N**

If **YES**, which state?   _____

If you are non-U S Citizen, please complete the following questions:

What is your alien registration number?   _____

On what date were you first authorized to work in the U. S.?   _____

When does your work authorization expire?   _____

IF YOUR ALIEN DOCUMENTATION DOES NOT CONTAIN AN ALIEN NUMBER, YOU MUST INCLUDE A COPY OF YOUR WORK AUTHORIZATION WHEN RETURNING YOUR APPLICATION.

If you worked for less than one year for your last employer, please complete the following question:

How long had you worked for your previous employer?   _____ years _____ months

If your social security number ends with the numbers "05", please complete the following questions:

What is your regular occupation?   _____

Did you get a definite date of recall from ANY of your past employers?   **Y**   **N**

UC- 42(I) Rev 01/ 11/ 2001

UA 1564-2 WR
(Rev. 2-01)

State of Michigan
Department of Consumer & Industry Services
UNEMPLOYMENT AGENCY

ADDITIONAL CLAIM BY MAIL

Authorized by MCL 421.1, et seq.
Completion of this form is required to qualify for benefits.

CISV

BYB Date							B.O. No.

OCC.
CODE

To the Claimant:
Begin this form with Item 1 below.

Follow all instructions very carefully.

1. PRINT Name: Last	First	Middle	2. Social Security Number — —	Ck. Digit

3. No. and Street

4. City-State-Zip Code	County	5. Telephone Number ( )

IMPORTANT: THIS FORM IS TO BE USED FOR FILING YOUR ADDITIONAL CLAIM BY MAIL ONLY IF ALL SEPARATIONS SINCE YOU LAST CLAIMED BENEFITS WERE DUE TO LACK OF WORK, OR IF YOU HAVE HAD NO EMPLOYMENT SINCE YOU LAST CLAIMED BENEFITS.

Have you returned to work since last claiming benefits? .... ☐ NO ☐ YES

If "NO," your claim is effective the beginning of the week in which this form is **received**.
If "YES," complete item 11 below.

It is your responsibility to complete and mail this form so that it is RECEIVED by your branch office no later than the Friday after the end of the week containing your last day of work. If you stopped claiming benefits for a reason other than a return to work, this completed form must be RECEIVED during the first week for which you wish to start claiming benefits again.

YOU MUST HAVE A PERSONAL IDENTIFICATION NUMBER (PIN) TO CALL MARVIN. IF YOU HAVE FORGOTTEN YOURS, GO IN TO THE BRANCH OFFICE *BEFORE* YOUR CALL-IN DAY. BE SURE TO HAVE PICTURE ID WITH YOU.

SINCE YOU LAST CLAIMED BENEFITS:

6. Unemployment benefits are subject to Federal and State income tax. Do you wish to have **both** Federal and Michigan State income tax withheld from the taxable portion of each weekly benefit payment? (You can choose to have taxes withheld only once per benefit year.) .... ☐ NO ☐ YES

    A. If "YES," you must enter the number of dependents/exemptions you claim for State income tax purposes. ☐

7. Have you applied for or received retirement benefits? .... ☐ NO ☐ YES

8. Have you moved or changed your name? (If name change, file your claim in person.) .... ☐ NO ☐ YES

9. Are you in training or attending school? (If "YES," give dates.) From _____ Thru _____ .... ☐ NO ☐ YES

10. Were you unable to file this claim due to injury, illness or hospitalization that lasted 14 days or more? ...... ☐ NO ☐ YES

11. List all employment since your last period of unemployment (whether in state or not). If more than 1 employer, use reverse side.

UA Account No. (DO NOT WRITE HERE)	Check Digit	☐ Hourly ☐ Salary	First Date Worked	Last Date Worked
		Plant or Location	
EMPLOYER – Firm Name		Telephone ( )	Reason for unemployment ☐ Lack of Work **IF THIS SEPARATION WAS FOR REASONS OTHER THAN LACK OF WORK, YOU MUST FILE IN PERSON.**
No. and Street		Position Title	Do you expect to return to work with this employer? ☐ Yes When: _____
City – State – Zip Code			☐ No ☐ I don't know
County & State Worked In	FIPS CNTY	Was Social Security taken out of your pay? ☐ YES ☐ NO	If your return to work date exceeds 120 days, you must register for work to be eligible for benefits.

LAST EMPLOYER

12. If you are not a citizen of the USA, enter the type of form or document issued to you: _____ Expiration Date: _____

13. Have you received or will you receive payments from your last employer for any period following your last day of work? .... ☐ NO ☐ YES
If "YES," show the amount of payment and period covered.

    (a) Vacation Pay $ _____ From _____ To _____

    (b) Holiday Pay $ _____ From _____ To _____

    (c) Wages in Lieu of Notice $ _____ From _____ To _____

    (d) Other_____ $ _____ From _____ To _____

14. **YOUR CERTIFICATION:** I certify that all of the information submitted by me on this form is true and correct to the best of my knowledge and belief. I UNDERSTAND THAT THE LAW PROVIDES PENALTIES OF FINE, AND/OR IMPRISONMENT, AND/OR COMMUNITY SERVICE FOR FALSE STATEMENTS TO SECURE BENEFITS.

15. Claimant's Signature _____ 16. Date Signed _____

17.	**BRANCH OFFICE USE ONLY**						
Add'l	R/O	Effective W/E Date	RSW/JAW Date	Reg. Req. Y N	UA 1002/APP	D/E Date	D/E Clerk

- - - - - - - - - - - - - - - - - - - FOLD HERE - - - - - - - - - - - - - - - - -

FROM:

_____

_____

_____

THIS WILL
NOT BE
DELIVERED
WITHOUT
FIRST CLASS
STAMP

- - - - - - - - - - - - - - - FOLD HERE FIRST - - - - - - - - - - - - - - -

Continuation of Item 11 from front of form.

UA Account No. Check Digit	☐ Hourly ☐ Salary	First Date Worked	Last Date Worked
(DO NOT WRITE HERE)	Plant or Location		
NEXT TO LAST EMPLOYER EMPLOYER – Firm Name	Telephone ( )	Reason for unemployment ☐ Lack of Work	
No. and Street	Position Title	**IF THIS SEPARATION WAS FOR REASONS OTHER THAN LACK OF WORK, YOU MUST FILE IN PERSON.**	
City – State – Zip Code	Was Social Security taken out of your pay? ☐ YES ☐ NO		
UA Account No. Check Digit	☐ Hourly ☐ Salary	First Date Worked	Last Date Worked
(DO NOT WRITE HERE)	Plant or Location		
THIRD LAST EMPLOYER EMPLOYER – Firm Name	Telephone ( )	Reason for unemployment ☐ Lack of Work	
No. and Street	Position Title	**IF THIS SEPARATION WAS FOR REASONS OTHER THAN LACK OF WORK, YOU MUST FILE IN PERSON.**	
City – State – Zip Code	Was Social Security taken out of your pay? ☐ YES ☐ NO		

273

STATE OF FLORIDA AGENCY FOR WORKFORCE INNOVATION
UNEMPLOYMENT COMPENSATION WORK SEARCH RECORD

Name: _____

Social Security Number: _____

DATE	EMPLOYER NAME, ADDRESS & TELEPHONE NUMBER	CONTACT METHOD	RESULTS	VERIFIED (AGENCY USE)

Continue to list additional work search contacts in this format on separate sheets of paper.
Examples of "Contact methods": in-person, resume, application, faxed application
Examples of "Results": hired, not hiring, call back, application on file.

I certify the information included on this report is correct and complete to the best of my knowledge.
I understand misrepresentation to obtain benefits to which I am not entitled is fraud and subject to prosecution.

Claimant Signature: _____ Date:_____
AWI Form UCB-20A

Weekly Earnings Worksheet

Weeks Claimed _____

First Week Days Worked	**Hours Worked Each Day**	**Second Week: Days Worked**	**Hours Worked Each Day**
Sunday	_____	Sunday	_____
Monday	_____	Monday	_____
Tuesday	_____	Tuesday	_____
Wednesday	_____	Wednesday	_____
Thursday	_____	Thursday	_____
Friday	_____	Friday	_____
Saturday	_____	Saturday	_____

Add up the hours shown for each day. This is your total hours for the week.

_____

Add up the hours shown for each day. This is your total hours for the week.

_____

Write down your pay rate per hour:

_____

Write down your pay rate per hour:

_____

Multiply the total hours for the week times your pay rate per hour. The answer shows your gross earnings for the week. _____

Multiply the total hours for the week times your pay rate per hour. The answer shows your Gross earnings for the week.

_____

form 7

Employment Development Department

State of California

EDD TELEPHONE NUMBERS:
ENGLISH   1-(800) 300-5616
SPANISH   1-(800) 326-8937
CANTONESE 1-(800) 547-3506
VIETNAMESE 1-(800) 547-2058
OUTSIDE CA   1-(800) 250-3913
TTY (NON VOICE) 1-(800) 815-9387

EMPLOYMENT DEVELOPMENT DEPARTMENT APPEAL FORM

If you want to appeal a Department determination, please explain why you disagree and return this form to the Department using the office address listed on the enclosed notice. You have 20 days from the date of the notice to file an appeal. The 20-day period may be extended for good cause. Reasons for filing an appeal after 20 days should be explained.

Please note that claimants for Disaster Unemployment Assistance have 60 days to file an appeal. Employers who are appealing the Department's DE 3807 Notice of Determination or Assessment have 30 days to file an appeal.

I disagree with the Department's decision dated _____ because:

(Attach an additional sheet if more space is required)

CLAIMANTS: While your appeal is pending, you must continue to file a continued claim form for the period that you want to claim benefits. If you are found eligible, you can be paid only for periods for which you have filed continued claim forms and have met all other eligibility requirements.

The following information must be provided by the party filing the appeal (Appellant) or an authorized agent of the party filing the appeal. Signature of the appellant or agent is required.

Do you need a translator? ☐ Yes   ☐ No   If yes, please give language and dialect: _____

Appellant Telephone No.: (____) _____

Appellant Name: _____

Appellant Fax No.: (____) _____

Appellant
Mailing Address: _____

Street No., Apt. No., or P.O. Box   City   State   ZIP Code

Claimant Name: _____

Claimant Social Security Number: _____ - ____ - _____

Employer Account Number: _____
(For employer appeal only)

Agent Name (If applicable): _____

Mailing Address: _____

Street No., Apt. No., or P.O. Box   City   State   ZIP Code

Signature

Appellant or Agent: _____   Date: _____

- Versión en español en el dorso -

Employment Development Department

State of California

FORMULARIO DE APELACIÓN DEL DEPARTAMENTO DEL DESARROLLO DEL EMPLEO (EDD)

Si usted quiere apelar una decisión del Departamento, por favor explique la razón por la cual no está de acuerdo y regrese este formulario al Departamento, usando la dirección que aparece en la notificación adjunta. Usted tiene 20 días a partir de la fecha de esta notificación para presentar una apelación. El plazo de 20 días puede extenderse por razón justificada. Se deben explicar las razones por presentar su aplelación después del plazo de 20 días.

Por favor, note que los solicitantes de Asistencia por Desempleo debido a Desastres (DUA) tienen 60 días para presentar una apelación. Los empleadores/patrones que están apelando la Notificación de Decisión o Evaluación (DE 3807) del Departamento, tienen 30 días para presentar una apelación.

Yo no estoy de acuerdo con la decisión del Departamento fechada el _____ porque:

(Adjunte una hoja adicional si necesita más espacio)

SOLICITANTES DE BENEFICIOS: Mientras su apelación esté pendiente, usted tiene que continuar presentando una solicitud para beneficios continuos por el período que usted desea solicitar beneficios. Si se determina que Ud. tiene derecho a beneficios, sólo se le puede pagar por los períodos para los cuales Ud. ha presentado solicitudes para beneficios continuos, y para los cuales haya reunido todos los otros requisitos.

La siguiente información tiene que ser suministrada por la persona que está apelando (Apelante) o el agente

¿Necesita un(a) traductor(a)? ☐ Sí   ☐ No   Si marcó sí, por favor, especifique el idioma y dialecto: _____

No. de Teléfono del/de la Apelante: (____) _____

Nombre del/de la Apelante: _____

No. de Fax del/de la Apelante: (____) _____

Dirección Postal del/de la Apelante: _____

| No. de Calle., No. de Dept., o Apartado Postal | Ciudad | Estado | ZONA Postal |

Nombre del/de la Solicitante de Beneficios:

_____

Número del Seguro Social del/de la Solicitante:

_____ - _____ - _____

Número de Cuenta del Empleador/Patrón: _____
(Para la apelación del Empleador/Patrón solamente)

Nombre del Agente (Si es pertinente): _____

Dirección Postal: _____

| No. de Calle., No. de Dept., o Apartado Postal | Ciudad | Estado | ZONA Postal |

Firma del

Apelante o Agente: _____   Fecha: _____

- English version on the other side -

INDEX

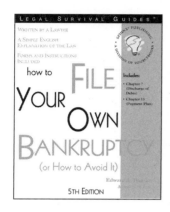
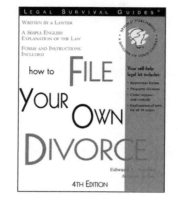
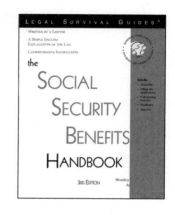

SPHINX® PUBLISHING'S NATIONAL TITLES
Valid in All 50 States

LEGAL SURVIVAL IN BUSINESS

The Complete Book of Corporate Forms	$24.95
How to Form a Delaware Corporation from Any State	$24.95
How to Form a Limited Liability Company	$22.95
Incorporate in Nevada from Any State	$24.95
How to Form a Nonprofit Corporation	$24.95
How to Form Your Own Corporation (3E)	$24.95
How to Form Your Own Partnership (2E)	$24.95
How to Register Your Own Copyright (4E)	$24.95
How to Register Your Own Trademark (3E)	$21.95
Most Valuable Business Legal Forms You'll Ever Need (3E)	$21.95

LEGAL SURVIVAL IN COURT

Crime Victim's Guide to Justice (2E)	$21.95
Grandparents' Rights (3E)	$24.95
Help Your Lawyer Win Your Case (2E)	$14.95
Jurors' Rights (2E)	$12.95
Legal Research Made Easy (2E)	$16.95
Winning Your Personal Injury Claim (2E)	$24.95
Your Rights When You Owe Too Much	$16.95

LEGAL SURVIVAL IN REAL ESTATE

Essential Guide to Real Estate Contracts	$18.95
Essential Guide to Real Estate Leases	$18.95
How to Buy a Condominium or Townhome (2E)	$19.95

LEGAL SURVIVAL IN PERSONAL AFFAIRS

Cómo Hacer su Propio Testamento	$16.95
Guía de Inmigración a Estados Unidos (3E)	$24.95
Guía de Justicia para Víctimas del Crimen	$21.95
Cómo Solicitar su Propio Divorcio	$24.95
How to File Your Own Bankruptcy (5E)	$21.95
How to File Your Own Divorce (4E)	$24.95
How to Make Your Own Will (2E)	$16.95
How to Write Your Own Living Will (2E)	$16.95
How to Write Your Own Premarital Agreement (3E)	$24.95
Living Trusts and Other Ways to Avoid Probate (3E)	$24.95
Manual de Beneficios para el Seguro Social	$18.95
Mastering the MBE	$16.95
Most Valuable Personal Legal Forms You'll Ever Need	$24.95
Neighbor v. Neighbor (2E)	$16.95
The Nanny and Domestic Help Legal Kit	$22.95
The Power of Attorney Handbook (4E)	$19.95
Repair Your Own Credit and Deal with Debt	$18.95
The Social Security Benefits Handbook (3E)	$18.95
Unmarried Parents' Rights	$19.95
U.S.A. Immigration Guide (3E)	$19.95
The Visitation Handbook	$18.95
Win Your Unemployment Compensation Claim	$21.95
Your Right to Child Custody, Visitation and Support (2E)	$24.95

Legal Survival Guides are directly available from Sourcebooks, Inc., or from your local bookstores.
Prices are subject to change without notice.
For credit card orders call 1–800–432–7444, write P.O. Box 4410, Naperville, IL 60567-4410
or fax 630-961-2168
Find more legal information at: **www.SphinxLegal.com**

SPHINX® PUBLISHING ORDER FORM

BILL TO:		SHIP TO:		
Phone #	Terms	F.O.B.	Chicago, IL	Ship Date

Charge my: ☐ VISA ☐ MasterCard ☐ American Express

☐ **Money Order or Personal Check**

Credit Card Number [ ][ ][ ][ ][ ][ ][ ][ ][ ][ ][ ][ ][ ][ ][ ]   Expiration Date

Qty	ISBN	Title	Retail	Ext.	Qty	ISBN	Title	Retail	Ext.
		SPHINX PUBLISHING NATIONAL TITLES				1-57248-220-6	Mastering the MBE	$16.95	
	1-57248-148-X	Cómo Hacer su Propio Testamento	$16.95			1-57248-167-6	Most Valuable Bus. Legal Forms You'll Ever Need (3E)	$21.95	
	1-57248-147-1	Cómo Solicitar su Propio Divorcio	$24.95			1-57248-130-7	Most Valuable Personal Legal Forms You'll Ever Need	$24.95	
	1-57248-166-8	The Complete Book of Corporate Forms	$24.95			1-57248-098-X	The Nanny and Domestic Help Legal Kit	$22.95	
	1-57248-163-3	Crime Victim's Guide to Justice (2E)	$21.95			1-57248-089-0	Neighbor v. Neighbor (2E)	$16.95	
	1-57248-159-5	Essential Guide to Real Estate Contracts	$18.95			1-57248-169-2	The Power of Attorney Handbook (4E)	$19.95	
	1-57248-160-9	Essential Guide to Real Estate Leases	$18.95			1-57248-149-8	Repair Your Own Credit and Deal with Debt	$18.95	
	1-57248-139-0	Grandparents' Rights (3E)	$24.95			1-57248-168-4	The Social Security Benefits Handbook (3E)	$18.95	
	1-57248-188-9	Guía de Inmigración a Estados Unidos (3E)	$24.95			1-57071-399-5	Unmarried Parents' Rights	$19.95	
	1-57248-187-0	Guía de Justicia para Víctimas del Crimen	$21.95			1-57071-354-5	U.S.A. Immigration Guide (3E)	$19.95	
	1-57248-103-X	Help Your Lawyer Win Your Case (2E)	$14.95			1-57248-192-7	The Visitation Handbook	$18.95	
	1-57248-164-1	How to Buy a Condominium or Townhome (2E)	$19.95			1-57248-225-7	Win Your Unemployment Compensation Claim (2E)	$21.95	
	1-57248-191-9	How to File Your Own Bankruptcy (5E)	$21.95			1-57248-138-2	Winning Your Personal Injury Claim (2E)	$24.95	
	1-57248-132-3	How to File Your Own Divorce (4E)	$24.95			1-57248-162-5	Your Right to Child Custody, Visitation and Support (2E)	$24.95	
	1-57248-100-5	How to Form a DE Corporation from Any State	$24.95			1-57248-157-9	Your Rights When You Owe Too Much	$16.95	
	1-57248-083-1	How to Form a Limited Liability Company	$22.95				**CALIFORNIA TITLES**		
	1-57248-099-8	How to Form a Nonprofit Corporation	$24.95			1-57248-150-1	CA Power of Attorney Handbook (2E)	$18.95	
	1-57248-133-1	How to Form Your Own Corporation (3E)	$24.95			1-57248-151-X	How to File for Divorce in CA (3E)	$26.95	
	1-57248-224-9	How to Form Your Own Partnership (2E)	$24.95			1-57071-356-1	How to Make a CA Will	$16.95	
	1-57248-119-6	How to Make Your Own Will (2E)	$16.95			1-57248-145-5	How to Probate and Settle an Estate in California	$26.95	
	1-57248-200-1	How to Register Your Own Copyright (4E)	$24.95			1-57248-146-3	How to Start a Business in CA	$18.95	
	1-57248-104-8	How to Register Your Own Trademark (3E)	$21.95			1-57248-194-3	How to Win in Small Claims Court in CA (2E)	$18.95	
	1-57248-118-8	How to Write Your Own Living Will (2E)	$16.95			1-57248-196-X	The Landlord's Legal Guide in CA	$24.95	
	1-57248-156-0	How to Write Your Own Premarital Agreement (3E)	$24.95				**FLORIDA TITLES**		
	1-57248-158-7	Incorporate in Nevada from Any State	$24.95			1-57071-363-4	Florida Power of Attorney Handbook (2E)	$16.95	
	1-57071-333-2	Jurors' Rights (2E)	$12.95			1-57248-176-5	How to File for Divorce in FL (7E)	$26.95	
	1-57071-400-2	Legal Research Made Easy (2E)	$16.95			1-57248-177-3	How to Form a Corporation in FL (5E)	$24.95	
	1-57248-165-X	Living Trusts and Other Ways to Avoid Probate (3E)	$24.95			1-57248-203-6	How to Form a Limited Liability Co. in FL (2E)	$24.95	
	1-57248-186-2	Manual de Beneficios para el Seguro Social	$18.95			1-57071-401-0	How to Form a Partnership in FL	$22.95	

Form Continued on Following Page   **SUBTOTAL**

To order, call Sourcebooks at 1-800-432-7444 or FAX (630) 961-2168 (Bookstores, libraries, wholesalers—please call for discount)

Prices are subject to change without notice.

Find more legal information at: **www.SphinxLegal.com**

SPHINX® PUBLISHING ORDER FORM

Qty	ISBN	Title	Retail	Ext.
_____	1-57248-113-7	How to Make a FL Will (6E)	$16.95	_____
_____	1-57248-088-2	How to Modify Your FL Divorce Judgment (4E)	$24.95	_____
_____	1-57248-144-7	How to Probate and Settle an Estate in FL (4E)	$26.95	_____
_____	1-57248-081-5	How to Start a Business in FL (5E)	$16.95	_____
_____	1-57071-362-6	How to Win in Small Claims Court in FL (6E)	$16.95	_____
_____	1-57248-202-8	Land Trusts in Florida (6E)	$29.95	_____
_____	1-57248-123-4	Landlords' Rights and Duties in FL (8E)	$21.95	_____

GEORGIA TITLES

Qty	ISBN	Title	Retail	Ext.
_____	1-57248-137-4	How to File for Divorce in GA (4E)	$21.95	_____
_____	1-57248-180-3	How to Make a GA Will (4E)	$21.95	_____
_____	1-57248-140-4	How to Start a Business in Georgia (2E)	$16.95	_____

ILLINOIS TITLES

Qty	ISBN	Title	Retail	Ext.
_____	1-57071-405-3	How to File for Divorce in IL (2E)	$21.95	_____
_____	1-57248-170-6	How to Make an IL Will (3E)	$16.95	_____
_____	1-57071-416-9	How to Start a Business in IL (2E)	$18.95	_____
_____	1-57248-078-5	Landlords' Rights & Duties in IL	$21.95	_____

MASSACHUSETTS TITLES

Qty	ISBN	Title	Retail	Ext.
_____	1-57248-128-5	How to File for Divorce in MA (3E)	$24.95	_____
_____	1-57248-115-3	How to Form a Corporation in MA	$24.95	_____
_____	1-57248-108-0	How to Make a MA Will (2E)	$16.95	_____
_____	1-57248-106-4	How to Start a Business in MA (2E)	$18.95	_____
_____	1-57248-209-5	The Landlord's Legal Guide in MA	$24.95	_____

MICHIGAN TITLES

Qty	ISBN	Title	Retail	Ext.
_____	1-57071-409-6	How to File for Divorce in MI (2E)	$21.95	_____
_____	1-57248-182-X	How to Make a MI Will (3E)	$16.95	_____
_____	1-57248-183-8	How to Start a Business in MI (3E)	$18.95	_____

MINNESOTA TITLES

Qty	ISBN	Title	Retail	Ext.
_____	1-57248-142-0	How to File for Divorce in MN	$21.95	_____
_____	1-57248-179-X	How to Form a Corporation in MN	$24.95	_____
_____	1-57248-178-1	How to Make a MN Will (2E)	$16.95	_____

NEW YORK TITLES

Qty	ISBN	Title	Retail	Ext.
_____	1-57248-193-5	Child Custody, Visitation and Support in NY	$26.95	_____
_____	1-57248-141-2	How to File for Divorce in NY (2E)	$26.95	_____
_____	1-57248-105-6	How to Form a Corporation in NY	$24.95	_____
_____	1-57248-095-5	How to Make a NY Will (2E)	$16.95	_____
_____	1-57248-199-4	How to Start a Business in NY (2E)	$18.95	_____

Qty	ISBN	Title	Retail	Ext.
_____	1-57248-198-6	How to Win in Small Claims Court in NY (2E)	$18.95	_____
_____	1-57071-186-0	Landlords' Rights and Duties in NY	$21.95	_____
_____	1-57071-188-7	New York Power of Attorney Handbook	$19.95	_____
_____	1-57248-122-6	Tenants' Rights in NY	$21.95	_____

NORTH CAROLINA TITLES

Qty	ISBN	Title	Retail	Ext.
_____	1-57248-185-4	How to File for Divorce in NC (3E)	$22.95	_____
_____	1-57248-129-3	How to Make a NC Will (3E)	$16.95	_____
_____	1-57248-184-6	How to Start a Business in NC (3E)	$18.95	_____
_____	1-57248-091-2	Landlords' Rights & Duties in NC	$21.95	_____

OHIO TITLES

Qty	ISBN	Title	Retail	Ext.
_____	1-57248-190-0	How to File for Divorce in OH (2E)	$24.95	_____
_____	1-57248-174-9	How to Form a Corporation in OH	$24.95	_____
_____	1-57248-173-0	How to Make an OH Will	$16.95	_____

PENNSYLVANIA TITLES

Qty	ISBN	Title	Retail	Ext.
_____	1-57248-211-7	How to File for Divorce in PA (3E)	$26.95	_____
_____	1-57248-094-7	How to Make a PA Will (2E)	$16.95	_____
_____	1-57248-112-9	How to Start a Business in PA (2E)	$18.95	_____
_____	1-57071-179-8	Landlords' Rights and Duties in PA	$19.95	_____

TEXAS TITLES

Qty	ISBN	Title	Retail	Ext.
_____	1-57248-171-4	Child Custody, Visitation, and Support in TX	$22.95	_____
_____	1-57248-172-2	How to File for Divorce in TX (3E)	$24.95	_____
_____	1-57248-114-5	How to Form a Corporation in TX (2E)	$24.95	_____
_____	1-57071-417-7	How to Make a TX Will (2E)	$16.95	_____
_____	1-57248-214-1	How to Probate and Settle an Estate in TX (3E)	$26.95	_____
_____	1-57248-228-1	How to Start a Business in TX (3E)	$18.95	_____
_____	1-57248-111-0	How to Win in Small Claims Court in TX (2E)	$16.95	_____
_____	1-57248-110-2	Landlords' Rights and Duties in TX (2E)	$21.95	_____

SUBTOTAL THIS PAGE _____

SUBTOTAL PREVIOUS PAGE _____

Shipping — $5.00 for 1st book, $1.00 each additional _____

Illinois residents add 6.75% sales tax _____

Connecticut residents add 6.00% sales tax _____

TOTAL _____

To order, call Sourcebooks at 1-800-432-7444 or FAX (630) 961-2168 (Bookstores, libraries, wholesalers—please call for discount)
Prices are subject to change without notice.
Find more legal information at: **www.SphinxLegal.com**